Thomas Wolke
Risk Management

Thomas Wolke
Risk Management

—

ISBN 978-3-11-044052-2
e-ISBN (PDF) 978-3-11-044053-9
e-ISBN (EPUB) 978-3-11-043245-9

Library of Congress Cataloging-in-Publication Data
A CIP catalog record for this book has been applied for at the Library of Congress.

Bibliographic information published by the Deutsche Nationalbibliothek
The Deutsche Nationalbibliothek lists this publication in the Deutsche Nationalbibliografie;
detailed bibliographic data are available on the Internet at http://dnb.dnb.de.

© 2017 Walter de Gruyter GmbH, Berlin/Boston
Cover illustration: scanrail/iStock/Thinkstock
Typestting: fidus Publikations-Service GmbH, Nördlingen
Printing and binding: CPI books GmbH, Leck
♾ Printed on acid-free paper
Printed in Germany

www.degruyter.com

Foreword

At the beginning of the 1990s many corporate crises occurred, which led to an expansion and a higher importance of corporate risk management. Since 2008 the global financial crisis dominates the economical media in theory and practice. Because of that the importance of a functioning company-wide risk management, and in particular for banks, is enormously increased. In recent years, the German edition of "risk management" has become a standard work in German-speaking science education and in German banking practice. For these reasons, I have decided to offer an English edition.

I thank Carlye Birkenkrahe for her excellent support in translating this German book into the English version. Without her help, the English edition could not have been achieved in such a short time and with such high quality. As for the content, formal and linguistic errors are my sole responsibility.

I am grateful for further recommendations, notification of errors, suggestions for improvement and would welcome emails at thomas.wolke@hwr-berlin.de

Thomas Wolke

Table of content

Foreword —— V

List of Figures —— XI

List of Tables —— XIII

List of Abbreviations —— XV

List of Symbols —— XVII

1 Fundamentals —— 1
1.1 The definition and reasons for risk management —— 1
1.2 Risk management as a process —— 4
1.3 Risk identification and risk types —— 5
1.4 References —— 8

2 Risk measurement and risk analysis —— 9
2.1 Simple loss measurements —— 10
2.1.1 Maximum loss —— 10
2.1.2 Expected loss —— 12
2.2 Key indicators —— 13
2.2.1 Volatility —— 14
2.2.2 Sensitivity —— 24
2.3 Value at Risk (VaR) —— 25
2.3.1 Statistical foundations —— 26
2.3.2 VaR of an individual risk position —— 30
2.3.3 VaR of portfolios —— 34
2.3.4 Additional calculation methods —— 52
2.3.5 Backtesting —— 57
2.3.6 Lower partial moments (LPM) —— 60
2.3.7 Critiques of the VaR concept —— 64
2.4 Stress tests, scenario analysis and worst case scenarios —— 67
2.5 Qualitative risk measurement techniques —— 70
2.6 Risk analysis —— 74
2.7 References —— 81
2.8 Technical appendix —— 83

3 Risk control —— 89
3.1 Risk provision —— 90
3.2 Risk avoidance and risk limitation —— 91

3.3	Risk distribution (diversification) and risk shifting —— 94	
3.4	Risk transfer and risk compensation —— 96	
3.4.1	Insurance —— 98	
3.4.2	Options —— 101	
3.4.3	Futures —— 108	
3.4.4	Swaps —— 111	
3.5	References —— 114	
4	**Financial risks —— 115**	
4.1	Market price risks —— 116	
4.1.1	Interest rate risk —— 117	
4.1.1.1	Basics of interest rate change risk —— 117	
4.1.1.2	Duration —— 123	
4.1.1.3	Convexity —— 125	
4.1.1.4	VaR calculation of interest positions —— 128	
4.1.1.5	Immunization of bond portfolios —— 135	
4.1.1.6	Interest rate swaps —— 139	
4.1.1.7	Interest rate options —— 142	
4.1.1.8	Interest rate futures —— 144	
4.1.2	Exchange rate risk —— 146	
4.1.2.1	Foundations of exchange rate risk —— 146	
4.1.2.2	Currency swaps —— 150	
4.1.2.3	Currency forward transactions —— 151	
4.1.2.4	Currency options —— 155	
4.1.2.5	VaR calculation of foreign exchange positions —— 157	
4.1.3	Stock price risk —— 158	
4.1.3.1	Portfolio theory —— 159	
4.1.3.2	Capital Asset Pricing Model (CAPM) —— 163	
4.1.4	Real estate price risk —— 167	
4.2	Default risk —— 169	
4.2.1	Measurement of individual transaction default risk —— 170	
4.2.2	Analysis of individual transaction default risk —— 172	
4.2.3	Risk-adjusted lending rates —— 176	
4.2.4	Control of individual transaction default risk —— 181	
4.2.5	Measurement and management of credit portfolios —— 188	
4.2.6	Country risk —— 191	
4.3	Liquidity risks —— 194	
4.3.1	Types of liquidity risk —— 195	
4.3.2	Measurement of the liquidity risks —— 197	
4.3.3	Control of liquidity risks —— 202	
4.4	The financial crisis (since) 2008 —— 203	
4.4.1	Dangers and causes of the financial crisis —— 204	

4.4.2	Solution approaches to avoiding and redressing financial crises —— 207
4.4.2.1	Laws and regulations —— 207
4.4.2.2	Human misconduct —— 216
4.4.2.3	Market failure —— 216
4.4.2.4	Mistaken decisions by politicians and regulators —— 220
4.4.2.5	Risk management —— 224
4.4.3	Basel III —— 226
4.4.4	Appraisal and outlook —— 232
4.5	References —— 237
4.6	Technical appendix —— 245

5	**Performance risks —— 249**
5.1	Operational risks —— 249
5.1.1	Measurement of operational risks —— 250
5.1.2	Internal operational risks —— 259
5.1.2.1	Personnel risks —— 259
5.1.2.2	Process risks —— 259
5.1.2.3	System risks (IT risks) —— 260
5.1.3	External operational risks —— 260
5.1.3.1	Legal risks —— 261
5.1.3.2	Natural risks —— 261
5.1.4	Management of climate change risks —— 262
5.2	Procurement and sales risks —— 266
5.2.1	Procurement risks —— 267
5.2.2	Sales risks —— 272
5.2.3	Cash Flow at Risk —— 279
5.3	References —— 287
5.4	Technical appendix —— 290

6	**Risk controlling —— 292**
6.1	Duties of risk controlling —— 292
6.2	Organization of risk controlling and risk management —— 294
6.3	Company-wide profit and risk aggregation —— 302
6.4	The external risk report —— 311
6.5	References —— 313
6.6	Technical appendix —— 315

7	**Profit-risk-based company management using a case study —— 317**
7.1	Description of the case study —— 317
7.2	Risk identification and risk measurement —— 323
7.3	Risk analysis —— 335

List of References —— 344

Glossary —— 351

Index —— 353

List of Figures

Fig. 1.1: Definitions and reasons for risk management —— 3
Fig. 1.2: The risk management process —— 4
Fig. 1.3: Classification of the types of business risk —— 7
Fig. 2.1: Overview of risk measurements —— 9
Fig. 2.2: Daily stock prices for BMW and MAN in 2005 —— 20
Fig. 2.3: Daily stock price returns, average and volatility for BMW —— 21
Fig. 2.4: Daily stock price returns, average and volatility for MAN —— 21
Fig. 2.5: Density function of theoretical normal distribution for example of BMW —— 27
Fig. 2.6: Empirical density function for the returns of BMW 2005 —— 28
Fig. 2.7: 2.5 %-quantile of the density function for BMW —— 29
Fig. 2.8: Formula for parametric calculation of the VaR —— 32
Fig. 2.9: Examples for correlation coefficients of +1 and −1 —— 40
Fig. 2.10: Example for a correlation coefficient of +0.6 —— 41
Fig. 2.11: Example for a correlation coefficient of 0 —— 41
Fig. 2.12: Calculation methods of Value at Risk —— 56
Fig. 2.13: Typical deviations from the normal distribution —— 64
Fig. 3.1: Overview of risk strategies and control instruments —— 88
Fig. 3.2: Example for a VaR limit system —— 92
Fig. 3.3: Overview of risk transfer and risk compensation —— 97
Fig. 3.4: Basic functioning of insurance —— 98
Fig. 3.5: Profit and loss profile of a call option —— 102
Fig. 3.6: Profit and loss profile of a put option —— 104
Fig. 3.7: Profit and loss profile of a put option and its associated underlying asset —— 105
Fig. 3.8: Profit and loss profile of a future —— 108
Fig. 3.9: Profit and loss profile of a future and its associated underlying asset —— 109
Fig. 3.10: General mechanism of swaps —— 111
Fig. 4.1: Example yield curves —— 119
Fig. 4.2: Example for present value calculation of a bond —— 120
Fig. 4.3: Present value, modified duration and convexity of a present value assessment —— 125
Fig. 4.4: Convexity in the immunization of the present value —— 135
Fig. 4.5: Example of the functioning of an interest rate swap —— 140
Fig. 4.6: Application of an interest rate swap as a control instrument in risk management —— 141
Fig. 4.7: Profit and loss profile of an interest rate option (put) and the associated bond —— 142
Fig. 4.8: Types of exchange rate risk and associated control instruments —— 147
Fig. 4.9: Functioning of a currency swap —— 149
Fig. 4.10: Calculation of the implicit forward exchange rate using a financial hedge —— 152
Fig. 4.11: Profit and loss profile of a currency option (put) and the associated foreign-currency position —— 154
Fig. 4.12: Transformation curves for BMW and MAN for various correlations —— 159
Fig. 4.13: Security Market Line based on the CAPM —— 164
Fig. 4.14: Example rating —— 172
Fig. 4.15: Measurement and distribution of default risk —— 177
Fig. 4.16: Classification and delineation of credit derivatives —— 183
Fig. 4.17: Credit Default Swap —— 185
Fig. 4.18: Total Return Swap —— 185
Fig. 4.19: Laws and regulations for the causes and solution approaches to the financial crisis —— 214

Fig. 4.20: Market failure for the cause and solution approach to the financial crisis —— 219
Fig. 4.21: Causes and solution approaches of the financial crisis —— 224
Fig. 4.22: Equity requirements of Basel II/III —— 228
Fig. 5.1: Categorization of operational risks and examples —— 249
Fig. 5.2: Construction of the total loss distribution for operational risks in an example —— 256
Fig. 5.3: Density function and 1 %-quantile for the procurement risk of crude oil —— 270
Fig. 5.4: Density function and 10 %-quantile for the sales risk as a function of the revenues —— 276
Fig. 6.1: Structural and procedural diagram for risk controlling and risk management —— 298

List of Tables

Tab. 2.1: Relative (observed) asset changes —— 14
Tab. 2.2: Results for maximum loss, expected loss, expected change in assets, volatility —— 17
Tab. 2.3: Prices and returns for BMW and MAN —— 19
Tab. 2.4: Maximum loss, expected asset change, volatility for examples A, B, C, and BMW, MAN stocks —— 22
Tab. 2.5: Number of standard deviations for quantile and intervals of standard normal distribution —— 29
Tab. 2.6: VaR for examples A, B and C —— 33
Tab. 2.7: VaR and features of a sample portfolio (BMW and MAN) —— 35
Tab. 2.8: Simple example for calculation of portfolio volatility —— 37
Tab. 2.9: Examples for different correlation coefficients —— 39
Tab. 2.10: Results of VaR calculation for a sample portfolio —— 44
Tab. 2.11: Example for the change to the portfolio VaR based on the respective given correlation coefficients —— 45
Tab. 2.12: Determining factors and results of Component Value at Risk (CoVaR) for BMW and MAN —— 50
Tab. 2.13: Example for a historical simulation —— 53
Tab. 2.14: Initial data backtesting for BMW and MAN for reporting date of January 3, 2005 —— 57
Tab. 2.15: Sample data for calculation of lower partial moments —— 61
Tab. 2.16: Results of VaR and stress tests or scenario analyzes —— 67
Tab. 2.17: Example scoring model for credit risk measurement —— 71
Tab. 2.18: Results of a scoring model for credit risk measurement —— 72
Tab. 2.19: Sharpe ratio and RoRaC for example portfolio (BMW and MAN) —— 76
Tab. 2.20: Risk analysis and action possibilities for various scenarios and risk attitudes —— 79
Tab. 3.1: Effects of the various control instruments on RoRaC and VaR —— 112
Tab. 4.1: Interest-bearing securities and types of interest —— 117
Tab. 4.2: Results of a present value assessment with modified duration and convexity —— 127
Tab. 4.3: Present value, modified duration and convexity of a bond portfolio —— 131
Tab. 4.4: Calculation of the individual VaR of a bond portfolio —— 132
Tab. 4.5: Cumulative probabilities of default (%) according to Standard&Poor's —— 174
Tab. 4.6: Risk-adjusted lending rate and its components —— 179
Tab. 4.7: Default probabilities as a function of rating class and number of standard deviations —— 200
Tab. 4.8: Risk weightings on the basis of Standard&Poor's —— 226
Tab. 5.1: Example of observed losses from hardware failure —— 253
Tab. 5.2: Distributions of the loss number and loss amount for an example of operational risk —— 254
Tab. 5.3: Aggregation of loss number and loss amount distribution —— 254
Tab. 5.4: Total loss distribution and cumulative probabilities for an example of operational risk —— 255
Tab. 5.5: Monte Carlo simulation of revenues —— 273
Tab. 5.6: Results for different analytical methods of calculating the revenue VaR —— 277
Tab. 5.7: Expected values, standard deviations and value at risk values for individual components of cash flow —— 283
Tab. 5.8: Expected values, standard deviations, and value at risk values for the assembled components of the cash flow —— 285

Tab. 6.1: Scheme for the risk aggregation of risk types and organizational units based on the VaR (in € mill.) —— 299
Tab. 6.2: Correlations and standard deviations (in € mill.) of the individual risk groups —— 306
Tab. 6.3: Company-wide profits, VaR, Component VaR (in € mill.), RoRaC and equity utilization —— 307
Tab. 7.1: Balance sheet and income statement of Bsp AG in € mill. for the year 01 —— 317
Tab. 7.2: Income statement of Bsp AG in € mill. for the year 01 —— 318
Tab. 7.3: Results of the risk measurement for Bsp AG in € —— 334
Tab. 7.4: Individual VaR, Component VaR, profits in €, RoRaC and equity utilization of Bsp AG —— 338

List of Abbreviations

(Abbreviations used in the text; in brackets the German term)

Abbreviation:	Explanation:
ABS	Asset Backed Securities
AQR	Asset Quality Review
BAS	Bid-Ask Spread
BCBS	Basel committee on Banking Supervision
BIS	Bank for International Settlement
bn	Billion
bp	Basis points
BS	Business sector
C	Call option premium
CA	Comprehensive Assessment, central administration
CFaR	Cash Flow at Risk
CoVaR	Component Value at Risk
CRD	Capital Requirements Directive
CRR	Capital Requirements Regulation
CVA	Credit Value Adjustment
CVaR	Credit Value at Risk
DRS	German Accounting Standard (Deutsche Rechnungslegungs Standards)
DRSC	German Accounting Standard Committee (Deutsche Rechnungslegungs Standards Committee)
E	Exercise price
EBA	European Banking Authority
ECB	European Central Bank
ESM	European Stability Mechanism
ESMA	European Securities and Markets Authority
EU	European Union
EURIBOR	Euro Interbank Offered Rate
FED	Federal Reserve System
FMSA	Financial Market Stabilization Authority (Bundesanstalt für Finanzmarktstabilisierung)
FMStFG	Financial Market Stabilization Fund Act (Finanzmarktstabilisierungsfondsgesetz)
FSB	Financial Stability Board (Finanzstabilitätsrat)
HGB	Commercial Code (Handelsgesetzbuch)
IAS	International Accounting Standards
IASB	International Accounting Standards Board
ICAAP	Internal Capital Adequacy Assessment Process
IFRS	International Financial Reporting Standards
InstitutsVerV	Institutional Remuneration Directive (InstitutsVergütungsVerordnung)
IRB	Internal Ratings Based (Approach)
KonTraG	German Act on Corporate Control and Transparency (Gesetz zur Kontrolle und Transparenz im Unternehmensbereich)
KWG	German Banking Act (Kreditwesengesetz)
L	Liquidity risk surcharge

Abbreviation:	Explanation:
LaR	Liquidity at Risk
LCR	Liquidity Coverage Ratio
M	Market portfolio
MaRisk	Minimum Requirements for Risk Management (Mindestanforderungen an das Risikomanagement)
MiFID	Markets in Financial Instruments Directive
MiFIR	Markets in Financial Instruments Regulation
mill	Million
MTF	Multilateral Trading Facility
NSFR	Net Stable Funding Ratio
P	Put option premium
pcs	Pieces
RoRaC	Return on Risk adjusted Capital
SME	Small and Medium sized Enterprises
SoFFin	Financial Market Stabilization Fund (Sonderfonds Finanzmarktstabilisierung)
SSM	Single Stability Mechanism
TLAC	Total Loss-Absorbing Capacity
US GAAP	Generally Accepted Accounting Principles
VAG	Insurance Supervision Act (Versicherungsaufsichtsgesetz)
VaR	Value at Risk

List of Symbols

(Symbols and abbreviations used in calculations)

Symbol:	Description:
A, Adm	Administration costs (distribution, administration)
BAS	Bid-ask spread
C	Convexity
CE	Credit equivalent
CF	Cash flow
CFaR	Cash Flow at Risk
Co	Copper
CoVaR	Component Value at Risk
$CR_{A,B}$	Correlation between A and B
CVaR	Credit Value at Risk
D^{Mac}	Macaulay Duration
D^{mod}	Modified Duration
EAC(A)	Expected asset change of position A
EaD	Exposure at Default
EL	Expected Loss
EL(A)	Expected loss of position A
Fin	Financial costs (risks)
FR	Forward rate (currency)
Grp	Gross profit
IE, Int	Interest expense
i_{rf}	Risk free interest rate
L	Liquidity risk surcharge
LCVaR	Liquidity-adjusted Credit Value at Risk
LGD	Loss Given Default
LPM	Lower partial moments
LVaR	Liquidity-adjusted Value at Risk
M	Maturity
ML(A)	Maximum loss of position A
O-Ext	External operating (operational) risks
Oil	Crude oil (Brent Spar)
O-Int	Internal operating (operational) risks
O-Tot	Total operating (operational) risks
PC	Production costs
PD	Probability of Default
PV	Present value
Q	Quantity, volume
r_A, μ_A	Expected value (average)/return of A
RB	Result from normal business activities
RE	Revenues (sales)
r^{mv}_P	Return of the portfolio P with the minimal volatility
RP	Risk position
RR	Recovery Rate (=1-LGD)

List of Symbols

Symbol:	Description:
s_A, σ_A, Vol(A)	Standard deviation, volatility of A
$s_{A,B}$	Covariance between A and B
s_A^2	Variance of A
SAC	Sales and administrative costs
s^{mv}_P	Standard deviation (volatility) of the portfolio P with the minimal volatility
$ß_A$	Beta factor of position A
Sw	Swap rate (currency)
T	Liquidation period in time units
TE, Tax	Tax expenses
VaR	Value at Risk
W, Wag	Wage (salaries) costs
w_A	Portfolio weight of position A
w^{mv}_A	Weighting of A of the portfolio with the minimal volatility
ΔVaR_i	Marginal Value at Risk of the i-th position
α	Alpha quantile of normal distribution (e.g. 1%)
λ	Parameter of Poisson distribution

1 Fundamentals

It is not necessary to emphasize the importance of risk management in view of the daily media information about the consequences of the worldwide financial crisis, company bankruptcies, and other emergencies. In the news coverage about risk, central concepts are often interpreted and applied in different ways. What follows is an overview of the different types of risk and a process-oriented description of risk management. Risk identification and an overview of the different types of risk will round off the fundamentals of risk management.

1.1 The definition and reasons for risk management

There is no unified **definition of risk** concepts applied in the business literature. The word "risk" derives from the early Italian risicare, which means "to dare". A relatively commonly used definition of risk is based on possible damage or the potential loss of a net asset position, with no potential gains to offset it. The neglect of potential gain is especially important because in further concepts, for example the RoRaC concept (see Section 2.6), the measurement of returns is separate and occurs independently of the risk measurement. There must be sharp distinctions between risk and return, otherwise it's possible for the same profit to be considered more than once, which could lead to inconclusive results.

In business **decision theory**, the concept of risk is based on knowledge of probabilities or probability distributions regarding uncertain future events.

Risk management includes the company-wide measurement and supervision of all business risk.

In particular, **consideration of the synergies** between different risks, the so-called diversification effect, represents an important distinction between the treatment of individual risks and of combined risks.

The term **risk controlling**, often used in both practice and theory in this context, is substantively distinct from risk management. In the following material, risk controlling is viewed as a component of risk management which supports the planning and steering of the company. From this perspective, risk controlling fulfills a strong organizational and oversight role. By contrast, risk management revolves around the concrete implementation of provisions for risk measurement and risk steering. Risk controlling is one part of the process-oriented description of risk management (see Section 1.2).

The **reasons** for risk management are manifold and complex. Ever since the 2008 financial crisis there has been a mutual consensus about the necessity of a functioning business risk management strategy. Since the grounds for pursuing risk manage-

ment have an effect on the way it is conducted, the reasons will be described and elucidated. The effects of the financial crisis on risk management will be handled in more detail in Section 4.4. The reasons can be divided into three categories:
- Legal framework
- Economic reasons
- Technological advances

Legal framework include first of all the respective national laws and regulations. For example, the following legislation applies in Germany: The German Act on Corporate Control and Transparency (KonTraG) from 27 April 1998, which expands the duty of care required from companies and stipulates disclosure of the business risks in the management report. The Corporate Governance Code contains non-legally-binding recommendations for risk management. The Risk Limitation Act of 12 August 2008 regulates the disclosure requirements of major company shareholders (financial investments) and is supposed to make company acquisitions by investors more transparent. The Commercial Code (Handelsgesetzbuch/HGB) and the German Accounting Standard (Deutscher Rechnungslegungsstandard/DRS) describe the most important laws regulating German reporting.

In America the Dodd-Frank Act constitutes an important legal framework in response to the financial market crisis. The goal of the Dodd-Frank Act is to promote stability of the financial market as well as increase responsibility and transparency in the US financial system. The US GAAP (Generally Accepted Accounting Principles) regulate, among other things, risk reporting for US companies.

However, there are also international laws and regulations that form a legal basis for risk management. For banks Basel III sets out the current and future international legal framework for structuring risk management. For the insurance industry, Solvency II is the corresponding counterpart to Basel III. Descriptions of industry-specific features will be omitted here and elsewhere in this book in favour of more generally accessible accounts. The IFRS 9 (International Financial Reporting Standards) applies to external risk reporting from 2018. The contents of the IFRS 9 as it applies to external risk reporting will be explored in more detail in Section 6.4 and with regard to the financial crisis in Section 4.4. The application of international laws depends on how they are integrated into national law and often represents a long process. Thus the USA has not so far adopted Basel III. The greatest alignment between national and international law being observed at the moment is with the IFRS, although the differences between the US-GAAP and the IFRS are also evident here.

Over the course of the financial crisis, numerous laws and regulations have been passed in the last few years which have especially changed the legal framework for banks and financial markets. Basel III is one example mentioned here and other pertinent laws and regulations are discussed in Section 4.4. The effects of the financial crisis on risk management for non-banking institutions will also be further clarified there.

The **economic reasons** for risk management lie basically in the strongly increasing globalization of the financial markets and the introduction of new financial products (especially in the area of derivatives). The launch of the Euro in combination with inadequate regulation of these new products was one cause of the financial crisis and therefore a reason to pursue risk management. In Section 4.4.2 these developments will be considered more closely in the context of market failure.

Finally, there is **technological advances**, primarily the quicker spread of information through digital media and the Internet. But also, businesses now make products that become obsolete faster, thus shortening the product cycle and increasing the product risks. As a result, the commodities and goods markets also grow faster due to the technological advances in spreading information and accompanying globalization. The result of the increasing globalization and shortened product cycles are seen in the numerous bankruptcies of the past years and not least also in the financial crisis.

The concept of risk management and the reasons for pursuing risk management are summarized in Figure 1.1.

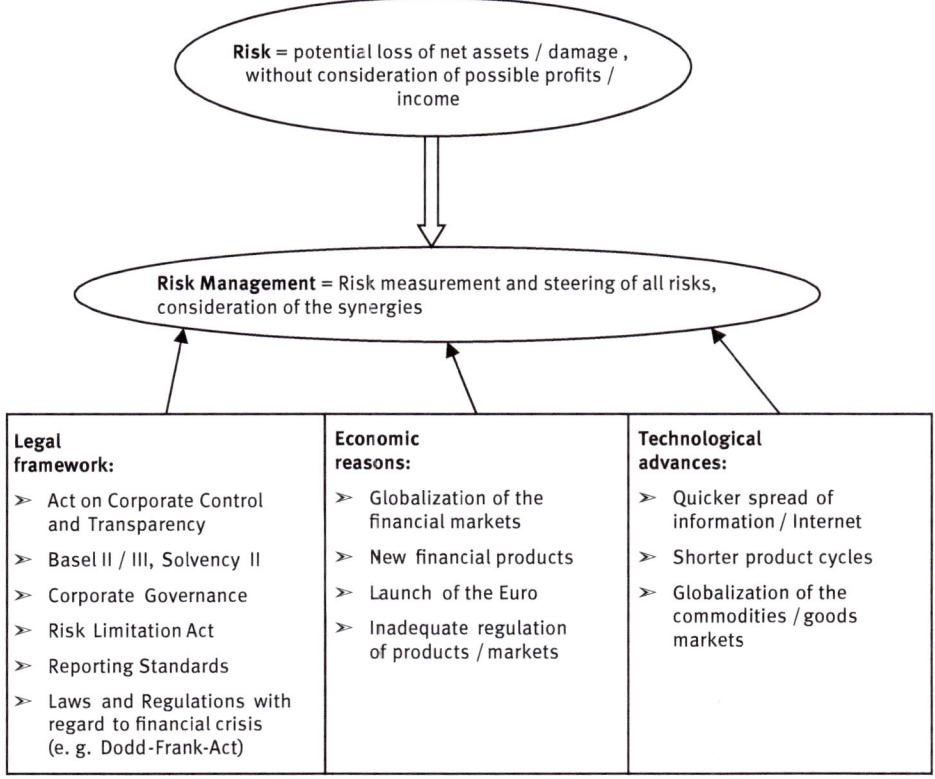

Fig. 1.1: Definitions and reasons for risk management

1.2 Risk management as a process

Starting from the concept of "risk management" as defined in Section 1.1, the topic of risk management will now be systematized. There are different criteria for doing this. One of the classifications that is used most often in the literature considers risk management as a process, i. e., as a sequence of events in time (dynamic). Risk management is a dynamic process and not a one-time event (static). The schematic representation of risk management processes shown in Figure 1.2 is often found in the current literature in this or slightly modified form (based on the classic management process). The structure of this book is oriented to this schema, so that the process-oriented perspective provides a red thread to lead the reader through the individual chapters.

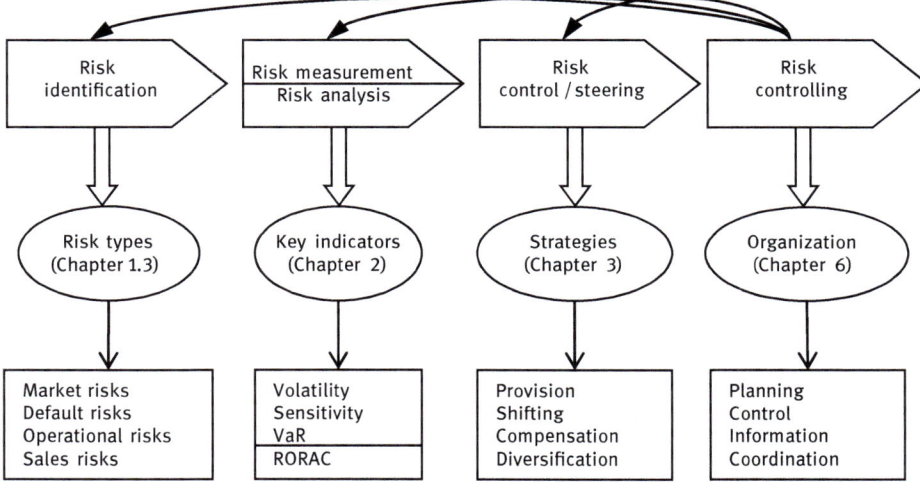

Fig. 1.2: The risk management process

Economic risks in the sense of the above definition (see Figure 1.2) will be included in the scope of **risk identification**. There are a number of different approaches for this purpose, which depend on the special features of the business and its organizational structures. Generalizations are simply not possible, yet there are different instruments that can be deployed. For a complete compilation of all risks see Section 1.3, where a systematization of business **risk types** (for example, market risks) can be found.

After risk identification comes **risk measurement** and the accompanying assessments or **risk analysis**. In the context of risk measurement it is then useful to distinguish between quantitative and qualitative measurement procedures. Quantitative measurement is largely about key figures (for example volatility), whose calculation is based on existing observable prices, rates and other market data (Sections 2.1 to 2.4). For many risks, however, such market data are not available, for numerous reasons. In these cases, qualitative measurement techniques are used (see Section 2.5). In the second chapter, fundamental functions of the different key indicators will be discussed, before these are adjusted to the specific features of different types of business risk (Chapters 4 to 7).

In **risk analysis**, the measurement results are evaluated (Section 2.6). Here, the risks are filtered for relevancy first. The central goal of the analysis is to answer the question of whether the measured and relevant risks require action. The core of risk analysis is the so-called concept of Return on Risk-Adjusted Capital (=RoRaC, see Section 2.6).

The outcome of the risk analysis is the foundation for the necessary **risk control** (risk steering). Because of the numerous and complex instruments and strategies for risk control, at this point the strategies will be roughly divided into
- provision,
- risk shifting,
- compensation and
- diversification.

In the third chapter the basic principles of different strategies and the corresponding instruments will be discussed. In chapters 4–7 these instruments as well as the measurement methods from the second chapter will be assigned to the different types of business risk.

In **risk controlling**, the organizational aspect of risk management will finally be considered (Chapter 6). This includes the question of how risk generating and risk controlling organizational units can be structurally and procedurally embedded in the company. The methodology of the measurement system as well as its organization and supervision are, next to risk reporting and support of management, the primary duties of risk controlling. Finally, in the context of the collaboration between risk controlling and corporate management, actual risk-based corporate management will be discussed. The described phases of risk management form an iterative feedback loop (see Figure 1.2), i. e., the outcomes or decisions in the context of risk strategy can lead to measurements or provisions or compensation (risk control), or to a renewed identification of yet unconsidered types of risk. Also within the scope of risk control is establishing new methods of risk measurement or changing the guidelines of the risk analysis.

1.3 Risk identification and risk types

Identification of **business risks** that exist in the context of corporate activities cannot be described in general form. Types of risk and especially their respective

importance for a business depend heavily on the specific features of the business, such as for example industry characteristics, regional peculiarities or product types. In order to be more accessible and comprehensible to a wider readership, this book will not delve further into these special features. Instead it will revolve around other principles and emphases. The interested reader will find references to the available specialist literature in the relevant sections where the various industries and other special features are mentioned. However, some general fundamental principles and basic tools can be applied to risk identification independently of that. For example,
- analysis grids,
- risk tables,
- interviews,
- analysis of operational processes.

A basic component and prerequisite of risk identification is the systematization of the types of business risk

There are various kinds of systematizations of the different **risk types** in the literature and in business practice. What decides the type of systematization and especially the related criteria is the corresponding question. The objective of this book is a general, business-wide discussion of risk management, independent of industry features, company size and region.

At the highest level, a distinction will be drawn between **scientific** and **economic risks**. This might seem banal at first glance. However, a fundamental problem will become apparent: the various risks cannot always be clearly separated from one another. Thus scientific risks like, for example, earthquakes are inextricably intertwined with the economic risks of reinsurance companies. This problem cannot be solved through systematization. Nonetheless what follows will try to minimize the problem by using the clearest possible definitions of the risk categories.

The **economic** and **business risks** will be suitably separated in a second step. Here the impossibility of precision will be seen again: cyclical risks directly affect the business sales risk.

On the corporate or business level a distinction in **financial** and **performance** risks will be drawn. This is in line with the goal of capturing all possible business risks based on internal accounting systems. The financial risks will be further divided into market, default and liquidation risks. The performance risks will be subdivided into operational and sales/procurement risks.

The **interdependence** between the various economic risks must be emphasized.

A default risk can lead to a liquidation risk if the agreed interest and principle payments can no longer be met by debtors. The stock price risk cannot be separated from the insolvency risk (=default risk), because a corporation threatened with insolvency also automatically carries a considerable amount of stock price risk. A production process that requires crude oil entails a procurement risk through rising oil prices. The crude oil must be bought in US-$, which along with the procurement risk creates a currency risk from appreciation of US dollars.

These examples illustrate the **allocation problem** of assigning various types of risk to transactions. Different methods and tools are used for different types of risk. Thus it is advisable to use the most precise categories possible. This allocation can be achieved with the help of the **causation principle** and the **control principle**. Both principles will also be applied in organizational risk controlling and risk management in Section 6.2. With the causation principle, transaction risks are assigned according to primary causal risk. Overdue debtor payments and threatened corporate bankruptcy are thus classified according to the primary causal principle of default risk. Increasing crude oil prices would be classified according to procurement risk. On the control principle, the risks are allocated where they can be most sensibly controlled. So the exchange rate risks arising from crude oil procurement is classified as a currency risk (currency management). The overdue interest and principal payments are classified as liquidation risks (liquidation management). The control principle is also necessary in the context of risk controlling, in order to grasp the compensation effect for, e. g., exchange rate risks or liquidation control throughout the **entire company** (see Section 6.2).

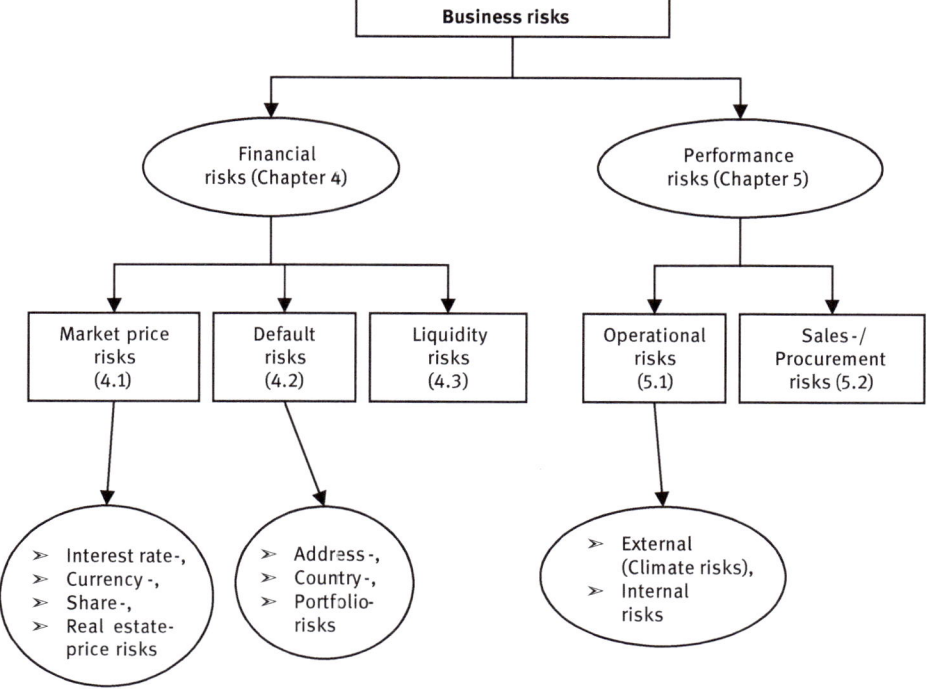

Fig. 1.3: Classification of the types of business risk

The classifications of business risk are compiled in illustration 1.3. The development of the fourth and fifth chapters can be understood on the basis of the given sections.

1.4 References

For a deeper consideration of the **concepts** of **risk management** and **risk controlling** as well as a **process oriented** discussion of risk management, see

Burger, Anton/Buchhart, Anton: Risiko-Controlling, Oldenbourg Verlag, München, 2002

and the English works

Bloss, Michael/Ernst, Dietmar/Häcker, Joachim/Sörensen, Daniel: "Financial Engineering", Oldenbourg Verlag, München, p. 501–506, 2012,

Jorion, Philippe: "Value at Risk: The New Benchmark for Managing Financial Risk", McGraw-Hill, 3rd ed., 2006.

Pojasek, Robert B.: "Organizational Risk Management and Sustainability: A Practical Step-by-Step Guide", Taylor&Francis Inc., 2017.

Various classifications of **risk types** can be found in many works on risk management, for example in

Crouhy, Michel/Galai, Dan/Mark, Robert: "The Essentials of Risk Management", McGraw Hill Education, New York, 2nd edition, 2014,

Jorion, Philippe: "Financial Risk Manager Handbook", Wiley, Hoboken, New Jersey, 6th edition, 2011,

Sartor, Franz J./Bourauel, Corinna: Risikomanagement kompakt – In 7 Schritten zum aggregierten Nettorisiko des Unternehmens, Oldenbourg Wissenschaftsverlag, München 2013.

and

Vanini, Ute: "Risikomanagement – Grundlagen, Instrumente, Unternehmenspraxis", Schäffer-Poeschel Verlag, Stuttgart, 2012

For an overview on different **risk topics** see

Allen, Steven: "Financial Risk Management: A Practitioner's Guide to Managing Market and Credit Risk", Wiley Finance, 2nd edition, 2012,

Malz, M. Allan: "Financial Risk Management: Models, History and Institutions", Wiley Finance, 2011,

2 Risk measurement and risk analysis

After risk identification in Section 1.3 comes risk measurement and, building on that, risk analysis. Risk measurement is the core of risk management. Only risks that can be identified or measured can be planned and controlled. Because it is so important, this book will attach a special significance to risk measurement and treat it with corresponding thoroughness. First the quantitative procedures (i. e. measurable numbers) will be discussed. At the same time the respective advantages and disadvantages will be derived from simple, easily understandable examples. From Chapter 4, risk measurement will be applied to special types of risk and specific adjustments will be made where appropriate. The same applies to the representation of qualitative measurement methods in Section 2.5. In particular, the transfer to credit risks (default risks) in Section 4.2 gets its own discussion because the rating procedure represents a special application for qualitatively measurable risk.Finally, the first job of risk analysis is to judge whether or not the previously measured risks require further steps (discussed in Chapter 3). The various risk measurements are shown in Figure 2.1.

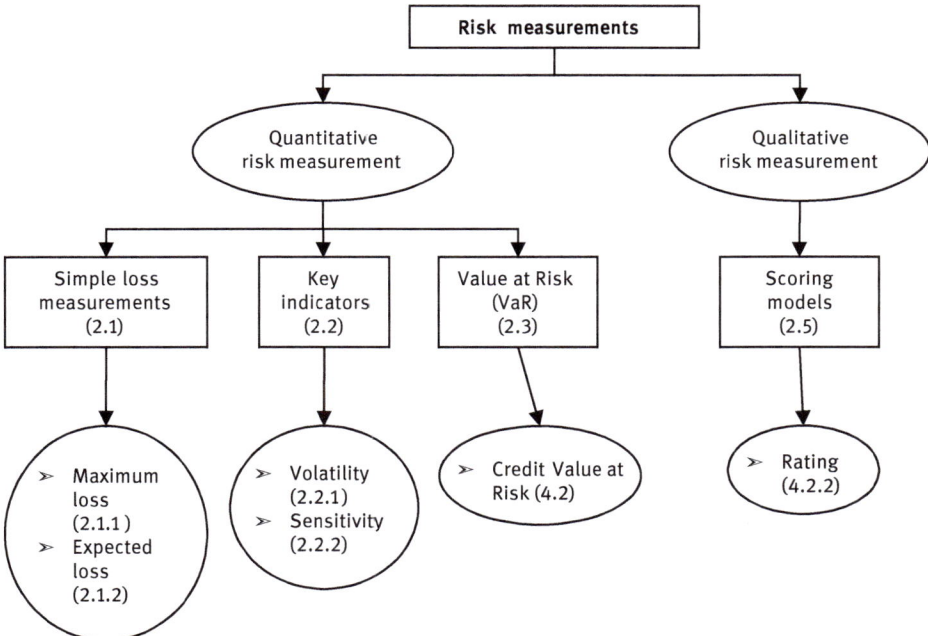

Fig. 2.1: Overview of risk measurements

2.1 Simple loss measurements

Simple loss measurements rely on long-known probability calculations (especially expected value) backed up by common sense. The disadvantage of simple loss measurements lies in the totally inadequate picture of the actual or relevant risk content, especially in view of a potentially necessary risk control. Because of this, these key indicators have a subordinate role in practice. There remains nonetheless an advantage: because they are easy to use and calculate, they can be used, despite their imprecision, as a rough estimate for forming a larger framework for plausibility considerations of complex measurements (like, for example, the Value at Risk in Section 2.3)

2.1.1 Maximum loss

A direct and very simple measurement of risk is the maximum loss.

The **maximum loss** refers to the greatest possible damage or loss of an asset position or start-up capital.

The mechanism of maximum loss will be demonstrated in two simple examples which will be referred to again later.

Example A:
Two players, S and T, play a game and start with capital of € 1,000 each. Their assets at the beginning of the game, then, amount to € 1,000 each. They throw **once**. If it comes up heads, player S has to pay player T € 500, and if it comes number, T has pay S € 500. It is assumed that the throw (and the coins) aren't manipulated and that the probability of either heads or tails coming up is 50 % respectively.

Example B:
Student C bought an asset worth € 1,000 from an arbitrarily chosen market. So his assets amount to € 1,000. In the future, he can sell these assets on the exchange for € 1,300 with a probability of 70 %. The probability of selling for only € 700 is 20 %, and the probability that his asset is worthless on the exchange is 10 % (that is, a total loss of € 1,000).

In example A, the maximum loss is obviously

$$ML(A) = \underline{-€\,500.00}$$

(since presumably they only play once.) If they play more than once, the maximum loss adds up to € 1,000. In that case the maximum loss corresponds to the start-up capital. In example B the maximum loss is

$$ML(B) = -€\,1{,}000.00$$

if the asset is no longer worth anything on the market.

The computation of the absolute maximum loss in monetary units is only suitable for certain purposes. **Absolute loss measurements** in currency units are necessary for the comparison of available risk capital or equity capital, since these amounts will also be determined in Euros. For comparisons of the various risk positions to each other, however, the **relative loss measurements** are necessary, in order to be able to assess the risks independently of the size of the asset position. Here we refer to the amount of the asset position or start-up capital. This results in a relative maximum loss of

$$ML(A) = -€\,500.00\,€\,/\,€\,1{,}000.00 = \mathbf{-\,50\,\%},$$
$$ML(A) = -€\,1{,}000.00\,€\,/\,€\,1{,}000.00 = \mathbf{-\,100\,\%}.$$

The advantage of maximum loss lies in its easy calculability, that is, no probability has to be included. The maximum loss is also suitable as a control figure, since a risk calculation with results greater than the maximum loss can't be correct.

The simplicity of the maximum loss is at the same time its crucial **disadvantage**. There is no qualitative assessment of the risk content, that is, what is riskier cannot be judged. It becomes immediately apparent that B is not necessarily riskier than A just because the maximum loss is much higher. The probability of the maximum loss occurring remains fully unconsidered. The maximum loss has a 50 % chance of occurring in example A, while in example B the greatest damage has only a 10 % chance of occurring! So this measurement should not, at least, be used for a qualified risk evaluation.

Furthermore, especially in the area of financial market instruments, there are positions for which the maximum loss cannot be computed. In particular this touches on **derivatives**, where an asset loss can be caused not by sinking prices but by increasing prices. However, as long as the price can rise arbitrarily, at least in theory, an upper limit in the sense of a maximum loss cannot be specified. This issue will be explored in more detail in Sections 3.4.2 and 4.4.2.

A maximum loss also cannot be determined for risks or damages with potentially incalculable monetary consequences. An example here would be the risks from the operation of a **nuclear power plant**. If there were a catastrophic nuclear accident, liability insurance (in Germany there is a ceiling of € 2.5 billion for damages) would fall far short of covering the potential maximum losses. The rest of the damages would have to be carried by the state or the taxpayers.

In relation to the financial crisis there is discussion of how much **equity capital** the **banks** must deposit in future for their balance sheet assets. Here one could apply a theoretical approach, using the maximum loss of all risk-related assets as a measurement for minimum capital requirements. Then it would be possible for the banks to bear all their business risk themselves. In practice this approach is not feasible. For one thing, the global capital markets don't have enough equity capital available for the banks to come anywhere near being able to cover the maximum loss. For another thing, the banks must earn interest on equity capital deposits, which they generate, for example, through interest rates on customer credit. With the maximum loss approach, the interest rates on credit would have to be raised so high that it would be economically and legally (ethically) unacceptable. In Sections 4.4.2 – 4.4.4 the question of capital requirements for banks in relation to Basel III will be considered more closely.

In summary, what can be said for **maximum loss** is that it can always be used as an additional **control variable** because it is very simple to calculate. In particular, it can be used as a warning indicator when its concrete calculation is not possible, for example with derivatives and nuclear power plants. Its **fundamental weaknesses**, however, must not be ignored. Additional more substantial risk measurements must be used, which will be discussed in the following sections.

2.1.2 Expected loss

To mitigate the grave disadvantages of maximum loss, it is obvious that probabilities must be included in the risk measurement. The simplest possibility is to calculate the expected loss in terms of the statistical expected value. The expected value corresponds to the "weighted average" of the values, which can express the uncertain "asset loss" figure.

With **expected loss**, the potential losses are multiplied by their respective chances of occurring and the results are added up.

In examples A and B, the expected losses (=EL) can be calculated by weighting their respective asset losses with their associated probabilities (relative expected loss in parentheses), so:

$$EL(A) = (0.5 \times -€\,500.00) = \underline{\boldsymbol{-€\,250.00\,(-25\,\%)}},$$
$$EL(B) = (0.1 \times -€\,1{,}000.00) + (0.2 \times -€\,300.00) = \underline{\boldsymbol{-€\,160.00\,(-16\,\%)}}.$$

The **advantage** over the maximum loss is immediately apparent: the risk assessment is much fuller when it includes the probabilities. Applying expected loss versus maximum loss it is now clear that example A is riskier than example B. The reason is obvious. The maximum loss occurs in B with a probability of only 10 %, while in A the probability is 50 %. Thus, this differential risk assessment takes into account the expected loss, as opposed to the maximum loss.

The expected loss nonetheless also has significant **disadvantages** with regard to the quality of the risk assessment. In expected loss, the origins of the risk are not reflected. In other words: the expected value does not adequately show the risk distribution (or the probability distribution). This issue become clear immediately when example B is modified as follows to example C:

Example C:
This time, a total loss of € 1,000 has a probability of only 5 %. Now the likelihood of an absolute loss of € 200 is 55 %, while a profit of € 525 has a 40 % probability.

Now the expected value of the loss again amounts to

$$EL(C) = (0.05 \times -€\,1{,}000.00) + (0.55 \times -€\,200.00) = \underline{-€\,160.00\ (-16\,\%)}.$$

Consequently, the risk bearer would, with the help of the expected loss, reach an identical risk assessment as that in Example B. However, this is a questionable result, because in case C the risk appears to be smaller, since the maximum loss occurs with a likelihood of only 5 % and the other loss potential of € 200 is smaller than example B's € 300. It is exactly this **varying quality** of the **risk structure** that is **not shown** by expected loss.

Comparing examples B and C shows **even further weaknesses** of expected loss. Because the various risk origins are not observable, the risk bearer's potential **risk attitude cannot** be adequately **mapped**. Thus a risk-averse student would prefer variant C because the potential losses are apparently smaller. Example B, on the other hand, would be preferred by the risk-friendly participants. Furthermore, when calculating expected losses it is possible to apply a **different basis** of **calculation** in each case. Thus in example A, only one loss measurement flows into the calculation from two observations in all. In examples B and C, on the other hand, two loss measurements come from a total of three observations. The factor of time has also been disregarded up till now, since only one singular action (static) has been examined. In practice, however, business activities consist of constantly repeated operations (e. g. ongoing buying and selling => dynamic consideration).

2.2 Key indicators

The weaknesses of the so-called "simple risk measurements" described in Section 2.1 lead to further risk measurements or key indicators, described below, which can be used to remedy these weaknesses. These approaches basically fall back on known statistical methods or key indicators.

2.2.1 Volatility

In the first step, the individual relative asset changes (changes of the assets in relation to the initial assets or start-up capital) are compared to the respective probabilities of occurrence. The examples cited above give the following values:

Tab. 2.1: Relative (observed) asset changes

A:		B:		C:	
Relative asset change:	Probability:	Relative asset change:	Probability:	Relative asset change:	Probability:
−50.00 %	50.00 %	−100.00 %	10.00 %	−100.00 %	5.00 %
+50.00 %	50.00 %	−30.00 %	20.00 %	−20.00 %	55.00 %
		+30.00 %	70.00 %	+52.50 %	40.00 %

The **expected relative asset losses** can be **calculated**. The above examples then give the following calculations and results:

$$EL(A) = (-50.00\,\% \times 50.00\,\%) = \mathbf{-25.00\,\%},$$
$$EL(B) = (-100.00\,\% \times 10.00\,\%) + (-30.00\,\% \times 20.00\,\%) = \mathbf{-16.00\,\%},$$
$$EL(C) = (-100.00\,\% \times 5.00\,\%) + (-20.00\,\% \times 55.00\,\%) = \mathbf{-16.00\,\%}.$$

These relative expected asset losses must correspond to the results in Section 2.1.2. As long as nothing else is specified, the following relative values are used. If it is explicitly stated that the values are relative, they will be omitted for simplicity in other versions.

Another weakness of the expected loss is the variable basis of the calculation. To rectify this weakness, the asset profits with their associated probabilities of occurrence must also be considered. Then there is no risk measurement any more, but an expected change in asset.

With expected asset change, all potential (observed) changes in assets are multiplied by their associated probabilities and added up.

With **expected asset change**, all potential (observed) changes in assets are multiplied by their associated probabilities and added up.

The expected change in assets therefore has the advantage that the same basis of calculation – namely all probabilities (which always add up to 100 %) – can be used as an underlying foundation for a comparison of alternatives. For the example, then, the following **expected asset changes** (=EAC) occurs:

$EAC(A) = (-50.00\% \times 50.00\%) + (50.00\% \times 50.00\%) = \textbf{0.00\%}$,
$EAC(B) = (-100.00\% \times 10.00\%) + (-30.00\% \times 20.00\%) + (30.00\% \times 70.00\%) = \textbf{+5.00\%}$,
$EAC(C) = (-100.00\% \times 5.00\%) + (-20.00\% \times 55.00\%) + (52,50\% \times 40.00\%) = \textbf{+5.00\%}$.

The expected change in assets also delivers no distinctive results for examples B and C.

The crucial weakness of the expected value is the lack of qualitative risk assessment, which can be seen in examples B and C. The question arises of how the various processes leading to the identical results (–16% for expected loss and +5% for expected change in assets) can be computationally captured and described. A more intuitive approach, which captures the risk better, would be to consider the summed **differences** between the individual **possible** (observed) **asset changes** and the calculated **expected asset changes** calculated above. Intuition would indicate that the higher the sum of the differences, the greater the risk. The differences measure the deviation from a particular expected value and thus describe the deviation from an expectation as risk. The respective results are:

A: $(-50.00\% - 0.00\%) + (50.00\% - 0.00\%) = \underline{\textbf{0.00\%}}$,
B: $(-100.00\% - 5.00\%) + (-30.00\% - 5.00\%) + (30.00\% - 5.00\%) = \underline{\textbf{–115.00\%}}$,
C: $(-100.00\% - 5.00\%) + (-20.00\% - 5.00\%) + (52,50\% - 5.00\%) = \underline{\textbf{– 82.50\%}}$.

This approach immediately exhibits significant flaws. For one thing, example A will show no risk, because the **positive** and **negative differences cancel** each other out exactly. Thus the simplest differences would not be a suitable risk measure, since it is obvious that in example A, as explained thoroughly above, there is an actual risk. Also, the results in both B and C clearly don't portray the risks correctly. **Negative values** arise, which is erroneous for a risk assessment, since it makes no sense to define a negative risk. What's more, the **dimension** of less than – 100% in example B is not a meaningful result since the maximum loss in B amounts to 100%.

There are two common mathematical approaches used to avoid positive and negative differences cancelling each other out. On the one hand, the **absolute value of the differences** can be calculated. In order to avoid values greater than 100% coming up, the absolute differences are still multiplied by the probabilities of the respective changes in asset (=likelihood of occurrence). This approach delivers the following outcomes:

A: $|-50.00\% - 0.00\%| \times 50.00\% + |50.00\% - 0.00\%| \times 50.00\% = \underline{\textbf{50.00\%}}$,
B: $|-100.00\% - 5.00\%| \times 10.00\% + |-30.00\% - 5.00\%| \times 20.00\% + |30.00\% - 5.00\%| \times 70.00\% = \underline{\textbf{35.00\%}}$,
C: $|-100.00\% - 5.00\%| \times 5.00\% + |-20.00\% - 5.00\%| \times 55.00\% + |52.50\% - 5.00\%| \times 40.00\% = \underline{\textbf{38.00\%}}$.

The results appear plausible at first glance, since no result is greater than 100 % and also, in particular, examples B and C have different outcomes. This mean absolute deviation is quite a common measure of dispersion and thus risk. However, its features have been controversial since the 1990s. Another disadvantage of the mean absolute deviation is the often difficult algebraic refinement of the figures. As a result, the following risk measurement procedures have been established world-wide (for a discussion of the two different distribution measurements, see the literature references in Section 2.7).

To avoid the positive and negative results cancelling each other out, the **differences** are first **squared**. These squared differences are then multiplied by their associated **probabilities**. This allows the various risk structures to be considered. The sums return the following values, which are designated by the statistical indicator "**variance**":

Variance(A) = $(-50.00\% - 0.00\%)^2$ x 50.00 % + $(50.00\% - 0.00\%)^2$ x 50.00 % = **0.25**,
Variance(B) = $(-100.00\% - 5.00\%)^2$ x 10.00 % + $(-30.00\% - 5.00\%)^2$ x 20.00 % + $(30.00\% - 5.00\%)^2$ x 70 % = **0.1785**,
Variance(C) = $(-100.00\% - 5.00\%)^2$ x 5.00 % + $(-20.00\% - 5.00\%)^2$ x 55.00 % + $(52.50\% - 5.00\%)^2$ x 40 % = **0.17975**.

The squaring stops any negative values from arising. However this results in data is no longer given as a percentage, but in percent squared. Also, after squaring, the dimensions are no longer open to sensible interpretation in relation to the changes in asset. These weaknesses can nonetheless be easily remedied by drawing the **roots** from the **variance**. Then the orders of magnitude can be meaningfully interpreted in relation to the expected values and the results are once again in the same units, namely **percent**. The values calculated in this way are the standard deviations of the expected changes in asset. In business administration and especially in finance this value is called **volatility**. For this example the following volatilities (=Vol) subsequently arise:

Vol(A) = **50.00 %**,
Vol(B) = **42.25 %**,
Vol(C) = **42.40 %**.

Volatility has become established worldwide as a measurement for the fluctuation range and therefore as a cornerstone of risk measurement. That is why the above derivation was described in such detail. All other instruments, methods and applications within risk management are fundamentally based on this volatility. **Volatility** can first of all be **technically** defined as follows:

Volatility is calculated as the square root of the sum of the squared differences of each individual observed change of assets and the expected change of asset multiplied by the respective probability. Volatility describes the average deviations of the expected change of assets upwards and downwards.

This allows the possibility of more valuable statements about the risk content. Version A is clearly riskier than B and C. On the other hand, B is only slightly less risky than C. Now a **different** possible **risk structure** can also be adequately mapped. At first glance, example C seems less risky, since the loss appears smaller. As shown above, this is a misjudgement. Only the volatility models the risk properly because it maps as risk not only losses but also the fluctuations around profits. This fluctuation around the gains is larger in example C that in example B because C is overall slightly riskier than B (and has a respectively higher volatility).

In Table 2.2, the results for the maximum loss, the expected loss, the expected change in assets and the volatility are summarized.

Tab. 2.2: Results for maximum loss, expected loss, expected change in assets, volatility

Example:	Maximum loss:	Expected loss:	Expected asset change:	Volatility:
A	−50.00 %	−25.00 %	0.00 %	50.00 %
B	−100.00 %	−16.00 %	+5.00 %	42.25 %
C	−100.00 %	−16.00 %	+5.00 %	42.40 %

For this example, the **volatility** can be **interpreted** as follows: In example A, the change in assets fluctuates around its expected value of 0 % on average by 50 percentage points upwards and downwards. This result is obvious, since only asset changes of +50 % or −50 % occur! In example B (C), the change in assets fluctuates around its expected value of 5 % by 42.25 (42.40) percentage points upwards and downwards.

In relation to the concept of **risk defined** in Section 1.1, which focuses on loss without comparison to profit, volatility appears at first glance to represent a contradiction. By this calculation an increase in assets (capital gains return) runs at +50 % in example A, +30 % in example B and +52.5 % in example C. This apparent contradiction can be resolved through the following remarks.

When only the observed losses are used (i. e. in example A −50 % and in example B −100 %, −30 %) there would be no statistically correct amount, because then the sum of the weights would not be 100 (or one). As mentioned above, there would be no **unified basis** of **calculation** for comparison. Also, there would be no statistically meaningful results when considering the development of changes in asset over time if only the losses were used in the calculation and hence many different points in time were to be compared. For a useful comparison, the whole time series together with the observed returns must be considered in each case.

On the other hand, the capital gains return is not used as a direct risk measurement in calculating the volatility, but rather the **fluctuation around** the **expected change in asset**, and only this fluctuation is treated as risk.

This interpretation of volatility will be especially significant in risk analysis, and particularly in dealing with the RoRaC concept (=Return on Risk-Adjusted Capital). The **profit** in the form of capital gains must then be grasped **independently** of the **risk measurement**. Specifically, the other types of profit (e. g. interest or dividend income) that don't relate to the volatility must also then be considered in the profit calculations. In this respect therefore the volatility represents no contradiction to the unilateral (loss-oriented) definition of risk.

The **consideration of time** is simply not included in this concept of volatility as it is described so far. On the basis of the above derivations this is now after all simple and easy.

In considering development over time, which is normal in business practice, a realistic example would now be useful. Examples B and C are based on the purchase of an asset in an arbitrary market, which can only be sold at **a point later in time** (static approach). Now for this transaction, the specific purchase of a single stock will do, which can however be bought or sold on every work day or trading day thereafter (dynamic approach).

The entire year of 2005 has been chosen as the historical observation period, with a total of 257 trading days and thus 257 observed stock prices. Which year of the past is used is irrelevant to the following procedures. It only matters whether the chosen data are representative for the given circumstances and the featured methods can be illustrated. Therefore the year 2005 can also be designated as the year X. The stock prices of **BMW** (the car manufacturer) and **MAN** (a machine manufacturer) will be used for comparison.

To be able to compare the changes in asset for both stocks, the calculation of the comparable **relative** information must be reconsidered. There are numerous methods which won't be considered here in order keep things simple (see Section 2.7). To illustrate the effect of volatility most simply and clearly, the principle of **daily stock price returns** will be used.

Instead of getting the price changes from the starting capital (assets) specified right at the beginning of the observation period, it is assumed that the stock is sold every day and then bought again the next day. The subsequent earnings or losses are then based on the previous day's purchase price, in order to get a relative win or loss statement. This value is called the **daily stock price return**. Possible profits from dividend payments are ignored in this process. In Table 2.3 the price data (closing prices) and the return calculations are given as an example.

Tab. 2.3: Prices and returns for BMW and MAN

	Prices:		Returns:	
Trading days:	BMW	MAN	BMW	MAN
03.01.2005	€ 33.75	€ 29.50		
04.01.2005	€ 34.42	€ 29.64	**1.985 %**	0.47 %
05.01.2005	€ 34.54	€ 29.22	0.35 %	−1.42 %
06.01.2005	€ 34.71	€ 29.50	0.49 %	0.96 %
.	.	.	.	.
.	.	.	.	.
.	.	.	.	.
29.12.2005	€ 37.41	€ 45.24	0.78 %	0.69 %
30.12.2005	€ 37.05	€ 45.08	−0.96 %	−0.35 %

On January 3, 2005 no return could be calculated, since by definition there was no price available from the previous day. On January 4 the **return** for **BMW** is calculated as:

The price difference between January 4 (sell day) and January 3 (purchase day) = € 34.42 − € 33.75 and this difference is based on the January 3 purchase price: € 0.67 / € 33.75 = **1.985 %**.

All further returns for BMW and MAN develop the same way on the other observed days. Thus the time series can be calculated in % with daily stock price returns for BMW and MAN for the year 2005 (without January 3, 2005). This data can now be used to **calculate** the **average stock price return** and its volatility. The only difference to the calculations described above is that no probabilities for specific price changes are available (like those used in examples A, B and C), but rather there are 256 observed individual stock price returns. In order to calculate the average, the various returns are not weighted with a probability, but rather the simple sum of all the returns is divided by the number of observations (i. e. 256). This corresponds to a probability of occurrence of each individual return of precisely 1/256. The daily stock price return thus calculated amount to:

BMW: **0.042 %**,
MAN: **0.175 %**.

The associated **volatilities** can be **calculated** analogously based on the average returns per day by taking the deviations between the individual observed daily returns and the average return calculated above, squaring the deviations and adding them up, and then dividing by the number of observations. The square root of these results represents the volatility around the average returns and amounts to:

BMW: **1.031 %**,
MAN: **1.386 %**.

So the BMW (MAN) stock **fluctuates** on **average** around its average daily return of 0.042 % (0.175 %) by 1.031 (1.386) **percentage points**.

Because the calculated volatility of the time series has such high importance in risk management and is therefore published daily, for example in the trade papers, this **interpretation** will be deepened further through **graphic** illustrations.

First, in Figure 2.2 the actual 2005 stock exchange prices for BMW and MAN are shown over time.

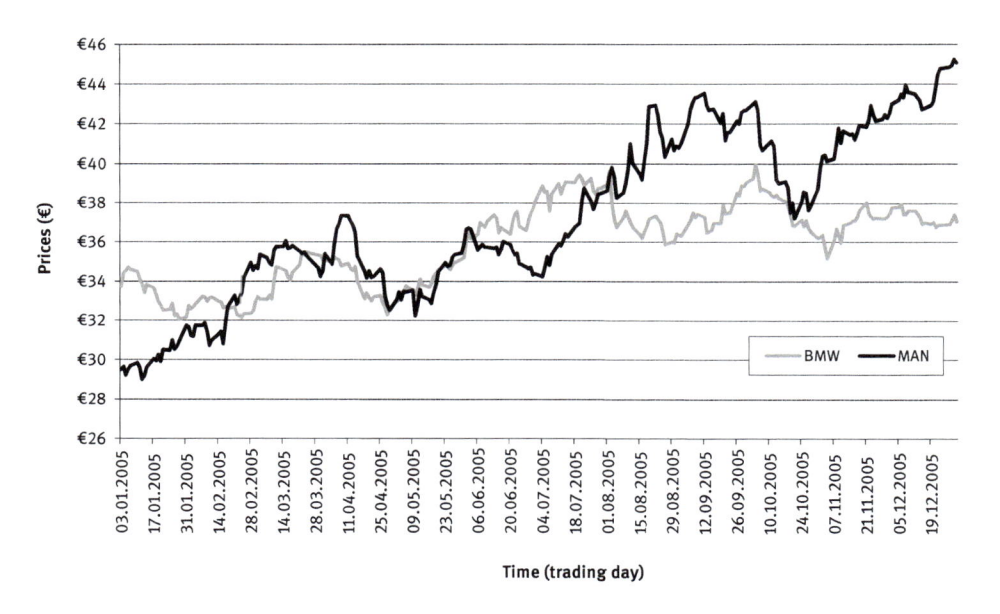

Fig. 2.2: Daily stock prices for BMW and MAN in 2005

At first glance, the stock performance graphic requires hard work to derive at best intuitive **claims** about the **risk content**. It seems reasonable to suppose that the MAN stocks fluctuate more strongly than the BMW stocks. Since big swings are observable in both stocks, it is not possible to derive a direct comparison about the risk content from Figure 2.2. It is also impossible to draw conclusions about the risk content for the entire year from the fact that the MAN stocks were lower than the BMW stocks at the beginning of 2005 and higher at the end of 2005. In Figures 2.3 (BMW) and 2.4 (MAN)

2.2 Key indicators — 21

therefore, the daily stock price returns with their averages and associated volatility are shown.

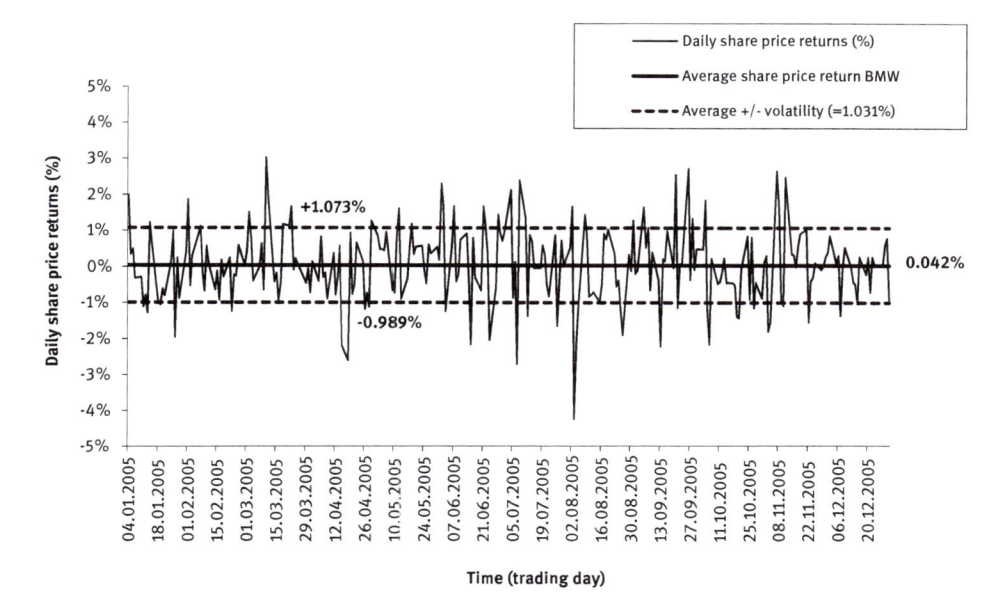

Fig. 2.3: Daily stock price returns, average and volatility for BMW

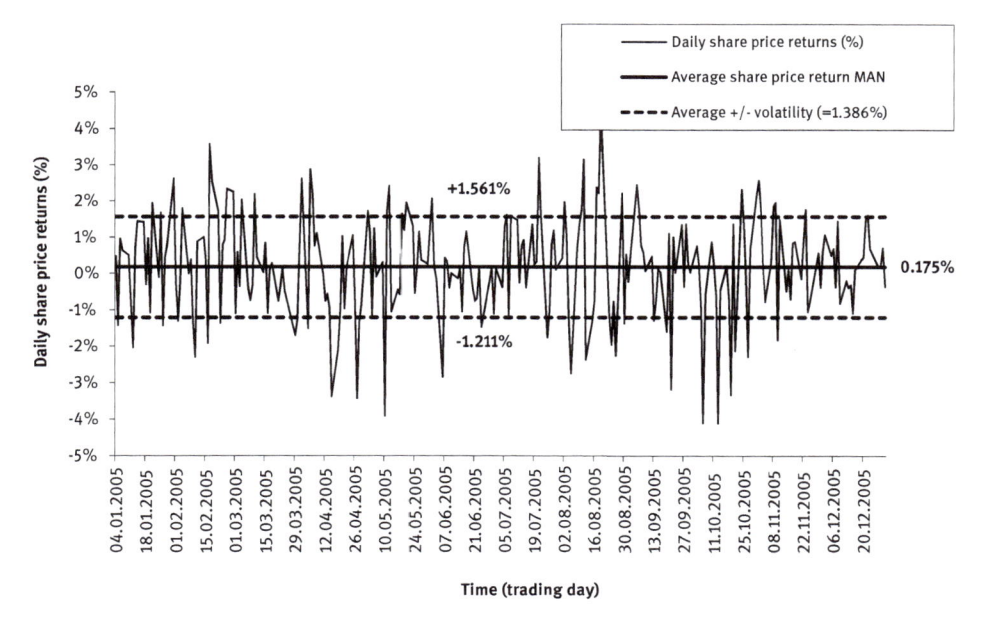

Fig. 2.4: Daily stock price returns, average and volatility for MAN

Through inspection and calculation of the volatility, the stronger fluctuations and thus the higher risk of MAN compared to BMW becomes clear and also measurable. Consideration of just the relative changes in the daily stock price returns shows the much more frequent and bigger fluctuations in the MAN stocks. Just looking at the graphic representation of the **relative changes** already leads to a **better possibility** of **risk assessment** than the absolute stock prices shown in Figure 2.2.

Also, the **interpretation** of the key indicator **volatility** as average fluctuation around the mean is especially clear in Figures 2.3 and 2.4. There are few big peaks lying above the volatility but many small ones lying underneath the volatility. On average, this results in the calculated volatility.

The volatility of the **BMW** and **MAN** stocks can now also be compared with examples A, B and C, since for purposes of **comparability** the expected change in assets (or the average stock price return) and associated volatilities are measured in percent. Additionally, for an even better comparison of the results, the ratio of the change in assets to the volatility is also calculated. There is a high expected change in assets and simultaneously the volatility (and thus the risk) is small, so this ratio assumes a high value. Thus high-value ratios coming from this comparison can be regarded as positive in terms of risk assessment. A detailed analysis of the results of risk measurement is presented in Section 2.6. In Table 2.4, all the important key indicators described up till now are summarized for examples A, B, and C as well as for the BMW and MAN stocks.

Tab. 2.4: Maximum loss, expected asset change, volatility for examples A, B, C, and BMW, MAN stocks

Key indicator:	Example A:	Example B:	Example C:	BMW:	MAN:
Maximum loss:	−50.00 %	−100.00 %	−100.00 %	−100.00 %	−100.00 %
Expected relative asset change (average stock return):	0.00 %	+5.00 %	+5.00 %	+0.042 %	+0.175 %
Volatility:	50.00 %	42.25 %	42.40 %	1.031 %	1.386 %
Expected asset change/volatility:	0.0000	0.1183	0.1179	0.0407	0.1263

Example A performs the worst, for there the expected change in assets is smallest and the risk greatest. Examples B and C vary only marginally due to the equal change in assets and only slightly different risk. The MAN stock turns out to be the most profitable and the BMW stock is only slightly better than example A.

There are many **challenges** in **calculating the volatility** for time series such as the stock price returns for the BMW and MAN stock, resulting in various calculation approaches. The most important problems will be briefly discussed here, without however digging too deeply into them.

The first question in calculating the volatility relates to the **choice** of the **observation period**. A calendar year consisting of a total of 257 trading days was chosen. It is certainly indisputable that had a longer period been chosen, it would have led to other volatility results. However, it is obvious that there probably is no "right" historical period length. Also, with longer observation periods the probability is greater that unusual events (i. e. shocks and crises located further in the past) must be taken into account. With a shorter period, on the other hand, current events and structures have a stronger influence on the calculation. Likewise, it can be argued in reverse that long historical periods contain events that are no longer relevant for the future. Since this discussion is still a controversy in science and business practice, only two alternative calculation methods will be briefly introduced here.

Empirical research has shown that with long historical periods, applying **logarithmic returns** leads to more stable results. Another way to consider different time structures in longer historical periods consists of **exponentially weighting** the past returns. Thus the most current values are weighted the most heavily and the oldest values are given the least weight. In the area of classic financial market risk, the banks have meanwhile implemented an **observation period of 250 trading days**, i. e., a year, as the default choice. For this reason, the further examples here will also use a year (with ca. 250 trading days) as the basis for calculations.

Other methods or means of identifying the volatility exist. These include, firstly, the so-called **implied volatilities**. These derive from the market data on options. Since this market data is generally only available for very few large businesses that are listed on the stock exchange, the range of application is very limited and will not be explored further here.

Various studies have also shown that volatility varies over different time periods, that is, it is not constant over the entire period under review. With the help of so-called parametric approaches, it is possible to make a **time-variant estimate of volatility** based on a stochastic process. At the center of this estimate is the GARCH model. For details of the GARCH model please refer to the relevant literature (see Section 2.7).

In the absence of time series, **volatility** would have to be **estimated**, for example on the basis of experience or expert knowledge. This approach will be necessary later in calculating the volatility for certain types of business risk, for example, for sales risk (see Section 5.2).

Although volatility has become a fundamental measure of risk, it still has three grave **disadvantages**:
- In the stock example described above, the prices were observed for regular intervals and the stocks could be sold or bought daily. However if the asset positions to be compared with each other must be held over varying time periods (the so-called holding period or liquidation period, i. e. for stocks as opposed to credits), then volatility is no longer suitable, because it can't map **uneven time periods**.
- Volatility is in the first place a relative fluctuation measure. This means however that it gives no direct conclusions about potential loss in monetary units. In par-

ticular there is no reference to the asset which is exposed to the corresponding risk (so-called Risk exposure). However, it is exactly risk-oriented management control that demands a **risk assessment in monetary units** in order to compare all the risks to the business liability (equity capital) available for offsetting those risks. With simple loss measures, the loss was measured directly in € (see Section 2.1.1 – 2.1.2) and then given as a percentage in reference to the assets. One could likewise do the same with volatility, measuring relative volatility and giving it in reference to the assets (or the risk exposure). In this respect, this disadvantage is not a technical problem. The much more pressing question to be answered is which date to use and how to value the assets. This question will be answered in the section about Value at Risk (2.3).
- In contrast to the maximum loss and to the expected loss, volatility represents indeed a more meaningful risk measure (in the sense that higher volatility means also a qualitatively higher risk), but the **risk philosophy of the decision maker** cannot be explicitly factored in to the volatility measure. This important problem is further illustrated by a simple example: A risk-averse investor has two investment alternatives, one with a volatility of 1% and one with a volatility of 0.5%. On the basis of his risk aversion he will choose the investment with the volatility of 0.5%. This could be a bad decision, since what is not considered is whether the volatility of 0.5% also has a better ratio to the possible profits from the investment. It is also conceivable that the alternative with the smaller volatility would indeed appeal to the investor's risk aversion, but the risk is still too high with respect to the investor's tolerance however it is measured, and then the investment should not be accepted.

2.2.2 Sensitivity

Along with the important key indicator of volatility, sensitivity or sensitivity analysis is often applied.

Sensitivity is a measure of how sensitively the asset reacts to changes in one or more influencing factors.

A central prerequisite for determining sensitivities is a model that can describe the relationship between the **factors influencing** the **changes in asset** and the size of the asset (in particular through a functional relationship). If this functional relationship is known or if it can be described through parameters, then the associated sensitivity is usually calculated by the **first derivative** of the function for the influencing factor. In many areas of economics, "sensitivity" appears under the synonym "elasticity" (i. e. price elasticity, quantity elasticity, demand elasticity).

When **calculating** the **volatility** of **the stock price returns** in Section 2.2.1, calculating the first derivative for the associated determining factors is **not possible** through the available stock prices alone. In reality, other factors influencing the stock price would have to be identified in order to establish a functional relationship between these determining factors and the resulting stock prices. Since numerous attempts have failed due to the complexity of the explanation and the abundant determining factors of stock prices, this will not be explored further here.

Nonetheless, sensitivity remains an important area of application in risk management in relation to **interest rate risk**. There is a clearly defined relationship between these influencing factors: interest rates and the present value (PV) of the interest position (a type of asset). Sensitivity answers the question, how much does the net present value change when the respective underlying interest rate climbs, for example, by a percentage point? The functional relationship is clearly described by the present value function. The result of the first derivative of the present value function as sensitivity is the **duration** (among other things as a key indicator for the average capital commitment period), which plays a central role in interest rate risk. Duration will be discussed in detail in Section 4.1.1.

Sensitivity should **not**, however, be a **sole evaluation criterion** in risk management. A substantial risk assessment is not possible with sensitivity analysis since the change applied to the respective influence factors (for example, interest rate changes of one percentage point) represents a purely arbitrary, subjective assumption without risk assessment. The chance of hidden changes entering into the determining factors is not considered. Use of sensitivity, therefore, should be limited, dependent on whether a particular determining factor is relevant to the risk management approach or not. In particular, with several influencing variables, risk management can be organized more efficiently with an eye on the relevant determining factors. Within risk analysis especially, sensitivity is a suitable aid in **risk factor analysis** (determining factors). In general, no risk control strategy is meaningful with sensitivity alone (with the exception of duration, see Section 4.1.1).

Consequently, the three disadvantages of volatility mentioned above also cannot be remedied by calculating the sensitivity. A more extensive approach is required to rectify these disadvantages. In the next section an approach will be defined using the **Value at Risk concept**.

2.3 Value at Risk (VaR)

With the VaR concept, the possible change to the asset position is considered.

Value at Risk (VaR) is a **loss-oriented risk measure**. Risk measures that remedy a possible change in assets in the loss area are also known as shortfall or **downside risk measures**.

In the Anglo-Saxon literature, VaR is also known as **capital at risk**. Other similar terms in use, which rely on the same principle as value at risk, are e. g. **credit value at risk**, which refers to credit or default risk, and **cash flow at risk,** which relates to business performance risk. The term **operational value at risk** is a measure for capturing the operational risks.

The measurement of risk by means of the volatility, introduced in Section 2.2.1, is in itself nothing new or special. VaR was originally developed as a risk measure especially for market risk by the investment bank Morgan Stanley in 1994, because of the strong increase in financial market risk. In the last years, VaR was further developed for other risks, in particular for default risk. **Two objectives** are central to the development and construction of VaR:

- With VaR, **various types of risk** should in particular be able to be compared or unified with a single risk measure.
- The **disadvantages** of the **volatility** risk measure described above in Section 2.2.1 (no consideration of the time period, no measurement in monetary units, no allowance for the risk attitude) should be remedied as much as is possible by the VaR concept.

Finally, VaR enables risk-adjusted risk-reward management by linking with earnings, known under the term RoRaC (Return on Risk adjusted Capital, see Section 2.6 and Chapter 6).

2.3.1 Statistical foundations

In pursuit of the stated objectives, it is obviously necessary to consider the relative changes in asset over time. To do so, the examples of BMW and MAN from Section 2.2.1 will be referred to (see Figures 2.3 and 2.4). Certain characteristics of the derivation of the volatility calculation can already be observed. Thus, the mean relative change in assets (stock return) lies close to 0 %. The average fluctuation corresponded to the calculated standard deviation (volatility). Significantly larger fluctuations than the volatility are rather rare, while slightly smaller fluctuations are frequently observed. The fluctuations run relatively symmetrically around the expected value. These properties lead to the conjecture that a **normal distribution** could be created for the observed stock returns. The approach of the normal distribution has two fundamental **advantages**:

- The normal distribution is described entirely through the two location parameters, **expected value** / mean ($=\mu$) and **standard deviation** / volatility ($=\sigma$).
- Numerous other types of distribution **converge towards** the **normal distribution** and are also derived from it. The principles derived from the normal distribution can also be applied to other types of risk whose normal distribution cannot be determined (e. g. the binomial distribution when applied to default risk).

The normal distribution was already discovered in 1733 and plays an important role in statistics. An especially noteworthy feature is the symmetrical and bell-shaped path (also known as the "Gaussian bell curve" after its discoverer). In Figure 2.5, the ideal path of the theoretical normal distribution is sketched for the above example of BMW (see Figure 2.3).

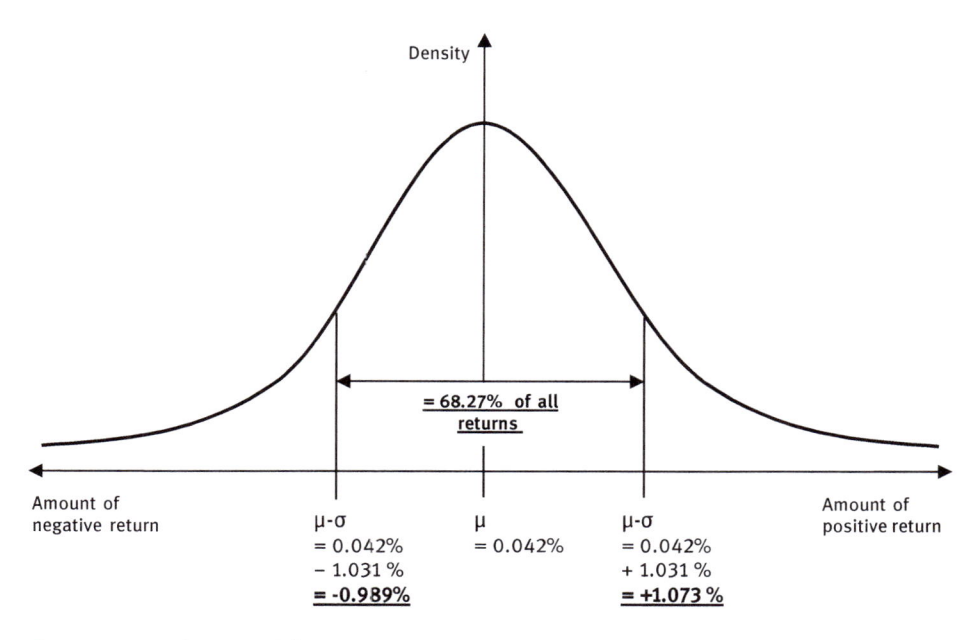

Fig. 2.5: Density function of theoretical normal distribution for example of BMW

The bell-shaped curve is called the **density function**. This expresses the probabilities that specific realizations, in this case particular rates of return, will occur. This **theoretical** assumption of the derivative of the normal distribution does **not match** the **actual returns** observed in the **sample** from the year 2005. The empirically factual observed distribution of the stock price returns generally always deviates from the theoretical idealized distribution assumptions. This is caused by the numerous factors influencing the stock prices and thus the stock price returns. Thus, the stock price returns are not formed based on an expected normal distribution assumption, but many different factors in the capital market. Agreement with the idealized normal distribution assumption would be pure coincidence here. To clarify this issue, the empirical density function for the returns on the BMW stocks is mapped in Figure 2.6.

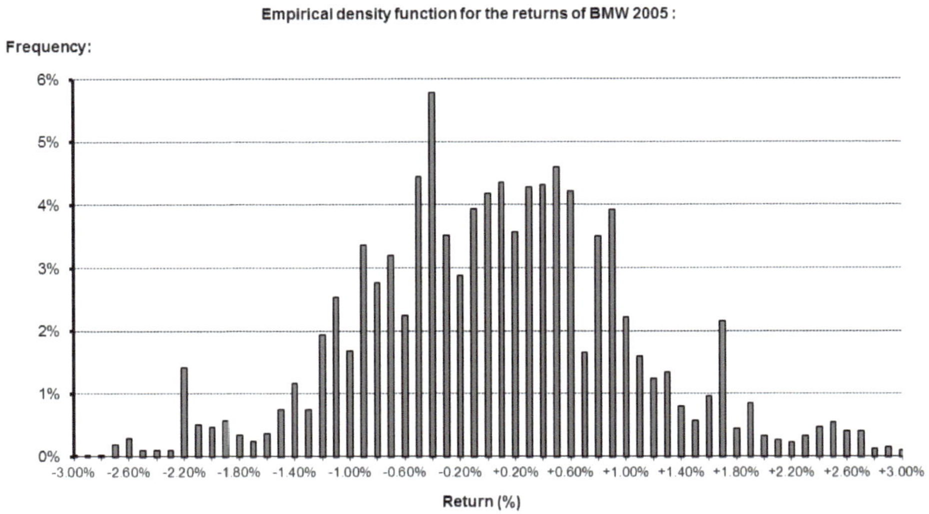

Fig. 2.6: Empirical density function for the returns of BMW 2005

To construct Fig. 2.6, **clusters** (groups) of return changes are generated. So, for example, the cluster −2.20 % contains the frequency of all changes to the observed returns between −2.15 % and −2.25 %.

It is evident that the actual observed returns partially deviate from the normal distribution assumption significantly. In particular in some individual observed returns the deviation is (coincidentally) especially large. However, the **basic structure** underlying the normal distribution can be fundamentally **identifie**d. A frequent correction, which is used when there are very large deviations in the basic structure, is to apply another distribution (e. g. the t-distribution), which is better suited to map the observed realizations.

For application within risk management, however, it is not the question of frequency of individual returns that is crucial, but rather the question of a particular **range of returns**. In Figure 2.5, for example, the range between the average minus volatility and the average plus volatility (the so-called **1 sigma interval**) was shown with the help of the density function. The value of 68.27 % comes from corresponding areas under the density function. To calculate the area under the density function, corresponding statistical tables of the standard normal deviation can be used. However, for risk management, the probability for an interval is not what's needed, but rather the probability of the (unilateral) drop below a certain value (return). For determining these values, a table with the number of standard deviations for a particular probability is required. This table is called the **quantile of the standard normal distribution**. The standard normal distribution says when the expected value is zero and the standard deviation is one. The functioning and use of the quantile of the standard normal distribution according to Table 2.5 will be demonstrated using the example of

BMW again. The values for quantile and the intervals can be interchanged with one another. Hence the number of standard deviations for intervals is also specified in Table 2.5.

Tab. 2.5: Number of standard deviations for quantile and intervals of standard normal distribution

Probability:	99.5%	99.0%	97.5%	95.0%	90.0%	84.13%	68.27%	50.00%
Number of standard deviations (quantile):	2.58	2.33	**1.96**	1.64	1.28	1.00	0.48	0.00
Number of standard deviations (interval):	2.81	2.58	2.24	1.96	1.64	1.41	1.00	0.67

For the purpose of risk management, the 2.5% lowest return of BMW stock is what is sought, which means, conversely, that the 97.5% highest return is likewise sought. In Table 2.5 the value of **1.96** can be read as a number of standard deviations for the quantile 97.5% (or 2.5%). As in Figure 2.5, the relationship shown for BMW in Figure 2.7 is graphically illustrated in the form of the density function.

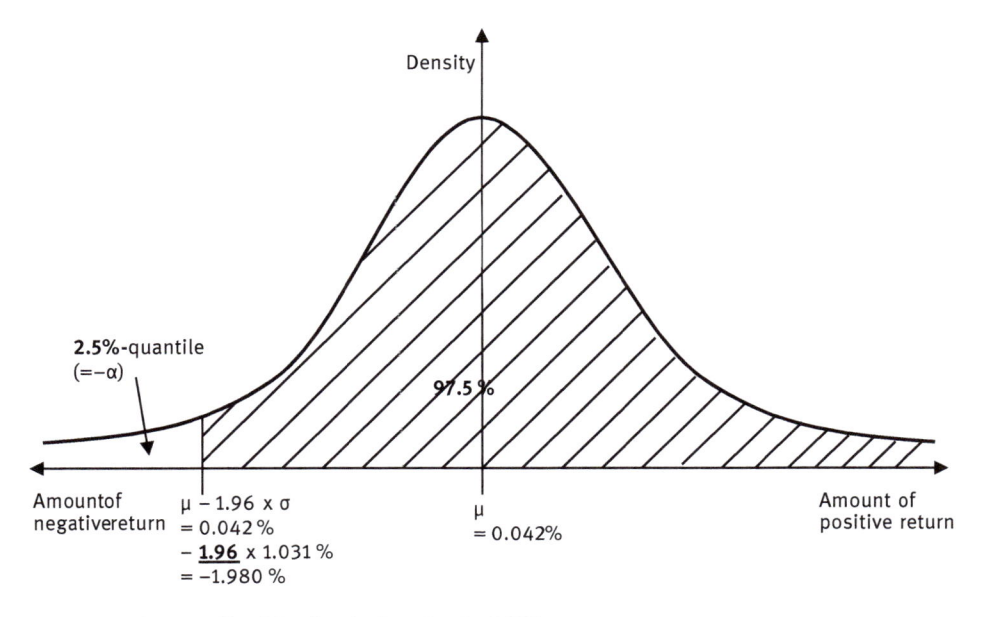

Fig. 2.7: 2.5%-quantile of the density function for BMW

The probability is 2.5% that the returns are smaller than −1.98%. Or to put it another way: the probability is 97.5% that the returns are greater than or equal to −1.98%. Whether the value of −1.98% is attributed to the area of 97.5% or 2.5% is all the same.

These statements correspond to the areas identified in Figure 2.7 (shaded area = 97.5 %, remaining area = 2.5 %). The entire area under the density function always represents 100 %. This approach and fundamental principle form the **statistical basis of VaR**. All further approaches in the context of VaR calculations constitute more or less complex or comprehensive modifications of this fundamental principle.

2.3.2 VaR of an individual risk position

On the basis of the principles set out above, a simple **definition** for the value at risk for an **individual risk position**, i. e., an asset position whose value is only influenced by a **single risk factor** (=determining factor), can be undertaken as follows:

The **Value at Risk** (VaR) is defined as the expected **maximum loss** of the **risk position** over a specific **liquidation period** for a fixed **confidence level**.

The **risk position** is the asset position valued at the current (prevailing) market prices (the so-called mark-to-market valuation) in local currency units (€). Currency positions (e. g. US-$ 100 mill., see Section 4.1.2) must therefore be converted into local currency units (€).

The **liquidation period** is the time required to close the affected risk position in case of a crisis (to sell). The liquidation period can, for example, depend on specific features of the business or the investors, or generally on particular decision-making bodies. Also, certain risk categories (i. e. credit risk) or governmental regulations can require different liquidation periods, for example, a day, two days, five days, 10 days, or a year.

An important **central assumption** is required for the mathematical consideration of the liquidation period within the VaR approach. The observed daily returns should be **chronologically independent**, meaning that the daily returns are statistically **uncorrelated** with each other. This means that the returns follow a so-called random path. From this we can deduce that the expected values can be converted in a fairly simple linear fashion for different time periods. Thus the daily returns can be converted into yearly returns by multiplying the daily average by the number of days per year (e. g. 256). Likewise, the yearly average values can be converted into daily or 10-day values. The linear conversion also applies to the variance as well as to the expected value, unlike the volatility, which requires use of the root function. For example if volatility for the daily returns amounts to 1.031 % (see e. g. BMW), then the volatility σ can be calculated for 10 days by multiplying by the square root of 10

$$\sigma_{T=10Days} = \sigma_{1Day} \cdot \sqrt{T} = 1.031\% \cdot \sqrt{10} = 3.26\%.$$

Conversely, the yearly volatility can be converted, for example, into daily volatility (through division by e. g. the square root of 256).

Another approach to the liquidation period that is worth considering is to calculate the volatility and the expected value **directly** from the observed data. So when there are daily data, the respective returns can be calculated based on lengths of 10 days (for a 10-day liquidation period). The volatility and expected values of the returns are measured from 1 to 11 working days, 2 to 12 working days, and so on. In the above example of BMW it follows that the volatility is 3.419 % (instead of 3.26 %) and the expected value is 0.38 % (instead of 0.42 %). These variations are based on the **root function** (respectively for the expected value of the time unit, here a factor of 10) only as an **estimate** for the conversion of the liquidation period (because here the returns are correlated with each other). The direct calculation however can only be made when converting to longer periods (e. g. 1 day to 10 days). When shorter liquidation periods are converted (for example the values are for a year but the liquidation period is a month), then the conversion is done with a root factor of 1/12 (respectively 1/12 for the expected value) and may not be exact (because of the possible correlation of the returns). Then there are no monthly data for direct calculation of volatility and expected values.

The **confidence level** is the probability defined by the risk bearer (the decider) according to the **quantile of the standard normal distribution** shown above. The number of standard deviations is derived from the confidence level. The number of standard deviations and therefore the worst possible returns are determined based solely on these two parameters: expected values and standard deviation. The resulting calculation of the VaR is therefore known as the **parametric calculation method**! The higher the chosen confidence level is, the greater the number of standard deviations (see Table 2.5) and thus the higher the potential maximum loss.

The choice of confidence level reflects the desired rating (see Section 4.2.2) of the risk bearer or the investor. So a confidence level of 99 % corresponds by implication to a default probability of 1 %. In turn, a default probability of 1 % corresponds to a **rating** of, for example, AA. The decision maker must verify a specific risk-bearing capacity (equity capital) for a specific rating and also e. g. for the amount of the finance charges.

Based on these conventions, the **parametric calculation of the VaR** can be calculated using the formula shown in Figure 2.8.

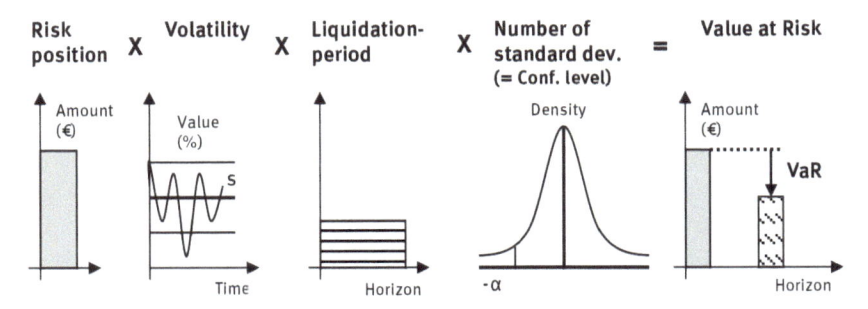

Fig. 2.8: Formula for parametric calculation of the VaR

The VaR cannot result in a value greater than the **maximum loss** (see Section 2.1.1). If the VaR calculation gives a result greater than the maximum loss, then the VaR of this risk position must be set at the maximum loss.

The BMW stock again serves as a calculation example. We consider an investor who owns exactly 10 BMW stocks with a due date of January 1, 2006. On the due date, the price of the BMW stocks was 37 euros, so the **risk position** is 370 euros.

To calculate the **volatility** we will use the historical period of the year 2005 as a basis. As was already shown in detail above, the BMW stocks have a volatility of 1.031 %.

The investor needs a **liquidation period** of 10 trading days, which means that the decision process to sell the stocks would normally take two calendar weeks. This approach is often used in e. g. banking practice.

The investor chooses a **confidence level** of 99 %. From Table 2.5 we get a number of 2.33 standard deviations for the quantile of the standard normal distribution.

Using the VaR formula shown in Figure 2.8, these data give the following calculation and the resulting outcome:

Risk position: x Volatility.: x Liquidation period: x Confidence level: = **VaR**:
€ 370.00   x 1.031 %   x $\sqrt{10}$ x 2.33   = **€ 28.11**.

The **VaR** of this single risk position of BMW stocks can be **interpreted** as follows:

A **VaR** of € 28.11 **means** that in the next 10 trading days the expected loss will have a 99 % probability of being less than € 28.11. In other words: a loss greater than € 28.11 has only a 1 % chance of occurring within the next 10 days.

In this simple calculation of VaR, an expected value (=average stock price return) of μ=0 %, required for the standard normal distribution, was assumed in applying the number of 2.33 standard deviations. As already calculated above, this is not the case. In order to get a statistically correct result, this **non-zero expected value** must be mathematically **corrected** in the **VaR calculation**! A general formula for calculating the VaR for the non-zero expected returns and the resulting correction computation is given in the Technical appendix (Section 2.8). For the expected return of 0.042 % for BMW, a corrected VaR emerges of:

$$€ 370.00 \times (2.33 \times 1.031\% \times \sqrt{10} - 10 \times 0.042\%) = \underline{€ 26.55}.$$

With an expected value >0 the VaR is reduced by the correction computation, with the expected stock price return sinking to >=0. With expected values smaller than zero, the corrected VaR subsequently increases. Since no new business knowledge is gained through this corrective computation, it will be dispensed with and the expected value will be assumed to be zero. The possible consideration of an average non-zero stock price return is a purely statistical corrective computation and does not therefore contradict the business definition of risk in Section 1.1, where the risk was defined without comparison to the possible profits (e. g. the average stock return). The same goes for the volatility calculation (see Section 2.2.1).

The high **significance** of the **normal distribution assumption** will become very clear when the calculation of the VaR for the original examples A, B and C from Sections 2.1.1 and 2.1.2 is attempted. If there had been a normal distribution for these examples, the factor could be set at 2.33 standard deviations for a confidence level of 99 %. With a liquidation period of a day, the following theoretical VaR would emerge for A, B and C:

Tab. 2.6: VaR for examples A, B and C

Key indicator:	Example A:	Example B:	Example C:
Asset position:	€ 1,000.00	€ 1,000.00	€ 1,000.00
Volatility:	50.00 %	42.25 %	42.40 %
VaR:	€ 500.00 (max. loss)	€ 984.43	€ 987.92

The dimensions of the calculated VaR are not plausible (in example A, the calculated VaR with the volatility and the number of standard deviations amounts to € 1,165.00, when it cannot be larger than the maximum loss of € 500.00). It is obvious that this is caused by the very high volatilities. The high volatilities are based on the respective distributions, which in these examples have no resemblance to the normal distribution.

From these principles and calculation results drawn from the VaR concept, the following essential **properties** of the **VaR** of an individual risk position can be derived.
– The **expectations** of the decision maker in relation to the future change in values have no influence on the VaR.

- Choosing **different observation periods** leads to different volatilities, which means that comparison is only possible between equal observation periods (usually, 250 trading days, that is one stock market year).
- The actual observed changes of the risk factors do not correspond to the **normal distribution assumption**. The expected value is often $\mu <> 0$, as with BMW (expected value of the price returns is $\mu = 0.042\%$!) and asymmetry, kurtosis, fat tails etc. are present. In the above VaR calculation, mathematical, purely statistical corrections that would have damaged the normal distribution assumption were ignored for purposes of simplification.
- The **influencing factors of the VaR** express in a **positive** direction (i. e. they are correlated positively with each other). The greater the risk position, the volatility, the liquidation period, the confidence level respectively is, the larger is also the VaR. The only exception: The higher the expected value of the returns μ is, the smaller is the VaR.

The next step is to transfer the insights and properties of the individual risk position VaR to **portfolios**, so to several related securities.

2.3.3 VaR of portfolios

In Section 2.3.2, the VaR of an individual asset position was calculated, which depends on only one risk factor. This parametric calculation of an individual risk position is indeed very easy, but naturally does not sufficiently map economic reality. Therefore it must first be established, how a portfolio is to be understood in the following remarks.

In a **portfolio**, a fixed number of individual asset positions are summarized, which are all evaluated in the same base currency (e. g. €).

It is assumed that cash and investments at risk-free interest rates don't belong to the portfolio. Thus the first discussion is focussed on portfolios that consist only of risk-bearing asset positions (a consideration of risk-free interest rates appears e. g. in CAPM in Section 4.1.3). The VaR can now also be determined for a portfolio whose value depends on several risk factors (asset positions). The above mentioned examples of BMW and MAN stocks will be used for calculating the VaR of portfolios. An investor will now be considered who has not only BMW stocks but also MAN stocks in his portfolio (total assets). The investor manages a portfolio with the individual position features described in Table 2.7.

Tab. 2.7: VaR and features of a sample portfolio (BMW and MAN)

Asset position:	Number of stocks:	Risk position (2. 1. 2006):	Weights:	Average stock price return (μ):	Volatility (σ):	VaR ($\mu = 0$):	VaR ($\mu <> 0$):
BMW	10	€ 370.00	45.12 %	0.042 %	1.031 %	€ 28.11	€ 26.11
MAN	10	€ 450.00	54.88 %	0.175 %	1.386 %	€ 45.96	€ 38.09

For MAN the risk position will be calculated based on a stock price of € 45.00 from the reporting date of January 2, 2006. A liquidation period of 10 days and a confidence level of 99 % were also used calculate the MAN VaR, so that the VaR for the MAN stocks, like the VaR calculation for the BMW stocks, is

Risk position: x Volatility.: x Liquidation period: x Confidence level: = **VaR:**
€ 450.00   x 1.386 %   x $\sqrt{10}$ x 2.33   = **€ 45.96**.

In Table 2.7, the VaR values are still specified based on an expected value (average stock price return) of $\mu <> 0$.

The central question that follows from this is: "How are the individual asset positions summarized in a **portfolio**?" To answer this question, each aggregated portfolio size (e. g. the portfolio return) will first be derived intuitively on its own.

Based on the data in Table 2.7, the **number of all portfolio stocks** in this case simply adds up to **20**. Since this quantity has no significance without an evaluation in monetary units, this value will not be explored further.

The total **risk position of the portfolio** likewise comes about through summation of the individual risk positions. The portfolio risk position amounts then to € 370.00 plus € 450.00 or **€ 820.00** on the reporting date. This assessment of the portfolio is based on the so-called mark-to-market evaluation. The value of the risk position is also of only limited significance. A more meaningful figure is the so-called **portfolio weight** of individual risk positions in the portfolio. The portfolio weight is calculated by dividing the individual risk positions by the total risk positions, so

Portfolio weight BMW = € 370.00 / € 820.00 = **45.12 %**,
Portfolio weight MAN = € 450.00 / € 820.00 = **54.88 %**.

It is immediately apparent that the **sum** of all the **portfolio weights** must add up to **100 %**. For portfolios that consist of bonds, the respective present value is used as the risk position.

The portfolio weights form the foundation for calculating the price return on the portfolio, the so-called **portfolio return**, from the average price returns on the individual risk positions.

For example, looking at the average **BMW** price return in the amount of 0.042%, this leads to an average increase in the risk position from € 370.00 by 0.042% to € 370.16. Likewise by **MAN** there is an 0.175% increase from € 450.00 to € 450.79. The sum of both risk positions, now increased by the average return, amounts to € 370.16 + € 450.79 = € 820.95. Based on the initial value of the whole portfolio in the amount of € 820.00 this gives a portfolio return of **0.115%**.

The results don't match exactly because the risk position is **rounded** to two decimal places. In some of the following calculation examples this is acceptable for reasons of clarity!

From this computation it can now be directly inferred that the portfolio return can be determined not only through the circuitous path of the absolute risk positions in euros, but also directly through the **percentage weighting of the individual returns**. In this manner, the portfolio returns can be calculated as follows:

(Portfolio weight BMW x Return BMW)   + (Portfolio weight MAN   x Return MAN)
= (45.12%   x 0.042%)   + (54.88%   x 0.175%)
= **0.115%**.

The following guideline can be formulated for calculating the portfolio return.

The **portfolio return** comes from the sum of the individual returns multiplied by the respective portfolio weight.

Thus the portfolio return must always be greater than or equal to the smallest individual return and smaller than or equal to the largest individual return. The only exception to this exists when there are also negative weights possible, for example, in short sales. In the following remarks, only **positive weights** will be assumed. For the principles of short sales see also Section 3.4.2 (options) and for the problem of short sale risk measurement compare also the maximum loss. Certain short sales were prohibited or newly regulated in relation to the financial crisis (see Section 4.4.2).

To determine the **portfolio volatility**, considerations similar to those used for the portfolio returns will be employed. A first intuitive approach to the calculation of portfolio volatility would be again the sum of the individual volatilities calculated with the help of the portfolio weights, so:

(Portfolio weight BMW x Vol. BMW)   + (Portfolio weight MAN   x Vol. MAN)
= (45.12%   x 1.031%)   + (54.88%   x 1.386%)
= **1.226%**.

A simple plausibility consideration nonetheless shows that this approach would be incorrect. This type of calculation would have the effect that **reciprocal fluctuations** and therefore risk reducing effects would not be accounted for at the level of the portfolio volatility.

A simple example shown in Table 2.8 illustrates this problem. The calculation of the individual volatility of stock A and stock B was executed as it was for the examples of BMW and MAN in Section 2.2.1. For the summary in the column entitled "aggregate portfolio return", a weight of 50 % each of the portfolio was taken for stocks A and B.

Tab. 2.8: Simple example for calculation of portfolio volatility

Time:	Stock A:	Stock B:	Aggregated portfolio return: (Stock A + Stock B)
1:	+2.00 %	−0.50 %	(50 % x 2.00 %) + (50 % x −0.50 %) = **+0.75 %**
2:	+3.00 %	−1.00 %	(50 % x 3.00 %) + (50 % x −1.00 %) = **+1.00 %**
3:	−3.00 %	+3.00 %	(50 % x 3.00 %) + (50 % x +3.00 %) = **+0.00 %**
4:	+1.00 %	−0.50 %	(50 % x 1.00 %) + (50 % x −0.50 %) = **+0.25 %**
Return:	+0.75 %	+0.25 %	+0.50 %
Volatility:	**2.28 %**	**1.60 %**	**+0.40 %**
Weights:	50.00 %	50.00 %	100.00 %
Return/Vol.:	0.329	0.156	1.25

For the portfolio in Table 2.8, the individual returns from stock A and stock B, corresponding to their respective weights of 50 % of the portfolio, are summarized. In this way, the **aggregated portfolio returns** emerge at individual points in time.

The return computations can be grasped directly and the validity of the calculation described above for determining the **portfolio return** is immediately apparent (50 % x 0.75 % + 50 % x 0.25 % = +0.50 %, it also corresponds exactly to the average of the aggregate portfolio returns).

If the **portfolio volatility** were now based on the aggregate portfolio returns, as described in Section 2.2.1, then the result of this would lead to a volatility of only **0.40 %**! A weighting of the individual volatilities of stock A and stock B would nonetheless lead to a much higher value of 1.94 % (50 % x 2.28 % + 50 % x 1.60 % = 1.94 %). The cause of this strong deviation is obvious. A **compensation effect** develops through the aggregation of the individual returns. The stock A positive returns at times 1, 2 and 4 oppose the respective negative returns of stock B at the same points in time. Likewise, the exact reverse at point 3. Precisely this effect can, however, not be considered through the weighted summation of the individual volatilities. Thus a **measure** must be applied which captures the **relationships of the individual returns** between the stocks at the respective times.

A measure for the consideration of the relationship between the two dimensions is the statistical **covariance**. Generally speaking, the covariance is the mean value of the products of the deviations for all the data point pairs.

While the variance measures the squared dispersion of the return of an individual stock around its own average return, so the covariance captures the variations between the returns of two stocks. To this end, in order to **calculate** the **covariance**, the difference between the observed individual return on the stock and its average return is calculated and multiplied by the corresponding difference of the other stock (= products of the deviations). To calculate the means, these products, as with the variance, are added up over all the time points and the sums are then divided by the number of time points. For the example shown in Table 2.8, the covariance is calculated as follows:

Time point: Deviation stock A:	x	Deviation stock B:		
1	(2% – 0.75%)	x	(–0.5% – 0.25%)	= – 0.00009375
2	(3% – 0.75%)	x	(–1% – 0.25%)	= – 0.00028125
3	(–3% – 0.75%)	x	(3% – 0.25%)	= – 0.00103125
4	(1% – 0.75%)	x	(–0.5% – 0.25%)	= – 0.00001875

The sum over all time points gives –0.001425 and division by the number of time points by four delivers for the **covariance**

$$\text{Covariance}(A,B) = s_{A,B} = \mathbf{-0.00035625}.$$

In contrast to variance and expected value, **time series** play an important role in detecting the compensation effect in the covariance, i.e. when an observed stock return is up against another observed stock return. As with the calculation of the variance, the statistical key indicator covariance has also some **weaknesses** with respect to **interpretation**. Thus the covariance, due to the multiplication of percent by percent has no dimension that can be interpreted. The dimension of the covariance is therefore also unsuitable for comparing different asset positions and their returns.

The covariance can be further developed into a normalized and thus interpretable indicator. This normalized indicator is the so called **correlation coefficient**.

The **correlation coefficient** between two quantities is calculated by dividing the covariance between the two quantities by the product of the two individual standard deviations (volatilities).

For the above example of the two stocks A and B, the correlation coefficient is calculated as follows:

Covariance[A,B] / (Volatility[A] x Volatility[B]) = Correlation coefficient[A,B] = $CR_{A,B}$
−0.00035625   / (2.28 % x 1.60 %)   = **−0.977**.

Normalizing the covariance by dividing the products by the two individual volatilities leads to the following useful **properties** of the **correlation coefficient**:
- The correlation coefficient can only take values between +1 and −1.
- A correlation coefficient of +1 means a completely positive relationship between both quantities (for example, returns).
- A correlation coefficient of zero indicates that neither positive nor negative relationship between the quantities is measurable.
- A completely negative relationship is established by a correlation coefficient of −1.

In the simple example of stocks A and B then, an almost completely negative relationship is established between the returns on stock A and stock B over time (so for time points 1, 2, 3 and 4). This rests on the obvious observation that positive returns on stock A oppose and reverse negative returns on stock B at the same time point. A **completely negative relationship**, i. e. a correlation coefficient of exactly −1, is reached when the stocks not only oppose each other exactly but also comprise a completely linear relationship between both returns (which is not the case in the above example of stocks A and B at time points 1 and 4). The linear relationships in the correlation coefficient are explained further with various examples below, since the correlation coefficient plays an especially important role in the aggregation of risk.

With this goal in mind the possible characteristics of returns on an arbitrary stock A are taken as a basis. For the individual features of stock A, the distinctive features of stock B will then be assigned. The respective varying correlation coefficients between stocks A and B will then arise out of these assignments. The various returns with the resulting respective correlation coefficients are shown in overview in Table 2.9.

Tab. 2.9: Examples for different correlation coefficients

Example:		I:	II:	III:	IV:	V:
Correlation coefficient (k):		k=+1	k=+1	k=−1	k=+0.6	k=0
Observation:	Return A:	Return B:	Return B:	Return B:	Return B:	Return B:
1	−4.00 %	−3.00 %	−7.00 %	4.00 %	−1.00 %	4.00 %
2	−3.00 %	−2.50 %	−5.00 %	3.00 %	−3.50 %	−3.00 %
3	−2.00 %	−2.00 %	−3.00 %	2.00 %	2.11 %	2.00 %
4	−1.00 %	−1.50 %	−1.00 %	1.00 %	−2.50 %	−1.00 %

Tab. 2.9 (continued)

Example:	I:	II:	III:	IV:	V:
5	0.00 %	−1.00 %	1.00 %	0.00 %	3.00 %	0.00 %
6	1.00 %	−0.50 %	3.00 %	−1.00 %	0.50 %	−1.00 %
7	2.00 %	0.00 %	5.00 %	−2.00 %	−0.50 %	2.00 %
8	3.00 %	0.50 %	7.00 %	−3.00 %	1.00 %	−3.00 %
9	4.00 %	1.00 %	9.00 %	−4.00 %	5.00 %	4.00 %

A **correlation coefficient** of +1 does not always mean that a positive return on a necessarily implies a positive return on be. The relationship is completely linear. A correlation coefficient of +1 says nothing about the slope or the ordinate of the straight lines of this relationship. This situation is shown graphically in Figure 2.9.

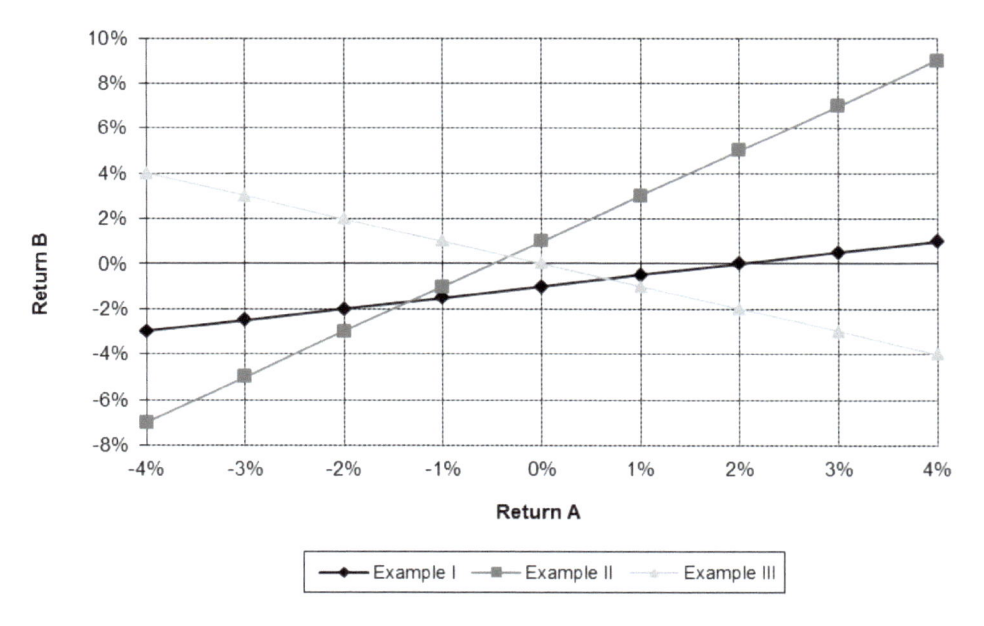

Fig. 2.9: Examples for correlation coefficients of +1 and −1

In Figure 2.9 it becomes clear that for all examples, the observed return pairs of A and B lie on a single line but these have different slopes or ordinates. So, for example, if A in example I has a return characteristic of 0 % then a return characteristic of −1.0 % is observed for B. In example II, on the other hand, a return of +1.0 % is observed for B, although in both examples of the correlation coefficient amounts to +1 respectively. Thus various slopes and ordinates are present. Conversely, the same goes for a correlation of −1 in example III. The relationship here is negative for mine has a negative slope. Conclusions cannot be drawn from the correlation coefficient of −1 about the gradient of the negative slope and the ordinate.

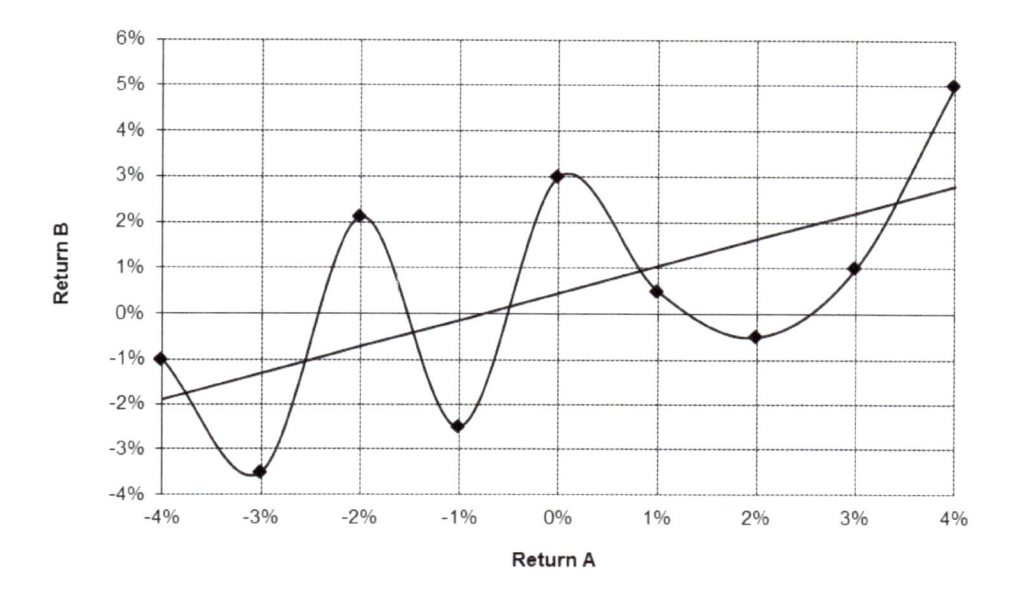

Fig. 2.10: Example for a correlation coefficient of +0.6

In Figure 2.10 a relationship for the **correlation coefficient** of **+0.6** is shown. A positive relationship is indeed still recognizable overall (visible through the regression line), however the relationship is no longer completely linear, but rather the observed return pairs are scattered around the regression line. The same would apply likewise in reverse for a negative correlation coefficient greater than −1 (which has been omitted for the sake of clarity in Figure 2.10).

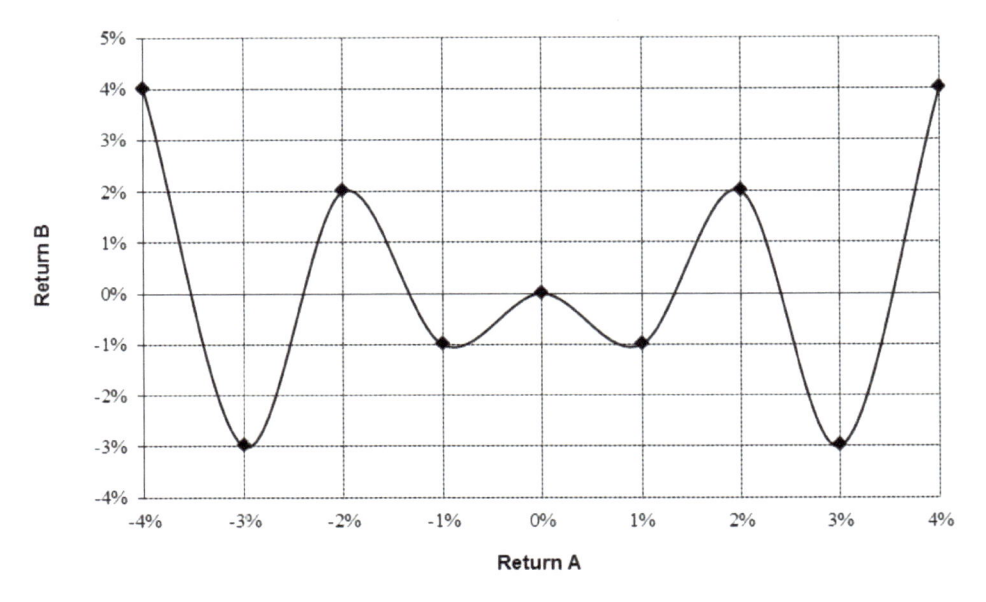

Fig. 2.11: Example for a correlation coefficient of 0

An example of an uncorrelated relationship is sketched in Figure 2.11. Here neither a positive nor negative tendency can be seen. The **correlation coefficient** is **zero**, which also means that stocks A and B are not dependent upon each other. The slope of the regression line through the observed return pairs amounts to zero.

Although the correlation coefficient has positive properties, the original goal of calculating the volatility of the portfolio has not been reached. Not only the covariance but also the correlation coefficient does not correspond to the portfolio volatility generated in Table 2.8 of 0.40 %! In order to calculate the portfolio volatility, the previously calculated determining factors

- portfolio weights of A and B (w_A=50 %, w_B=50 %),
- volatilities or variances of A and B (s_A=2.28 %, s_B=1.6 % or s^2_A, s^2_B),
- and covariance or correlation coefficient ($s_{A,B}$=−0.00035625 or $CR_{A,B}$=−0.977)

go into a mathematical model, which for purposes of clarity (and the lack of additional business knowledge gain) will not be derived here. The derivation of this model rests on the **portfolio theory** developed by Markowitz in 1952. The application of portfolio theory specifically to stock price risk in the context of risk management will be addressed explicitly in more detail in Section 4.1.3. Here, the necessary instruments will first be provided for the calculation of the VaR. For **calculating** the **portfolio volatility** on the basis of portfolio theory, the following apply:

$$\textit{Portfolio volatility (A,B)} = s_P = \sqrt{w_A^2 \cdot s_A^2 + w_B^2 \cdot s_B^2 + 2 \cdot w_A \cdot w_B \cdot k_{A,B} \cdot s_A \cdot s_B}$$

For the example of stocks A and B, the **portfolio volatility** can be determined as follows with the help of this equation:

$$s_P = \sqrt{0.5^2 \cdot 0.0228^2 + 0.5^2 \cdot 0.016^2 + 2 \cdot 0.5 \cdot 0.5 \cdot -0.977 \cdot 0.0228 \cdot 0.016} = \mathbf{\underline{0.40\,\%}}.$$

This result likewise corresponds to the fluctuation for the portfolio, obtained through the portfolio returns, of 0.40 % (see Table 2.8). With the help of the correlation coefficient and the portfolio volatility, the compensation effect between the individual returns can then be considered. If this **compensation effect is large enough**, the portfolio volatility falls below the minimum individual volatility. Through this, an increase in the return to volatility portfolio ratios can be achieved compared to the individual stocks A and B. The portfolio return, on the other hand, cannot be smaller than the smallest individual return (see the derivation of the portfolio returns above). Thus, through this compensation effect on the portfolio level, a significantly higher ratio of return to volatility of 1.25 arises, as compared to 0.329 for stock A and 0.156 for stock B (see Table 2.8).

The account coming from the portfolio volatility equation has some crucial advantages over the aggregated portfolio account in **interpreting** the **portfolio structure**, which will be discussed in more detail in the following sections.

The correlation coefficient is defined as the covariance divided by the product of the individual volatilities. If this expression replaces the correlation coefficient in the equation for the portfolio volatility, the product of the volatilities is cancelled out and one gets:

$$s_P = \sqrt{w_A^2 \cdot s_A^2 + w_B^2 \cdot s_B^2 + 2 \cdot w_A \cdot w_B \cdot s_{A,B}}$$

This is a computational simplification, but the interpretation through the correlation coefficient gets lost. So the initial equation of the portfolio volatility given above can, with help from the binomial formula (a² + b² + 2ab = [a + b]²), be simplified for a correlation coefficient of +1 to:

$$s_P = w_A \cdot s_A + w_B \cdot s_B.$$

If there is then a correlation coefficient of +1 and therefore no compensation affect, the portfolio volatility corresponds to the sum of the weighted individual volatilities. This corresponds to the intuitive approach to calculating the portfolio volatility which was described above in the derivation of the aggregated portfolio sizes in the example of MAN and BMW (s_P = 1.226 %). Likewise, for a correlation coefficient of –1 (so with the greatest possible compensation effect) results in a portfolio volatility of

$$s_P = |w_A \cdot s_A - w_B \cdot s_B|.$$

Since the volatility is only defined for values greater than or equal to zero, this is ensured by taking the absolute value.

With the help of the portfolio volatility, the VaR can now also be calculated for the entire portfolio, which consists of BMW and MAN stocks, in a manner similar to the VaR calculation for individual risk positions. In the first step, as in the example of stocks A and B, the portfolio volatility is calculated from BMW and MAN stocks. For this purpose, the covariance between the BMW and MAN returns will first be calculated. As with the above described approach, this amounts to

$$Covariance\ (=s_{BMW,MAN}) = \mathbf{+0.00005158}.$$

From this the correlation coefficient between the BMW and MAN returns will be calculated:

Covar.[BMW,MAN] / (Vol.[BMW] x Vol.[MAN]) = Correlation coefficient[BMW,MAN]
+0.00005158   / (1.031 % x 1.386 %)   = **+0.36** = $CR_{BMW,MAN}$.

The correlation coefficient for BMW and MAN is significantly higher than in the above example for stocks A and B. The compensation effect is very much weaker. Because of this the portfolio volatility doesn't sink so sharply in relationship to the individual volatilities as in the example of A and B. This can be read from the ratios of return to volatility. Through the portfolio formation the portfolio return fall below the individual MAN returns and at the same time the portfolio volatility doesn't fall sharply enough. The quotient for MAN is therefore somewhat higher than it is for the portfolio (see Table 2.10). The correlation coefficient $CR_{BMW,MAN}$ is the basis for calculating the portfolio volatility of BMW and MAN:

$$= \sqrt{w_{BMW}^2 \cdot s_{BMW}^2 + w_{MAN}^2 \cdot s_{MAN}^2 + 2 \cdot w_{BMW} \cdot w_{MAN} \cdot k_{BMW,MAN} \cdot s_{BMW} \cdot s_{MAN}}$$

$$= \sqrt{0.4512^2 \cdot 0.01031^2 + 0.5488^2 \cdot 0.01386^2 + 2 \cdot 0.4512 \cdot 0.5488 \cdot 0.36 \cdot 0.01031 \cdot 0.01386}$$

$$= s_P = Portfolio\ volatility\ (BMW,MAN) = \mathbf{1.025\,\%}.$$

With help from the portfolio volatility the VaR can now be calculated for the portfolio. The risk position of the portfolio is then composed of the sum of the two individual positions and results in € 370.00 + € 450.00 = € 820.00. The portfolio is based on the same liquidation period of 10 days and a confidence level of 99 %. The **calculation** of the **portfolio VaR** is then:

Risk position: x Volatility.: x Liquidation period: x Confidence level: = **VaR:**
€ 820.00   x 1.025 %   x $\sqrt{10}$ x 2.33   = **€ 61.93**.

For a better overview and a practical interpretation of the results, the results for BMW, MAN and the portfolio (consisting of the BMW and MAN stocks) are summarized in overview in Table 2.10.

Tab. 2.10: Results of VaR calculation for a sample portfolio

Asset position:	Risk position (2.1.2006):	Portfolio weights:	Average price return:	Volatility:	VaR:	Average return/volatility:
BMW	€ 370.00	45.12 %	0.042 %	1.031 %	€ 28.11	0.041
MAN	€ 450.00	54.88 %	0.175 %	1.386 %	€ 45.96	0.126
Portfolio	€ 820.00	100.00 %	0.115 %	1.025 %	€ 61.93	0.112

The effects of the reciprocal compensation between the return fluctuations of BMW and MAN are conspicuous. This is expressed in a portfolio VaR of € 61.93, while on the other hand the sum of the VaR for the individual asset positions amounts to € 74.07. That means that the **portfolio analysis** leads to a **€ 12.14** smaller VAR and thus also to a **smaller risk** than does the **summation** of the **individual risks**. This effect is often **planned** in building a portfolio and is also part of the business design.

The **diversification effect** is defined as risk limitation through an appropriate combination of specific asset positions in a portfolio. The strength of the diversification effect is based on the correlations between the individual asset positions or the correlations between their returns.

To illustrate the strength of the diversification effect, various (theoretical) correlations are calculated for the respective corresponding VaR values of the portfolio in Table 2.11. The basis for these calculations is again the above portfolio, consisting of BMW and MAN stocks. The portfolio weighting, the liquidation period, the volatility of the individual positions and the confidence level are left constant. Only the theoretical **change to the correlation coefficient** and the resulting change (all other things being equal) to the portfolio volatility and thus also the **change to the portfolio VaR** are given in Table 2.11. The "Difference" column specifies the difference between the sum of the VaR of the individual positions and the portfolio VaR, based on the respective given correlation coefficients (so for a correlation coefficient of +0.36 this would be the € 12.14 calculated above).

Tab. 2.11: Example for the change to the portfolio VaR based on the respective given correlation coefficients

Correlation coefficient:	Portfolio volatility:	Portfolio VaR:	Difference to sum of individual VaR (€ 74.07):	Difference to sum of individual VaR (in %):
−1.00	0.295 %	€ 17.85	€ 56.22	75.90 %
−0.80	0.478 %	€ 28.90	€ 45.16	60.98 %
−0.60	0.609 %	€ 36.77	€ 37.30	50.35 %
−0.40	0.716 %	€ 43.23	€ 30.84	41.63 %
−0.20	0.808 %	€ 48.84	€ 25.22	34.06 %
0.00	0.892 %	€ 53.87	€ 20.19	27.26 %
0.20	0.968 %	€ 58.47	€ 15.59	21.05 %
0.36	**1.025 %**	**€ 61.93**	**€ 12.14**	**16.39 %**
0.40	1.038 %	€ 62.74	€ 11.33	15.30 %
0.60	1.104 %	€ 66.73	€ 7.34	9.91 %
0.80	1.167 %	€ 70.49	€ 3.57	4.83 %

From Table 2.11 and through mathematical transformations of the above equation for the portfolio volatility (see Technical appendix Section 2.8), the following central **properties** of the **diversification effect** can be derived in relation to the VaR.

Because of the possible diversification effect, the **VaR** summarized on the **portfolio level** is **smaller** than or equal to the **sum of the individual risk position VaR**.

If the **correlation coefficient is smaller than 1**, then a diversification occurs, i. e. the portfolio risk and thus also the portfolio VaR sink below the sum of the individual risk positions.

If the returns on the asset positions are **completely positively correlated** (correlation coefficient = +1), the portfolio VaR is equal to the sum of the individual risk position VaR.

With a **fully negative correlation**, the diversification effect is at its largest, i. e. the portfolio volatility is at its smallest and therefore the portfolio VAR is also smallest compared to the sum of the individual risk position VaR.

In practice in the capital market, correlations in the neighborhood of −0.4 to +0.8 can frequently be observed. From Table 2.11 it is evident that with positive correlations the relative difference to the sum of the individual risks can also be substantial (up to 27 %, see Table 2.11, last column). The extent of this relative difference depends on the number constellations and thus may vary from case to case. Further work with the VaR and the diversification effect is then warranted.

In the previous remarks, the Value at Risk concept focused in particular on calculating a **measurement** for capturing **portfolio risk**. With the help of the VaR, however, much more is possible than just computing a single number in monetary units. As was shown in the section on risk analysis, light **modifications** to the previous strategies for calculating the **VaR** considerably widen the interpretation possibilities and the resulting action recommendations on the basis of the VaR. Some meaningful modifications are described here with an eye towards the later **risk analysis**.

A common question in the analysis of portfolios is the **change** in the **VaR**, i. e. the portfolio risk, when the **individual asset positions change**. The volatility or the VaR of the individual positions cannot provide any significant information when considered in isolation, since these values contain no information about possible effects of the correlations or the portfolio structure. For this reason, we will now pursue the question of how the contribution to portfolio risk changes when a portfolio position increases by one unit.

The **marginal VaR** is the (dimensionless) factor of a portfolio position that indicates how sharply the overall portfolio risk increases when this portfolio position increases by one unit.

This question can be solved mathematically by forming the first derivative of the portfolio risk with the weighting of the observed position (see Section 2.2.1 sensitivities). The mathematical derivation will be omitted here (see Section 2.8), and only the results will be economically interpreted. For the marginal VaR of an asset position i (=ΔVaR_i) inside the portfolio, the derivative provides the value of

$$\Delta VaR_i = \alpha \times Covariance\ (Position\ i,\ Portfolio)\ /\ Portfolio\ volatility\ (=s_p).$$

The marginal VaR then follows by multiplying the number of standard deviations α corresponding to the quantile of the standard normal distribution multiplied by the covariance between the position i returns and the aggregated portfolio returns, divided by the portfolio volatility.

For application to the example portfolio example containing the BMW and MAN stocks, the calculation must first be established as a **time series** with the **aggregated portfolio returns** corresponding to the portfolio weightings (BMW=45.12% and MAN=54.88%). This occurs as already described above. Then the covariance between the BMW return and the portfolio as well as between MAN and the portfolio is calculated, which gives the following value:

$$Covariance\ (BMW,\ Portfolio) = \mathbf{\underline{0.00007627}},$$
$$Covariance\ (MAN,\ Portfolio) = \mathbf{\underline{0.00012872}}.$$

With the help of these covariances, the number of standard variations of 2.33 for a confidence level of 99% and the portfolio volatility of 1.025% already calculated above, the marginal VaR factors for BMW and MAN can now be established as per the above equation:

ΔVaR_i = α × Covariance (Position i, Portfolio) / Portfolio volatility,
ΔVaR_{BMW} = 2.33 × 0.00007627 / 1.025 % = **0.01734**,
ΔVaR_{MAN} = 2.33 × 0.0012872 / 1.025 % = **0.02926**.

As already discussed, the **covariance** is, as an absolute number, **not very informative**. However, since the findings from the equation for the marginal VaR will be applied later for yet other purposes, it is possible to illustrate the marginal VaR even more clearly. For these purposes, the so-called **beta factor** (=$ß_i$) for the individual asset positions i will be defined as follows:

$$ß_i = \text{Covariance (position i, portfolio) / Portfolio } \mathbf{variance}.$$

This beta factor measures the influence of the risk of position i against the entire portfolio risk. The higher the beta factor is, the greater the influence of the associated asset position risk on the portfolio risk. The beta factor was derived in the context of the **CAPM** from Sharpe (1968). In the context of applying portfolio theory to stock price risk (Section 4.1.3), the use of the beta factor will be further explored in more detail. For BMW and MAN the beta factor respectively comes to:

$$ß_{BMW} = 0.00007627 / 0.00010506 = \mathbf{0.726},$$
$$ß_{MAN} = 0.00012872 / 0.00010506 = \mathbf{1.225}.$$

The MAN stock is rated as riskier because of its higher volatility and so it is also not surprising that it has a higher influence on the portfolio risk. With help from several transformations (see Technical appendix 2.8), the marginal VaR factors can now be calculated using the beta factors, and identical results emerge for BMW and MAN:

ΔVaR_i = α × $ß_i$ × Portfolio volatility (=s_p)
ΔVaR_{BMW} = 2.33 × 0.726 × 1.025 % = **0.01734**,
ΔVaR_{MAN} = 2.33 × 1.225 × 1.025 % = **0.02926**.

Thus the marginal VaR, simply formulated, consists of the confidence level, the systematic risk of the portfolio position and the overall portfolio risk (expressed through the portfolio volatility) taken together. The marginal VaR can be used for various purposes and risk management. In particular, it will be discussed in more detail as a **sensitivity measure** in **risk analysis** (Section 2.6). However, if the entire portfolio risk is supposed to be reduced merely by selling an asset position, then the largest marginal VaR or the largest beta factors can easily identify which asset position is most effective with regard to the overall risk.

The marginal VaR is now the foundation for developing the so-called incremental value at risk as another possible application.

The **incremental value at risk** is that value at risk that emerges when the original value at risk increases due to taking on an additional risk position or due to an increase in an existing position.

When the portfolio consisting of BMW and MAN stocks is used as an initial position, this portfolio has a VaR of € 61.93 before a possible change. The incremental value at risk gives approximately the increase in this previous VaR, if e. g. a new BMW stock were bought into the portfolio at a valuation price of € 37.00 per stock. The new VaR for the whole portfolio is then simply calculated by multiplying the corresponding marginal BMW VaR by the amount of the increase of the associated position (so of stock of € 37.00) and that gives:

$$\text{Incremental VaR}_{BMW} = \Delta VaR_{BMW}\ (=0.01734) \times €\ 37.00 = \mathbf{0.64\ €}.$$

If this incremental BMW VaR is added to the old portfolio VaR then the new portfolio VaR comes out to € 61.93 + € 0.64 = **€ 62.57**. This calculation of the new VaR is nonetheless only an **approximate calculation,** by which a **linearity** between the increase of an individual risk position and the increase in the portfolio VaR is implied. However, because of the portfolio volatility property (root of the squared summands) this is not given. If the exact VaR is calculated for the new portfolio, this then delivers a value of **€ 63.98**. The incremental VaR can then be just a simple estimate that requires little computation to determine how a change to one individual portfolio position roughly changes the overall VaR.

The so-called Component VaR has, on the other hand, a fundamentally more important function and significance, which is also built on the marginal VaR or draws on the relationships derived there.

The diversification effect plays a fundamental role in analyzing a portfolio by means of the VaR. In the example, the diversification effect is expressed in the amount of € 12.13. The sum of the individual VaR amounts to € 74.06 while the portfolio VaR, by taking the correlation into account, is then only € 61.93. An analysis of the individual position VaR is therefore insufficient, since the diversification effect is neglected. It is exactly this defect that is remedied by the component VaR.

The **Component Value at Risk** is the VaR of an individual position i in this diversified portfolio, reduced by the proportional diversification effect of the portfolio.

The calculation of the Component Value at Risk of an individual position i is carried out with the help of the beta factor $ß_i$ as follows:

$$CoVaR_i = \text{Portfolio VaR } (=VaR_p) \times \text{Beta factor of i } (=ß_i) \times \text{Weight of i } (=w_i).$$

Inserting the values already calculated for BMW and MAN into this formula gives:

$$CoVaR_{BMW} = €\ 61.93 \times 0.726 \times 45.12\,\% = \mathbf{€\ 20.29},$$
$$CoVaR_{MAN} = €\ 61.93 \times 1.225 \times 54.88\,\% = \mathbf{€\ 41.64}.$$

This form of the calculation can be transformed into a yet simpler version by applying the **correlation coefficient** ($=CR_{i,p}$) between the position i and the portfolio. The correlation coefficient is calculated by taking the covariance between position i and the portfolio, and dividing it by the product of the volatility of position i and the portfolio P. The results for BMW and MAN are:

$$CR_{BMW,P} = 0.00007627 / (1.031\,\% \times 1.025\,\%) = \mathbf{0.722},$$
$$CR_{MAN,P} = 0.00012872 / (1.386\,\% \times 1.025\,\%) = \mathbf{0.906}.$$

With the help of the correlation coefficient the Component VaR can be represented in a simpler form, namely:

$CoVaR_i$ = VaR of Position i ($=VaR_i$) x Correl. coeff. (Position i, Portfolio P) ($=CR_{i,p}$)

The Component VaR for BMW and MAN can then also be calculated from this account, as follows:

$$CoVaR_{BMW} = €\ 28.11 \times 0.722 = \mathbf{€\ 20.29},$$
$$CoVaR_{MAN} = €\ 45.96 \times 0.906 = \mathbf{€\ 41.64}.$$

The **sum** of both the **Component VaR** gives the **VaR** of the **diversified portfolio** in the amount of € 20.29 + € 41.64 = **€ 61.93**. The proportional diversification effect is already taken into account for each of the two Component VaR. When the individual portfolio positions are compared with each other, then the CoVaR is more significant, since the proportional diversification effect is included. Otherwise the diversification effect is only taken into account on the aggregated overall portfolio level. This precise advantage will play a fundamental role in the later risk analysis (Section 2.6).

The simpler form of the calculation of the correlation coefficient is nonetheless not so well suited to interpretation of the CoVaR. The determining factors (weights, beta factors) and the VaR values are show in overview in Table 2.12.

Tab. 2.12: Determining factors and results of Component Value at Risk (CoVaR) for BMW and MAN

Asset position:	Weights:	Beta factor:	Value at Risk:	Component VaR:	Proportional div. effect:
BMW	45.12 %	0.726	€ 28.11	€ 20.29	€ 7.82
MAN	54.88 %	1.225	€ 45.96	€ 41.64	€ 4.32
Portfolio	100.00 %	1.000	€ 74.07	€ 61.93	€ 12.14

From Table 2.12 it is immediately evident that the **proportional diversification effect** depends on the amount of the component value at risk. The smaller the component value at risk is compared to the value at risk, the larger the proportional diversification effect. The component value at risk is in turn smaller when the respective beta factors and weightings are smaller. The BMW stocks then have a much higher proportional diversification effect because they have a somewhat smaller portfolio weighting and a considerably lower beta factor than the MAN stocks have. In other words: if the price of the BMW stocks sink, it will have a significantly smaller effect on the portfolio value than if the MAN stock prices drop. The beta factor arises out of the observed returns and cannot be actively influenced. On the other hand, the decision makers can influence the portfolio weighting. The design of the portfolio structure (portfolio weighting) is the subject of risk analysis (see Section 2.6).

The fundamental principle of the **VaR of a portfolio** which consists of two individual asset positions can be transferred to portfolios with **any number of asset positions**. Nothing changes in the economic derivation and the gain in business insights; only the technical account will become correspondingly more complex. The mathematical representation will therefore be omitted here and referred to in the Technical appendix (2.8 and 6.6).

The VaR calculation of several asset positions will later fall back on this fundamental principle, when the topic is a business-wide risk measurement based on the VaR. In this case all the asset positions or comparable positions of the business are considered as a type of portfolio, in order to calculate the VaR for the entire business from it.

The conclusion can be noted that the VaR concept **remedies** many **disadvantages** of other risk measurement methods and is also particularly suitable through application of **portfolio theory** for business-wide risk measurement and control. Because of these advantages of the VaR approach, yet more possibilities of the VAR calculation will be briefly described. Finally, still another alternative (lower partial moments in Section 2.3.6) to the VaR concept will be presented and briefly discussed.

2.3.4 Additional calculation methods

The calculation described above for determining the value at risk is also called the **"variance-covariance method"** and is also synonymously called the **parametric** or the **analytic** method. This method rests in principle on the expected values, volatilities and correlations of the risk factors (standard method). For simple portfolios or asset positions which are only influenced by one risk factor (with a linear relationship to the asset position), the calculation as it was described above is relatively simple. In the context of the variance-covariance method, this method is therefore also simply called the standard method. More difficult is the VaR calculation of, for example:
- Derivatives,
- Portfolios with various distribution types of the risk factors,
- Risk positions which do not have a linear relationship to the risk factor.

The value of the derivatives depends on several risk factors simultaneously (i. e. interest rates, maturity, stock prices). The VaR calculation of portfolios or individual risk positions may also depend on various distributions of the risk factors, e. g. from interest rate risk and from default risk with government bonds. The present value of fixed interest risk positions does not depend on the interest rate risk factor in a linear way. The following **various approaches** can be used to calculate the VaR in these cases.

One solution approach that takes into account non-linearity and the multifactorial dependency consists of the analytical development or application of corresponding **mathematical models**. These models are very complex and require demanding mathematics. Thus they are only comprehensible with great difficulty and for a small circle of decision-makers and users. There are also on top of that issues (for example, the combination of default risk and interest-change risk) for which there are scarcely any usable analytical approaches. Here, numerical (statistical) methods can be applied. With a view towards the financial crisis (see Section 4.4), however, simple and easily comprehensible risk measurement models should rather be sought, since this can be better communicated to a wide audience (and not only specialists). Thus we refer here to the literature in Section 2.7 for these advanced approaches.

Non-linear relationships can be considered through the method of **linearising** with the simple standard method. The methods of linearising, as with the sensitivities (see Section 2.2.2), is based on the first derivative of the respective evaluation function of the risk factor. Examples of this are the duration for interest-bearing asset positions (see Section 4.1.1) or the delta in the evaluation of derivatives (see Section 3.4.2). With linearising, however, a **margin of error** does arise, the amount of which depends on the curvature of the respective evaluation function. If this margin of error can be accepted by the decision-maker or user, then the simple standard method with linearized values can be applied (for a numerical example see Section 4.1.1). If the decision-maker cannot accept the margin of error, then mathematical models of the advanced standard method or **simulation models** must be applied.

In the **approximation method**, the expected values, volatilities and risk factor correlations are approximated (estimated) and not calculated from historical data. The approximation method is applied when no historical data is available. The parameters can also be estimated when the available data do not appear representative of the future or are flawed in some way. Estimates can be made on the basis of existing comparable historical data or can be carried out by experts. The disadvantage of the approximation method consists in the subjectivity of the parameter assessment. Objectivity is a great advantage of the value at risk calculation which is partially lost in applying the approximation method. The results of the approximation method can be incorporated into the simple and advanced standard methods as well as the Monte Carlo simulation.

With the **historical simulation**, every asset position at each observed time point in the past, together with the corresponding characteristics of the underlying risk factors, is evaluated and added to the total value of the portfolio at the observed time point. This procedure is especially easy because no volatilities, correlations and other statistical parameters have to be calculated or estimated. The historical simulation proceeds in the following steps:
- First the historical risk factors (e. g. daily) are determined.
- Then the historical market values of the portfolio are calculated based on the historical data of the various risk factors.
- The relative market value changes of the portfolio are calculated based on the simulated values, and the corresponding quantile determined for the chosen confidence level (or the corresponding VaR of the portfolio).

The historical simulation is frequently used in practice because it is simple to execute! In particular, the disadvantage of linearising in evaluating asset positions and the resulting margin of error (with the variance-covariance method) is eliminated. For this reason, the procedure will be illustrated by a simple example for a better depiction of the crucial disadvantages. The following asset positions of a portfolio are considered:
- A zero bond has a term of 10 years and a maturity redemption of € 100.00. The current interest rate for assessing this zero bond amounts to 4.5 %. This gives a current risk position for the zero-coupon bond of € 100.00 / 1.045^{10} = **€ 64.39**.
- The second asset position consists of 30 American stocks which will be traded in US-$. The current stock price amounts to US-$ 35.00 and the current exchange rate is US-$/€ 1.45 (indirect or quantity quotation: 1 € = US-$ 1.45). From this comes a risk position of (30 x US-$ 35.00) / 1.45 = **€ 724.14**.

The overall current risk position of the portfolio therefore amounts to **€ 788.53** (€ 64.93 + € 724.14). Extracts of the specified historical values for the three risk factors (10-year interest rate, stock price in US-$, exchange rate in US-$ – €) could be observed in Table 2.13 for the 10 historical time points.

Tab. 2.13: Example for a historical simulation

Time point:	Interest rate 10 y.:	Stock price:	Exchange rate:	Portfolio value:	Portfolio change:
1	4.76 %	$ 35.30	$ 1.4329	€ 801.87	–
2	4.54 %	$ 34.70	$ 1.4456	€ 784.26	−2.20 %
3	4.89 %	$ 33.00	$ 1.4892	€ 726.82	−7.32 %
4	4.56 %	$ 33.20	$ 1.4532	€ 749.41	3.11 %
5	4.25 %	$ 34.10	$ 1.4294	€ 781.64	4.30 %
6	4.93 %	$ 36.00	$ 1.4383	€ 812.69	3.97 %
7	4.44 %	$ 35.90	$ 1.4652	€ 799.82	−1.58 %
8	4.50 %	$ 34.20	$ 1.4777	€ 758.72	−5.14 %
9	4.45 %	$ 34.00	$ 1.4553	€ 765.59	0.91 %
10	4.78 %	$ 33.90	$ 1.4309	€ 773.43	1.02 %
Expected value: 4.61 %		$ 34.43	$ 1.4518	€ 775.43	−0.33 %
Volatility: 0.22 %		$ 1.03	$ 0.0205	€ 26.29	4.07 %

In the column "portfolio value", the values for the corresponding historical risk factors are calculated in a way similar to the calculation of the risk position above. Thus it is assumed that the remaining maturity of the zero bond is exactly 10 years for all 10 of the time points. The portfolio values or the associated relative changes form the basis for calculating the VaR. The following various approaches are possible for this:

- The VaR for a confidence level of, for example, 90 % can practically be determined by "**counting**", using the historical portfolio values. So in 10 % of the worst cases the value of the portfolio is € 726.82. That is, with a confidence level of 90 %, the portfolio's decrease in value is not worse than € 749.41 (the second worst value). From that comes a VaR of **€ 39.12** (€ 788.53 current risk position – € 749.41). For other confidence levels, either 100 observations are necessary in order to determine the second worst value. Or, for example, a linear interpolation for an approximate determination of the second-worst value can be carried out. In the literature, the method of "counting" is also sometimes synonymously called historical simulation. This method has, however, another grave disadvantage: the amount of the VaR is exclusively dependent on the amount of the second-worst value. The distribution and structure of all other value changes are not taken into account at all. Thus this calculation has only very limited significance.
- The calculation of the VaR with the help of the **volatility** parameter is more significant, since here all value changes are included. The calculation can be done

directly on a **euro basis** using the historical portfolio values. The volatility has a value of € 26.29 and that, with a confidence level of 90 %, gives a VaR of € 26.29 x 1.28 = **€ 33.65**. However this method also has a disadvantage. Thus the volatility is calculated as the deviation from the mean of the historical portfolio values. The amount of the risk position then has no influence on the amount of the VaR.
- The calculation of volatility as a function of the relative historical portfolio changes represents the best method. The volatility amounts in this case to 4.0655 %. In this case what comes out is VaR = risk position x volatility (in %) x number of standard deviations = € 788.53 x 4.0655 % x 1.28 = **€ 41.03**. This method has the advantage that not only the amount of the risk position but also the distribution of the historical value changes are both included.

The example shows that all correlations between the risk factors are included in the calculation of the portfolio value. Non-linear relationships between the portfolio and the risk factors (here, the 10-year interest rate) are also accurately taken into account. The disadvantages of the historical simulation are the low flexibility in terms of sensitivity to changing volatilities, correlations and the necessary large volumes of data, as well as the effort required to do the computations. The crucial **disadvantage** emerges nonetheless in the practical application. The calculation and the procedure may seem easy, but are even more restricted than the interpretation possibilities for decision-makers. If different historical data are used, the result also changes. The problem lies in the lack of research into the cause. The basis for the different portfolio VaR cannot be deduced. The historical simulation acts like a so-called "black box". In contrast to the analytical calculation, one cannot determine how strongly the VaR changes when the volatility of a risk factor changes around a specific value (sensitivity of volatility).

Compared to the historical simulation, the **Monte Carlo simulation** is fundamentally more flexible. Here, possible future changes in risk factors are simulated on the basis of various distribution assumptions, which therefore don't have to correspond to the past rates of change. At the same time is assumed that individual risk factor develop randomly (random walk) and are not auto-correlated.
- In the first step, the risk factors are determined and their corresponding expected values, volatilities and covariances are calculated from historical data or estimated through the approximation method. This procedure corresponds to the variance–covariance method.
- Then, correlated random numbers are generated from the standard normally distributed uncorrelated random number of each individual risk factor using the Cholesky decomposition of the covariance matrix, which reflects the correlations between the various risk factors. The Cholesky decomposition is a procedure from numerical mathematics, in which a symmetrical positive definite matrix (here the matrix with the variances and covariances) is decomposed into its factors. The

multiplication of these factors by the uncorrelated random numbers then gives the random numbers with the desired correlations.
- The thus simulated correlated random numbers are used to simulate the changes to the risk factors. The market values of the individual positions are calculated using the simulated risk factors and evaluation models and then from that the value of the aggregated portfolio. The VaR (or the corresponding quantile) can then again be calculated for a specific confidence interval, as with the historical simulation, from a corresponding number of simulated portfolio valuations.

With the Monte Carlo simulation, the distribution assumptions can be varied at will, and the sensitivity with regard to the changed volatilities and correlations can also be calculated. Uniform distributions can also be simulated in this way by, for example, generating equally distributed random numbers in the interval from 0 to 1 and converting these into corresponding changes in the risk factors. A possible **example of use** from the area of the financial crisis is calculation of the VaR for Greek government bonds, for example, where various types of distribution of the interest change risk and the default risk (see Sections 4.1.1 and 4.1.2) were pooled (the so-called **folding** of distributions). The advanced standard method provides no practicable analytical solution approach to this problem. The greatest disadvantage of the Monte Carlo simulation consists in the limited possibilities for analyzing the results with regard to the aggregated portfolio value (as with the historical simulation above). More flexibility, however, is associated with more effort and requires more understanding of statistics (e. g. for the Cholesky decomposition).

The various methods have the **advantages and disadvantages** described above. The choice of method should therefore depend on
- the available data,
- the mathematical statistical target level and
- the required analysis options and the desired flexibility.

of the users or decision-makers. In Figure 2.12, the summaries and application possibilities of the various calculation methods are shown in overview.

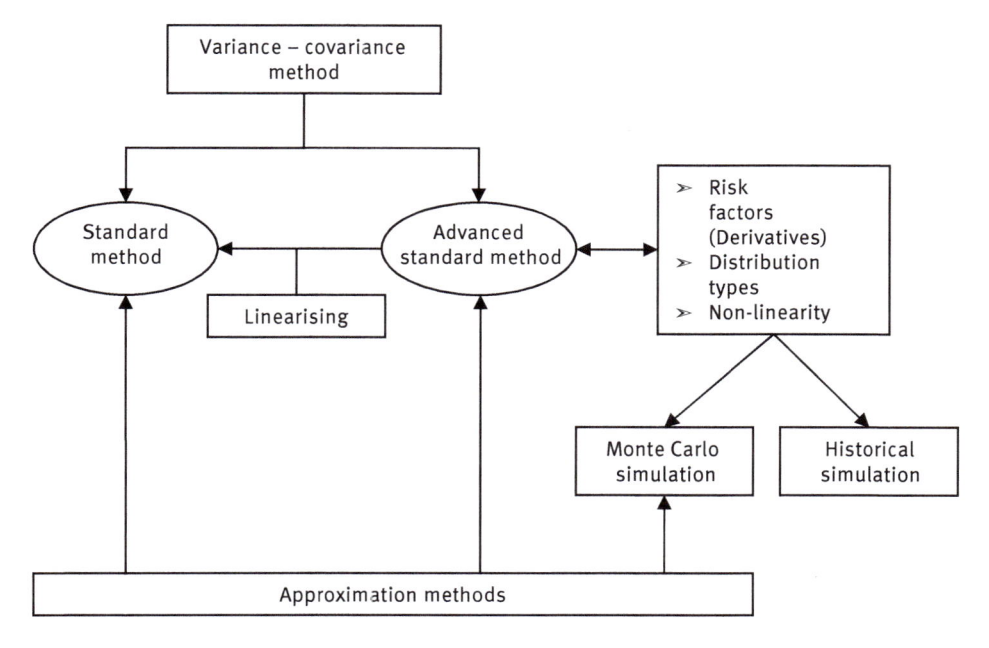

Fig. 2.12: Calculation methods of Value at Risk

Quantitative risk measurement was not newly invented with the value at risk method. With duration, delta and gamma there were already much earlier similar risk measurement instruments which are also found in the VaR concept. The decisive advantage of the VaR consists in the **business-wide consolidation of various risk types** in a systematic and **aggregated treatment**. Certainly the value at risk does not represent a complete risk management system, but is rather a valuable and established auxiliary instrument in the overall context of business-wide risk management (see Section 6.3).

2.3.5 Backtesting

As well as investigating whether the VaR represents a robust risk measure even in extreme situations, it can be tested for how reliable the computational method would have been in predicting actual losses incurred in the past.

Testing the statistical accuracy of the value at risk using historical data is called **backtesting**.

In doing so the question is posed whether the statistical model from which the VaR came (e. g. variance – covariance method or simulation approaches) could have **adequately predicted** reality in the past.

For example, the statistical reliability of a VaR that at some point in the past predicted the maximum loss per day with a confidence level of e. g. 95 % can be tested. It is nothing more than **the prediction** that in the future, 95 % of the daily losses will not exceed the VaR, but there may still be major losses in fewer than 5 % of the cases. If the computational model is adequate, then the actual incurred losses should have only exceeded the VaR on around 5 % of the observed days and been less than the VaR on all the other days.

However, only in the rarest cases will an exact match be observable in such a comparison between forecast and reality. Rather, it is important to investigate whether the observed deviations are **still tolerable**. Thus losses that exceed the VaR on 30 % of the days lead to the conclusion that the method used to calculate the VaR is defective. If the losses exceed the VaR on e. g. fewer than 7 % of the days (instead of the predicted 5 %) than the **reliability of the VaR** can be regarded as given. How high the overrun rate can be and the reliability of the VaR still be accepted lies within the subjective discretion of the decision maker or risk carrier. In practice, the rule of thumb is that overruns of 4 to 7 percentage points (so in the above case 9 % to 12 % of the days exceeded the VaR) are taken as acceptable.

For the portfolio of BMW and MAN stocks, it can be tested whether the VaR which on January 3, 2005 had been based on available data from 2004 would have been confirmed by reality. The VaR for the portfolio would have been determined on that day through the components risk position, volatility, liquidation period and confidence level, as in Section 2.3.2.

$$\text{VaR} = \text{Risk position} \times \text{Volatility} \times \text{Liquidation period} \times \text{Confidence level}$$

The risk position and volatility would have been based on the following initial data that was available for the reporting date of January 3, 2005.

Tab. 2.14: Initial data backtesting for BMW and MAN for reporting date of January 3, 2005

	BMW:	MAN:
Stock price:	€ 33.75	€ 29.50
Number of pieces:	10 pcs.	10 pcs.
Risk position:	€ 337.50	€ 295.00
Portfolio weights:	53.40 %	46.60 %
Volatility:	1.635 %	1.274 %
Correlation coefficient:	0.58	

The risk position of the portfolio arises from the sum of the individual risk positions of BMW and MAN:

$$€\ 337.50 + €\ 295.00 = \underline{\boldsymbol{€\ 632.50}}.$$

For the calculation of the **portfolio volatility**, the variance–covariance method, as in Section 2.3.3, gives the following result for this reporting date:

$$\begin{aligned} s_P &= \sqrt{w_{BMW}^2 \cdot s_{BMW}^2 + w_{MAN}^2 \cdot s_{MAN}^2 + 2 \cdot w_{BMW} \cdot w_{MAN} \cdot k_{BMW,MAN} \cdot s_{BMW} \cdot s_{MAN}} \\ &= \sqrt{0.534^2 \cdot 0.01635^2 + 0.466^2 \cdot 0.1274^2 + 2 \cdot 0.534 \cdot 0.466 \cdot 0.58 \cdot 0.01635 \cdot 0.01274} \\ &= \underline{\boldsymbol{1.281\,\%}}. \end{aligned}$$

For a daily VaR with a confidence level of 95 %, the factor 1 must be used for the liquidation period and the factor 1.645 for the confidence level. Under these conditions, the VaR on January 3, 2005 would have been the following:

$$\begin{aligned} VaR &= €\ 632.50 \times 0.01281 \times 1 \times 1.645 \\ &= \underline{\boldsymbol{€\ 13.32}}. \end{aligned}$$

The claim of the value – that after January 3, 2005, 95 % of the portfolio losses would probably not be greater than € 13.32 – can now be tested against the actual losses in 2005. In reality, the VaR was exceeded on 8 trading days; while on 248 trading days there were losses smaller than or equal to € 13.32 or else there were profits. This means that the VaR was not exceeded in 96.88 % of the cases. The **computational method** used can therefore be classified as **reliable**.

The **disadvantage** of backtesting (in particular with respect to the **financial crisis**) lies in the subjectivity of the decision-maker regarding which loss overruns are still acceptable. Backtesting shows numerous unacceptable overruns in times of financial crisis (e. g. 2008). Objective reasonable conclusions cannot be drawn from backtesting alone about which contribution to the volatility or the VaR must be increased. For periods without crisis–driven outliers, back testing could again give overruns within the acceptable range. Back testing, therefore, is suitable as an additional instrument for testing the statistical robustness of the VaR. The VaR makes no claim about the amount and distribution of the loss in excess of the confidence level (particularly during crises). The methodology of the lower partial moments, described in the following section, starts at precisely this critique point of the VaR.

2.3.6 Lower partial moments (LPM)

An approach to risk evaluation that is related to the value at risk concept is represented by the so-called lower partial moments. It is also assumed that the probability distribution for an uncertain future target figure, i. e. the market price of a securities portfolio, is known. In contrast to the LPM, however, the value at risk first requires a confidence level to be established which can form a basis for determining a value at the left edge of the distribution function which can be interpreted as maximum loss. The lower partial moments approach goes the opposite way:
- First, a **loss limit** is defined in € (or some other interesting threshold) for the risk position under investigation.
- In a second step, the **properties** of the **distribution function** below this value are investigated.

Thus the **lower partial moments** can be described as a research tool for examining the shortfalls from a target value. They provide, in contrast to the value at risk, information about the left side of a distribution function.

So along with the shortfall probability for a reference value, the average scope of the shortfall as well as the dispersion measures can also be determined.

The basic principle of the lower partial moments is the development of a mean for all observed reference value shortfalls. The individual LPM differ only in that they add **different exponents** to the shortfalls. So the "LPM zero" describes the mean with the zero potentiated shortfall, the "LPM 1" describes the mean with the shortfalls raised to the first exponent, the "LPM 2" describes the mean with the shortfalls raised to the second. By using the different potentials, the meaning of the respective results changes, which from a business point of view is especially interesting for the zero, first and second orders (for a mathematical description of lower partial moments, look in the Technical appendix in Section 2.8).

With **LPM 0** all of the shortfalls are converted to the value of one by applying the null exponent (raising any number to zero gives the value one). The expected value then delivers a result between zero and one, which can be interpreted as a probability that there will a shortfall at all. The determining of a probability for the shortfall from a reference value indicates that a **strong analogy** exists between the information content of **LPM 0** and **VaR**. The complement of the LPM 0 (1-LPM 0) corresponds methodologically to the confidence level in VaR, since it expresses the probability that the reference value will not be undershot.

The **LPM 1** gives information on top of that about how large the reference value shortfalls are on average. Thus it is the crucial additional information that distinguishes the lower partial moments from the value at risk: the LPM approach not only says that a specific percentage of shortfalls is calculated, but also what **magnitude** of **shortfalls** can be expected. Note that in determining the LPM 1, not all characteristics of the random variables are still included (i. e. the whole probability distribution) in the calculation, but only the cases in which a shortfall actually exists. Only thus can the calculated mean answer the economically interesting question of which **average shortfall amount** to calculate with.

Also, with **LPM 2** only the cases with actual shortfalls are considered. Through the formation of the average from squared values comes a result that is related to the variance. However, while the dispersion above and below the observed reference value is included in the variance, the LPM 2 only takes account of a one-sided view of the shortfalls. Through the squaring, the shortfalls receive increasingly stronger weighting in the formation of the expected value. Overweighting large values, however, is only useful from a business perspective when high losses are subjectively perceived, despite a relatively low probability of occurrence, as a greater threat than smaller scale losses with a much higher probability of occurrence. The LPM 2 is therefore an indicator for the **presence of especially high losses** even if they have a **low frequency**. However, it is only useful to interpret the result when the subjective perception of risk differs from the statistical risk expectation (expressed through the LPM 1), i. e. when the amount of the loss is attributed a larger role than the probability of occurrence. For purposes of a better interpretation it is useful to extract the roots from the LPM 2 because, as with the variance, the LPM 2 delivers a result in a unit that is not interpretable (squared euros). However, through the extraction of the roots the nonlinear modelling of especially large losses does not get lost. The root from the LPM 2 can therefore be well compared with other euro amounts, i. e. the LPM 1.

In principle, the lower partial moments approach methodologically follows the concept of **moments in statistics**, which allows the description of the distribution functions. As a result, all values of a distribution can theoretically be regarded as reference values. The so-called central moments have particular significance in statistics, where the expected value of the distribution is used as a reference value. Here, the central moment of the second order corresponds to the variance, the central moment of the third order corresponds to the skew and the central moment of the fourth order corresponds to the curvature (kurtosis), a measure of the peakiness of a distribution function. When examining lower partial moments in the context of risk management, however, only **moments of the order of k ≤ 2** lend themselves to **meaningful economic** interpretation.

The following calculations will make clear for the **example** of the BMW and MAN stock portfolios how the lower partial moments of the zero, first and second orders are determined.

Asset position:	Number of pieces:	Price per stock:	Risk position on 1.2.2006:
BMW	10	€ 37.00	€ 370.00
MAN	10	€ 45.00	€ 450.00

The value of the portfolio on January 2, 2006 corresponds to the sum of the risk positions (€ 370 + € 450 = € 820). A loss limit of € 15.00 is established for a single day. The portfolio value reduced to € 15.00 will serve as a reference value for calculating the lower partial moments (€ 820 − € 15 = € 805).
- Risk position (2.1.2005): € 820.00
- Loss limit: € 15.00
- Reference value: € 805.00

Now, to determine the expected number of days and the expected extent of the shortfall below the reference value, all the percentage value changes of the portfolio observed in the year 2005 are first multiplied by the portfolio value from the reporting date of January 2, 2006. This results in a distribution simulated on the basis of historical data of the expected value changes for the current portfolio (historical simulation), which has a range of 256 values. The simulated scenarios are then ranked by the size of the value changes, so all values that go over the loss limit of € 15.00 can be counted.

Table 2.15 shows that in 11 of 256 cases the reference value of € 805.00 was undershot. The **calculation** of the lower partial moments can now be carried out as follows:

$LPM\ 0\ = 11 / 256 = \underline{\mathbf{4.3\%}}$,
$LPM\ 1\ = [(805.00-804.24) + (805.00-803.79) + \ldots + (805.00-794.06)] / 11 = \underline{\mathbf{€\ 3.84}}$,
$LPM\ 2\ = [(805.00-804.24)^2 + (805.00-803.79)^2 + \ldots + (805.00-794.06)^2] / 11 = \underline{\mathbf{23.43}}$
or
$\sqrt{LPM2}\ = \underline{\mathbf{€\ 4.84}}$.

Tab. 2.15: Sample data for calculation of lower partial moments

Rank:	Value change:	Portfolio value:	Rank:	Value change:	Portfolio value:
1	+€ 23.49	€ 843.49	247	−€ 16.21	€ 803.79
2	+€ 21.25	€ 841.25	248	−€ 16.46	€ 803.54
3	+€ 17.88	€ 837.88	249	−€ 17.06	€ 802.94
4	+€ 16.97	€ 836.97	250	−€ 17.29	€ 802.71
(...)	(...)	(...)	251	−€ 18.15	€ 801.85
242	−€ 13.87	€ 806.13	252	−€ 18.94	€ 801.06
243	−€ 14.00	€ 806.00	253	−€ 19.18	€ 800.82
244	−€ 14.09	€ 805.91	254	−€ 19.35	€ 800.65
245	−€ 14.38	€ 805.62	255	−€ 22.91	€ 797.09
246	−€ 15.76	€ 804.24	256	−€ 25.94	€ 794.06

The following **conclusions** can be drawn for the **portfolio** from the determined values:

The likelihood of occurrence that a loss will exceed € 15.00 on one day is **4.3 %**. In such a case, an average overrun of the loss limit is calculated at **€ 3.84**, which corresponds to an expected overall loss of **€ 18.84** (€ 15.00 + € 3.84). However, it cannot be excluded that in some cases the overruns will be significantly higher than **€ 4.84** ($\sqrt{\text{LPM 2}}$). A more meaningful way towards the LPM 2 is to calculate the average fluctuations around the LPM 1. For the above example this gives:

$$\text{LPM } s^2 = [(0.76-3.84)^2 + (1.21-3.84)^2 + \ldots + (10.94-3.84)^2] / 11 = \underline{\mathbf{8.68}} \text{ or}$$
$$\text{LPM } s = \sqrt{\text{LPM } s^2} = \underline{\mathbf{€ 2.95}}.$$

So the average overrun of the € 3.84 loss limit fluctuates on average above and below by **€ 2.95** (=LPM s).

Thus the LPM describes the losses through shortfalls from a reference value (e. g. the Value at Risk). The LPM can therefore be used to measure possible losses in **crisis times** (e. g. the financial crisis 2008). A normal distribution is taken for the observed values under the reference value so, as with the VAR, the following claim can be made for the above example with the help of the LPM: if the reference value is undershot (crisis scenario), then the occurring losses will not be greater than € 10.71 (€ 3.84 + 2.33 x € 2.95) with a probability of 99 %. How high the chosen confidence level is set and which distribution is the basis must depend on further examination of the available data and on the preferences of the decision-maker. For capital requirements in normal times, the VaR calculation above will serve. How high a possible capital buffer must be for crisis times can be described through the LPM. If an investor had put aside € 20.00 for the above portfolio, then € 15.00 represents the capital requirement for "normal" times (loss limit or VaR) and the remaining € 5.00 form a buffer for crisis times. The buffer of € 5.00 can also be represented in another way. In the assumption of a normal distribution, this buffer absorbs 65.30 % (number of standard deviations = 0.3934) of the possible losses in crisis times. In order to cushion 99 % of the losses in crisis times he would have to put aside capital of € 25.71 (€ 15.00 + € 10.71). LPM therefore represents an objectively transparent loss criterion for crisis times in addition to the VAR.

From these statements, the following **properties** and **critique points** can be established for lower partial moments:

A **historical simulation** is necessary for calculating lower partial moments. Calculating the volatilities is (as with the VAR) not possible.

The calculation of the zero order lower partial moments is **tightly bound** with the Value at Risk content.

Consideration of **correlations** and diversification effects is not directly possible through lower partial moments (only indirectly through simulations) and also conceptually not intended. Also, varying liquidation periods cannot be methodologically considered. The lower partial moments can always only refer to the number of days on which the boundary value shortfall could be observed.

Lower partial moments can only **complement** the **VAR**, not replace it. A business-wide risk steering based on the lower partial moments is not sensible, since this would result in providing capital resources for extreme situations or crisis times (instead of on the basis of confidence levels). In business practice this is economically not reasonable and also not actionable (for more information see also the sections on maximal loss (2.1.1), on the stress test (2.4), and on the financial crisis (4.4) and Chapter 6).

Despite the possibilities for reinforcing the **significance** of the **VaR** statistically through back testing and expanding it through the complementary calculation of the lower partial moments for crisis times, there remain still some central critique points of the VaR concept, which will be discussed even more precisely below.

2.3.7 Critiques of the VaR concept

The critique points most often posed in business practice and in business literature against the VaR concept are the following:
- A central critique of the VaR method consists in the **assumption** of **the normal distribution** and, in particular, the often empirically observed abnormalities in the form of "fat tails", exaggerated peaks (leptokurtosis) and also skewness, compared to the idealized theoretical development of the normal distribution curve. In Figure 2.13 these typical abnormalities are shown graphically.
- The objection to the principle difficulties of entering the **future** from the **past** applies not only to the VaR concept but to nature itself.
- Another critique refers to the **short-term** nature of the VaR approach. This short-termism refers to the choice of liquidation periods of 2 to 10 days for the typical application to financial market risk.
- The VaR concept consists of only one value. The possible **extreme values** in the form of losses (i. e. in times of crisis) that are higher than a VaR value for the specified confidence level are not considered.

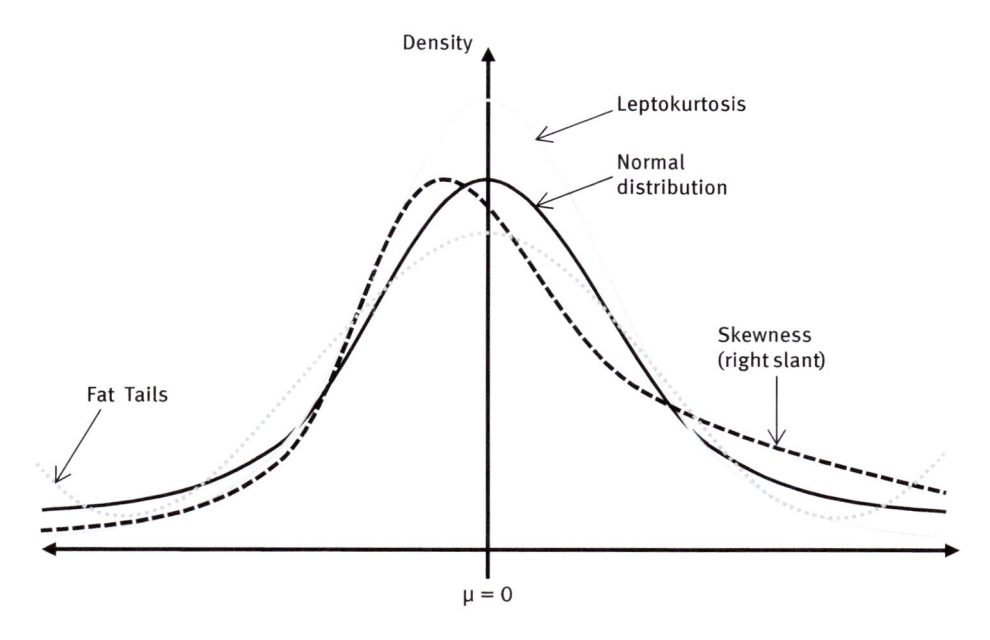

Fig. 2.13: Typical deviations from the normal distribution

Although these critiques are **discussed heatedly** in connection with the financial crisis and in scientific literature as well as in business practice, some **responses** to the above-mentioned points should be made here:
- The **assumption** of the **normal distribution** is indeed not always empirically sustainable, but it can be largely remedied through statistical means. The student's- or t-distribution offers a possibility for treating the fat tail problem. But also, the historical simulation or the "counting of the worst observable asset losses" (in the context of the lower partial moments) corrects this disadvantage. Finally, the VaR concept can also in principle be used when no normal distribution is available at all, in which case determining the quantile is more difficult (one possibility is the so-called full enumeration, see Section 5.1.1). But the core message of the VaR remains: even with a uniform distribution, it is the maximum possible asset loss compatible with the confidence level.
- The fundamental problem, **inferring** the **future** from **past data**, cannot be fully rectified by a statistical process. Nonetheless there is at least the question about the respective advantages and disadvantages of statistical methods compared to subjective, individual prediction models that don't rest on any past data. Proponents of statistical methods cite the objectivity and therefore the greater transparency. Stress tests (see Section 2.4), for example, can also partially eliminate the neglect of unexpected risk situations.

- The obvious **short-term** nature of the VaR approach can be easily remedied by multiplying the corresponding root factor (for example, in comparing market and default risks, the market risks can be multiplied by the root factor from 250 days). That this multiplication reduces the accuracy of the possible maximum loss estimate is indisputable! However, this is not a special problem of the VaR concept, but rather a general difficulty that emerges with long-term forecasts. So, for example the weather forecast for the next few days is always much more accurate than the forecast for a day two weeks away.
- Possible extreme values will be considered in Section 2.3.6 through the **lower partial moments** (a similar method is the calculation of the value at risk based on **extreme value theory**), which nonetheless cannot replace the VaR concept, but rather can only complement it. Thus in considering extreme values, the diversification effect cannot be directly taken into account. Therefore extreme values are also not for use in business-wide risk measurement and steering, but merely for additional informational purposes. Furthermore, extreme values are not suitable for business-wide risk control because a business can't and doesn't want to reserve capital for very rare (extreme) losses. Rather, a "normal" measure for possible losses is needed. A normal measure is precisely what the VaR approach offers, and not extreme losses. In times of financial crisis, for example, the lower partial moments can be used to get information about how well the business is girded against extreme losses in crisis situations.

This last critique was discussed intensively and controversially in reference to the financial crisis. Therefore this point will be illustrated in the following example. Suppose someone wants to know, with a confidence level of 99 %, how many roof tiles at most can land on his head when he leaves the house. Then the answer (i. e. one tile) corresponds to the **principle** of the **value at risk**. A steering measure will now be taken based on the answer. So, for example, the only safety measure might be to check for loose roof tiles. Now the extreme values are observed and it is determined, for example, that three tiles at once could fall from the roof, which might happen every 50 years. Since this could lead to death, an appropriate precaution would be to wear a helmet every day when leaving the house. It is obvious that this measure would not be taken into serious consideration because it would not be **proportionate**! And it is precisely this proportionality that the VaR concept is about in the context of business-wide risk measurement and risk steering.

Although the main critiques of the VaR concept can be refuted, it makes absolute sense, as with the lower partial moments, to apply complementary statistical methods. To these **additional methods** belong, among others, the stress tests, which will be described in the following section.

2.4 Stress tests, scenario analysis and worst case scenarios

The fact that projection of past data into the future is often refuted is a more significant criticism of the VaR concept which is often put forward in scientific literature and business practice. This leads to the question of how **robust** the previously introduced **risk measures** are for future unexpected risk situations (e. g. financial crises), especially the VaR. It is exactly this question (in addition to backtesting and lower partial moments) that the so-called stress tests, scenario analysis and worst-case scenarios are supposed to try to answer.

Considering the robustness of the VaR key indicator leads to a core problem of the VaR concept. The VaR only makes a claim about the size of the expected maximum loss for a specified confidence level. It allows no statement, however, about how much the **loss exceeds the confidence** level. Or to put it another way: when the maximum loss is not greater than € 1 million with a confidence level of, for example, 95 % under normal market conditions, how great is the possible loss above this 95 %? So the lower partial moments are about capturing the so-called **outliers**, in particular for coping with future **financial crises**. This is the reason for stress testing, which attempts to take into account extremely unusual situations in order to support the concept of the VaR.

Stress tests can be described as a process in which situations can be identified and controlled which could cause extraordinary losses (exceeding the VaR).

For this purpose, a so-called **scenario analyses** is carried out, where the portfolio is evaluated under the assumption of various scenarios or environmental conditions. For this, various **very large changes** are assumed for the respective **key risk factors**, and from that the respective resulting portfolio losses are determined. In this case, however, the **correlations** between the risk factors are **ignored**.

On the other hand, **worst-case scenarios** can be done where different scenarios are not analyzed but rather always just the worst imaginable scenario. A possible risk measure for determining the highest possible loss was already described in detail with the maximal loss in Section 2.1.1.

The crucial problem when performing stress tests of any kind is **determining** the **extraordinary changes** in the relevant risk factors. Here, basically two procedures can be distinguished.

First, the e. g. four highest reductions can be determined from **historical changes** over a very long observation period. Empirical investigations have shown that these changes (in particular the stock return drops) are seldom exposed by the VaR based on the empirical normal distribution of the previous 250 trading days. The maximum number of standard deviations that can be statistically verified over a long period, e. g. 10 years, can also be derived from empirical studies.

Another approach is to derive the extraordinary losses on the basis of assessments from experts and decision-makers with regard to the **future development** of important key **indicators** such as, for example, stock indices, oil prices, base interest rates etc.

Performing stress tests by means of various scenarios will be illustrated using the above examples of the BMW and MAN stock portfolios. For the daily changes in the BMW and MAN stock returns, the following **example** scenarios could be used:

1. The highest relative daily **drop** in the **DAX** stock index in the past 20 years was on October 16, 1989 and amounted to **−12.81 %**.
2. The average of the three lowest daily price returns of the previous six years was for **BMW −9.49 %** and for **MAN −10.10 %**.
3. Bookstaber's rule (1997) says to choose **10 standard deviations** as an approach. In the context of the volatility determined by the VaR calculation of 1.031 % for BMW, 1.386 % for MAN and 1.025 % for the portfolio, we get a result of **−10.31 % for BMW**, **−13.86 % for MAN** and **−10.25 % for the Portfolio**. Bookstaber's approach is not a VaR calculation, that is, it is not multiplied by the liquidation period and the number of standard deviations, but rather uses only the calculated percentage losses (volatility times 10).
4. Experts estimate (a completely freely chosen assumption) a future sales decline of 30 %, based on sharply climbing oil prices and a recession threatening the world automobile and machine manufacture economy, which changes the corresponding stock prices by **−15 %**.
5. As a worst-case scenario, the maximum loss will be set at **−100 %** of the total assets.

The stock value from January 2, 2006 is again set as the initial value for calculating the asset losses in the context of the respective scenarios, so for BMW € 370.00, for MAN € 450.00 and for the portfolio € 820.00. The outcomes of the scenarios and the resulting losses are summarized together with the above calculated VaR results in Table 2.16.

Tab. 2.16: Results of VaR and stress tests or scenario analyzes

Scenario:	BMW stocks:	MAN stocks:	Portfolio:
VaR (according to Section 2.3.3):	€ 28.11	€ 45.96	€ 61.93
1. Highest drop in the DAX:	−€ 47.40	−€ 57.65	−€ 105.05
2. Lowest returns for BMW, MAN:	−€ 35.11	−€ 45.45	−€ 80.56
3. Number of standard deviations = 10:	−€ 38.15	−€ 62.37	−€ 84.05
4. Experts estimate:	−€ 55.50	−€ 67.50	−€ 123.00
5. Maximum loss:	−€ 370.00	−€ 450.00	−€ 820.00

With the exception of Scenario 3, "Number of Standard Deviations", **no** possible **correlations** are considered, i. e. the portfolio losses always arise out of the **sum of the individual losses** of the BMW and MAN stocks. In scenario 3, "Number of Standard Deviations", the correlations are taken into account by using the portfolio volatility, which does indeed show the correlations. With the VaR results and in scenario 3, the portfolio loss is thus smaller than the sum of the individual risks. In the other scenarios, due to the assumptions and the neglect of the diversification effect, the portfolio losses compared to the portfolio VaR are clearly higher than are the individual BMW and MAN position losses compared to the individual VaR.

However, the **subjectivity** in creating scenarios and the resulting significant differences in the amount of the losses is especially striking. In particular, the calculations for the relative asset changes inside the individual scenarios are not usually objectively transparent. Thus, significant differences arise just through
- the choice of different historical periods for determining the minimum returns (scenario 1. and 2.),
- the number of underlying returns for calculating averages (scenario 2.),
- the selection of the author of various capital market studies (scenario 3.) and
- the interviewing of various experts (scenario 4.).

The significance of the maximum loss is referred to in Section 2.1.1.

This means that stress tests exhibit the following **disadvantages** compared with the VaR concept. They are unsuitable for **comparisons** between different businesses and also for comparisons between different departments and risk types inside of a single business when respectively different **subjective scenario assumptions** are made. However, this is exactly what the ECB did with stress testing (e. g. making different assumptions about real estate markets in Spain and Germany; see Section 4.4). In addition, **no plausible likelihood of occurrence** can be specified for the determined extreme losses, which also hampers comparability. Conversely, this is exactly the fundamental advantage of the VaR concept. By establishing the parameters of confidence level, historical period (a trading year with ca. 250 trading days) and liquidation period, it is possible for the risk measurement to be almost objective across different risk types by means of the VaR. In later chapters, this objective transferability of the VaR approach will thus be in the foreground for different types of business risk.

Stress tests have another **disadvantage** that lies in the methodology or **application** of the method **itself**. A stress is described as, among other things, something unexpected or an unplanned event or an acute threat, which cannot be offset. A stress test uses specific assumptions, which are then no longer unexpected or no longer pose an acute threat. So this contradiction lies in the planning and execution of the stress test itself. When one tests the simulated assumptions in advance, then these are no longer a stress when they occur. For example, if the students are told in advance that the VaR method will be on their risk management exam and they prepare for it, then it causes the students no stress when the VaR method is on the exam. If the measurement of reputation risk is part of the exam, that will mean stress for the students because they probably did not prepare themselves for it (since it wasn't announced ahead of time). In this respect, the term scenario analysis is more meaningful, since the term scenario does not include stress resistance testing.

Nonetheless, **stress tests** have their justification for **being used**. Thus they are suitable as a risk indicator, to at least **add information** (as with the lower partial moments) about the purely theoretical extreme loss which is not represented by the VaR. The lower partial moments have as their great advantage over the stress tests that they are much more objective and therefore more transparent. Within the various design possibilities demonstrated as examples of scenario building, the Bookstaber approach still represents the best possibility with regard to objectivity and consideration of the correlations. Following the Bookstaber approach, the maximum observable number of standard deviations is measured at the largest asset losses during a sufficiently long historical period and used as a basis.

Since the performance of stress tests is very subjective, the specific design depends on the particulars of the respective users (business, investor, regulatory authority). There can be crucial differences due to varying industries, regions, business sizes and so on. For this reason, the various subjective design possibilities in the context of stress tests will not be further explored here.

2.5 Qualitative risk measurement techniques

The risk measures discussed so far all have as a feature that the risk is evaluated in monetary units. This important characteristic rests on an economic reality which in practice is only relevant to a few business situations. Here it involves asset positions that are traded daily on functioning capital markets and evaluated through that. Risks that arise in the form of possible asset losses based on price fluctuations in the financial markets are also summarized in the risk category of **financial market risks**. Financial market risks are directly quantifiable through risk measurements and therefore also easier to deal with than qualitative (in the sense of not quantifiable) risks. In typical business dealings, financial market risks don't arise due to business operations but rather are motivated by profit or security considerations of some sort or another. Consequently, with the exception of banks, insurance and financial service providers (for whom dealing with financial market risk is part of their core business), qualitative risks have therefore a greater significance. For this reason, an approach will now be introduced that makes it possible to quantify risks that are not directly measurable.

The necessity of measuring qualitative risks will first be illustrated through some relevant business **examples**.
- **Credit risk** (default risk; see Section 4.2) consists of the possibility that one customer (out of e. g. three clients A, B and C in total) doesn't repay the trade credit

and thus the business (the supplier) suffers an asset loss for the amount of the unpaid credit.
- A business sells three different products A, B and C. The company is subject to **sales risk** (see Section 5.2.2) for each product. The sales risk consists in the possibility that fewer products will be sold than was planned, resulting in an asset loss.
- A business plans new production plants, with three alternatives A, B and C to choose from. Production with a new plant is subject to so-called **operational risk**. If customers don't get their ordered products delivered on time due to a failure at the production plant, this can lead to an asset loss for the business. Asset losses can also arise through defective production or damage at the plant.

These examples illustrate very well the **difference** from **financial market risks**. With the credit risks outlined here, the value of the claim is not assessed in monetary units daily in a market. Consequently, a deterioration of assets, e. g. due to downgrading of the borrower, also cannot be directly measured in monetary units. The measurement and the assessment of creditworthiness are called the (credit) rating (see Section 4.2.2).

With this, the second key problem becomes clear. When there can be no evaluation in monetary units in a functioning market, then the **influencing factors** must be **quantified** for a risk evaluation. All influencing factors relevant for the asset value must be captured and aggregated into a single total figure. This total figure must be assigned to an asset value in order to be able to capture the possible asset losses again in the sense of the VaR concept.

The quantifying of influencing factors in particular can be based on a well-known principle. The **application** of this **basic principle** is called the **scoring model**. The modern concept of the scoring model is also used as a generic term. There are numerous variations to be found, especially in investment decision-making under the terms **cost-benefit analysis** or value analysis.

The **basic structure** of scoring models consists, in the first step, of **weighting** the various **influencing factors**. Influencing factors with a large impact are given a high weight (e. g. 60 %) and vice versa. In the second and crucial step, the characteristics of the various influencing factors are evaluated depending on the respective alternatives, being given a **rating** on a **scale** of 1 to 10. In the third and last step, the weighted points of all the influencing factors are added up for each alternative and this sum constitutes the **target value** (the score) used for assessment.

An **example** of the credit risk mentioned above illustrates the procedure. Three credit customers A, B and C are assessed. For this assessment, the following four influencing factors and their respective possible ratings will be used as an:
- the borrower's previous **solvency** (very good, good, satisfactory, sufficient, poor),
- the borrower's current **financial situation** (good, medium, poor),

- the amount of the borrower's existing **liquid funds** in relation to the credit amount (in %),
- the general current **state of the business** and the **future business prospects** in relation to product sales (excellent, good, moderate, poor).

The solvency should, with 40 %, have the strongest influence on the credit risk. The financial situation should influence the credit risk with 30 %, the liquid funds with 20 % and the state of the business with 10 %. Table 2.17 shows possible example ratings of the individual influencing factors for the respective borrowers.

Tab. 2.17: Example scoring model for credit risk measurement

Influencing factors:	Solvency:	Financial situation:	Liquid funds:	Business prospects:
Weighting:	40 %	30 %	20 %	10 %
Credit customer A:	Good	Good	30 %	Moderate
Credit customer B:	Satisfactory	Poor	20 %	Good
Credit customer C:	Very good	Medium	40 %	Poor

In the next step, the different characteristics are assigned points from 1 to 10. The best possible rating is given 10 points and the worst is given 1 point. The best possible rating in this case, from the perspective of the user (the lender), stands for a small risk; one point is given when the rating has a strong influence on a high risk (e. g. when the payment habits are very bad). **Point scales** are assigned to the individual influencing factors as follows:

Solvency: very good=10, good=8, satisfactory=6, sufficient=4, poor=2,

Financial situation: good=9, medium=6, poor=3,

Liquid funds: <10 %=1, 10–20 %=2, ... , 80–90 %=9, 90–100 %=10,

Business prospects: excellent=10, good=8, moderate=5, poor=2.

Table 2.18 shows the results when the points given in the previous step are weighted and added up to a target value.

2.5 Qualitative risk measurement techniques

Tab. 2.18: Results of a scoring model for credit risk measurement

Influencing factors:	Solvency:	Financial situation:	Liquid funds:	Business prospects:	Target value:
Weighting:	40 %	30 %	20 %	10 %	
Credit customer A:	8	9	3	5	=0.4x8+0.3x9+0.2x3+0.1x5 =**7.0**
Credit customer B:	6	3	2	8	=0.4x6+0.3x3+0.2x2+0.1x8 =**4.5**
Credit customer C:	10	6	4	2	=0.4x10+0.3x6+0.2x4+0.1x2=**6.8**

With a target value of 7, borrower A has the smallest **credit risk**; borrower C has an only slightly higher risk with 6.8 and borrower B has the significantly highest credit risk with 4.5. The procedure would be similar for other areas of **sales risk** mentioned as examples (for products A, B C, the influencing factor would be e. g. customer service) and **operational risk** (for plants A, B, C the influencing factor would be e. g. the maintenance quality).

Using this example, the most important **characteristics** of the scoring models can be summarized for **risk management**:
- Scoring models offer the possibility to consider **qualitative and quantitative influencing factors** of a risk and to make alternatives comparable by calculating a target value.
- The target value of scoring models can serve as a **basis** for further **quantifying** of the relevant risks.
- The **correlations** between various influencing factors are **not** explicitly **considered** with scoring models.
- The allocation of points on a **scale** of 1 to 10 is made **subjectively** by the user, which means the comparability of the risks between different users is limited.
- The choice of **influencing factors**, their respective **weightings** and the **setting** of the point scales are carried out by each individual user. Because of this the results become even less comparable.

The **disadvantages** of the scoring models show considerable similarity to those of the **stress tests**. Thus a question arises with regard to the use of scoring models in the context of risk management. While stress tests are simply an additional criterion to the VaR calculation, the importance of the scoring models is much greater.

Only through the use of scoring models can important business risks be quantified at all and thus integrated into business-wide risk management. So the use of **scoring models** is not an additional criterion but rather a *sine qua non*, especially for VaR-based **risk management**. It will be shown later that scoring models are required for establishing the comparability of the VaR concept. Ultimately this is the only way to pull together and manage the most disparate business risks under one overall concept. Given the importance of scoring models, the previously mentioned **disadvantages** must always be considered and kept in focus by the user. The behaviour and the credit rating methods of the rating agencies (as the primary users of scoring models) during the financial crisis illustrates this need (see Section 4.4).

2.6 Risk analysis

After risk measurement, the question of analysis of the measurement results immediately follows, and the action plan to be derived from those results. Risk analysis depends first of all on the **risk attitude of the business** or the investor. The spectrum ranges from completely risk-averse to totally risk-taking. Complete risk aversion is not appropriate for entrepreneurial activity, since every business activity is usually also linked to a business risk. Complete risk avoidance would, however, abandon any **profit expectations**. This demonstrates that with risk analysis, no unified applicable standards can be derived for all companies. Since it is not very practical to derive action plans for single individuals, the following will only show risk analysis for risk-averse and risk-taking approaches.

A first rough **sorting** of the measurement results into various **risk categories** is often carried out in business practice. In the first step, it can be divided into the following categories:
- **Critical risks** which could lead to a threat to the business.
- **Important risks** which may not endanger the continued existence of the company but can lead to short-term capital measures in order to sustain the business.
- **Insignificant risks** which might require no special measures, but can be managed in the course of running the business.

However, the question immediately arises as to when and how explicitly a risk is rated as critical, important or insignificant on the basis of its measurement result. For this purpose it is necessary to examine the VaR with a view to active risk management.

Thus the **VaR** can be interpreted as **risk capital** or also as economically necessary capital for business activities. Thus the VaR stands opposite the **equity capital** as an important factor for necessary reserves against possible future losses. The VaR indicates the necessary equity capital needed as a buffer for covering potential losses. With this approach it is also now easier to using the VaR from different positions to sort the above risk categories into a rough classification. So, for example, positions with a VaR up to e. g. 5 % of the equity capital can be classified as insignificant, positions with a VaR between 5 and 20 % of the equity capital as important and positions with a VaR greater than 20 % of the equity capital as critical. The amount of the respective VaR as a percentage of the equity capital again depends on the individual risk approach and company specific's and is listed here only as an example for a generic company.

Nonetheless, such a classification into risk categories is extremely insufficient for a risk analysis. The decisive factor is the **inclusion** of the **profits** or **profit expectations**. So, first of all, the profits that can be assigned to the asset positions must be captured and taken into account. On the other hand, the (necessary) **interest return** on the **equity capital** is to be considered. For an alternative investment of the equity capital in the capital market, the risk-free interest rate (e. g. $i_{rf} = 3\%$) will be used as an interest benchmark.

A first intuitive approach to pulling together the **profit** and **risk** in a single **key indicator** consists in dividing the average price return by the associated volatility. For BMW and MAN (see Table 2.4) this gives:

$$BMW = 0.042\% \ / 1.031\% = \mathbf{0.0407},$$
$$MAN = 0.175\% \ / 1.386\% = \mathbf{0.1263},$$
$$Portfolio = 0.115\% \ / 1.025\% = \mathbf{0.1122}.$$

Interpretation of the two **results** suggests the conclusion that it would be more worthwhile to invest in MAN stocks than in BMW stocks because a much higher return (0.175 % compared to 0.042 %) is achieved only with a disproportionately higher risk (1.386 % compared to 1.031 %). In other words: the greater the ratio, the greater the expected returns for equal risk. Also, the portfolio ratio is somewhat smaller than for MAN, because the diversification effect isn't sufficient to compensate for BMW's lower portfolio return. This calculation has the immediately obvious disadvantage that the interest rate on the equity capital is not considered in terms of the opportunity cost. By contrast, the Sharpe Ratio explicitly considered the risk-free rate and calculated it as:

Sharpe Ratio = (average price return − risk-free rate) / volatility

---

To consider the risk-free rate of 3 % per annum, this must be still converted to a daily rate since the return and volatility determined above are likewise daily values. For the daily risk-free rate, that is 3 % / 256 trading days = 0.012 %. The Sharpe ratio of BMW, MAN and the portfolio then amount to

Sharpe Ratio BMW = (0.042 % − 0.012 %) / 1.031 % = **0.0294**,
Sharpe Ratio MAN = (0.175 % − 0.012 %) / 1.386 % = **0.1178**,
Sharpe Ratio Portfolio = (0.115 % − 0.012 %) / 1.025 % = **0.1008**.

Using a year as the reference period must give identical results since the denominator and the numerator of the ratio are multiplied by the same factor (number trading days; Sharpe Ratio BMW = (10.752 % − 3.00 %) / 263.936 % = 0.0294). Nothing has changed about the favorability (compared with return to volatility ratio), but the rela-

tions of the quotients to each other have changed somewhat. With certain number constellations, favorability can also change by taking into account the risk-free rate. The **Sharpe ratio** has nonetheless the following **disadvantages:**
- In calculating the Sharpe ratio, there are **no** figures evaluated in **monetary units**, but only in relative amounts. Because of this no claims about the absolute effects (e. g. on the equity capital) in monetary units can be derived from the Sharpe ratio.
- The **volatility** as a risk measure has **disadvantages** described in Section 2.2.1, which can largely be resolved by the VaR.
- The average asset change or price return is not the only profit component of an asset position. Rather, **dividend payments** or **interest payments**, for example, must also be considered in the profits, in addition to exchange gains. The Sharpe ratio by definition **does not take this into account.**
- The Sharpe ratio does **not** consider correlations and the resulting **diversification effects** for individual positions.

These disadvantages of the Sharpe ratio can be eliminated by using the **component value at risk** as a risk figure. This eliminates several disadvantages. Firstly, it involves a risk figure in monetary units. Secondly, diversification effects are also considered proportionally for individual positions. And finally, the CoVaR lacks the other disadvantages of the volatility (see Sections 2.2.1 and 2.3). If the profit in currency units rather than the percentage price return is now used, consisting of the components exchange profit plus dividend- or interest payment minus the risk free interest payment in currency units, this leads to the following calculation for the so-called **Return on Risk adjusted Capital (=RoRaC):**

RoRaC = (price gain + distribution gain − risk-free interest rate) / Component VaR

Here the term "return" is used for the profit and the Component Value at Risk is used for the risk-adjusted capital. For these or lightly modified variations, the terms **RaRoC** (=**R**isk **a**djusted **R**eturn **o**n **C**apital) and **RaPM** (=**R**isk **a**djusted **P**erformance **M**easurement) are also used in literature and practice. Because calculations are involved here which can be transposed in each case and always show the same business situation, the different variations and terms will not be explored further.

The **application** of this **key indicator** will be developed further using the **portfolio** with the BMW and MAN stocks. To calculate the RoRaC, the data from Table 2.10 are additionally extended by the following information and calculations:
- To determine the **yearly price gains** in Euros, the price return is projected onto a year and based on the risk position. For BMW that gives
  0.042 % x 256 trading days = 10.752 % of € 370.00 = **€ 39.78**.
  0.175 % x 256 trading days = 44.800 % of € 450.00 = **€ 201.60** for MAN and

€ 39.78 € + € 201.60 € = **€ 241.38** for portfolio.
- For the **dividend payment**, 2% (= **€ 7.40**) is estimated for BMW and for MAN 1% (= **€ 4.50**) on the risk position per 2.1.2006), which gives **€ 11.90** for the portfolio.
- From the sum of the yearly price gain and the dividend payment and minus the **risk-free interest rate**
BMW: 3% of € 370.00 = **€ 11.10**,
MAN: 3% of € 450.00 = **€ 13.50**,
Portfolio: 3% of € 820.00 = **€ 24.60**,
comes for BMW an **overall profit** of **€ 36.08** and for MAN **€ 192.60** for one year. For the portfolio the overall profit amounts to **€ 228.68**.
- The **Component VaR** already determined in Section 2.3.3 must also be projected onto a year in order to be compared with the yearly profit, so it must be multiplied by the square root of 256 instead of the square root of 10 (trading days). For BMW the CoVaR amounts to **€ 102.64** for 1 year, for MAN **€ 210.68** and for the portfolio **€ 313.32**.

The resulting key indicators and calculation bases are summarized in Table 2.19.

Tab. 2.19: Sharpe ratio and RoRaC for example portfolio (BMW and MAN)

Key indicator:	BMW:	MAN:	Portfolio:
Return (1 day):	0.042 %	0.175 %	0.115 %
Volatility (1 day):	1.031 %	1.386 %	1.025 %
Profit (overall 1 year):	€ 36.08	€ 192.60	€ 228.68
VaR (1 year):	€ 142.21	€ 232.54	€ 313.32
Component VaR (1 year):	€ 102.64	€ 210.68	€ 313.32
Relative Component VaR (1 year): (in relation to portfolio)	32.76 %	67.24 %	100.00 %
Beta factor:	0.726	1.225	1.000
ΔVaR:	0.01734	0.02926	0.02388
Weights:	45.12 %	54.88 %	100.00 %
Return/Volatility (1 day):	0.0407	0.1263	0.1122
Sharpe ratio (1 day):	0.0294	0.1178	0.1008
RoRaC (1 year):	0.3515	0.9142	0.7299

The following **properties** and **analysis possibilities** in the context of risk management can be derived from the results in Table 2.19:

A classification of the various risk positions or business areas into **risk categories** (e. g. low, middle, high) can be carried out using the **relative Component VaR**. It is clear from the relative Component VaR that the MAN stocks carry approximately twice as much risk as the BMW stocks. The weighting of the risk positions is, however, clearly more balanced. For further analysis, the profits and the effects of the weighting changes (e. g. with the help of the beta factor or the Incremental VaR) must be included in the portfolio var.

The **value at risk** of the overall portfolio delivers a first **risk assessment** through comparison with the **equity capital.** If the portfolio VaR lies significantly below the available equity capital than a high credit rating is given. If, depending on the risk appetite, the VaR is close to or at the equity capital, then measures based on further analysis are needed.

An assessment can be carried out with the help of the **Incremental VaR** (ΔVaR) or the beta factor where dismantling the risk position **reduces** the overall **portfolio VaR** the most quickly.

The **RoRaC** is best suited for a **comparison** of **risk positions** or of business units. The portfolio RoRaC can only take values between the smallest and the largest individual RoRaC values (see Technical appendix 2.8). The MAN RoRaC value is higher than the portfolio's and much higher than BMW's. As with the Sharpe ratio explanations, it can be inferred that increasing the MAN stocks would be advantageous.

For a **risk analysis** of the results in Table 2.19, **three scenarios** are suggested:
1. The equity capital of € 314.00 stands at the same level as the portfolio VaR.
2. The portfolio is underfinanced with 50 % of the equity capital in the amount of € 157.00.
3. A coverage of the VaR is available for the portfolio with equity capital of € 471.00 (150 %).

Within these three scenarios, possible instructions will be derived respectively for both **risk-averse** and **risk-taking** approaches. So altogether six decision-making areas emerge (see Table 2.20).

In **scenario 1**, the credit rating or the necessary capital reserves would be given and measures to reduce the overall portfolio VaR would not be necessary for the time being. However, there is no buffer for possible crises (for example, an amount given by the lower partial moments). A **risk-averse investor** would make the effort to build up such a capital buffer. For this purpose, he could either reduce the portfolio VaR or increase the equity capital. Capital increases are one possible measure in the context of risk steering and should first be excluded at this point (see Section 3.1). In order to lower the portfolio VaR, the portfolio must be dismantled or rearranged in such a way that the portfolio VaR drops by the desired amount. If a capital buffer of € 30.00 e. g. is needed, then the portfolio VaR must drop to € 284.00. Based on the higher incremental VaR and beta factor of the MAN stocks (see Table 2.19), a risk-averse investor would first sell two MAN stocks. This would lower the portfolio risk most quickly and effectively. His portfolio VaR would then amount to € 271.90 and his portfolio RoRaC would be reduced to 0.6994. The portfolio RoRaC drops since with the sale of the MAN stocks the portfolio risk decreases, but at the same time the portfolio's return stock also decreases disproportionately. A risk-averse investor would thus have a better diversified portfolio with a portfolio volatility reduced to 0.999 %. In return he would have to accept a lower portfolio return of 0.108 %.

The **risk-taking** investor would, for example, be content with a capital buffer of € 15.00 (portfolio VaR = € 299.00). To this end, he would sell two BMW stocks because of the smaller individual RoRaC. His portfolio VaR would in this case amount to € 293.46, with the BMW stocks still only having a portfolio weighting of 39.68 %. Based on the increased return stock through the higher MAN weighting, his RoRaC would have climbed to 0.7547. In return for that, however, because of the increased risk element from the MAN stocks and the smaller diversification, he must accept a higher portfolio volatility of 1.055 %.

In **scenario 2**, there would be an acute need for action related to a drastic reduction of the portfolio VaR. A **risk-averse** investor would again, as in scenario 1, sell MAN stocks because of the higher incremental VaR. At the same time, however, he would also be eager to achieve a low portfolio volatility through a corresponding diversification. To achieve a portfolio VaR of, for example, under € 150.00 (a capital buffer of at least € 7.00 for crises) he could sell all 10 MAN stocks. Then his portfolio would not be at all diversified and his RoRaC would sink to 0.2537 (individual RoRaC of BMW stock). It would be substantially better to sell only six MAN stocks and instead sell another four BMW stocks. He would then also have a portfolio VaR of under € 150.00 (€ 147.18) but a RoRaC of 0.6705. But because of the diversification, the portfolio volatility would still only amount to 0.982 %!

The **risk-taking investor** would, as in scenario 1, sell all BMW stocks. In order to reduce the portfolio VaR under € 150.00 he would still have to additionally sell four MAN stocks (then portfolio VaR = € 139.53). His RoRaC would then climb to 0.8282. However, his undiversified portfolio would then also have a volatility of 1.386 % (individual volatility of MAN). If he were to mix in BMW stocks according to his risk propensity (e. g. not completely risky), then he would, for example, with a total of one BMW stocks and six MAN stocks, reach a portfolio VaR of € 145.27. Thus his portfolio RoRaC would have dropped only slightly to 0.8203 but his portfolio volatility would have dropped to 1.269 %.

In **scenario 3**, the **risk-averse investor** would augment his portfolio as necessary with attention to sufficient diversification. He would not, as in scenario 1, sell MAN stocks but rather buy BMW stocks, so long as a good diversification is maintained. If the BMW stock portion of the portfolio were to get too high, then he would also still buy MAN stocks corresponding to his potential equity capital. With a portfolio of, for example, 20 BMW stocks and 11 MAN stocks he would have a portfolio VaR of € 445.92, a portfolio RoRaC of 0.6369 and a portfolio volatility of only 0.969 %.

The **risk-taking** investor, by contrast, would buy MAN stocks and, depending on his risk appetite, perhaps mix BMW stocks into the portfolio (as in scenario 2). If he were to buy six MAN stocks (altogether 10 BMW stocks and 16 MAN stocks), he would come to a portfolio VaR of € 443.68, a portfolio RoRaC of 0.7759 and a portfolio volatility of 1.092 %.

The respective **decision-making areas** and **action possibilities** for the various scenarios and risk attitudes are summarized in Table 2.20.

Tab. 2.20: Risk analysis and action possibilities for various scenarios and risk attitudes

Scenario: (previous portfolio VaR: € 314.34)	Risk attitude:	Action:	New portfolio VaR:	New portfolio RoRaC:	New portfolio volatility:
Equity = € 314.00	Risk-averse	Sell 2 MAN	€ 271.90	0.6994	0.999 %
	Risk-taking	Sell 2 BMW	€ 293.46	0.7547	1.055 %
Equity = € 157.00	Risk-averse	Sell 6 MAN Sell 4 BMW	€ 147.18	0.6705	0.982 %
	Risk-taking	Sell 4 MAN Sell 9 BMW	€ 145.27	0.8203	1.269 %
Equity = € 471.00	Risk-averse	Buy 2 MAN Buy 10 BMW	€ 445.92	0.6369	0.969 %
	Risk-taking	Buy 6 MAN	€ 443.68	0.7759	1.092 %

The results in Table 2.20 show rudimentary analysis possibilities based on the value at risk, the beta factor, the incremental VaR and the profit expectations. There are many **more ways** to derive **possible action plans** from the results. For example, as already mentioned, there is the possibility of increasing the equity capital (see Section 3.1) or also the portfolio theory approach of minimizing the volatility of stock portfolios (see Section 4.1.3). In particular, risk distribution (diversification) in Section 3.3 deals with further approaches to deriving optimum action possibilities. There, the various strategies and instruments of risk management in the third chapter will also be represented with regard to possible changes of the RoRaC value.

2.7 References

The worldwide **standard** on the topic of **Value at Risk** is the work of

Jorion, Philippe: "Value at Risk: The New Benchmark for Managing Financial Risk", McGraw-Hill, 3rd ed., 2006.

In this book can be found not only extensive discussions on the topic of value at risk, but also about such related issues as, for example, sales risk, operational risk, risk-adjusted profit measurement, basics of business-wide risk management etc. are discussed clearly and illustrated in detail with numerical examples.

Along with the work of Jorion, there are yet other **English speaking works** that may not have the same significance but show certain similarities in the treatment of the key areas (especially the VaR). The following works are especially worth highlighting here:

Alexander, Carol: "Market Risk Analysis: Volume IV: Value-at-Risk Models", Wiley Finance Series, 2008
Dowd, Kevin: "Beyond Value at Risk", John Wiley and Sons, 1999,
Holton, Glyn A.: "Value-at-Risk. Theory and Practice", Academic Press, 2nd ed., 2009.
Penza, Pietro/Bansal, Vipul K.: "Measuring Market Risk with Value at Risk", Wiley, New York, 2000,

The work of Holton in particular stands out for its **very technical** and **mathematical explanations** and is therefore especially recommended for the mathematically inclined reader. More or less detailed representations of the **GARCH models** can be found in all the works.

For a correction factor of **auto correlated returns** and further discussions of the overarching theme of credit risk management, see

Hull, John C.: "Risk Management and Financial Institutions", Wiley, Hoboken, New Jersey, 4th ed., 2015.
Jorion, Philippe: "Financial Risk Manager Handbook", Wiley, Hoboken, New Jersey, 6th edition, 2011,

For a **critical analysis** and **limitations** of the **VaR concept** and possible alternatives, the discussions of

Franke, Günter: "Gefahren kurzsichtigen Risikomanagements durch Value-at-Risk", in: Johanning, Lutz/Rudolph, Bernd (Hrsg.): "Handbuch des Risikomanagements", Band 1, S. 53–85, Uhlenbruch Verlag, 2000,
Jorion, Philippe: "Value at Risk: The New Benchmark for Managing Financial Risk", McGraw-Hill, 3rd ed., 2006.

and

Pfingsten, Andreas u. a.: "Armutsmaße als Downside-Risikomaße: Ein Weg zu Risikomaßen, die dem Value-at-Risk überlegen sind", in: Johanning, Lutz/Rudolph, Bernd (Hrsg.): "Handbuch des Risikomanagements", Band 1, S. 85–107, Uhlenbruch Verlag, 2000.

are suitable by way of example.

Both approaches grapple with the critique of the value at risk concept in a very mathematical and statistical manner. The contribution of Pfingsten et al. recognizes that before a planned application of value at risk, there are many questions and problems to be resolved with regard to the use of poverty measures.

For a development of the **statistical basis**, in particular the normal distribution in Section 2.3.1, the books from

Alexander, Carol: "Market Risk Analysis: Volume I: Quantitative Methods in Finance", Wiley, 2008,
McNeil, Alexander J./Frey, Rüdiger/Embrechts, Paul: "Quantitative Risk Management – Concepts, Techniques and Tools", Princeton University Press, Princeton and Oxford, 2015,
Miller, Michael B.: "Mathematics and Statistics for Financial Risk Management", Wiley Finance, 2nd ed., 2014,

and

Poddig, Thorsten/Dichtl, Hubert/Petersmeier, Kerstin: "Statistik, Ökonometrie, Optimierung", Uhlenbruch Verlag, 2. Auflage, 2001

are recommended. In particular, the reference and application in portfolio management is explained in examples. The calculations of empirical volatilities, correlation coefficients etc. are also constructed very clearly.

For a discussion about the dispersion measures, **mean absolute deviation** versus standard deviation, see:

Gorard, Stephen: "Revisiting a 90-year-old debate: the advantages of the mean deviation", in: http://www.leeds.ac.uk/educol/documents/00003759.htm.

The discussion about the **lower partial moments** are based on

Alexander, Carol: "Market Risk Analysis: Volume IV: Value-at-Risk Models, Wiley Finance Series, 2008,
Angermüller, Niels O./Eichhorn, Michael/Ramke, Thomas: "Lower Partial Moments: Alternative oder Ergänzung zum Value at Risk?", in: Finanz Betrieb, Heft 3, S. 149–153, 2006,
Holton, Glyn A.: "Value-at-Risk. Theory and Practice", Academic Press, 2nd ed., 2009.

An approach to calculating the value at risk on the basis of **extreme value theory** can be found in

Hakenes, Hendrik/Wilkens, Sascha: "Der Value-at-Risk auf Basis der Extremwerttheorie", in: Finanz Betrieb, Heft 12, S. 821–829, 2003.

For the **extreme value theory** in **general** and its **applications**:

Longin, Francois M.: "Extreme Events in Finance: A Handbook of extreme value theory and its Applications", Wiley, Hoboken, New Jersey, 2017,
McNeil, Alexander J./Frey, Rüdiger/Embrechts, Paul: "Quantitative Risk Management – Concepts, Techniques and Tools", Princeton University Press, Princeton and Oxford, 2015,

For the choice of number of standard deviations in the context of **stress tests**, the approach of

Bookstaber, Richard: "Global Risk Management: Are We Missing the Point?" in: Journal of Portfolio Management 23 (Spring), S. 102–107, 1997

is suitable.

An excellent insight and overview to the problem of **calculating** the **stock price returns** is also provided by

Alexander, Carol: "Market Risk Analysis: Volume I: Quantitative Methods in Finance", Wiley, 2008,
Capinski, Marek/ Zastawniak, Tomasz: "Mathematics for Finance: An Introduction to Financial Engineering", Springer, London, 2nd edition, 2011,
Uhlir, Peter/Steiner, Helmut: "Wertpapieranalyse", Physica-Verlag, 2001.

For another numerical example with detailed explanations on the topic of **risk analysis,** for a maximum **RoRaC** with a non-zero portfolio weighting, see

Wolke, Thomas: "Die Fallstudie – Risikoanalyse eines Aktienportfolios anhand von Portfoliotheorie, Beta-Faktor, Value at Risk und Return on Risk adjusted Capital", in: WISU, Heft 7/14, S. 886–889, 2014,

and for a **RaRoC** analysis see

Jorion, Philippe: "Financial Risk Manager Handbook", Wiley, Hoboken, New Jersey, 6th edition, p. 677–679, 2011.

The **historical capital market data** used (stock prices, DAX) were taken from the websites of the respective companies (BMW, MAN) and the website of the Austrian national Bank (www.oenb.at).

2.8 Technical appendix

The calculation of the expected loss and the expected asset changes is carried out through the **expected value** E (also called the theoretical mean):

$$E(X) = \mu = \sum_{i=1}^{N} x_i \cdot p_i$$

with
X: random variable (e. g. for the loss or asset change),
N: number of possible events,
x_i: the i-th event,
p_i: probability of occurrence for the i-th event.

On the basis of the expected value, the **variance** V will be defined as follows:

$$V(X) = \sigma^2 = \sum_{i=1}^{N} (x_i - E(X))^2 \cdot p_i$$

From that arises the **standard deviation** S (volatility):

$$S(X) = \sigma = \sqrt{V(X)} = \sqrt{\sum_{i=1}^{N} (x_i - E(X))^2 \cdot p_i}$$

The calculation of the **stock price returns** r_t from the stock price k_t in euros at time point t is carried out according to

$$r_t = \frac{k_t - k_{t-1}}{k_{t-1}}$$

and used for long time series

$$R_t = \ln\left(\frac{k_t}{k_{t-1}}\right).$$

Here possible dividend payments are neglected.

The expected value of empirical time series (also called empirical mean value), e. g. the calculation of the **average return** r, arises from

$$r = \hat{\mu} = \frac{1}{T} \cdot \sum_{t=1}^{T} r_t$$

included are
T: number of time points in the time series,
r_t: observed return at time point T.

Let s^2 be used for the unbiased estimate of the **empirical variance**:

$$s^2 = \hat{\sigma}^2 = \frac{1}{T-1} \cdot \sum_{t=1}^{T} (r_t - r)^2$$

Extracting the roots from the empirical variance s^2 gives the risk measure standard deviation s (mean variation), which represents the **volatility** around the return:

$$s = \hat{\sigma} = \sqrt{\frac{1}{T-1} \cdot \sum_{t=1}^{T}(r_t - r)^2}.$$

One approach to considering different time structures consists in using **exponential weighting** within the **standard deviation** $s^{\exp}$ according to

$$s^{\exp} = \hat{\sigma}^{\exp} = \sqrt{(1-\lambda) \cdot \sum_{t=1}^{T} \lambda^{t-1} \cdot (r_t - r)^2}$$

Through the so-called **decay factor**, the current data are more strongly weighted than the older observations. Values between zero and one can be chosen for the factor λ. In practice, decay factors between 0.90 and 0.99 are frequently chosen.

The **density function** of the **normal distribution** has the form

$$f(x) = \frac{1}{\sqrt{2 \cdot \pi} \cdot \sigma} \cdot e^{\left(\frac{(x-\mu)^2}{2 \cdot \sigma^2}\right)}$$

and is uniquely determined through the expected value μ and the standard deviation σ.

The calculation of the **VaR** with an **expected value** of **μ<>0** has the form:

$$VaR = RP \cdot (\alpha \cdot s \cdot \sqrt{T} - r \cdot T)$$

with
RP: amount of the risk position in euros,
α: number of standard deviations based on the confidence level (quantile from the standard normal distribution),
s: volatility,
T: liquidation period in days,
r: average return (expected value).

The variable r_p is taken for the **portfolio return**:

$$r_p = \sum_{i=1}^{N} w_i \cdot r_i$$

and there is also

$$w_i = \frac{RP_i}{RP_p} \text{ with } \sum_{i=1}^{N} w_i = 1,$$

where
N: number of individual asset positions,
r_i: average return of the i-th asset position,
w_i: percentage weighting of the i-th asset position (risk position RP_i) at the portfolio risk position (RPp)

The empirical **covariance** $s_{1,2}$ between the returns of two asset positions 1 and 2 is calculated as follows:

$$s_{1,2} = \hat{\sigma}_{1,2} = \frac{1}{T-1} \cdot \sum_{t=1}^{T}(r_{t,1} - r_1) \cdot (r_{t,2} - r_2)$$

with
$r_{t,1}$ or $r_{t,2}$: observed return of the asset position 1 or 2 at time point t,
r_1 or r_2: average return of asset position 1 or 2.

With the covariance the **correlation coefficient** $CR_{1,2}$ can be calculated

$$CR_{1,2} = \frac{s_{1,2}}{s_1 \cdot s_2}$$

Here we have
s_1 or s_2: The volatility of asset position 1 or 2.

With the help of the covariance or the correlation coefficient, the **portfolio variance** can generally be found for N positions using

$$s_p^2 = \sum_{i=1}^{N} w_i^2 \cdot s_i^2 + \sum_{i=1}^{N} \sum_{j=1, i \neq j}^{N} w_i \cdot w_j \cdot s_{i,j}$$

and the associated **portfolio volatility** can be calculated using the root of s_p^2.

For a portfolio which only consists of **N=2 asset positions**, the **portfolio volatility** can be represented more simply through

$$s_p = \sqrt{w_1^2 \cdot s_1^2 + w_2^2 \cdot s_2^2 + 2 \cdot w_1 \cdot w_2 \cdot s_{1,2}}$$

When applying the **correlation coefficient**, this form arises:

$$s_p = \sqrt{w_1^2 \cdot s_1^2 + w_2^2 \cdot s_2^2 + 2 \cdot w_1 \cdot w_2 \cdot k_{12} \cdot s_1 \cdot s_2}$$

By representing the portfolio volatility using the correlation coefficient for two asset positions, the **portfolio VaR** (VaR_p) can be calculated following:

$$VaR_p = RP_p \cdot \alpha \cdot s_p.$$

RP_p is the total asset position of the portfolio, since the liquidation period is set at one day and the expected value is ultimately taken as $\mu=0$. With the help of the equation for the portfolio volatility s_p, this equation of the VaR calculation can be transformed into

$$VaR_p = \sqrt{RP_p^2 \cdot \alpha^2 \cdot w_1^2 \cdot s_1^2 + RP_p^2 \cdot \alpha^2 \cdot w_2^2 \cdot s_2^2 + RP_p^2 \cdot \alpha^2 \cdot 2 \cdot w_1 \cdot w_2 \cdot k_{12} \cdot s_1 \cdot s_2}$$

For a **correlation coefficient** of $CR_{1,2}=0$, a **portfolio VaR** then arises of

$$VaR_p = \sqrt{VaR_1^2 + VaR_2^2}.$$

If the correlation coefficient amounts to $CR_{1,2}=-1$, then we get:

$$VaR_p = |VaR_1 - VaR_2|.$$

And for a correlation coefficient of $CR_{1,2}=+1$, this follows

$$VaR_p = VaR_1 + VaR_2.$$

The **marginal VaR** (ΔVaR_i) of an asset position i in a portfolio p is calculated by means of

$$\Delta VaR_i = \alpha \cdot \frac{s_{i,p}}{s_p}.$$

The **beta factor** of the an asset position i in a portfolio p is defined as

$$\beta_i = \frac{s_{i,p}}{s_p^2} = \frac{CR_{i,p} \cdot s_i \cdot s_p}{s_p^2} = CR_{i,p} \cdot \frac{s_i}{s_p}$$

With help from the beta factor the **marginal VaR** can also be **simplified** to

$$\Delta VaR_i = \alpha \cdot (\beta_i \cdot s_p)$$

The **Component VaR** of an asset position i ($CoVaR_i$) in a portfolio p is calculated according to

$$CoVaR_i = VaR_p \cdot \beta_i \cdot w_i = VaR_i \cdot CR_{i,p}$$

and there is also

$$\sum_{i=1}^{N} CoVaR_i = VaR_p.$$

The **lower partial moments** are mathematically described as follows:
 a) for discrete distributions:

$$LPM_k(r; X) = E[\max((r-X); 0)^k]$$

and for the average fluctuations (s) around LPM_1 there is:

$$LPM_s(r; X) = \sqrt{E[\max((r-X-LPM_1); 0)^2]}$$

b) for continuous distributions:

$$LPM_k(r; X) = \int_{-\infty}^{r} (r - X)^k f(x) dx$$

with:
r = defined reference value (loss limit) in €,
X = random variable (e. g. portfolio value),
k = order of the lower partial moments,
E = expected value,
f(x) = density function of the random variable X.

In order to be able to describe the shortfalls from the defined limit r, the difference between r and all possible values of X will first be determined in the formula. If the difference is negative, then the reference value was not undershot. However, since only the shortfalls, i. e. all differences with a positive sign, are supposed to be considered, the maximum of null and the respective difference is generated.

Proof that the **portfolio RoRaC** can only take values between the **smallest** and **largest individual RoRaC**, thus $R_1 <= R_P <= R_2$, is:

It is sufficient to show that $R_P >= R_1$ applies. The proof for $R_P <= R_2$ will then be conducted analogously. The profit or loss is g_1, g_2, g_P, the risk is s_1, s_2, s_P respectively, in €. It is

$$R_i = g_i/s_i \text{ for } i = 1, 2, p;$$
$$g_p = g_1 + g_2 \text{ and } s_p = s_1 + s_2$$
$$s_1, s_2 >= 0 \text{ and } R_1 <= R_2.$$

From the requirement that $R_1 <= R_2$ follows:

$$g_1/s_1 <=> g_2/s_2$$
$$<=> g_2 \cdot s_1 >= g_1 \cdot s_2$$
$$<=> g_2 \cdot s_1 >= g_1 \cdot s_2 + g_1 \cdot s_1 - g_1 \cdot s_1$$
$$<=> g_2 >= \{g_1 \cdot (s_2 + s_1) - g_1 \cdot s_1\}/s_1$$
$$<=> g_2 >= \{g_1 \cdot (s_2 + s_1)\}/s_1 - g_1$$
$$<=> g_2 + g_1 >= \{g_1 \cdot (s_2 + s_1)\}/s_1$$
$$<=> (g_2 + g_1)/(s_2 + s_1) >= g_1/s_1$$
$$<=> R_P >= R_1$$

3 Risk control

The results of risk analysis lead to the question of which measures to undertake in the context of corporate management in order to control the measured and analyzed risks. The possible control instruments are so numerous and complex that they must first be narrowed down. Discussion of instruments that are reserved for certain businesses on legal and industry specific grounds (in particular, banks) will be omitted. Rather, the **fundamental functioning** of general **control instruments** within **risk strategies** that can be applied to nearly every business will be discussed.

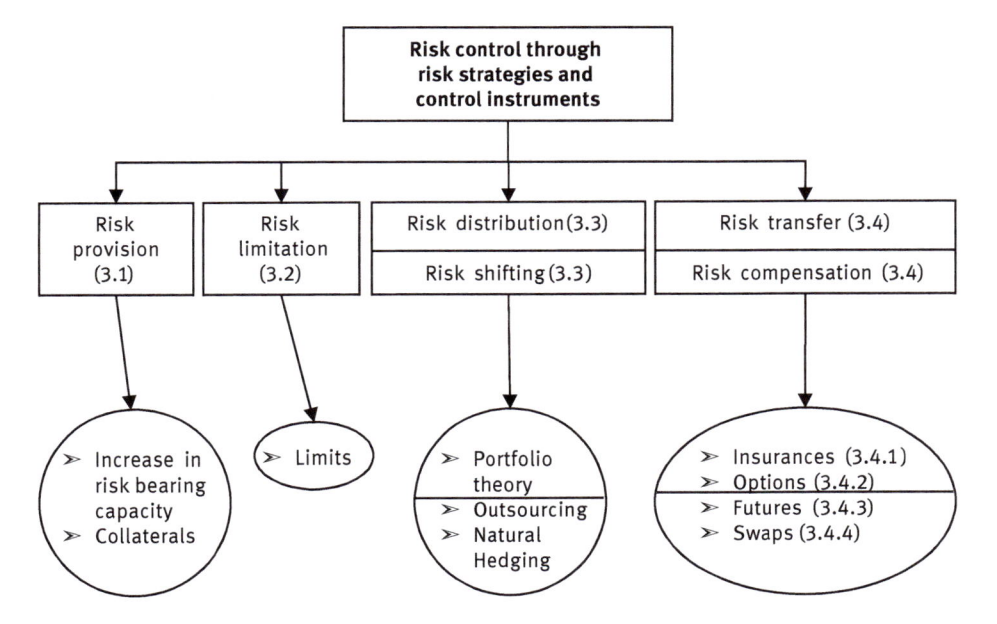

Fig. 3.1: Overview of risk strategies and control instruments

Figure 3.1 shows a possible breakdown of the various risk strategies and the associated control instruments. The **"no holds barred" risk strategy** (full risk-taking) is not listed here, since in this case, strictly speaking, there is no risk control and therefore it also follows that no control instruments can be assigned. The business consciously opts to take full risk in order to remain open to all the associated profit possibilities. In the following, the strategies and associated instruments are discussed and their effects on the Return on Risk adjusted Capital (RoRaC) are explained.

3.1 Risk provision

Risk provision means planning future risks with a view to present and future required risk bearing capacity. In Section 2.6, "risk analysis," the crucial economic figure for **risk bearing capacity** of a company was already represented, namely as **equity capital**. An increase in the equity capital means an increase in the risk bearing capacity to respond to any new risks (for example, in the context of planned investment) or to provide better provisions against risks already deliberately taken.

Along with the equity capital showing on the balance sheet, **provisions** and **hidden reserves** also represent a buffer for risk bearing capacity. To what extent hidden reserves and provisions are suitable for covering incurred risks is worth assessing critically against the background of the financial crisis. Risk tolerance and with it **risk provision** can be **increased** through the following **procedures**:
- Increasing the equity capital on the capital market or by the partners (shareholder),
- Putting profits in retained earnings or other reserves,
- Building hidden reserves through excessive depreciation and/or increased liability estimates.

These various risk provision possibilities are nonetheless to be judged differently according to their significance as risk buffers. An **equity capital increase** is not accepted by capital markets and capital made available to better cover existing risks (especially in times of financial crisis); rather, long-term investments in the business performance area are usually linked to equity capital increases.

The **operating income** (so, **no capital gains**) should be available for the assessable business risk potential. This is only the case when the profit is not paid out but rather put into the **profit reserves**. For crisis times when, as a rule, no profit is realized, the profit reserves are not available for risk provision.

The establishment of **provisions** is usually bound up with a concrete existing risk (tax payments, guarantee claims etc.) and is thus not available as a general risk buffer.

Hidden reserves are also only conditionally suitable as risk provisioning, since they are not explicitly valued and thus their size can only be known or they can only be made available through realization. Hidden reserves are also unsuitable for times of crisis.

Risk provision through increasing the risk bearing capacity has no direct effect on the **RoRaC** of a risk position. The amount of the equity capital has no influence on the risk or the expected profit of a risk position. In the RoRaC calculation, the amount of the risk position enters into the risk-free equity capital interest rate. Thus there is only an indirect connection between the equity capital and the risk-free equity capital interest rate as a part of the profit. Increasing the equity capital directly affects the risk analysis in the comparison of VaR with equity capital (see Section 2.6).

A further possibility of risk provision consists in acceptance of **collaterals**. Collaterals play an especially important role in managing credit risk (see Section 4.2.4). Although management of credit risk through collateral represents a core competence of credit institutions, this form of risk provision is also irrelevant for many non-banks. Here in particular collateral plays an important role in the form of
- trust receipts,
- ownership reservations and
- guarantees

in connection with the granting of **loans to customers** (e. g. to encourage the sale).

The acceptance of collateral affects the creditor's **RoRaC** in two ways. First, his default risk in the amount of the additional collateral sinks, through which his RoRaC, all other things being equal, climbs. On the other hand, the debtor will demand a more favorable interest rate for his additional collateral. A lower interest rate would diminish the profit and thus the RoRaC of the creditor. How the creditor's RoRaC changes overall then depends on the bargaining positions between creditor and debtor. The RoRaC would e. g. climb when the default risk of the creditor sinks more sharply than his profit through a possible lowering of the interest rate.

Risk provision is tightly **bound up** with **risk limitation**, since with risk provision the risk buffer in the form of equity capital is increased and thus the proportion of the business's total VaR decreases in relation to the risk buffer. If, however, an increase in the equity capital as discussed above is not possible or reasonable then the proportion of the VaR to the equity capital can only be reduced if the VaR is reduced through e. g. risk limitation. This form of risk management is the subject of the following Section 3.2.

3.2 Risk avoidance and risk limitation

Risk avoidance and risk limitation have the goal of limiting or even reducing the VaR of the entire company. Thus the term **risk avoidance** should not be used in its absolute sense, as every business activity is afflicted per se by risk. In this respect the terms risk avoidance and risk limitation amount to the same situation or control objective, namely, risk limitation reduction through **limits**.

Limits for the limitation of risk come in the most diverse forms and variations. As an overview, only some types of risk limits for **financial positions** will be briefly discussed:
- **Nominal limits** restrict financial positions that are exposed to a market price risk. However, there is no consideration of the risk amount and risk content of the underlying position, rather the package of financial assets is limited to its nominal value (e. g. € 10 mill. nominal value). Limitation by means of the nominal value does not, however, reflect the risk content in the background. So,

for example, fixed income securities with a nominal value of € 10 mill. have, as a rule, a smaller risk content than stock options with a nominal value of likewise € 10 mill.
- With **stop-loss limits** the financial position is sold when a certain market price is under- or overshot. This type of risk limitation also allows no meaningful risk limitation, since such limits may prevent a worst possible case, but the probability of occurrence of this stop-loss event is ignored.
- With **sensitivity limits**, the position is not further increased or decreased when a particular sensitivity is reached (such as the percentage of value decrease in the asset position when the associated risk factor sinks by 1%; see Section 2.2.2). In contrast to nominal limits and stop-loss limits, a substantial risk assessment can indeed take place with sensitivity limits; however, sensitivity alone is not sufficient for risk control. Thus the amount of change in the risk factors must be more or less arbitrarily determined without being able to explicitly consider the risk factor distribution. On top of that, sensitivity limits are relative figures, i.e. the risk limitations are not in monetary units, which means that a comparison with the equity capital as a risk buffer is not appropriate.
- With **scenario limits**, loss limitation through selling asset positions is carried out for particular scenarios (for example, global financial crisis => all major stock indices falling by 30% in a certain time period, the 10 year Bund-Future falls below € 95). Scenario limits are very similar to stop-loss limits. The difference consists in the manner of establishing the limit amount. There is the same crucial disadvantage of not taking the likelihood of occurrence into account.

The disadvantage of these limits is remedied through a **limit system** based on the **Value at Risk**. Here the maximum VaR is defined as the limit for every business unit, asset position or other specified risk unit. A possible VaR limit system is shown as an example in Figure 3.2.

```
                    ┌─────────────────────────────────┐
                    │ Equity of the corporate: € 100 Mio. │
                    │  => VaR limit: € 80 Mio.         │
                    └─────────────────────────────────┘
                              │
            ┌─────────────────┴─────────────────┐
            ▼                                   ▼
  ┌──────────────────┐                ┌──────────────────┐
  │ Business unit A  │                │ Business unit B  │
  │ VaR limit: €50 Mio.│              │ VaR limit: €40 Mio.│
  └──────────────────┘                └──────────────────┘
        │                                   │
   ┌────┴────┐                         ┌────┴────┐
   ▼         ▼                         ▼         ▼
```

Business unit element A1 — VaR limit: €20 Mio.
Business unit element A2 — VaR limit: €35 Mio.
Business unit element B1 — VaR limit: €30 Mio.
Business unit element B2 — VaR limit: €15 Mio.

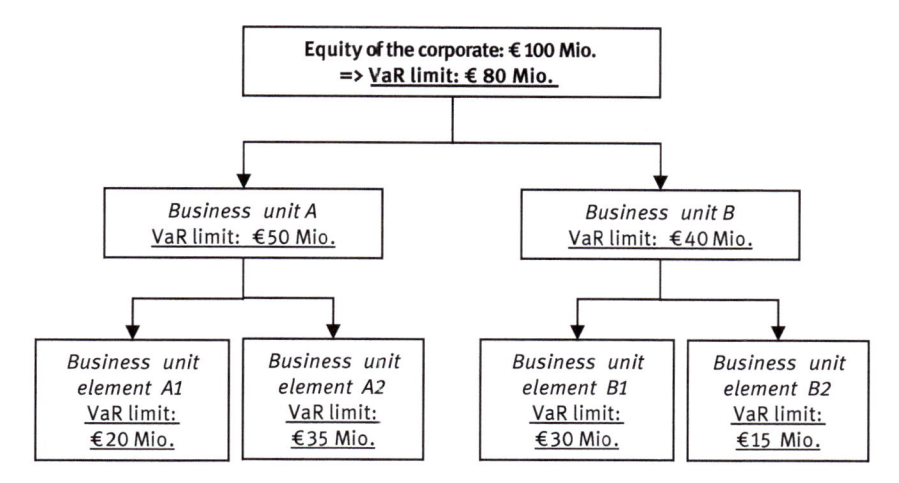

Fig. 3.2: Example for a VaR limit system

The sum of the business unit element VaR is respectively higher than the associated business unit VaR limit. The difference of respectively € 5 mill. takes into account the **diversification** or the correlation between **business unit elements,** for which the unit leader is responsible. The same applies at a higher level for the company leadership in the diversification between the business units (VaR for A + VaR for B = € 90 mill. compared with a VaR limit for the entire company of € 80 mill.). The **Component Value at Risk** may **not** be used for the VaR limit, therefore, since otherwise the diversification effect, for example, would already have been taken into account on the level of the business unit elements. For diversification, however, the division leader has responsibility on the division level (one level higher). Managing correlations and consciously accepting diversification effect can only happen on the higher portfolio level. The risk which is reduced through the diversification effect must therefore also be assigned to the VaR limit on the portfolio level (= business unit).

The difference between the equity capital of € 100 mill. and the total VaR limit of € 80 mill. represents a buffer in the amount of € 20 mill. for **crisis times**. The sum of the VaR limits of all the business unit elements in turn amounts to 100 mill. €. This corresponds to the total equity capital of the company. The buffer of € 20 mill. also stands available for the crisis case when all risks on the level of the business unit elements would happen simultaneously (so there would be no correlations and diversification).

Risk limitation has, like risk provision, no direct effect on the **RoRaC** through the increase in the risk bearing capacity. A VaR limit has no direct influence on the profit or the Value at Risk of an individual asset position. However, there is an indirect connection when existing risk positions within a portfolio would have to be dismantled in the course of a VaR limit. This could have an effect on the portfolio structure and thus also on the portfolio risk or the VaR (for an example see risk analysis in Section

2.6). Introducing a VaR limit and with that a possible associated reduction of an existing VaR has an effect in the context of risk analysis when comparing equity capital and VaR.

One disadvantage remains with risk limiting strategies in every case. Through the limitation, the condition is indeed fulfilled that the risk does not exceed the risk bearing capacity. However, management of the **profit-risk ratio** is **not taken into account** by any form of limitation. Management of the profit-risk ratio is therefore the focus of the following sections.

3.3 Risk distribution (diversification) and risk shifting

Risk distribution involves the **exploitation** of **diversification effects**. Diversification effects are achieved when the risks of at least two asset positions offset each other and thus the risk of the combined asset positions (= portfolio) is smaller than the sum of the individual risks. If at the same time the profit of the combined positions is not so sharply reduced as the aggregate risk then the **RoRaC** can **increase**. This possible increase is also aimed at by risk distribution strategy. However, if an investor has a risk-averse attitude, a portfolio structure can also be sought in which the portfolio RoRaC neither rises nor falls (see Section 2.6). It is the objective of the risk distribution strategy to determine the maximum or optimal RoRaC for a particular risk attitude and a given equity capital.

On the one hand, the new portfolio structure can be determined **heuristically** for this purpose (see the example I Section 2.6). On the other hand, the optimal portfolio can be determined **analytically** (as long as there is a clear analytical solution). An example of an analytical calculation, in the context of portfolio theory, is determining portfolio weightings with minimal volatility. In contrast, analytical determination of the optimal RoRaC while taking account of the given equity capital and respective risk attitude is more difficult and complex. For certain numerical combinations of volatility and zero covariance, there are portfolio weightings for which the RoRaC will be maximal (in contrast to the example in Section 2.6 where the RoRaC for a BMW stock weighting of 0 % assumes a maximum; for an example with a maximum RoRaC see Section 2.7).

Portfolio theory is the theoretical basis for diversification, whose base calculations were already used in Section 2.3.3 for calculating the portfolio VaR. The findings of portfolio theory are primarily derived from its application to stock portfolios. The special features arising from stock portfolios and their use in risk analysis will be explored further in Section 4.1.3, "stock price risk". These include e. g. determining the minimal portfolio volatility and considering investments for risk-free rates.

Since the beginning of the 1990s, companies have not only tried to exploit the diversification effect in the context of stock portfolios. The principle of **diversification** can also be used on **business units**, **products**, **services** and so on. In this respect, the application of the diversification effect in the context of risk management has a far greater significance than would be the case only for stock portfolios. The most famous example of this in Germany was the Daimler Group at the end of the 1980s under the leadership of Edzard Reuter. As the CEO, Reuter rebuilt the Daimler Group from an automobile company into a conglomerate. Reuter's goal and method consisted in distributing risk away from autos to other products (aerospace, aircraft, industrial equipment, electrical appliances, etc.) in order to become an integrated technology company. That was supposed to mitigate profit declines due to a poorly running automobile business. Edzard Reuter was not successful with this strategy. There are many more examples worldwide of unsuccessful business diversification strategies. Using the example of Daimler, some basic **difficulties** of risk distribution or diversification will be discussed in the context of risk management:

- The most crucial difference in using the diversification effect in risk management of various products consists in the necessary **management** of the **diversified products**. With a product portfolio, this management is perceived by the company leadership, which usually has the corresponding expertise about their products (e. g. expertise only about autos or only about electrical appliances). It was exactly this missing expertise with regard to the new products taken into the Daimler product portfolio that in the eyes of many observers caused the diversification strategy to fail.
- The success of risk distribution and thus the extent of the diversification effect is based on the measured **correlations** between the stocks and the individual asset positions (product sales). But this is exactly what is usually **not reliable** and constant over time. While with stock portfolios stable estimates for the correlations (or volatilities, see Section 2.2.1) can be calculated using various (complex) statistical methods based on extensive daily observable prices, this is naturally impossible when introducing new products and later eliminating them.
- The derivation of the diversification effect from portfolio theory is based on other key assumptions. These assumptions include, among others, the **neglect of transaction costs** for the purchase and sale of stocks, the determination of **constant time periods**, as well as the **arbitrary divisibility** of stocks. But it is exactly these assumptions that largely don't apply to product diversification within a company.

With **risk shifting** the idea in the foreground is that certain risks can be relocated outside of the business to other non-business areas, organizations or regions. A fundamental feature of risk transfer as distinct from other risk strategies (in particular risk compensation and risk transfer) is that not only is the risk transferred but also the associated assets or risk basis and thus also the possibly related profit opportunities. One typical possibility for risk shifting that is also often pursued in practice is the so-called **outsourcing** of e. g. business functions and business areas like, for example

- the IT area,
- logistics functions or
- facilities management.

After outsourcing, the required services and products in the outsourced areas are then bought back in by the outsourcing companies in the context of so-called service-level agreements. Through that, the profit-risk ratio changes, and must be recalculated in order to be able to assess the **favorability of outsourcing**. The profit is reduced by the cost of buying the outsourced services and products, but at the same time the associated risk (VaR) is also eliminated. If the profit sinks lower than the risk then the RoRaC increases. This is usually the case with simple activities in specialized companies (e. g. cleaning companies). For more complex activities (e. g. software development), outsourcing for example to IT companies has in the past often not been worth it. The **opportunities** and **risks** of **outsourcing** of business functions are controversial. This discussion will not be explored here, but rather referred to the relevant literature on the subject (see References Section 3.5).

Another **typical risk shifting** is pursued in the context of **exchange rate risk**, in which whole value chains from purchase to distribution are partially transferred to the respective foreign currency zone (e. g. to the US-$ currency zone). This form of exchange rate risk shifting is also called **natural hedging**. How the RoRaC can change through natural hedging cannot generally be articulated, since this depends on too many uncertain influencing factors (exchange rate, the cost of building value chains) and their development. The possibilities of risk control of currency risk in particular are discussed in Section 4.1.2.

Risk distribution and risk shifting each have **grave disadvantages** in the context of risk control. Some of these disadvantages can be remedied with the help of derivatives. The applications of derivatives in the context of risk management are therefore the central focus of the following section (Section 3.4) on risk transfer and risk compensation.

3.4 Risk transfer and risk compensation

With risk transfer, the risk causing asset position (risk position) remains in the portfolio (or company) and only a potential future asset loss is passed on by taking out a policy. For this a consideration must be paid, usually in the form of a premium. In contrast e. g. to risk shifting there is thus still the opportunity to also achieve profits through the asset position. Taking out **insurance** is still the most important and most frequently used **control instrument** for **risk transfer**.

However, **factoring**, **leasing** and **franchising** also allow risk transfer with certain types of contract (for example, from the perspective of the lessee with so-called finance leasing, or with a factoring contract with a *del credere* function). Since with factoring, leasing and franchising, however, the financing activity rather than the risk management potential stands in the foreground, these three themes will not be further explored here. There is extensive relevant literature on these topics.

With **risk compensation**, an additional finance position (financial securities) is purchased against the risk causing asset positions, which compensates the possible losses of the original asset position by simultaneous gains for a specified amount. Financial securities for compensation involve **derivatives**, i. e. financial instruments derived from original base securities. For risk transfer through insurance, risk compensation by derivative is an essential difference. While with insurance the potential profits of the original hedged asset position remain untouched, as a rule the use of derivatives **influences** not only the risk but also the **profit profile** of the hedged position in some specific way.

Derivatives can be used for **many purposes**. In the following discussions in this section, the focus is on risk compensation in the context of risk control. The trading of derivatives on the financial markets takes place in different categories and in various ways. For widespread **use** in **risk control**, in particular by non-banks, a limitation must first be imposed. Thus the so-called OTC derivative (OTC = over-the-counter) is excluded from the broader discussion, since it usually involves individual contracts agreed by financial institutions, which are unsuitable for widespread use within risk management in the non-banking sector. Also, certain elements of OTC derivative transactions were revised in the wake of the financial crisis (see Section 4.4). Therefore the following discussion will limit itself to the basic operation of exchange-traded and standardized options, swaps and futures for use as management tools. Figure 3.3 shows a summarized overview of all essential management tools and selected application examples in the context of risk transfer and risk compensation.

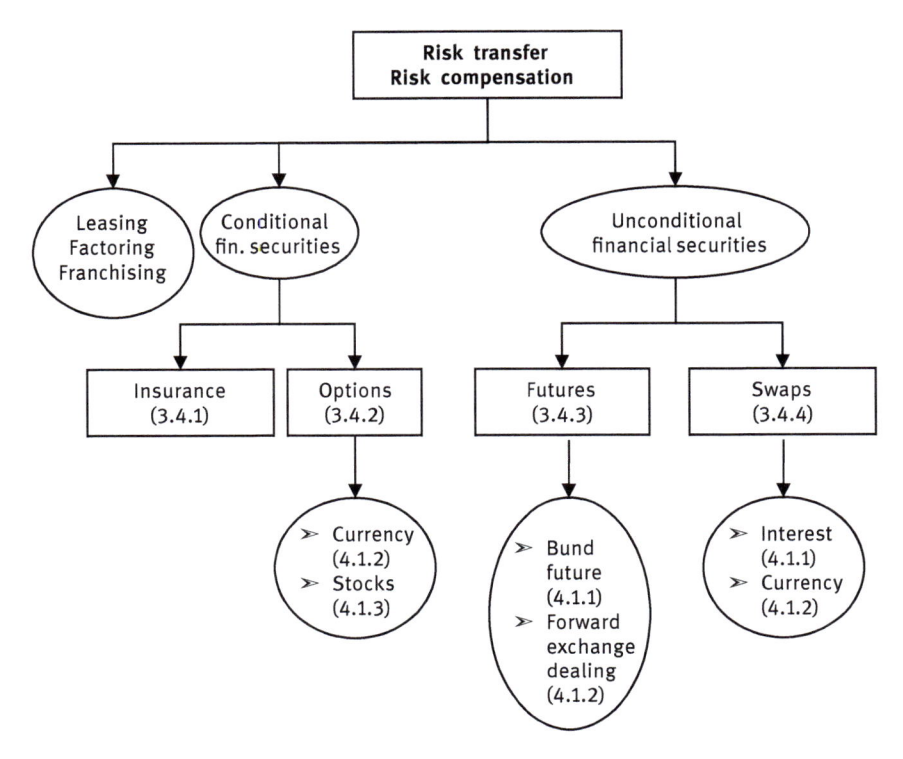

Fig. 3.3: Overview of risk transfer and risk compensation

3.4.1 Insurance

For employing insurance in risk transfer, it is first useful to briefly demonstrate the basic **functioning** of **insurance transactions**.

Insurance involves a contractual agreement between one or more policyholders (insurance collective) and an insurance company (insurer) that the insurer pays an agreed insurance benefit upon occurrence of an insured event, against payment of insurance premiums by the policyholder/s (see Figure 3.4).

The basic functions and interrelationships of the insurance principle are graphically illustrated in Figure 3.4.

3.4 Risk transfer and risk compensation

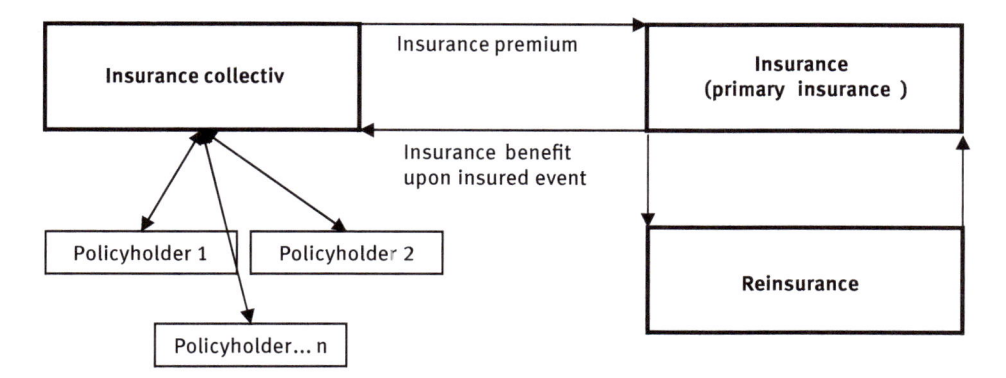

Fig. 3.4: Basic functioning of insurance

The **policyholders** transfer the risk of asset losses through the **collective** onto the **insurance**. Insurance is also called **conditional financial security**, since the insurance benefit payable only under the condition that the insured event occurs. Insurance can implement **risk balancing** by combining a multitude of risks into a collective. The variation of the actual damage to the expected value of the collective's total damage is thus clearly smaller than with the individual risks.

The **insurance premium** plays an important role in the context of **risk control**. It reduces the profit and at the same time reduces or transfers on the associated risks by taking out insurance. For the profit-risk ratio, the size of the risk premium is also the crucial factor, in relation to the reduced risk, in deciding whether insurance should be taken out to control risk or not. The insurance premium is made up of the following components:
- the **net risk premium** for covering the expected value of the total damage,
- the **gross risk premium** which consists of the net risk premium and the safety margin (The **safety margin** covers typical insurance risks that are not covered already by the net risk premium. This includes the risk of deviation of actual total damages from the expected value.),
- the **operating cost surcharge** and a possible **profit margin**.

The **net premium** is the sum of all these components. If the insurance tax is added to the gross premium, one gets the **gross premium** to be paid by the policyholder.

The following **numerical example** illustrates the calculation of the individual components for determining the gross premium:

Damage amount:	€ 1,000.00
Net risk premium (e. g. 10 % of damage amount):	€ 100.00
+ Safety margin (e. g. 1 % of damage amount):	€ 10.00
= **Gross risk premium:**	**€ 110.00**
+ Operating cost surcharge:	€ 3.00
+ Profit margin:	€ 7.00
= **Net premium:**	**€ 120.00**
+ Insurance tax (19 %):	€ 22.80
= **Gross premium:**	**€ 142.80**

Various **reference points** for **taking out an insurance policy**, from the perspective of **risk control**, can now be derived from the calculation of the insurance premium.

The **larger** the **collective** is, the smaller is the difference between the expected and the actual occurring total damage and thus also, from the perspective of insurance, the necessary gross risk premium. This principle corresponds to the so-called granularity principle, which is also used in calculating the lending rate in the context of default risk. Behind this connection stands the law of large numbers or the resulting statistical convergence between expected and actual total damages. A smaller gross risk premium also reduces the insurance premium overall and thus makes taking out insurance more lucrative from the perspective of risk control.

A general premium calculation is problematic if there are significant differences between the damage expectancy values of individual policyholders. In these cases, so-called **premium differentiation** is frequently applied, in which the premium is based more closely on the risk of the individual policyholder. This is often the case with industrial insurance. Through premium differentiation, risk balancing by the collective moves to the background, and thus insurance with a sharp premium differentiation is less attractive from the policyholder's risk control perspective, since he always also has to carry the operations cost surcharge and the profit margin of the insurance in addition to the premium.

Taking out insurance is all the more interesting when the **operations cost surcharge** and **profit margin** are **lower** based on e. g. the size, legal status or other properties of the insurance company.

Regardless of the discussed guides for the use of insurance to improve the profit-risk ratio, the **main area** of insurance from the business perspective is in property and casualty insurance (e. g. against climate change risk, see Section 5.1.4). To what extent the use of insurance increases the **RoRaC** can be difficult to evaluate. On the one hand, advantages of reduced risk can arise by insuring through sufficiently large insurance collectives, but their profit margin and operating costs surcharge elements of the premium are offsetting disadvantages on the cost side. So the RoRaC will probably sink sharply, especially for the industry insurance with premium differentiation described above. Nonetheless, it can be quite useful to take out industry insurance when it passes on risks that would strongly threaten the continued existence of the business (for example, a fire in a company warehouse).

From the standpoint of the business that considers insurance in the context of risk management, it is primarily only asset losses of **tangible fixed assets** and **material positions** that can be passed on by taking out insurance. Asset losses coming from financial positions cannot usually be covered by insurance with the exception of credit risks. For risk management of financial positions, derivatives come into use, whose general functioning will be explained in the following sections.

3.4.2 Options

Taken literally, **derivatives** are "derived" financials, also called second order financials, which consist of contractual agreements about first order financials (=base positions, underlying assets). **Base positions** are understood to include financial positions like equities, foreign currency, fixed-income securities and so on. The various characteristics of derivatives can be divided into the two categories "conditional financial securities" (whose insurance can also be assigned) and "unconditional financial securities".

Options are the main instruments of **conditional financial securities** for risk management of financial positions. The following general **definition** of an **option** is the first starting point for further use as an instrument in risk management:

The acquirer or buyer of an option (= long position) has the **right** but not the obligation to buy or sell the **underlying asset** from the option seller at an agreed **exercise price** within a certain **period** (=American option) or at a specific **maturity** (=European option). The option buyer pays an **option premium** to the option seller for this right.

The general definition refers to some central **properties** of options for use in **risk management**:
- Options are **forward transactions**, whereby an agreement is made today about the right to buy or sell an underlying asset at a specific price in the future. Forward transactions are characterized by a separation of the commitment transaction (today) and the fulfillment transaction (in the future). **Future asset losses** of base positions can only be compensated at all through possible fulfillment in the future.
- The **difference** between **American** and **European** options is only reflected in the valuation of the options. The difference between American and European options is first of all not significant for the basic functioning of options in risk management. For this reason, further discussions will explore European options exclusively.

– The differing legal status of the option buyer and seller also has an effect on the broadest possible application in risk control. The buyer of an option can lose, at most, the already rendered option premium. The option writer has, in contrast, delivery obligations with regard to the underlying asset, whose value under certain circumstances is not fixed until the maturity date. While the purchase of standardized options is therefore usually possible by any company, the **function of options writer** (= short position) is only possible for certain people in certain organizations (exchanges) under fairly restrictive conditions (for fulfillment of future delivery obligations). For this reason, the position of writer will not be included as a control instrument in further discussions of risk management. The option writer's position is only contrasted to the option seller's position in order to illustrate the mechanism.

In order to be able to represent functioning of **options** for **risk management** of financial positions, in theory and practice, a so-called **profit and loss profile** is often constructed. This involves a **static instrument** for evaluating options, which means the possible changes to the option premium (=option value) over time is not taken into account.

The following **example** will be the basis for generating a profit and loss profile for a **call option**:
– Call option premium (=C): € 10.00,
– Exercise price (=E): € 100.00,
– Maturity: in three months.

So the buyer of this call option pays an options premium of C = € 10.00 in return for the right to **buy** the underlying asset in three months for a price of E = € 100.00. The possible profit or loss of this call option arises out of the actual market price of the underlying asset at maturity in three months.

If the **price** of the underlying asset at maturity is **lower** than the **exercise price** of E = € 100.00, then the call option buyer will not exercise the option, since he could buy the underlying asset more cheaply in the market than through the call option. His loss, therefore, consists in the previously paid option premium of C = € 10.00. Conversely, the writer makes a profit from the unexercised option in the amount of the option premium, which is € 10.00.

If the **price** of the underlying asset is **higher** than the **exercise price** at maturity, then the option buyer can make a profit if he exercises the option, i. e. buys the underlying asset for € 100.00 and immediately sells it again for the new price over € 100.00. His profit then consists of the difference between the actual price and the exercise price, less the paid option premium. Thus, from the perspective of the option buyer, the break-even point is reached when the underlying asset is priced at exactly € 110.00, since then the profit(€ 110.00 – € 100.00) and the option premium cancel each other exactly. A corresponding profit is realized starting from a price of € 110.00

(e. g. if the underlying asset has an actual price of € 120.00: € 120.00 – € 100.00 € exercise price – € 10.00 option premium = € 10.00 profit). When the underlying asset is priced between € 100.00 and € 110.00, the option should also be exercised in order to at least partially cancel the loss of the option premium. The option writer experiences symmetrically opposite corresponding losses.

In Figure 3.5, a graphic **profit and loss profile** illustrates the example calculations for a **call option**.

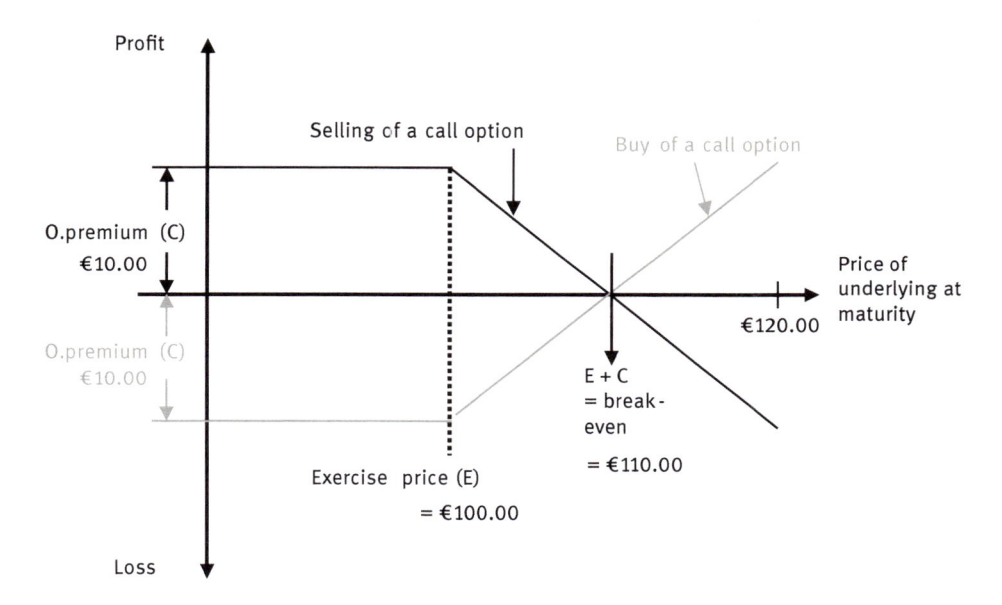

Fig. 3.5: Profit and loss profile of a call option

Risk control statements can be taken directly from the profit and loss profile. A call option buyer profits if the underlying assets increase in price, i. e. the expectation of increasing prices opens up **opportunities for additional profits** when buying call options. Due to the so-called **leverage effect** these profit opportunities are disproportionately larger than if the underlying assets were bought directly. The leverage effect is based on the smaller capital investment through the option premium compared with the direct purchase of the base position. Despite the smaller capital investment, with options the buyer can nonetheless fully participate in the profits through price increases in the base position.

The purpose of **risk control**, however, is to compensate for potential losses that come about through falling prices. So buying call options is unsuitable for direct use as a risk control tool (this is, however, indirectly possible with call options by combining various options, the so-called option strategies). From the writer's point of view, on the other hand, selling a call option can be used as a management instrument for offsetting sinking prices. If the prices of the underlying asset drop below € 100.00, the writer realizes a constant profit of € 10.00 from the collected option premium. This profit can therefore offset at least a small portion of asset position losses. Since loss compensation, from the perspective of the **call option writer**, is only partially possible through the option premium, and because of the previously mentioned special features of the writer, this risk control possibility will **not** be **dealt with** further.

The call option writer has yet other characteristics that also played a role in the capital markets and in the **financial crisis**. If the writer has sold the call option and the underlying assets are not yet in stock, because he speculated that this would be cheaper to buy at maturity, then he theoretically has an unlimited loss potential. If several writers speculate simultaneously to the same due date on the same underlying asset, then this can lead to sharp price increases which no longer have anything to do with the fundamental value of the underlying asset. Furthermore, the writer must purchase the underlying asset at the sharply raised price on the due date, which can in turn perhaps lead to liquidity and credit rating problems for the writer. A vivid practical example was the uncovered short selling of US hedge funds by German automaker Volkswagen in the autumn of 2008 (in the wake of speculations about the takeover of Volkswagen by Porsche). This principle is called **uncovered** (because the underlying asset is not in stock) **short selling** (= the call option writer), which in crisis times can accelerate certain negative developments described above. Because of this, short sale regulations in the EU were revised (see Section 4.4.2.1 g)).

A much better opportunity for risk management is offered by the **put option**, whose functioning will be demonstrated in the following simple example:
- Put option premium (=P): € 10.00,
- Exercise price (=E): € 100.00,
- Maturity: in three months.

Thus the buyer of this put option pays an option premium payment of P = € 10.00 for the right to **sell** the underlying asset in three months for a price of E = € 100.00. The possible profit or loss on this put option again arises out of the market price of the underlying asset at maturity in three months.

If the **price** of the underlying asset is **lower** than the **exercise price** of E = € 100.00 at maturity, then the option buyer realizes a profit by exercising the option, i. e. buying the underlying asset on the market for less than € 100.00 and then selling it again using the put option for E = € 100.00. His profit is the difference between the exercise price and the actual price, less the option premium. For an underlying asset priced at exactly € 90.00, that is the break-even point from the perspective of the option buyer, since there the profit (€ 100.00 – € 90.00) and the option premium cancel each other out exactly. A corresponding profit is realized when the price drops below € 90.00 (e. g. price for underlying = € 80.00: € 100.00 – € 80.00 exercise price – € 10.00 option premium = € 10.00 profit). For underlying asset prices between € 90.00 and € 100.00, the put option should still be exercised in order to at least partially cancel out the loss of the option premium. If the underlying asset is worthless at maturity (total or maximum loss), then the put option buyer realizes a corresponding profit of € 90.00 (€ 100.00 exercise price – € 0.00 market price – € 10.00 option premium). The writer again experiences symmetrically opposite corresponding losses.

If the **price** of the underlying asset at maturity **overshoots** the **exercise price** of E = € 100.00, then the put option buyer will not exercise the option, since he would be able to sell the underlying asset for more money on the market then he could by exercising the put option. His loss, consequently, consists in the previously paid option premium of P = € 10.00. Conversely, the writer has realized a profit of € 10.00, the amount the option premium, by not exercising the option.

The corresponding **profit and loss profile** of a **put option** is graphically represented in Figure 3.6.

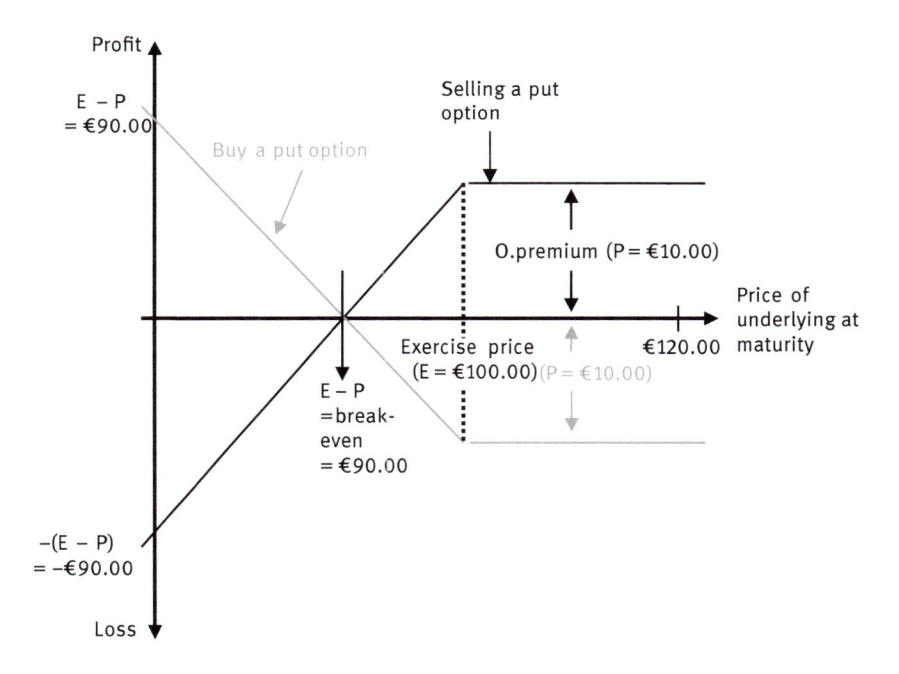

Fig. 3.6: Profit and loss profile of a put option

From the descriptions of the profit and loss profile for put options, one can derive the finding for risk management that buying put options can completely or at least partly offset asset position losses (this function of put options is called the **protective put**). The greater the loss of the underlying asset through falling prices, the greater the profit from the put option. In the context of **risk control**, the **purchase of put options** is a **suitable instrument** for compensating asset losses. From the profit and loss profile in Figure 3.6 it is also immediately apparent that the put option writer's position is unsuitable for risk control.

The use of the put option obviously has a great advantage with regard to the profit-risk ratio. Thus, although potential losses are compensated proportionally to their size, at the same time potential assets profits are only reduced by the option premium. When the losses are more sharply reduced than the associated profits, then one begins to suspect that the use of **put options improves** the **profit-risk ratio** or the **RoRaC** of the underlying asset position (base position). To examine the mechanism of a put option in relation to an existing asset position, the above example of a put option will be expanded as follows:
- Put option premium (=P): € 10.00,
- Exercise price (=E): € 100.00,
- Maturity: in three months,
- Actual price of the underlying asset: € 110.00,
- The underlying base position or asset position (=B) is already present in the portfolio at the time of put option purchase.

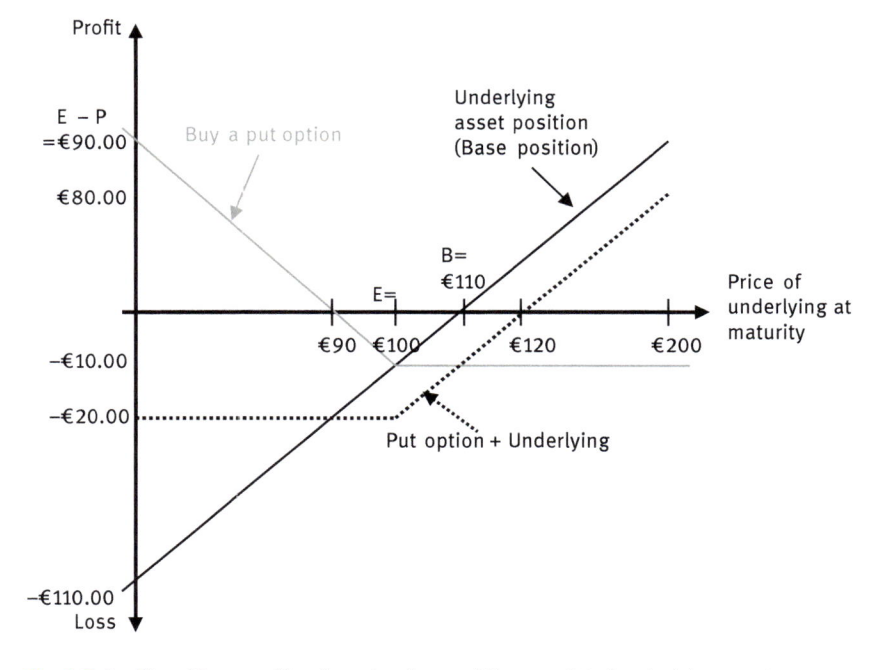

Fig. 3.7: Profit and loss profile of a put option and its associated underlying asset

If only the **profit and loss profile** of the existing **underlying asset** is now considered, then the profit or loss at maturity in three months runs proportional to the price of the underlying asset. At a price of € 110.00 there is no profit or loss; with prices below or above that there is a corresponding loss or profit. If the put option profile is added to the underlying assets, then a **total profit and loss profile** results from adding up the respective profits and losses of the underlying asset and the put option. The corresponding profile is illustrated in Figure 3.7.

If the underlying asset has a price of € 110.00 at maturity, it has realized no profit or loss with regard to the current price. With a total loss, when the base position is no longer worth anything, the loss amounts to € 110.00, and at a price of € 200.00 the profit amounts to € 90.00. Nothing has changed in the profit and loss profile of the put option purchase. It is carried over one to one from Figure 3.6.

The following features and conclusions can be derived from the composite **profit and loss profile** of the **put option** and **underlying** asset shown in Figure 3.7:
- If the price of the underlying asset is under € 100.00 at maturity, the profits from the put option **offset** the losses from the underlying asset. This compensation is nonetheless not complete, rather there remains a constant loss of € 20.00.
- This **constant loss of € 20.00** for underlying asset prices under € 100.00 consists of **two components** together: 1. The option premium for the put option in the amount of € 10.00. 2. The loss from the actual evaluation of the base position at € 110.00 and the put option's smaller exercise price of € 100.00, which gives likewise a difference of € 10.00. Both components together give the loss of € 20.00.
- Starting at a price of € 100.00 for the underlying asset at maturity, the **result** of the **composite position** increases linearly (parallel to the course of the individual base position). This result is nonetheless **diminished** by the **option premium** of € 10.00.
- At a price of € 120.00 and above, the composite position reaches a **profit zone** (€ 120.00 – € 10.00 option premium gives the actual evaluation price of the base position of € 110.00).

These general correlations are nonetheless not sufficient grounds for using the put option to improve the profit-risk ratio in the context of risk control. The following **aspects** should also be taken into account for a possible application:
- In the above explanations, only the so-called **intrinsic value** is considered, which results from the difference between the exercise price and the price of the underlying asset at maturity as well as taking the option premium into account. The fair value of an option is ignored. The **fair value** of an option basically reflects expectations of market participants that the option value can change in future due to changes in various influencing factors, e. g. term, risk-free interest rates, volatility and base price. Option value (which comes from the intrinsic value and the fair value combined) is determined as a function of these factors by means of complex so-called **option pricing models** (e. g. the Black and Scholes model). The influencing factors and their processing within the option pricing models depend on the characteristics of the underlying asset and therefore will not be further explored here.

- With help from the option pricing models, measures can be derived for compensating the underlying asset losses by simultaneous option profits even during the option's term, e. g. through the so-called **Delta hedge**.
- For analysis of the profit and loss situation of options, it is furthermore significant whether the **underlying asset exists** on the due date (the so-called covered option) or whether this must first be bought on the market at maturity when possibly exercising the option (uncovered option). In risk control it is assumed that options are used for offsetting losses of already existing asset positions. Thus only the case of **covered options** will be considered in the context of **risk control**. This differentiation is not yet necessary for the above simple reflections on the profit-loss profiles.
- Options can be used for **many purposes**, for example, for arbitrage and speculation. In these cases, more complex and extensive models are used to assess options. These models and strategies are irrelevant for risk management and thus will not be further explored here in this book. For interested readers who wish to deal more intensively with the models and application possibilities of derivative instruments, the relevant literature is listed in Section 3.5.

Using the options described above in the context of risk compensation results in a decrease in the underlying asset's VaR. The extent to which the underlying asset's RoRaC and the option change together cannot be directly inferred without further work. On the one hand, this depends on the amount of the option premium, since this diminishes the profit. On the other hand, the RoRaC also depends on the fair value of the option, and the fair value's influencing factors, whose determination must use more complex option pricing assessment models.

3.4.3 Futures

While options are categorized as conditional financials, futures belong to the unconditional financials. The condition with options is that the buyer exercises the option. Only under this condition will fulfillment take place in the future. With futures, this condition falls away, i. e. there is a mutual "unconditional" commitment between buyer and seller. The future fulfillment always takes place. The starting point for further use of the instrument in risk control is first the following **general definition** of a **future**:

With **futures**, the buyer **commits** to buy (= long hedge position) an agreed number of the underlying assets from the seller (= short hedge position) at the **forward rate** (future rate). Conversely, the purchaser simultaneously commits himself to deliver the agreed number of underlying assets at the forward rate. The effective delivery of the underlying assets is often omitted and replaced instead by a cash settlement.

3.4 Risk transfer and risk compensation

This definition of a future immediately shows some important features for risk control.
- The **premium payment** is **no longer necessary** because of the mutual commitment of buyer and seller, since neither contractual party has an advantage in the sense of a right (an option).
- The theoretical **profit potential** is boundless for the buyer of the base position, just as the **loss possibilities** are **unlimited** for the seller. This is because there is no possibility of stepping back from the transaction for certain price developments of the underlying asset (as was the case with the option, by not exercising it).
- The unlimited loss potential requires more restrictive conditions for the transaction participants (like those for option writers) or else certain **legal** and **organizational measures** for the processing of futures. For this reason, only certain futures transactions that have been developed for particular risks are suitable for wide use in risk management (especially for non-banks).
- While the exercise price and the option premium were the **relevant parameters** when applying options for risk control, for futures it is only the **forward rate**.

As with options, the functioning of futures in risk management can also be illustrated using the profit and loss profiles. For this purpose, a forward rate of € 120.00 will be chosen, based on a given underlying asset and an agreed due date of three months. The resulting **profit and loss profile** is **graphically** represented in Figure 3.8.

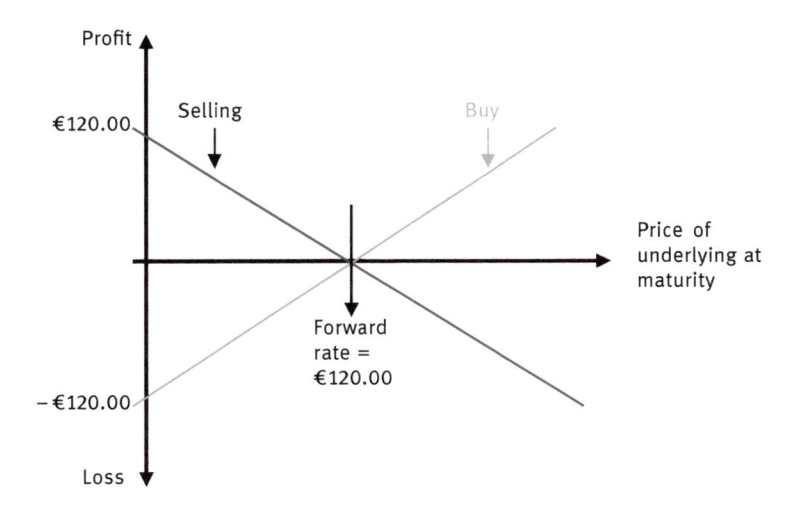

Fig. 3.8: Profit and loss profile of a future

It is immediately clear that only the **selling** of underlying assets is a **suitable control instrument** for application in risk control. The further the price is at maturity from the forward rate of € 120.00, the larger the profit or cash settlement (for example, an asset price of € 90.00 at maturity would deliver a cash settlement of € 30.00). With the cash settlement, the losses are already compensated by property positions in existence at completion of the futures transaction. The mechanism of this compensation is graphically illustrated by the fact that the price for the already existing assets at completion is assumed to be € 110.00. Figure 3.9 shows the result of the combination of selling at due date (future date) and base position.

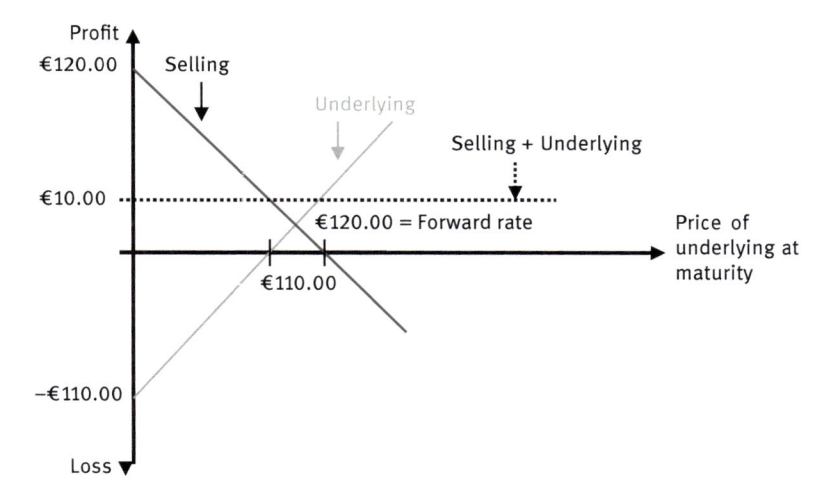

Fig. 3.9: Profit and loss profile of a future and its associated underlying asset

Using the illustration in Figure 3.9, the characteristics for risk control can be described:
- **Profits** and **losses always** balance out to a **constant profit** in the amount of € 10.00. This effect of futures is also called the "closing" of a position. The constant profit results from the difference between the forward rate and the current base price.
- (€ 120.00 – € 110.00). The closer the forward rate is to the current underlying asset price, the smaller the profit. If the forward rate and the current base price are identical, then neither profit nor loss is realized.
- Limiting losses while maintaining profit opportunities is not possible with futures as it is with options, since there is **no option premium** and no maturity right (i. e. not exercising the option).
- A **future** should be used as a **risk control instrument** when the constant profit is high and a similarly profitable construction with a put option is not available on the market. A future works particularly well if no profit is connected to the base position. This is conceivable e. g. with strategic shareholdings where the main focus is the exercise of voting rights.
- The forward rate is the decisive factor for futures prices in the financial markets due to the so-called **cost of carry**. The cost of carry is added to the current base

price, resulting in the forward rate. The profit calculated above therefore does not represent a pure profit, but rather the compensation for the cost of carry. The cost of carry can be composed of various components depending on the underlying assets, e. g. such as storage costs or interest on financing the base position minus income (e. g. dividend payment) from the base position.
– The higher the **actual cost of carry** of the base position and the smaller profit goal, the more it pays to use futures for risk control over put options.

Upon completion of the future, the risk (the VaR) of the base position sinks to (almost) null. The RoRaC of this position changes in relation to the amount of the forward rate. The higher the forward rate is, the more the RoRaC increases.

Most futures contracts are usually negotiated between bank representatives or financial brokers on the exchanges and are thus, as already indicated above, only possible for many non-banks through the involvement of banks. Nonetheless, futures were constructed for broad practical application to certain risks, which can be used simply and directly by every business. These include, on the one hand, **forward exchange transactions** for managing exchange rate risk (see Section 4.1.2) and, on the other hand, the so-called **Bund-Future** for use in the area of interest rate risk (see Section 4.1.1). The specifics of these risks and the resulting ungeneralizable properties of these special futures will therefore only be discussed in detail in the fourth chapter.

3.4.4 Swaps

Swaps, like futures, belong to unconditional financials. First, the general principle of swaps will be discussed independently of special areas of application. The concrete configuration of swaps will follow in later examples, in the corresponding Sections 4.1.1 and 4.1.2. The basic principle of swaps can generally be described as follows:

Swaps are agreements about **exchange transactions** in the future to exploit **comparative advantages** on the financial or commodity markets.

With **forwards** an exchange dealing is agreed for only **one time point** in the future, while **swaps** are negotiated for **several time points in the future**.

The general mechanism of using swaps to exploit comparative advantages can be illustrated using Figure 3.10. Two contracting parties (companies) A and B negotiating a swap will be considered. Both companies can negotiate contracts on different markets or the same markets, with their customers or with other institutions, under **certain conditions**. These can contain various items (X and Y), such as e. g. **goods, financial securities** and **cash flows**.

```
                    Delivery of X ( step [2])
┌─────────────────────────┐  ◄·········►  ┌─────────────────────────┐
│                         │  [2]+[3] = Swap │                         │
│      Company  A         │ ◄────────────► │      Company  B         │
│                         │                │                         │
└──┬──────────────────┬───┘                └──┬──────────────────┬───┘
   ▲            For-  │    Delivery of Y [3]     ▲            For-
 Acquisition  warding │                      Acquisition   warding
 of X         of Y    │                      of Y          of X
                      ▼
   Step [1]     [4]
┌─────────────────────────┐                ┌─────────────────────────┐
│  Market, customer or    │                │  Market, customer or    │
│  other institution      │                │  other institution      │
└─────────────────────────┘                └─────────────────────────┘
```

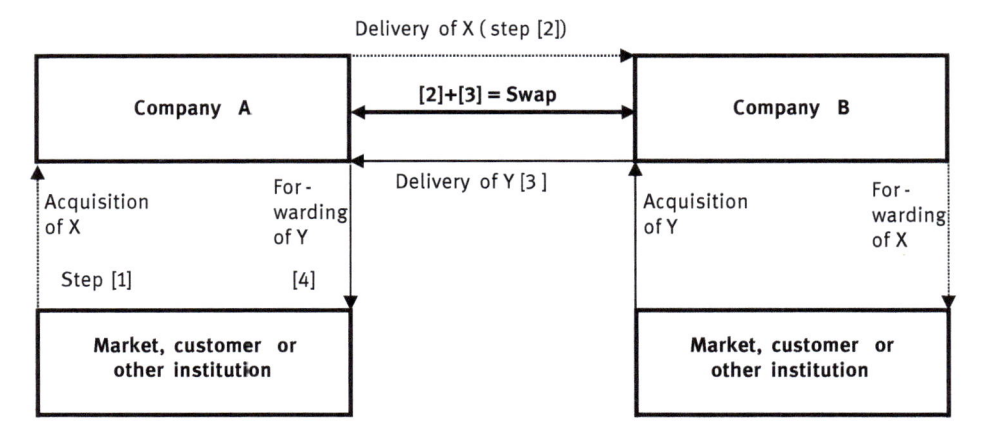

Fig. 3.10: General mechanism of swaps

The **comparative advantage** for both companies can be explained by describing the mechanism of swaps, as shown in Figure 3.10 based on the following features:
- Company A acquires through business activities a certain number of items X in the future (step [1]). This **item X** is **risky**, i. e. it can lose value in the future compared with its current price (**asset loss**). Company A agrees with company B to deliver this item in a specified condition and a determined amount on several dates in the future (step [2]).
- As a **consideration** for delivery of item X, company A receives item Y from company B on the same dates in the future, in a specified condition and a determined amount [3]. From A's perspective this consideration is equivalent to or better than the supply of X for its present business calculations or future planning. The possible **advantage** rests on the possibility that company A could turn item Y to advantage under certain conditions in the future [4].
- Through the swap ([2] + [3]), company A has **avoided** the future danger of an **asset loss** through item X, by simultaneously getting a possible advantage by utilizing item Y.
- Conversely, for **company B** the **advantage** rests likewise on getting item X and passing it on profitably to certain markets or customers. In return for obtaining X, company B delivers item Y, which will also be acquired in the future through business activities and would have been exposed to risk without the swap.

The crucial **basic concept** of swaps consists therefore in exploiting mutual advantages. This results in the frequently used concept of the comparative advantage, i. e. the **advantages** of both contracting parties to the swap (here A and B) are **compared** to each other.

This also results in a special advantage for the use of **swaps** as an instrument in the context of **risk control**. Thus risks can be avoided without incurring any costs for the avoidance (like those that occur e. g. with options in the form of the option premium). On the contrary, there may even be monetary benefits in addition to the risk avoidance (depending on the utilization possibilities of the swap items). In this respect, swaps represent a very good way of financially **improving** the **profit-risk ratio** or the RoRaC when corresponding advantages are available for both swap partners.

Identifying the **advantages** between possible swap partners is crucial for the **successful negotiation** of swaps. Potential advantages are recognized more and more frequently in the markets when market participants have access to a great deal of information about the potential advantages of companies. The rapid spread of information is increasing enormously on the market thanks to technological advances, in particular the Internet, and this massively promotes information exchange. This is also a reason why swaps are enjoying **dramatic growth** in business practice. If the above described advantages can be contractually realized, then the RoRaC generally rises through the swap.

In conclusion, the effects of the various control instruments on the RoRaC and the VaR are summarized in overview in Table 3.1.

Tab. 3.1: Effects of the various control instruments on RoRaC and VaR

Instrument:	RoRaC:	Risk/VaR:	Influencing factors:
Increase in risk bearing capacity:	No effect	No effect	Equity
Acceptance of collaterals:	Changes	Falls	Lending rate
Risk limitation:	Stays the same or changes	Stays the same or falls	Reduction of risk positions, risk attitude, portfolio structure, correlations
Risk distribution:	Increase is sought	Stays the same or falls	Risk attitude, portfolio structure, correlations
Risk shifting: (Outsourcing)	Changes	Falls	Purchase price of the outsourced services
Risk transfer: (Insurance)	Seldom increases Usually falls	Falls	Amount of the insurance premium
Options:	Changes	Falls	Option premium, influencing factors on the option price valuation
Futures:	Changes	Falls	Forward rate
Swaps:	Usually increases	Falls	Swap conditions

3.5 References

On the topic of **outsourcing** see the following works:

Burkholder, Nicholas C.: "Outsourcing: The Definitive View, Applications and Implications", Wiley, 2006,
Ebert, Christof: "Outsourcing kompakt – Entscheidungskriterien und Praxistipps für Outsourcing und Offshoring von Softwareentwicklung", Spektrum Akademischer Verlag , 3. korr. Nachdruck, 2011,
Fink, Dietmar/Köhler, Thomas/Scholtissek, Stephan: "Die dritte Revolution der Wertschöpfung", Econ, 2004,
Hermes, Heinz-Josef/Schwarz, Gerd: "Outsourcing-Chancen und Risiken, Erfolgsfaktoren, rechtssichere Umsetzung", Haufe Verlag, 2005,
Scholtissek, Stephan: "New Outsourcing – Die dritte Revolution der Wertschöpfung in der Praxis", Econ, 2004.

For a **deeper** discussion about the **functioning** of **insurance** and the risk transfer built upon it, see the standard works of:

Doff, Rene: "Risk Management for Insurers", Risk Books, London, 3rd ed., 2015,
Farny, Dieter: "Versicherungsbetriebslehre", Verlag Versicherungswirtschaft, 5. Auflage, 2011,
Hull, John C.: "Risk Management and Financial Institutions", Wiley, Hoboken, New Jersey, 4th ed. p. 45–69, 2015,
Nguyen, Tristan/Romeike, Frank: "Versicherungswirtschaftslehre", Springer Gabler, Wiesbaden, 2012

and

Saunders, Anthony/Cornett, Marcia Millon: "Financial Markets and Institutions", McGraw Hill Education, 6th edition, p. 469–493, 2015.

The worldwide standard on **derivatives** is

Hull, John C.: "Options, Futures, and Other Derivatives", Prentice Hall, 8th Edition, 2011.

Another possibility, which deals with **derivatives** more intensively, is also offered by

Eller, Roland/Heinrich, Markus u. a. (Hrsg.): "Handbuch Derivativer Instrumente: Produkte, Strategien, Risikomanagement", Schäffer Poeschel, Stuttgart, 3. Auflage, 2005

and

Stulz, Rene M.: "Risk Management & Derivatives", South-Western, 2002.

4 Financial risks

Based on the general account of risk measurement methods, risk analysis and risk control instruments, they can now be applied to various types of risk. The focus is on application of the methods and instruments to **specific characteristics** of the individual risk types (see Figure 1.3).

Every business activity that is associated with a risk can generally be categorized as either a financial risks or a performance-related risks. In principle, the two main categories can be distinguished from each other by the following definitions, although there are interfaces that cannot be clearly assigned. The **financial risks** include
- Asset losses that can occur through uncertainty about future cash flows (=**cash flow risks**),
- Losses that can arise through negative performance of financials securities (stocks, fixed income securities, foreign exchange positions) (= **financial value risks**).

Performance-related risks are possible losses that can arise through business activities in the areas of
- purchasing / procurement,
- production and
- sales.

The **difficulty** of **distinguishing** between the two **categories** can be well illustrated with the example of "falling sales". If a company doesn't achieve its planned sales volume, a loss results which is assigned to performance-related risk. At the same time, a sales decline leads to a reduction in the future cash flow (cash flow risk) and thus also represents a financial risk. In order to solve this allocation problem, the fourth and fifth chapters will explore the differences between the respective **necessary risk-management instruments**. Thus the risk of "falling sales" is first assigned to performance-related risks, since sales risk is controlled with marketing instruments and methods. Managing the cash flow risks resulting from the falling sales leads to a liquidity risk and is controlled with corresponding financial planning instruments, and is consequently classified as a financial risk.

Financial risks are further divided into three categories
- market price risks,
- credit risks and
- liquidity risks.

Market price risks fundamentally involve financial risks, however cash flow risks can also result from financial securities (e. g. with interest-rate payment claims from interest rate positions). With **credit risks** there are ultimately financial and cash flow risks to carry. On the one hand, loans also have a financial value, which, for example, can drop through a downgrading of the credit rating; on the other hand, loan repayment and interest rate losses lead directly to reduced cash flows in the future (cash flow risk). What is crucial for **distinguishing** between **market price risk** and **credit risk** is, again, the instrument originally applied. With credit risks, credit assessment is the focus of rating procedures, while market price risks focus on measuring value changes in the asset position through the present value method or comparable approaches. **Liquidity risks** primarily involve instruments for measuring and managing cash flow risks.

4.1 Market price risks

Developments in risk management are **most advanced** in the most important area of **market price risks**. The reason lies in historical developments of the early 1990s, when market price risks were especially prevalent in investment banking and brought many banks into difficulties. The resulting efforts to develop appropriate measurement methods and control instruments led to the current state of affairs in the area of market price risk.

The **importance** of **market price risks** depends chiefly on the respective industry. For banks, market price risks (especially interest rate risk) and credit risk represent the core risks. For nonbanks, the importance depends on the extent of the existing financial assets and the amount of the interest expense for servicing the borrowed capital.

Market price risks are divided into
- interest rate risk,
- foreign exchange risk,
- stock price risk and
- real estate price risk.

Interest rate risk is generally the most important risk. It affects various balance sheet and income statement items. Fixed income securities in financial assets can lose value through changes in market interest rates. Receivables from current assets (receivables from deliveries and services) can also cause interest rate risks. Increased interest on borrowed capital leads to a higher interest expense, which then also indirectly represents an asset loss. Furthermore, variable interest payments can lead to a cash flow risk. In addition to these direct effects of market rates, interest rate risk also has an indirect effect. Thus market interest rates are used for many evaluation purposes. A fundamental application is company valuation. So along with other influencing factors, increased market interest rates can lead to a lower company value in the context of company valuation (due to greater discounting of the cash flow).

Interest rate risk acts, therefore, in **varying degrees,** and in particular influences interest rate positions at the same time in **different directions**. Since, however, there are also appropriate instruments available for interest rate change risk, comments will be largely about interest change rate risk as part of market price risks.

Foreign exchange risk plays an important role in Germany for export-oriented companies. Measurement and management of exchange rate risk mainly concentrates on the question of how much foreign exchange positions can depreciate from export transactions through future changes in the exchange rate. Financial value risk control of foreign exchange positions is therefore in the foreground.

In the case of non-banks, **stock price risk** manifests primarily in the form of stocks, which are also reported under financial assets. Thus the focus is on controlling the financial risk. Risk control based on portfolio theory forms the basis for various control approaches.

The last category within market price risks is **real estate price risk**. At first glance this seems misleading, since real estate is understood to be immovable property. Consequently, real estate risk must be dealt with under the performance-related risks of operating risks (e. g. building fires). It is advisable to apply various instruments in order to obtain meaningful distinctions. It makes sense to apply the instrument of property insurance for dealing with the risks of **owner-occupied real estate** and this should be categorized as operating risk. When dealing with real estate price risk within market risks, purchasing **real estate** as an **investment** (including e. g. equities and fixed income securities) is considered. For managing property as a capital investment, the financial value risk is crucial and therefore the control instruments used are similar to those for e. g. stock price risk.

4.1.1 Interest rate risk

4.1.1.1 Basics of interest rate change risk

A general definition for interest rate risk is:

Interest rate risk can be defined as asset risks caused by market interest rates, either in the form of **net interest income risk** and/or **present value risks**.

For measuring interest rate risk, a distinction is made between interest rate position (interest exposure) and market interest rate volatilities. The **interest rate position** is the volume, to which the interest payment refers. The interest rate position is determined by the company, i. e. in which volume e. g. government bonds will be bought for the investment assets.

The **market interest rate volatilities** influence the value of an interest-rate position and arise on the financial markets. Interest-rate volatilities cannot, therefore, be controlled by the company, but are rather exogenous quantities from the standpoint of business. Market interest rate volatilities can change in various ways.

- The volatilities of individual market interest rates may fluctuate.
- The correlations between interest rates of various terms may change.
- Interest rates for different maturities vary in amount (change in the yield curve).

Risk analysis of **net interest income** in the form of e. g. increased interest expense or decreased interest income was long the focus of research into interest rate risk in the past. Nowadays, analysis of the present value risk has thoroughly prevailed. The net interest income (income statement orientation) and present value change of interest rate positions are identical in the total period (=the longest maturity) of all interest rate positions considered). However, it has become widely acknowledged that the **present value** is more accurate and **meaningful** for controlling interest rate risk. Thus the successive methods of present value, duration and value at risk are now used for measuring interest rate risk.

As already explained in the introduction to market price risks, and as can be seen from the description of market rate volatilities, interest rate risk works in various ways. For this reason it is appropriate to first **systematize** various **basic principles** of **interest rate risk**. Table 4.1 lists the most important **interest-bearing securities** and corresponding **types of interest**.

Tab. 4.1: Interest-bearing securities and types of interest

Interest-bearing securities:	Interest rate type:	Features:
Government bonds	Coupon rates	Usually risk free, long term
Corporate bonds, loans	Coupon rates, lending rates	Risky, long term
Money market securities	Variable (floating) rates (EURIBOR)	Usually risk free, short-term
Zero coupon bonds	Zero coupon rates	Risk-free/risky (discount factor)

There are many more types of interest-bearing securities over and above those named in Table 4.1, which are however irrelevant for the discussions in this book concerning interest rate risk management and therefore will not be further explored.

Government bonds are fixed income securities issued by the government for financing the state budget. Since the government is the debtor, the securities are classified as **risk free** (AAA rated) in the sense of default risk, i. e. it is always assumed that interest and redemption will be paid on time. Since government bonds include no credit risk, coupon interest rates are also lower compared with risky bonds such as e. g. **corporate bonds** or bonds from other countries with lower credit ratings (for example, Greek government bonds). From a business perspective this means that the interest income from capital investments (purchase of government bonds) is smaller than the interest expense on capital borrowed by issuing corporate bonds or taking out loans.

Money market securities and **variable interest rates** involve interest-rate positions with a very short maturity (at most a year, frequently 1 day, 1 month, 3 months, or 6 months maturity). Due to this short-term character there is no or very little interest rate risk, depending on the maturity. The **EURIBOR** is often used as a so-called **reference interest rate** in many interest rate risk control instruments.

The feature of **coupon interest** consists in the regular payment of a fixed interest rate based on the nominal value of the bond. With **zero bonds** and **zero coupon interest**, no interest (zero interest) is paid annually, rather the return consists in the difference between repayment and disbursement. Zero coupon interest stems from the financial mathematical distribution (see Technical appendix Section 4.6) of the difference between repayment and disbursement over the respective maturity. This zero coupon interest rate has one **crucial advantage** over coupon interest:

The zero coupon interest rate is the interest rate for a monetary sum for a certain period, with the interest and capital to be paid back all at once at the end of the term. There are therefore no interim payments within the maturity that could distort the results at maturity, which is however exactly the case with coupon interest rates. For this reason, **zero coupon interest rates must** also be used, conversely, to calculate future payments to the present date again (**discounting**!). Zero coupon interest rates are thus used for calculating **discounting factors**. In the following discussions, zero coupon interest rates will always be used for discounting without being explicitly mentioned.

On the one hand, zero coupon interest rates can be calculated on the capital market using financial mathematical methods, based on the prices of zero bonds. There are often not enough zero bonds traded or issued on the capital markets to determine consistent interest rates for all maturities. For this reason, zero coupon interest rates are, on the other hand, calculated using the numerous available coupon bonds in which the so-called **coupon effect** (which causes the distortion described above) is eliminated. The description of this calculation will be omitted here since it does not lead to any additional business insights. The relevant literature is listed for interested readers (see Section 4.5).

The calculation of zero coupon rates can be used to generate a definition of the present value, which is fundamental for the interest rate risk.

The **present value** (PV) of an interest rate position is the sum of the term-dependent **capital market interest rate discounted** contractually agreed **cash flows** (payment series) of the interest position up to **today's date**. The respective term-dependent zero coupon rates determined on the capital market are then used for the term dependent capital market rates.

The present values of interest rate positions calculated in this way can nonetheless deviate from market values. The **market value** is the actual interest position price (rate) agreed between market participants in money and capital markets. This possible difference is irrelevant to development of interest rate risk methods and will be omitted in the following discussion.

The **interest rate structure** or **yield curve** can be understood as the relationship or the graphical representation of market interest rates as a function of maturity. Different prices and thus also different interest rates are paid on the capital market for interest-rate positions with different terms. For dealing with interest rate risk, three basic forms of yield curves on the capital market are important:
- normal yield curve,
- flat yield curve and
- inverse yield curve.

Figure 4.1 shows three example yield curves.

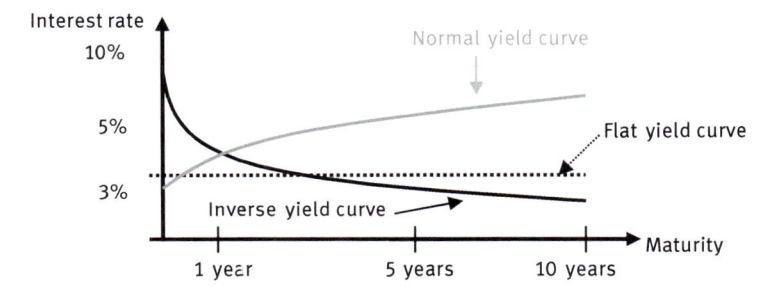

Fig. 4.1: Example yield curves

A **normal yield curve** is discussed when higher rates are paid for longer maturities and lower rates are paid for shorter maturities. With **flat yield curves**, the same interest rates are observed for all maturities. When lower interest rates are paid for shorter terms than for longer terms, then an **inverse yield curve** exists, which is relatively rare in capital market practice.

Changes to **yield curves** on the capital markets pose for banks in particular a central problem for dealing with interest rate risk. Consideration of the non-flat yield curves (which are the most frequent in practice) is for some issues so extensive and complex that a corresponding representation must be omitted in the framework of this book (see References Section 4.5). Further discussions here will refer to a non-flat yield curve where it is possible to describe it well. For some further questions a flat rate infrastructure is then assumed.

The thus far formal and partially abstract definitions will be illustrated with a concrete **numerical example**.

A company plans to purchase a coupon bond A from the government for financial assets from retained earnings. The government bond A has the following features:

- Face value: € 100.00 per unit,
- Nominal volume: 10 units per € 100.00; € 1,000.00 in total,
- Maturity: 3 years,
- Coupon rate: 4 % p. a. annual dividend,
- Repayment: face value due at maturity,
- Capital market rates: 1 year: 3 %, 2 years: 4 %; 3 years: 5 %.

The present value of bond A (PV_A) can be calculated on the basis of these givens. For these and all further calculations it will always be assumed that
- repayment at face value will always occur at maturity,
- there will only be annual payments and no sub-annual payments (particularly interest payments),
- payments always occur at the same time point in the year (such as January 1) and thus interpolations within a year are not necessary (e. g. no interest rate and no discount for 2.5 years, i. e. only whole years and no so-called broken terms).

While these assumptions are highly simplistic, deviations from them can be taken into account using financial mathematical methods without changing the following derivations with regard to the business content. For clarity, please refer to the literature for consideration of these assumptions (see Section 4.5).

In the first step, the associated cash flows are calculated from the information given about bond A. Next, the future payments are discounted with the corresponding capital market rates. The total of the discounted future payments is then the present value of the bond. The procedure is shown graphically in Figure 4.2. (for a financial mathematical description see Section 4.6)

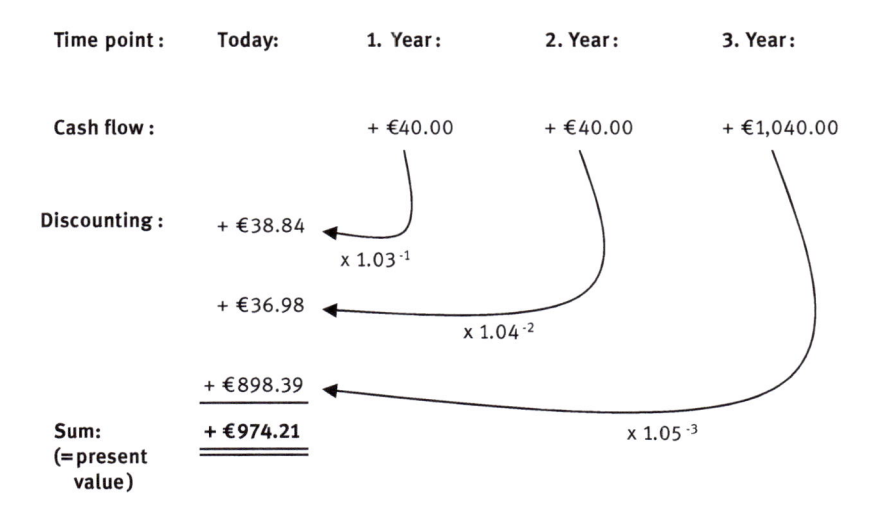

Time point:	Today:	1. Year:	2. Year:	3. Year:
Cash flow:		+ €40.00	+ €40.00	+ €1,040.00
Discounting:	+ €38.84	× 1.03^{-1}		
	+ €36.98		× 1.04^{-2}	
	+ €898.39			× 1.05^{-3}
Sum: (=present value)	+ €974.21			

Fig. 4.2: Example for present value calculation of a bond

The cash flow is calculated by paying 4 % interest on the nominal volume of € 1,000.00 for the first three years, with an additional repayment in the third year in the amount of the nominal volume. The discounting of the payments delivers a present value in the amount of **€ 974.21**. Based on the nominal volume of € 1,000.00 this value corresponds to 97.42 %.

This is the asset value of bond A, if the company buys the government bond at the current capital market interest rates.

The **present value** represents an equivalent to the future contractually promised payments relative to today's date.

In other words: if today the company were to invest € 38.84 on the capital market for a year at 3 %, € 36.98 for two years at 4 % and finally € 898.39 for three years at 5 %, it would in the future receive the exact payments which the government bond also promises! The investor would therefore theoretically have to invest the present value today in order to generate the payment series in the future (to duplicate it).

This simple example can now be used to derive the **interest rate risk** of **a bond** purchase. If the capital market rates climb, the future payments are discounted more sharply and the present value sinks! Or to put it another way: at higher interest rates, less would have to be invested in the capital market today in order to duplicate the bond payments. This **present value reduction** is tantamount to an **asset loss**.

In order to **measure** the **interest rate risk**, the question directly arises as to how sharply the present value sinks when the interest rate rises to a specific value. For this purpose, an increase was assumed in the capital market interest rate of one percentage point for every maturity. Such an increase of capital market rates is called a **parallel shift** in the **yield curve**. In capital market practice, the term **basis points** is used for percentage points (basis points = bp). An increase of one percentage point corresponds to 100 basis points. The increase is to be effective immediately (an assumption so that the term of the future payments does not have to be adjusted to the later interest rate change). The calculation of the present value for the interest rate increased by 100 basis points (so 4 %, 5 % and 6 %) gives:

Present value after rate increase
$= € 40.00 \times 1.04^{-1} \quad + € 40.00 \times 1.05^{-2} \quad + € 1,040.00 \times 1.06^{-3}$
$= € 38,46 € \qquad\qquad + € 36,28 € \qquad\qquad + € 873.20 € \qquad\qquad\qquad = \underline{€ 947.94}$.

The present value has therefore fallen from € 974.21 to € 947.94, which corresponds to an **asset loss** of **−€ 26.27** (or −2.697 % relative to the original present value). This method of measuring the interest rate risk has one crucial disadvantage. A specific interest change must be assumed, for which the associated specific present value reduction is then calculated. This is on the one hand very computationally intensive and, on the other hand, such a comparison with other interest rate positions makes no sense.

4.1.1.2 Duration

For measuring interest rate risk and subsequent comparisons, the question arises of how the **present value** reacts to **interest rate changes**. The question is answered through the **sensitivity** of the interest rate position. The term sensitivity is based on the first derivative of the underlying function for the relationship between the asset sizes and the influencing factors on the assets changes. The sensitivity thus arises through the first derivative of the present value function on the interest rate (see Section 2.2.2). The calculation of the **first derivative** of the **present value function** for current capital market interest rates gives a sensitivity which depends upon the amount of the absolute present value. Thus the possibilities for comparison would be once again very severely limited (e. g. only for comparing interest rate positions with the same present value). This disadvantage can be remedied if the sensitivity in the form of the first derivative is divided by the present value. Through that, a normalization takes place which enables any comparison between the most disparate interest rate positions. The result is the so-called modified duration.

The **modified duration** of an interest rate position is the first derivative of the present value function on the current capital market interest rates (= sum of the partial derivatives) divided by the current present value of this interest-rate position.

The mathematical representation of the modified duration will be omitted here (see Section 4.6). A simplified representation can be derived from the mathematical definition of the modified duration.

The modified duration (=D^{mod}) is calculated by multiplying the discounted payments by the **number of years** over which the payment occurs. The discounting is carried out for the number of years **plus one**.

The sum of these factors is then divided by the present value and gives for the above example:

D^{mod} = [1 x € 40.00 x $1.03^{-(1+1)}$ + 2 x € 40.00 x $1.04^{-(2+1)}$ + 3 x € 1,040.00 x $1.05^{-(3+1)}$] / € 974.21
 = [€ 37.70 + € 71.12 + € 2,566.83] / € 974.21 = € 2,675.65 € / € 974.21 = **2.747**.

The modified duration is a measure of the interest rate risk independent of the absolute amount of the present value. The significance of the modified duration is especially clear when an **evaluation** of the **change** in **present value** is carried out through some mathematical transformations (see Section 4.6), with help from the modified duration, as follows:

Present value change ≈ −1 x mod. duration x current present value x interest rate change

---

Multiplying by a factor of −1 shows the economic fact that interest rate decreases lead to a cash increase and vice versa.

Evaluation of the change in present value using the modified duration for an interest rate increase of 100 basis points gives:

$$\text{Present value change} \approx -1 \times 2.747 \times €\ 974.21 \times 0.01 = \underline{\mathbf{-€\ 26.76}}.$$

If the absolute present value change is divided by the current present value, this gives for the **relative present value change**:

$$\text{Relative present value change} \approx -1 \times 2.747 \times 0.01 = \underline{\mathbf{-2.747\,\%}}.$$

The **exact present value change** was already calculated above at −€ 26.27 (= −2.6975 %) for an interest rate increase of 100 basis points. Thus there is a **margin of error** in the amount of € 0.49. The evaluation using the modified duration has, however, the advantage that some important statements about the interest rate risk can be derived which are not evident from the above calculations of the exact present value change. From the calculation of the modified duration and the evaluation of the present value change and using the latter under the following **conditions**:
- **interest rate changes** are considered to be effective immediately after the current evaluation of the bond and
- for interest rate changes a **parallel shift** in the yield curve is assumed, i. e. the respective interest rates change by the same value for all terms,

then the following basic **properties** of the modified duration can be derived:
- The amount of the modified duration depends on, among other things, the payment structure of the interest-rate position. Long-term payments are weighted more strongly than short-term. High **long-term payments** lead therefore to a sharper **increase** in the modified **duration**. This corresponds to the **compound interest effect,** where the discounting of long-term payments leads to a disproportionately sharper reduction of the present value than it would with a shorter-term discounting of the same amounts.
- The earlier and the higher the **interest payments** on the bond, the smaller the modified duration is.
- An **increase** in the **capital market rates** leads to a decrease in the modified duration. In other words: if an interest rate increase leads to a decrease in the present

value, then the modified duration decreases simultaneously based on the higher interest rate. The higher the interest rate, the smaller the interest rate risk from repeated interest rate changes.

From the above **application** of the present value change **estimation,** with help from the modified duration, the following statements can also be derived about the interest rate risk:
- The higher the modified duration, the higher the change in the present value. Thus the modified duration can be used to **compare** the **risk content** of various **interest positions,** regardless of the absolute amounts of the respective present value.
- With an interest rate change of 100 basis points, the **relative present value change** corresponds exactly to the **modified duration.**
- The **amount** of the **interest rate change** has an immediate effect on the amount of the present value change.
- The **lower** the **interest rates**, the **higher** the modified **duration** usually is, all other things being equal.
- The relationship between the change in present value and the change in interest rate is exactly **inversely** proportional (thus the multiplication by –1 in the above formula). Interest rate increases lead to a drop in present value and vice versa.
- The evaluation of present value change overestimates the drop in present value through interest rate increases and underestimates the rise in present value based on interest rate decreases. The evaluation, therefore, corresponds to the cautionary principle. The **modified duration** is therefore known as the **conservative** (cautious) **estimator** for changes in present value.

The **margin of error**, which always comes up when applying the modified duration to the present value changes, is based on a linearization of the present value function. The modified duration converts the interest rate change linearly to its present value change. The actual present value function, however, has a curved profile due to the compound interest effect. The greater the interest rate change and the stronger the curvature of the present value function, the greater the margin of error.

4.1.1.3 Convexity

The curvature of the present value function is also referred to as convexity. The strength of the curvature can be measured by the **convexity** indicator. At first glance, the consideration of the convexity appears to represent only a computational refinement of the above evaluation using the duration. However, further statements about the interest rate risk can also be derived using the convexity indicator. For this reason the convexity will be briefly described below.

The **convexity** of an interest position is the second derivative of the present value function on the interest rate at the point of the current capital market interest rate, divided by the current present value of this interest position.

The relationship between present value assessment, exact present value change, modified duration and convexity is illustrated in Figure 4.3.

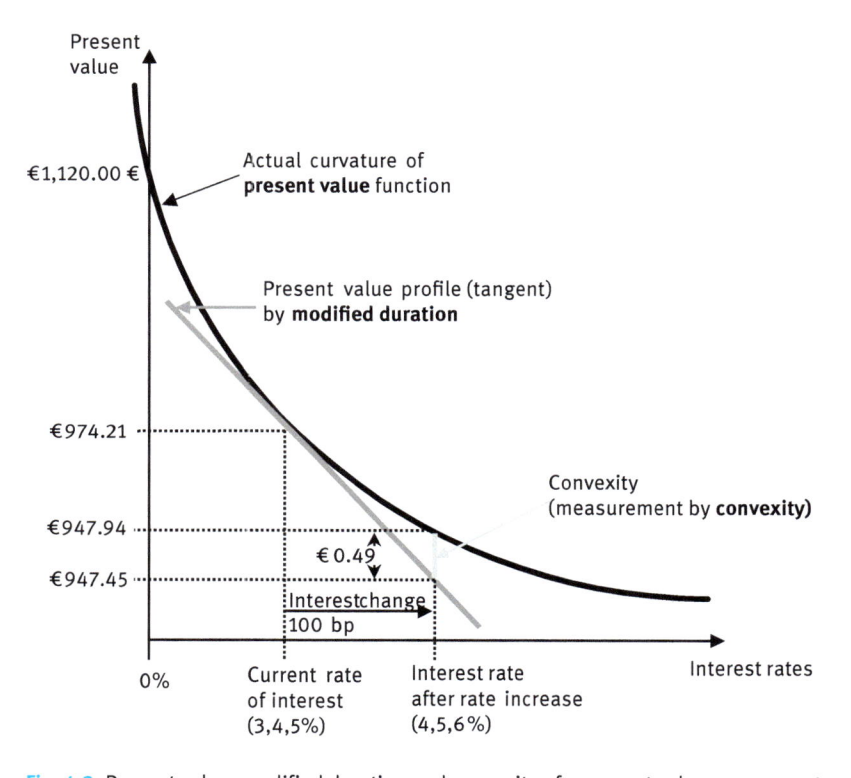

Fig. 4.3: Present value, modified duration and convexity of a present value assessment

The exact present value decrease from € 974.21 to € 947.94 arises from the curved profile of the present value function. The present values assessed over the modified duration represent a straight line (tangent) to the actual present value function, which results in the estimated change to € 947.45. The **present value decrease** is therefore **overestimated by € 0.49** through the modified duration. This overestimate (or conversely also underestimate with interest rate decreases) is all the greater, the stronger the actual curvature of the present value function.

From Figure 4.3 yet another connection becomes discernible, which is important in **overcoming financial crises**. A much debated approach for reviving the economy during and after crisis is an expansive monetary policy with low interest rates (see Section 4.4.2.4). With low interest rates or an interest rate of zero, the present value function has a very steep profile. Interest rate decreases cause a high present value increase but, conversely, interest rate increases trigger a sharp present value decrease. Thus when, because of inflationary tendencies, an **expansive monetary policy** is transformed into a restrictive monetary policy with appropriate interest rate increases, the consequence is correspondingly **high present value losses** for interest-dependent asset positions. Likewise, interest rate changes when the interest rates are already high conversely trigger only minor present value changes. In other words: Figure 4.3 clearly shows that the duration (as a measure of the slope of the present value function) increases with falling interest rates, all other things being equal.

While the modified duration approximately describes the reaction of the present value to interest rate changes, the convexity (C) gives information about how the associated margin of error reacts to interest rate changes, i.e. how strong the curvature of the present value function is. For the computational derivation and mathematical description of convexity, again please refer to the Technical appendix (Section 4.6). For the above example the **convexity** is **calculated** as follows:

$$C = [\mathbf{1 \times 2} \times €\ 40.00 \times 1.03^{-(1+2)} + \mathbf{2 \times 3} \times €\ 40.00 \times 1.04^{-(2+2)} + \mathbf{3 \times 4} \times €\ 1{,}040.00 \times 1.05^{-(3+2)}] /\ €\ 974.21$$
$$= [€\ 73.21 + €\ 205.15 + €\ 9{,}778.41] = €\ 10{,}056.77 / €\ 974.21 = \underline{\mathbf{10.323}}.$$

Convexity is also a dimensionless measure, which can be used for comparison with the curvature of the present value function of different interest positions. The **change in the present value** can be more **precisely evaluated** using the **convexity**.

Using a mathematical transformation (development of a Taylor series) results in the following improved assessment of the present value change in general terms:

Change in present value ≈   −1 x mod. duration x current present value x change in interest rate
+ 0.5 x convexity x current present value x change in interest rate^2

The calculation for the example delivers as a result:

present value change ≈   −1 x 2.747 x € 974.21 x 0.01
+ 0.5 x 10.323 x € 974.21 x 0.01^2 = −€ 26.76 + € 0.50 = **−€ 26.26**

and the relative present value change amounts to:

relative present value change ≈ −1 x 2.747 x 0.01 + 0.5 x 10.323 x 0.01^2 = **−2.696 %**.

The evaluation with convexity is thus much more precise, i. e. instead of a deviation of € 0.49 from the exact present value this now amounts to only € 0.01 (or instead of a relative deviation of 0.05 % it is only 0.001 %). The results of the example calculations are summarized in overview in Table 4.2.

Tab. 4.2: Results of a present value assessment with modified duration and convexity

	Exact calculation:	Evaluation with modified Duration and Convexity (C = 10.323):	Evaluation with modified Duration (D^{mod} = 2.747):
Present value before interest rate change:	€ 974.21	€ 974.21	€ 974.21
Present value after interest rate change:	€ 947.94	€ 947.95	€ 947.45
Absolute change in present value:	–€ 26.27	–€ 26.26	–€ 26.76
Relative change in present value:	– 2.697 %	–2.696 %	–2.747 %

The following **properties** can be determined for the **convexity** indicator:
- The higher the convexity, the **stronger** the **curvature** of the present value function.
- The **lower** the **interest rates**, the **higher** the **convexity**, all other things being equal.
- A much more **precise estimate** of the present value change is possible using convexity as compared to using only the modified duration by itself.
- Bonds with a **higher** (positive) **convexity** are **more advantageous** in the case of interest rate changes than bonds with a smaller convexity. Interest rate decreases result in a higher present value and interest rate increases cause a smaller present value loss.
- A **positive convexity** is always necessary to successful strategies for composing **portfolios** from interest positions.

4.1.1.4 VaR calculation of interest positions

Modified **duration** is not only appropriate for present value estimates and comparison of interest positions, but is also useful for calculating the **value at risk**. Calculation of the VaR is shown in Chapter 2 using stocks as an example. In the case of stocks, a change in the risk factor (=stock price) of e. g. 1% leads directly to a 1% change in the stock. This is not the case with interest positions, since a change to the interest rate risk factor of e. g. +100 bp (one percentage point) does not lead to an increase of one percentage point in the asset position. The asset change, in particular the interest rate position due to an interest rate change, must therefore be converted from an **interest rate change** into an **asset change**. This is exactly what can be achieved with the help of the modified duration.

For **calculating** the **value at risk**, e. g. for the above government bond, the volatility of the corresponding interest rate must first of all be calculated. The risk factors of the government bond are the zero coupon rates for one year, two years and three years maturity.

The issues resulting from multiple risk factors will not be dealt with here (the procedure follows the derivation for the bond portfolios), but instead a **flat yield curve** will be assumed. The number of risk factors can then be reduced, when not only the same amounts but also the same volatilities are assumed for all durations. Possible **correlations** between the interest rates for the different maturities will be **ignored**. For the example, the only risk factor is the zero coupon rate for a three-year duration.

An empirical review will be based on the euro interest rate swap with a three-year term. The year 2005 will again be used as the period for calculating the volatility. First, the **absolute differences** of the daily interest rate changes are calculated, and the volatility determined for these interest rate changes. This approach deviates from the described method for calculating the volatility of stock returns. When calculating volatility for stock price risk, the absolute differences were compared with the stock price of the previous day in order to obtain a relative magnitude. However, interest rates already involve relative sizes. Thus they no longer have to be compared to the previous day's interest rate (= relative interest rate changes). The **volatility** for the **daily absolute rate changes** of the **interest rate** for a **three year term** amounts to **0.032 %** (3.2 basis points), based on the absolute changes in interest rate for the year 2005.

Using the modified duration, the volatility of the daily interest rate changes can be converted into the corresponding present value change. For a liquidation period of 10 days and confidence level of 99 %, the calculation of the VaR for the bond is:

present value: x mod. duration x volatility: x liq. period: x conf. lev.: = **VaR:**
€ 974.21   x 2.747   x 0.032%   x √10   x 2.33   = **€ 6.31**.

The very low value compared to the stocks rests on the significantly smaller price fluctuations of fixed interest securities, which rest on the reliability of future cash flows. That is also why the profit potential is smaller with bonds compared to stocks. The RoRaC (see Section 2.6) is again crucial for a comparison of advantages. In order to apply the RoRaC concept, it is first necessary to consider bond portfolios. Also, consideration of the correlations between interest rates for different maturities and a non-flat yield curve must still be discussed.

The **margin of error** of the modified **duration** also effects the **calculation** of the **VaR**. It can be reduced again using convexity. However, since the effects are small and also the volatility calculation is only an estimate from historical data, this will be omitted.

In practice, a company will frequently buy not just one government bond but generally several bonds. A **bond portfolio** contains a **fixed number** of **fixed income securities** (bonds). The consideration of the effect of bond portfolios on present value, modified duration and VaR is continued for the above example, with the addition to **government bond A** of yet another **zero coupon government bond B** with the following features:
- Face value: € 1,000.00 per unit,
- Nominal volume: 1 unit for € 1,000.00,
- Maturity: 6 years,
- Coupon rate: 0 %! (**zero coupon**),
- Repayment: face value due at maturity,
- Capital market rate: 1 year: 3 %, 2 years: 4 %; 3 years: 5 %; 6 years: 8 %.

First the modified duration and convexity will be calculated for **bond B** as it was in the above calculations for the present value:

present value (PV) $= € 1,000.00 \times 1.08^{-6}$ = **€ 630.17**,
duration (D^{mod}) $= [6 \times € 1,000.00 \times 1.08^{-(6+1)}] / € 630.17$ = **5.556**,
convexity (C) $= [6 \times 7 \times 1.000.00 \times 1.08^{-(6+2)}] / € 630.17$ = **36.008**.

The very much smaller present value of only 63.02 % based on the nominal volume compared to 97.42 % for bond A is due to two important features of interest rate risk. Firstly, the discounting or compound interest effect is greater for B then for A because of the **longer duration** and the **higher interest rate** for 6 years. Apart from that, no **interest** is paid out with B, but rather the return is contained in the **difference** between **nominal volume** and **present value**. This difference must therefore be greater with zero coupon bonds than with comparable coupon bonds. In the case of a fixed nominal volume this can only be done using a lower present value. Using the modified **duration** it is apparent that with the zero coupon bond, the interest rate risk is **double** that of bond A. Based on the convexity, it can be seen that the curvature of the present value function is also much greater for bond B that it is for bond A.

Next, the central question follows of how the **present value, modified duration** and **convexity** can now be calculated for the bond portfolio consisting of bonds A and B. For this there are **two** basic **possibilities**:
- All future contractually agreed payments (cash flow) are additively combined into a total cash flow (so-called **cash flow mapping**). All payments at time one are added up to a new total payment at time one, all payments at time two are added up to a new total payment at time two, and so on. This total cash flow

is then treated almost like a bond with a particular payment structure, and the present value, modified duration and convexity are calculated for this cash flow.
- The **portfolio weighting** is determined using the present value, similar to the procedure with stock portfolios (see Section 2.3.3), and with the help of this weighting the modified duration and convexity for the entire portfolio can be calculated (see Technical appendix Section 4.6).

Both options respectively have a crucial **advantage** and **disadvantage**. Cash flow mapping has the great advantage of a much simpler computational operation. Its great disadvantage is that the aggregated cash flow makes it impossible to draw conclusions directly about the effect of individual bonds on the entire portfolio. With the calculations using the portfolio weighting the situation is exactly reversed. The advantage of the option of analyzing individual bonds in the portfolio counterbalances increased computational complexity.

For the example, the following cash flow mapping results:

1. Year:	2. Year:	3. Year:	4. Year:	5. Year:	6. Year:
+€ 40.00	+€ 40.00	+€ 1,040.00	€ 0.00	€ 0.00	+€ 1,000.00

For this cash flow, the present value, modified duration and convexity can simply be determined similarly to the above calculation method, and this yields the following results:

portfolio PV = € 40.00 x 1.03^{-1} + € 40.00 x 1.04^{-2} + € 1,040.00 x 1.05^{-3} + € 1,000.00 x 1.08^{-6}
= € 974.21 + € 630.17 = **€ 1.604,38**.

portfolio duration = [1 x € 40.00 x $1.03^{-(1+1)}$ + 2 x € 40.00 x $1.04^{-(2+1)}$ + 3 x € 1,040.00 x $1.05^{-(3+1)}$
+ 6 x € 1.000,00 x $1.08^{-(6+1)}$] / € 1,604.38 = **3.850**.

portfolio convexity = [1x2 x € 40.00 x $1.03^{-(1+2)}$ + 2x3 x € 40.00 x $1.04^{-(2+2)}$
+ 3x4 x € 1,040.00 x $1.05^{-(3+2)}$ + 6x7 x € 1,000.00 x $1.08^{-(6+2)}$] / € 1,604.38 = **20.412**.

If the present values of the individual bonds A and B are divided by the total portfolio present value, then it gives the following portfolio weightings (w_A and w_B):

portfolio weighting bond A (w_A) = € 974.21 / € 1,604.38 = **60.72 %**,
portfolio weighting bond B (w_B) = € 974.21 / € 1,604.38 = **39.28 %**.

With the help of the portfolio weightings, the modified duration and convexity for the portfolio can be calculated by multiplying the modified duration and convexity for bonds A and B by their associated portfolio weightings and then adding them up:

$$\text{portfolio duration} = 60.72\% \times 2.747 + 39.28\% \times 5.556 = \mathbf{3.850},$$
$$\text{portfolio convexity} = 60.72\% \times 10.323 + 39.28\% \times 36.008 = \mathbf{20.412}.$$

The values agree with the results of the cash flow mapping. However, it now becomes immediately clear from the description of the portfolio duration that the cause of the interest rate risk lies with B, which is not directly recognizable from the cash flow mapping. Table 4.3 summarizes the results for the present value, modified duration and convexity of the individual bonds and the entire portfolio.

Tab. 4.3: Present value, modified duration and convexity of a bond portfolio

	Bond A:	Bond B:	Bond portfolio (A+B):
Present value:	€ 974.21	€ 630.17	€ 1,604.38
Duration:	2.747	5.556	3.850
Convexity:	10.323	36.008	20.412

Using the portfolio duration and portfolio convexity, the **present value change** of the **portfolio** can now be easily **estimated** for a parallel shift of the yield curve by 100 basis points, as follows (for the application of duration and convexity to **non-parallel shifts** in the rate structure, see the literature references in Section 4.5):

$$\text{portfolio present value change} \approx -1 \times 3.850 \times €1,604.38 \times 0.01$$
$$+ 0.5 \times 20.412 \times €1,604.38 \times 0.01^2 = -€61.77 + €1.64$$
$$= \mathbf{-€60.13}.$$

Along with the present value assessment for the portfolio, there is now the question of how the **bond portfolio's VaR** can be calculated as a function of several influencing factors. The influencing factors are the **maturity-dependent interest rates**, which **correlate** more or less strongly with each other.

A simpler approach is to assume a **completely positive correlation** between the maturities and consider the volatilities for the individual maturities. Along with the above-mentioned volatility of 0.032% for the three-year maturity, the total required volatilities of the daily interest rate changes for the various maturities amount to:

1 year: **0.019%**; 2 years: **0.029%**; 3 years: **0.032%**; 6 years: **0.035%**.

Then the VaR can be calculated for every maturity from the present values for the individual maturities, as already described above in simplified form for bond A, as follows:

VaR = present value x mod. duration x volatility x liquidation per. x level of confidence.

Since the calculation is carried out in isolation for each maturity separately, the expression "present value x modified duration" is yet further simplified to:

(present value x number of years (of the respective maturity)) / (1 + interest rate of the maturity).

The calculation of the VaR for the individual years is given in Table 4.4.

Tab. 4.4: Calculation of the individual VaR of a bond portfolio

Maturity (number of years):	Present value x number of years:	x (1 + interest rate)⁻¹:	x Level of confidence x Liquidation period:	x Volatility:	= VaR:
1	€ 38.84 x 1	x 1.03⁻¹	x 2.33 x √10	x 0.019 %	= **€ 0.05**
2	€ 36.98 x 2	x 1.04⁻¹	x 2.33 x √10	x 0.029 %	= **€ 0.15**
3	€ 898.39 x 3	x 1.05⁻¹	x 2.33 x √10	x 0.032 %	= **€ 6.05**
6	€ 630.17 x 6	x 1.08⁻¹	x 2.33 x √10	x 0.035 %	= **€ 9.03**

The sum of the individual VaR gives an amount of **€ 15.28** for the **entire portfolio VaR**, taking into account different volatilities for interest rates of different maturities. However, this assumes a **completely positive correlation** of interest rates between the durations. Possible **diversification effects** are thus **ignored**.

In order to take into account possible correlations between the changes to different interest rates, the procedure is similar to that described for the portfolio VaR in Section 2.3.3. There, the VaR is calculated or the procedure clarified using a stock portfolio consisting of two stocks, BMW and MAN. In the above bond portfolio, however, there are not two risk factors but four (interest rates). For four risk factors, a manageable description of the computations is no longer possible. For a technical representation of the VaR calculation for more than two risk factors, see the Technical appendix from Chapter 6 (6.6). For this reason, the sample calculation to illustrate **correlations** between two interest rates is based on a **simpler portfolio**. This portfolio should have the following features:

- The portfolio consists of only two bonds or payments 1 and 2. There is a return of € 100.00 after one year, and also a return of € 100.00 after two years (so two zero coupon bonds with 1 year and 2 years maturity and a repayment of € 100.00 respectively).
- The current interest rates for calculation of the present value amount to 3 % for one year and 4 % for two years, as above.
- The volatility of the daily interest rate change adds up to 0.019 % for a one year term and to 0.029 % for two years.
- The correlations between the interest rate changes from one year and two year terms come to +0.7.

Analogously to the above procedure, the following results then emerge

PV of the portfolio = € 100.00 x 1.03^{-1} + € 100.00 x 1.04^{-2} = € 97.09 + € 92.45 = **€ 189.54**, portfolio weightings (w_1, w_2): w_1 = € 97.09 / € 189.54 = **51.22 %**; w_2 = **48.78 %**, modified duration (D^{mod}_1, D^{mod}_2, D^{mod}_p): D^{mod}_1 1 / 1.03 = **0.971**; D^{mod}_2 2 / 1.04 = **1.923**; D^{mod}_p = 51.22 % x 0.9709 + 48.78 % x 1.923 = **1.435**.

For a confidence level of 99 % and a liquidation period of 10 days, using a method similar to the one above without taking the correlations into account, we get the following values for the individual VaR:

$$VaR_1 = € 97.09 \times 0.971 \times 2.33 \times \sqrt{10} \times 0.019\% = \mathbf{€\ 0.13},$$
$$VaR_2 = € 92.45 \times 1.923 \times 2.33 \times \sqrt{10} \times 0.029\% = \mathbf{€\ 0.38}.$$

The simple sum gives a VaR of **€ 0.51** for the portfolio. The correlation between the interest rate changes is considered using only two interest rates, by means of the portfolio volatility s_p for the portfolio consisting of both bonds (payments 1 and 2):

$$s_p = \sqrt{w_1^2 \cdot s_1^2 + w_2^2 \cdot s_2^2 + 2 \cdot w_1 \cdot w_2 \cdot k_{1,2} \cdot s_1 \cdot s_2}$$
$$= \sqrt{0.5122^2 \cdot 0.00019^2 + 0.4878^2 \cdot 0.00029^2 + 2 \cdot 0.5122 \cdot 0.4878 \cdot 0.7 \cdot 0.00019 \cdot 0.00029}$$
$$= \mathbf{0.022\%}.$$

Using the portfolio's volatility, duration and present value, the portfolio VaR can now be calculated using the portfolio volatility, taking the correlation into account:

$$VaR_p = € 189.54 \times 1.435 \times 2.33 \times \sqrt{10} \times 0.022\% = \mathbf{€\ 0.44}.$$

The **diversification effect** then amounts to € 0.51 − € 0.44 = **€ 0.07**. The difference with **bond portfolios** compared to stock portfolios always consists in the conversion of interest rate changes into the associated present value changes using the modified **duration**. In the process the modified duration's margin of error is acceptable.

4.1.1.5 Immunization of bond portfolios

Risk control of a **bond portfolio** can be carried out in various ways. On the one hand, opposite positions can be developed in the form of interest rate swaps, interest rate options or interest rate futures for **risk compensation** (for general functioning, see Section 3.4). On the other hand, the **risk** can be **distributed**.

With risk distribution (see Section 3.3), so-called immunization strategies are applied to bond portfolios. Immunization means that the present value is immune to interest rate changes, so it is protected. There are two fundamentally different approaches to immunization strategies:
- immunization of the present value,
- immunization of the end value.

The idea of **immunizing** the **present value** is based on the above-derived estimate of a change in the present value through interest rate changes using duration and convexity:

change in present value ≈ −1 x mod. duration x current p. v. x change in interest rate
+ 0.5 x convexity x current p. v. x change in interest rate^2.

Immunization means that no present value decrease takes place through a change in interest rates. It can be directly derived from the estimate that this can only be the case when the modified **duration** is **zero**. Since the modified duration is a measure of the amount of the interest rate risk, this conclusion is immediately obvious. A modified duration of zero can be achieved in two ways:
- An interest position with a **duration** of **zero** or near zero is included the portfolio. This is possible through short-term money market instruments (e. g. with an interest rate equal to the 3-month EURIBOR). Due to the short term adjustment of the interest rate there is (almost) no interest rate risk, but only a correspondingly lower interest rate (profit) is afforded. When certain goals are pursued with a bond portfolio, such as e. g. long-term high yearly payments, this strategy is not suitable.
- With long-term payments through the purchase of bonds, these can be offset by issuing bonds (**selling of bonds**) and thus a **portfolio can be constructed** which has a modified duration of zero despite higher interest payments. This approach is a strategy often considered by banks. Since the construction of such a portfolio is subject to very many restrictions (especially due to the transaction costs as a result of the necessary restructuring of the portfolio) and often can only

be achieved by banks, this strategy and in particular the construction of such a portfolio will not be explored further (see References in Section 4.5).

The application of immunizing the present value requires yet another condition. It is also evident from the estimate of the present value change that with a modified duration of zero and a (normally) positive present value, the convexity must be positive, since otherwise a present value decrease could arise from a negative convexity. This condition was already mentioned above under the properties of convexity and is further clarified in connection with the immunization of the present value in Figure 4.4.

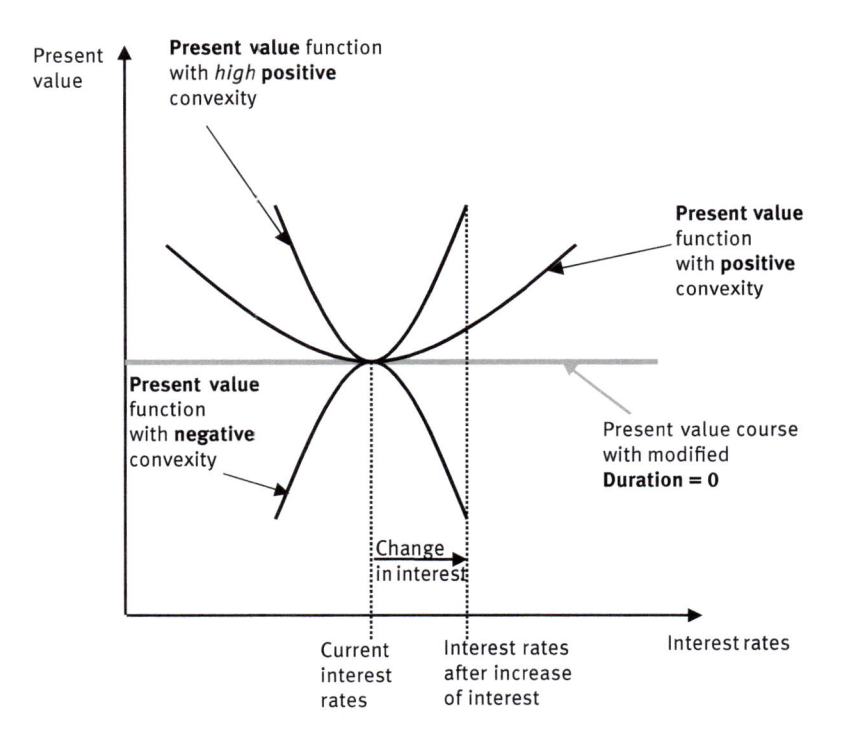

Fig. 4.4: Convexity in the immunization of the present value

The present value is based on the modified duration, so if modified duration is zero, then the course of the present value is horizontal (slope of zero). An interest rate change would at first glance have no effect on the present value. With a negative convexity the present value would, however, decrease with every interest rate change. By contrast, a positive convexity would cause a present value increase in every case. The higher the positive convexity, the higher the present value increase. For a **successful**

immunization, a **positive convexity** is also required along with the modified duration of zero.

The **immunization** of the **end value** is based on the characteristics of the Macaulay duration.

The **Macaulay duration** is the weighted average capital commitment of an interest position or bond portfolio in years

---

The calculation of the Macaulay duration ($= D^{Mac}$) is done by multiplying the discounted payment by the **number of years** over which the payment is made. The sum of these products is then divided by the current present value. Because the discounting is not carried out for the number of years +1, the discounted payments are weighted by the number of years. Therefore the units of the Macaulay duration can also be given in years. For the above bonds A and B the Macaulay duration amounts to:

D^{Mac}_A = *[1 x € 40.00 x 1.03⁻¹ + 2 x € 40.00 x 1.04⁻² + 3 x € 1,040. x 1.05⁻³] / € 974.21*
  = *[€ 38.84 + € 73.96 + € 2,695.17] / € 974.21 = € 2,807.97 / € 974.21 = **2.882 (years)**.*
D^{Mac}_B = *6 x € 1,000.00 x 1.08⁻⁶ / € 630.17 = **6.000 (years)**.*

The Macaulay duration of the zero coupon bond B corresponds exactly to the term of the zero coupon bond, because no payments occur before the end of the maturity. The Macaulay duration is also interpreted as an **average capital commitment period**.

The McCauley duration enables the immunization of the end value of a financial security against interest rate changes.

The **end value** of a financial security (or a portfolio) is **immune to interest rate changes** if the investor's planning horizon corresponds exactly to the financial security's Macaulay duration.

The main application of immunizing the end value thus lies with businesses and/or projects that are **time limited**.

The **basic idea** relies on the results of a change in interest rates: increasing interest rates cause a lower present value of the financial, while at the same time interest payments can be invested again at a higher interest rate. When the end value is immunized, both effects of an interest rate change overcompensate each other, so that the planned end value forms a lower limit! For the financial mathematical proof of the immunization, please see the relevant literature in Section 4.5. Through the choice of appropriate financials with regard to duration and portfolio holdings (measured by the ratio of the individual present value to the portfolio present value), the investor or business can immunize any portfolio for a specific planning horizon.

For the example portfolio containing bonds A and B, assuming that an immunization is desired for a **planning horizon** of **5 years**, the weightings w_A and w_B are sought such that:

$$w_A \times D^{Mac}_A + w_B \times D^{Mac}_B = \text{planning horizon} = 5.$$

The portfolio's Macaulay duration, weighted with the individual portfolio stocks, must correspond to the planning horizon with immunization. Since the total of the portfolio weightings must yield one, the **calculation** of the **weightings** can also be put in the form (for the derivation see Section 4.6):

$$w_A = (5 - D^{Mac}_B) / (D^{Mac}_A - D^{Mac}_B) \text{ and } w_B = 1 - w_A.$$

If the above values for the Macaulay duration are plugged into this equation, it delivers

$$w_A = (5 - 6) / (2{:}882 - 6) = \underline{\mathbf{32.07\,\%}} \text{ and } w_B = 1 - w_A = \underline{\mathbf{67.93\,\%}}.$$

This weighting refers, as mentioned above, to the present value of the interest position and not to the nominal volume. The new present value amounts can now be **converted** into the associated **nominal volumes**, by multiplying the old portfolio present value by the new weighting, so:

$$\text{Bond A: } €\,1{,}604.38 \,€ \times 32.07\,\% = \underline{\mathbf{€\,514.52}},$$
$$\text{Bond B: } €\,1{,}604.38 \times 67.93\,\% = \underline{\mathbf{€\,1{,}089.86}}.$$

These new present values can then be converted into the associated nominal volumes by dividing them by their current respective (present value) prices:

$$\text{Bond A: } €\,514.52 \,/\, \text{present value: } 97.42\,\% = \underline{\mathbf{€\,528.15}},$$
$$\text{Bond B: } €\,1{,}089.86 \,/\, \text{present value: } 63.02\,\% = \underline{\mathbf{€\,1{,}729.38}}.$$

If the portfolio is restructured according to the newly determined weightings, this delivers a new aggregated cash flow for the entire portfolio as compared to the original portfolio of:

	1. Year:	2. Year:	3. Year:	6. Year:
Old portfolio:	+€ 40.00	+€ 40.00	+€ 1,040.00	+€ 1,000.00
New portfolio:	+€ 21.13	+€ 21.13	+ € 549.28	+€ 1,729.38
	(= 4 % of € 528.15)		(=€ 21.13 + € 528.15).	

For **calculating** the portfolio's **end value** in five years, the payments of the first through third years are compounded at the fifth year using the corresponding **forward interest rates**, and the payment of the sixth year is discounted to the fifth year. The description of the calculation of the forward interest rates will be omitted, since the calculations are quite extensive and complex and produce no useful gain in knowledge for the further discussion. The forward interest rates are automatically determined when calculating zero coupon interest from existing capital market coupons. As already stated above, reference should be made to the corresponding literature, especially to the so-called **bootstrap method** (see Section 4.5).

With an **interest rate increase** in the maturity-linked interest rates of e. g. 100 basis points respectively, the sum of the compounded payments at the higher interest rates in the first three years will be larger for the immunized portfolio than the loss due to discounting the payment from the sixth year at the higher rate. It results in a new end value which is at least as large as the old one.

Both the **immunization** of the present value as well as the immunization of the end value have considerable **disadvantages** as **instruments** for controlling **interest rate risk**.
- Both immunization strategies require a one-off interest rate change immediately after the evaluation. In practice, however, interest rate changes happen all the time, which would result in a permanent restructuring of the portfolio.
- Beyond that, immunizing the present value has the disadvantage that combining corresponding immunized portfolios is quite difficult, especially for non-banks.
- On the other hand, immunization of the end value is only suitable for temporary projects or companies with a limited lifespan. However, in business practice most companies have unlimited lifespans.

Because of these disadvantages of immunization strategies and the importance of interest rate risk, the functioning of risk compensation of the interest rate risk through **interest rate swaps**, **interest rate options** and **interest rate futures** will be discussed below.

4.1.1.6 Interest rate swaps

An **interest rate swap** represents a contractually agreed exchange of several future different interest payment streams between two contractual parties. The swap agreement refers only to the interest payments, the associated nominal volumes are not exchanged.

With an interest rate swap, one party (e. g. company A) wants to exchange **fixed interest payments** against **variable interest payments** with another partner. The fixed interest payments are based on bonds with a long maturity and the variable interest rates refer to the short-term (e. g. 3 months) money market securities with an interest rate that is oriented toward EURIBOR. The **default risk** for **swap partners**, i. e. when one partner can no longer make the payments because of insolvency, is not taken into account in the following discussion.

The following example illustrates the functioning of the **comparative advantage** and interest rate swap for the two companies A and B. A and B can borrow on the capital market at the following respective interest rates:

	Fixed interest rate:	Variable interest rate (3 months):
A:	6.5 % p. a.	EURIBOR+0.5 %
B:	5.0 % p. a.	EURIBOR

At first glance, a profitable contract between A and B does not seem possible, since A must pay a higher interest rate for both the fixed and variable interest rates. The comparative advantage is that the **interest rate differences** are at respectively **different** levels for the various types of financing. That is the case here. While the fixed rate disparity amounts to **150 basis points**, the variable interest rate disparity adds up to **50 basis points**. **Company A** has a **comparative advantage** over company B with the variable interest rate, since A has to pay 150 basis points more for the fixed interest rate as compared to only 50 points more for the variable interest rate. Conversely, B has a comparative price advantage over A with the fixed interest rate, because B pays 150 basis points there while B is only 50 basis points lower with the variable interest rate. Both sides can use these advantages by agreeing, for example, to the following interest rate swap.

- The **nominal volume** is set at **€ 1 mill.** for A and B respectively. This amount is not exchange, but rather merely serves as the basis for the calculation.
- The **maturity** of the swap is **10 years**.
- **A pays** B a yearly **fixed interest rate** of 5.5 % (= € 55,000.00) on January 2.
- Likewise, on January 2, **B pays** A an annual **EURIBOR**-established variable interest based on the nominal volume. If the EURIBOR amounts to e. g. 3 % on January 2, then B pays A € 30,000.00.

The comparative advantages can now be used if A borrows on the capital market at EURIBOR plus 0.5 %, and B procures the same amount on the capital market at a fixed rate of 5 % per annum. The resulting cash flows are shown graphically in Figure 4.5, as with the general account of a swap in Section 3.4.4 (see Figure 3.10).

Company A pays EURIBOR for the borrowed funds [1] plus 50 basis points [4]. At the same time, A pays B the fixed interest rate and the amount of 5.5 % p. a. [2] and receives from B in return the EURIBOR [3]. So in total, A pays a fixed 6 % per annum (EURIBOR + 5 % – 5.5 %). Company A would normally have to pay a fixed interest rate of 6.5 %, i. e., A has achieved an **advantage** of **0.5 %** through the interest rate swap.

Company B pays A for the borrowed funds at a fixed interest rate of 5 % and at the same time the variable interest rate EURIBOR [3]. So in total, B pays EURIBOR minus 50 basis points (EURIBOR + 5% − 5.5%) for the borrowed funds. Normally, B would have to pay EURIBOR for the borrowed funds. So, B likewise achieves an **advantage** of **0.5%** through the interest rate swap.

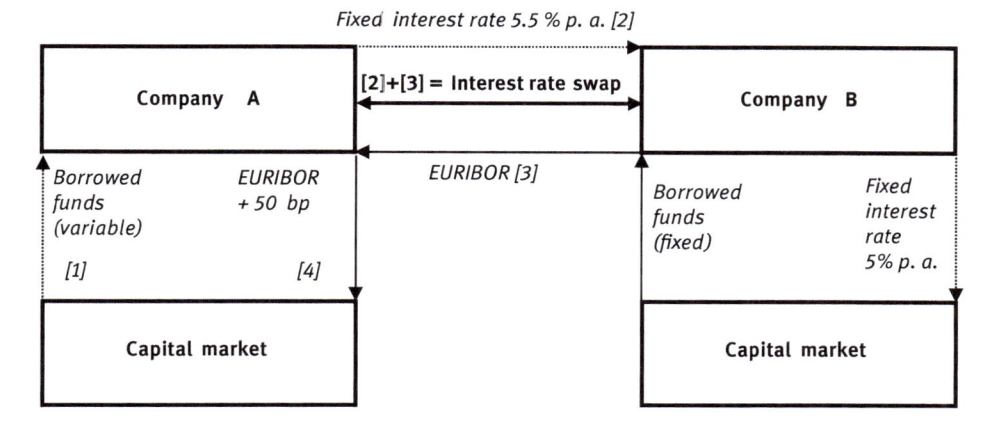

Fig. 4.5: Example of the functioning of an interest rate swap

Thus in this case the **overall advantage** from the various financing options amounts to 1% or 100 bp, **half** of which is distributed to each party. The entire advantage arises from the disparity between the differences in conditions for the fixed interest rates and the variable interest rates (6.5% − 5% = 1.5% and EURIBOR + 0.5% − EURIBOR = 0.5%; the gap between 1.5% and 0.5% gives the total advantage).

How this advantage between the parties is distributed depends on the respective **negotiating positions**. If, for example, company A is in a better negotiating position compared to B, then this could be reflected in A only paying B a fixed interest rate of 5.3% per annum. The advantage for B would then only amount to 0.3% and for A, in contrast, to 0.7%. Nonetheless overall it would still remain at 1% (100 bp).

Along with the negotiating position, the **expectations** of the contractual parties regarding the **future interest rate developments** still plays a role in the design of the interest rate swap. Thus, in the above example, company A will expect rising interest rates (since A will then receive a higher EURIBOR rate and will continue to pay only 5.5%) and B, on the other hand, will count on falling interest rates (since B continues to receive 5.5% but only has to pay a smaller EURIBOR rate). This motivation to close specific swaps has a rather **speculative character** and will not be dealt with further.

Swaps are of greater importance for **control** in **risk management**, for example, if the cash flows from a swap are used to avoid an interest rate risk resulting from original customer transactions. The following **example** will be taken to clarify this possible application of swaps:

Let's assume that company A is the financing company of a car manufacturer. Its customers have granted **loans** to A, with a **fixed interest rate** of 7% and with a maturity of 10 years, for financing car purchases. Company A refinances these loans through the above-mentioned funds borrowed on the capital market at EURIBOR plus 0.5 %. Without closing the above described interest rate swap, A would have an **interest rate risk** if the EURIBOR rate rose, since then the difference to the fixed interest rate of the loan would decrease from 7 %. By closing the interest rate swap, company A always has a constant profit of 1 % without any interest rate risk. This profit margin results from the difference between the fixed interest rate of 7 % minus the interest rate payment from the swap of 5.5 % and minus the premium for the variable refinancing on the capital market in the amount of 0.5 %. Because of this possibility, interest rate swaps in commercial (banking) practice are very popular. The relationship is graphically illustrated in Figure 4.6.

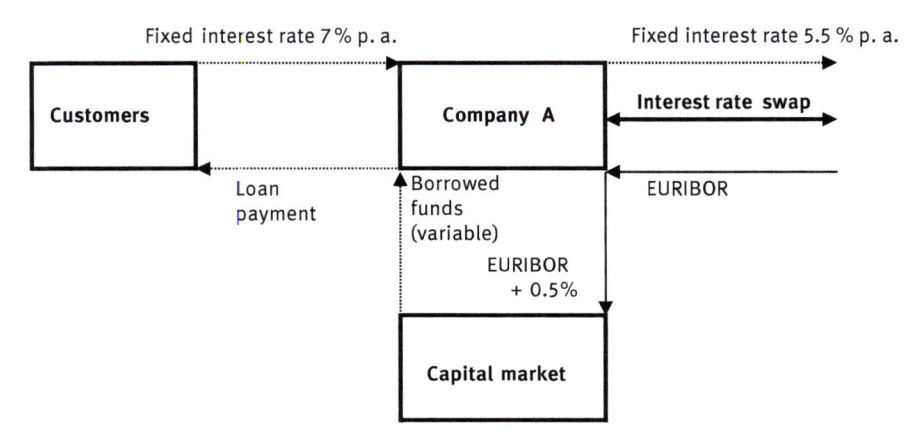

Fig. 4.6: Application of an interest rate swap as a control instrument in risk management

Along with interest rate swaps, interest rate options can also be applied to compensate interest rate risk.

4.1.1.7 Interest rate options

The basic principles discussed in detail in Section 3.4.2 apply to the **functioning** of **interest rate options**. With regard to the **base position** of interest rate options, there are different design possibilities, of which the following four types are important:
1. Options on the purchase or sale of interest positions (e. g. **government bonds**),
2. Options on the later transactions of **interest rate dependent derivatives**, such as e. g. interest rate swaps (so-called swaptions or swap options) or interest rate futures (bund future),
3. Options on an **interest rate upper limit** for variable interest rate positions (so-called caps),

4. Options on an **interest rate lower limit** for variable interest-rate positions (so called floors).

For application in risk management to control interest rate risks, which can arise through e. g. the purchase of government bonds, the first type of interest rate option plays the most important role. The immediate **effects** of an interest rate option is illustrated using the example of a put option purchase (long-put) based on the underlying asset of a government bond. The above government bond A will be used again as the underlying asset
- Nominal volume: € 100.00 per unit,
- Maturity: 3 years,
- Coupon rate: 4 % p. a. annual dividend.

With the current capital market interest rates (1 year: 3 %, 2 years: 4 %, 3 years: 5 %), the bond has a present value of PV = € 97.42. With the put option, the right is acquired to sell this bond in three months at an exercise price of E = € 97.00. The option premium amounts to P = € 0.50. The purchaser uses the put option to hedge against falling prices due to **climbing capital market interest rates**. Potential profit opportunities due to falling interest rates are at the same time maintained. The associated profit and loss profile for the government bond plus the put option is represented in Figure 4.7.

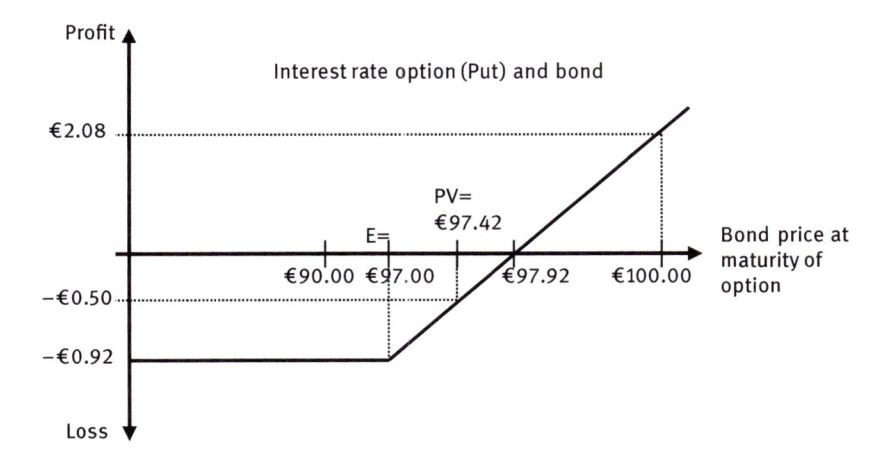

Fig. 4.7: Profit and loss profile of an interest rate option (put) and the associated bond

With **falling interest rates** and rising prices, the bond will achieve a profit when its value rises above a market value (price) of € 97.92. With **rising interest rates** and a price under € 97.00, the **loss** will be limited to a total of € 0.92 (€ 0.50 option premium and price loss from current price (present value) and exercise price of € 97.42 – € 97.00 = € 0.42).

Figure 4.7 assumes a constant option premium over time, i. e. only the option's **intrinsic value** is taken into account, which results from the difference between the base position price and the exercise price. The **fair value** of the interest rate option is **ignored**.

From the definition and functioning of interest rate options, the following **special properties** of **interest rate options** compared to general properties of options (see Section 3.4.2) can be derived:
- When **determining** the **fair value** of an interest rate option, there are particular difficulties with determining the change to individual interest rates, the yield curve and the correlations of the interest rates to each other, as well as their effects on the fair value.
- When **analyzing stock options** (or foreign exchange positions) the fluctuation of the stock prices is in the foreground. For other influencing factors, such as e. g. the risk free interest rate, therefore, a simplifying time constant could be assumed. When analyzing the interest rate options, this is not possible anymore because of interest rate sensitivity, which means that special **consideration** must be given to the **fluctuating volatilities** of interest rates. This hampers analysis of interest rate options.
- Over time, the bond's remaining **maturity** decreases automatically. The key feature of maturity for evaluating the underlying asset thus automatically varies between the time of the option purchase and the time of the option's exercise or maturity.
- Within the time limit of the interest rate position (maturity, remaining term) there is a further peculiarity of interest rate options. If the bond redemption amounts to 100, then it becomes clear immediately that as the maturity decreases the **fluctuation** of the **bond price drops** more and more, since the sure repayment of 100 becomes ever more probable (so-called pull to par effect). On the day of maturity, the volatility must ultimately amount to zero.

The issue with the time limitation of bonds or automatically decreasing duration is remedied in the case of standardized **interest rate futures**, in which a **theoretical bond** is constructed as the underlying asset whose **maturity** is always **the same**.

4.1.1.8 Interest rate futures

Interest rate futures will be discussed in various versions. On the one hand, so-called **OTC** (over the Counter) contracts are transacted in which individual agreements are made in order to take into account the different needs of the contractual parties. These freely negotiated contracts will not be further explored since they are basically agreed between banks or financial intermediaries, and are thus not suitable for wide application in risk management for non-banks. The **Euro-Bund-Future** (shortened to the Bund-Future) is by contrast especially appropriate for a wide range of risk management applications.

The **Bund-Future** is an exchange-traded, standardized forward transaction with the obligation to buy or sell a specific nominal volume of a synthetic German government bond on a specific date.

The standardized Bund-Future is characterized by the following **features**:
- A government bond serves as a synthetic bond with an **interest rate coupon** of 6 % and a **maturity** of exactly **10 years**.
- The standardized **settlement dates** are March 10, June 10, September 10 and December 10 respectively, with the next three delivery dates always available (so three, six and nine months maturity).
- The futures price for the synthetic bond is permanently traded on the stock exchange.
- Due to its standardization, the Bund-Future has a **high liquidity** on the exchanges.
- The transaction between the contracting parties is carried out by a **clearing house,** which guarantees the settlement and completion.
- The futures contracts are **evaluated daily** and any gains or losses must be settled up immediately via the clearing house.
- The synthetic bond is traded in place of actual deliverable bonds with a maturity between 8.5 and 10.5 years. So-called **conversion factors** (also called price factors) are used to link the synthetic bonds and the actually deliverable bonds.
- A futures contract always refers to a **nominal volume** of **€ 1 mill.**
- A futures contract can be closed (neutralized) every day by transacting an **offsetting position**.

The **functioning** and possible application of a Bund-Future for risk management will be illustrated in the following **example**:

A company has purchased investment goods in the amount of € 1 mill. Since the purchase price is payable in 6 weeks, these funds are invested in a government bond with a maturity of 10 years. The purchase price of the bond amounts to 98 %. To protect against the interest rate risk of this bond, **a futures contract** (€ 1 mill.) is **sold** at a future price of **97.90 %**. After six weeks, the **interest rates** have **risen** by 50 basis points, which means that the futures price (maturity price) has dropped to 97.45 % and the bond is listed at 97.50 %.

Through closing the futures contract, the company gets paid a profit of € 4,500.00 (97.90 % − 97.45 % based on a nominal volume of € 1 mill.). At the same time, the sale of the **bond** will result in a **loss** against the purchase price of € 5,000.00 (98.00 % − 97.50 % based on a nominal volume of € 1 mill.). The loss from the sale of the bond will then be in large part compensated by the Bund-Future, which suffers a total loss of only € 500 (the difference of € 500 is based on the **interest rate sensitivities** between actual bonds and the synthetic bond of Bund-Futures).

Conversely, in the case of falling interest rates the company would likewise have to balance a loss from the Bund-Future that would offset the simultaneous profit from the sale of the bond. In **consequence**, the following **properties** can be established from the risk management perspective:
- Bund-Future contracts are appropriate for **hedging** against **price losses** of existing bonds.
- At the same time, potential **price gains** are **sacrificed**, since these would likewise be offset by corresponding losses of the futures contracts.
- Due to high liquidity and their flexibility (possibility of daily settlement or closing out), Bund-Futures are a suitable instrument for **hedging existing bond portfolios**.
- Through the use of Bund-Futures, existing liquid funds can also be invested for short periods at higher interest rates (than would be possible through short-term money market securities) using coupon income from long-term bonds.

With that, the most important aspects of interest-rate risk are discussed. The following section will deal with exchange rate risk, which is likewise a very significant market price risk.

4.1.2 Exchange rate risk

After interest rate risk, exchange rate risk plays an important role, especially for **export-** or **import-oriented national economies**. German companies especially, with their high export stock, are strongly affected by exchange rate risk.

Exchange rate risk is defined as the negative deviation from a planned target (assets, profit) due to uncertain future developments in exchange rates.

4.1.2.1 Foundations of exchange rate risk

When using control instruments in the framework of exchange rate risk management, various **types** of **exchange rate risks** must be distinguished, to which various instruments are then assigned. The various types of exchange rate risk include the following forms:
- **Strategic exchange rate risk** arises due to fundamental exchange rate changes, which can permanently endanger future competitive abilities of export-oriented domestic companies. With strategic exchange rate risk, the long-term nature and stability of a specific exchange rate level are in the foreground.
- **Translation risks** are risks that result from currency conversion by international firms. These deal merely with asset-related conversion risks which are visible, for

example, in the preparation of a consolidated (world) balance sheet. It does not involve, however, exchange rate risk in the classical sense of the above definition. The firm as a whole suffers **no damage** through exchange rate changes, but only within the firm do specific positions shift through the evaluation of changed exchange rates.
- **Transaction risks** include open foreign currency positions, which can lose value through changes in the exchange rate. Transaction risks also include term risks (also called swap rate risks in the case of exchange rate risk), which may arise due to timing differences between various foreign-currency positions. With transaction risks, the short-term nature and volatility of the exchange rates are in the foreground.

When analyzing and controlling exchange rate risk, the following **features** must be taken into account and premises established:
- With the introduction of the euro on January 1, 1999 (cash launch on January 1, 2002) **price quotation (also called direct quotation)** was changed to **quantity quotation (also called indirect quotation)**. Before the euro launch, for example, the Deutschmark was quoted against the dollar in the form DM 2.40 / US-$ 1 as the exchange rate. The price of the US dollar amounted to DM 2.40, thus **price quotation**. Since the introduction of the euro, the US dollar is quoted in the form of one US-$ 1.20 / € 1. One euro (domestic currency unit) gives a quantity of US-$ 1.20 in foreign currency, thus quantity quotation. For all further explanations in this book, the **quantity or indirect quotation** will be used and the **euro** will be the **domestic currency** basis.
- For **measurement** of **exchange rate risk**, a distinction will be made between the currency position (currency exposure) and exchange rate volatilities.
- The **currency position** is defined as the number of foreign exchange exposures which are open in terms of time and/or amount in foreign currency units.
- The fluctuation of the exchange rates (**exchange rate volatilities**) influences the value of a currency position. The exchange rates form on the financial markets based on, among other things, economic influencing factors and thus cannot be controlled by companies, but are rather exogenous quantities from the business perspective.
- The **volatilities** of individual exchange rates may fluctuate.
- The **correlations** between the exchange rates of different currencies may change.

The various types of exchange rate risk and the associated risk management control instruments are shown in overview in Figure 4.8.

```
                    ┌─────────────────────────┐
                    │ Types of exchange rate risk │
                    │   and control instruments   │
                    └─────────────────────────┘
                                │
          ┌─────────────────────┼─────────────────────┐
          ▼                     ▼                     ▼
    ┌───────────┐         ┌──────────────┐      ┌──────────────┐
    │ Strategic │         │ Translation risks │  │ Transaction risks │
    │ exchange rate risk │ └──────────────┘      └──────────────┘
    └───────────┘                                      │
          │                                            ▼
          ▼
```

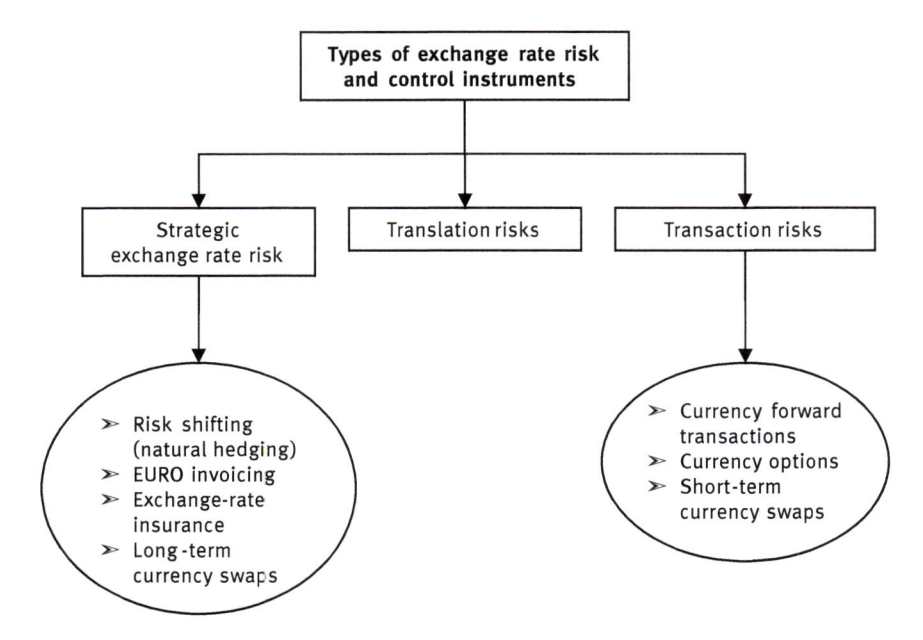

- Risk shifting (natural hedging)
- EURO invoicing
- Exchange-rate insurance
- Long-term currency swaps

- Currency forward transactions
- Currency options
- Short-term currency swaps

Fig. 4.8: Types of exchange rate risk and associated control instruments

The analysis and control of **strategic exchange rate risk** will be illustrated in the following **example**:

Auto SE builds cars in Germany and sells them predominantly in the USA (export) under the following conditions:
– The **sales price** in Europe amounts to € 20,000 per auto. In the USA this corresponds to a current exchange rate of US-$ 1.15 / € 1 for a planned sales price of US-$ 23,000 (US-$ 20,000 x 1.15).
– With a sales price of € 20,000 the **profit margin** in Germany amounts to € 3,000.

A strategic appreciation of the euro would mean a **long-term sustained increase** in the exchange rate to, for example, US-$ 1.30 / € 1 and would have the following consequences:
– If because of the market situation in the USA the cars could only be sold for US-$ 23,000 each, then due to **appreciation** this value in Germany would only amount to € 17,692.31 (US-$ 23,000 / 1.30).
– The **damage** for Auto SE would consist in a reduction in the profit margin from € 3,000 to only € 692.31 (€ 17,692.31 – € 17,000 €)!
– Alternatively, Auto SE could try to get a **higher sales price** of US-$ 26,000 (in order to get an equivalent of US-$ 26,000 / 1.30 = € 20,000 again), in so far as this

would be possible in terms of the market and competition, or would be strategically desired at all.

One possibility for managing the strategic exchange rate risk is **risk shifting** of whole value chains from purchasing to distribution into the respective foreign currency zone (usually a US-$ currency zone). In that case revenues obtained in US-$ are used in order to finance goods manufacturing (wages, supplies, materials and so on) in the foreign-currency country in the same currency (US-$). This form of foreign exchange risk shifting is therefore also called **natural hedging** (see Section 3.3). This concept is also based on the potential to buy raw materials that are invoiced based on US-$ more cheaply when the euro appreciates.

This form of risk management also has, nonetheless, a crucial **disadvantage**. Thus the question of earnings appropriation arises. If the profit gained in US-$ is kept in the outsourced company organization, then there is only a **translation risk** when preparing the consolidated balance sheet. If the profits, however, are exchanged for EURO, then an **exchange rate risk arises** again and the original exchange rate risk was not completely eliminated, but was simply limited to the amount of the profit transfer. However, the exchange rate risk is also not completely eliminated when the US-$ profits are kept, rather it is merely postponed until they are exchanged back into EURO. The advantage in this strategy consists in waiting for a favorable **moment** to get an **advantageous exchange rate**.

In order to completely **transfer** the **exchange rate risk** there are two possibilities:
- The exports and imports are **billed** in **EURO** (invoiced). Then the exchange rate risk is completely transferred to the business partner.
- **Exchange-rate insurance can** be obtained from e. g. Euler Hermes or the German AGA (the Auslandsgeschäftsabsicherung der Bundesrepublik Deutschland, the export guarantee scheme of the Federal Republic of Germany). This publicly promotes certain commercial developments.

Closing sales contracts in EURO is primarily a question of the respective **negotiating positions** and thus only a very **specific control option**. There is also the possibility that the foreign buyer will accept the currency risk in return for a corresponding discount. The extent to which the potential for risk transfer can be applied at all depends very heavily on the product and the industry. When applying this form of risk transfer, the exchange risk exchange rate risk decreases and at the same time the RoRaC increases if there is no offsetting loss of earnings due to e. g. price reductions.

Taking out exchange rate insurance in the form of **guarantees** and **warranties** serves longer-term hedging or transfer of exchange rate risks. Taking out exchange-rate insurance is tied to **certain conditions** such as eligibility and a lack of other hedging options. Therefore this control instrument is also only available in specific situations and for certain companies. The effect on the RoRaC depends on the size of the premium for the exchange rate insurance (see Section 3.4.1).

4.1.2.2 Currency swaps

Closing **long-term currency swaps** offers the possibility of compensating for strategic exchange rate risk. In a currency swap, the contractual partners agree
- to begin the **exchange** of capital in **different currencies** at a specific exchange rate (for example, German company A pays € 1 mill. to the US company B and B pays (at an exchange rate of US-$ 1.15 / € 1) US-$ 1,150,000 to A),
- the yearly exchange of **interest payments** on the originally exchanged capital at the agreed interest rates in the respective local currency (A pays 3 % = US-$ 34,500 interest to B and B pays 4 % = € 40,000 interest to A) and
- the **re-conversion** of the original capital at a specific exchange rate (e. g. the original rate of US-$ 1.15 / € 1 or the forward rate) after a long-term **maturity** (e. g. 10 years).

The functioning of the currency swap is illustrated in Figure 4.9.

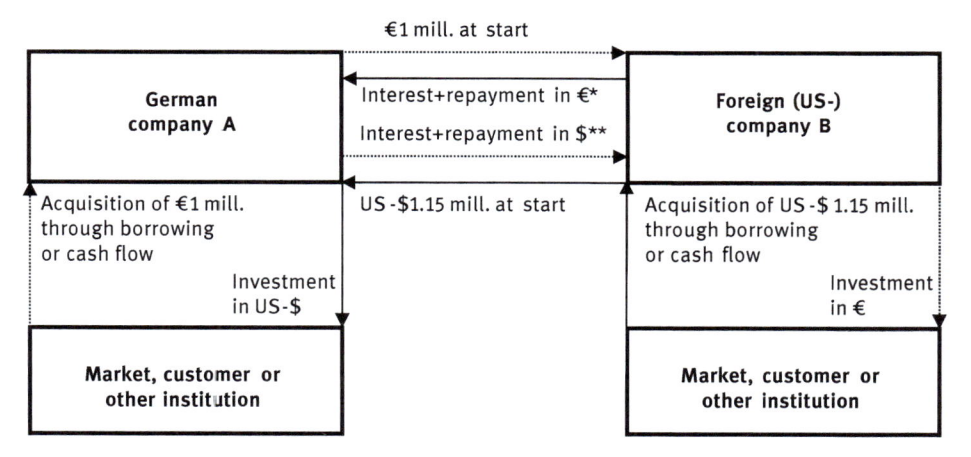

*: Annual interest payments of €40,000 + €1 mill. repayment after 10 years
**: Annual interest payments of US-$34,500 + US-$1.15 mill. repayment after 10 years

Fig. 4.9: Functioning of a currency swap

So the German company pays € 1 mill. at the start to swap partner B. The German company obtains these funds through borrowing or through generated cash flow. At the same time, company B pays US-$ 1.15 mill. to A. The advantage for both companies consists in the potential to **procure funds more easily** in their respective homelands than in the foreign currency region.

The German company A invests the US-$ 1.15 mill. obtained from company B and through that realizes long-term **repayments** in US-$ (for example, from the export of autos to the USA). The repayments are used to pay interest rates and amortizations to B and are thus **not** exposed to long-term **exchange rate risks**. Conversely, company B is likewise trading on a euro basis.

Insurance of strategic exchange rate risk through currency swaps has two **disadvantages**:

- The companies grant the swap partner credit in the local currency. There is thus a risk of credit default. If the swap partner becomes unable to pay, then the injured partner can fall back on the bankrupt partner's credit and not service it (i. e. discontinue the interest and redemption payments as well). Thus the **credit risk** of a currency swap is very **limited**. Nonetheless there remains a potential, non-negligible **exchange rate risk**, especially due to the long-term character of a partner's failure.
- The utilization of comparative advantages through a long-term currency swap requires the **existence** of **companies** with **corresponding interests** (regarding the amount of the payments, the currencies and the maturities) and especially also mutual awareness. Currency swaps, therefore, are not generally available and easily accessible in every desired form for every company with exchange rate risk, since there may not be a partner company for every form of currency swap.

See Section 3.4.4 to compare the effects of a currency swap on the RoRaC. **Currency swaps** with **short terms** (three months to two years) can also be used to control **transaction risks** of currency positions. The functioning is identical to the above explanations of a long-term currency swap. With a shorter duration, a swap partner's failure is merely likely to have a smaller impact on the exchange rate risk.

In the context of control and analysis of exchange rate risk through transactions (transaction risk), currency forward transactions play an important role.

4.1.2.3 Currency forward transactions

Currency forward transactions function like **futures** (see Section 3.4.3).

A **currency forward transaction** is the commitment to buy or sell foreign exchange positions at some specified point in the future at a previously established exchange rate.

For the application of currency forward transactions in the context of risk compensation, exchange rate risk is distinguished from other market price risks by one **fundamental property**. In the case of stocks, the risk lies in future asset changes, since the stock position already exists. In the case of currency, the risk is that asset positions (foreign exchange positions) will flow to the company whose future value in the home currency cannot be known today and is therefore subject to risk.

For this reason, currency forward transactions play a special role, since they allow future foreign-exchange positions to be hedged to a specific forward rate based on current calculations. Falling back on the initial example of strategic exchange rate risk, the profit margin can thus be hedged through future purchase of autos. This **example** will be supplemented with the following information in order to **apply** and illustrate the **functioning**:

- Investment and borrowing in US-$ can occur at an interest rate of 3 % p. a.
- Investment and borrowing in € can occur at an interest rate of 4 % p. a.
- The current exchange rate (spot exchange rate) amounts to US-$ 1.15 / € 1.

Auto SE is now planning sales in the USA of 50 cars at US-$ 23,000 (= € 20,000) each based on today's calculation (i. e. in particular a profit margin of € 3,000). After exactly a year, US-$ 1.5 mill. flows to Auto SE from the car sales.

Auto SE could now use a forward transaction to hedge a future currency position of US-$ 1.15 mill. For this purpose, the question arises at which forward rate would this possible on the currency markets. The calculation of the forward rate is done by constructing a so-called **financial hedge**.

The execution of the financial hedge consists of the following two financial transactions, which must be of equal value and out of which then comes the forward rate:

1. Auto SE takes out a credit today of US-$ 1,116,505 for a year. After one year, US-$ 1,150,000 (US-$ 1,165,505 x 1.03) must be paid back, including 3 % interest rate, for which the sales revenue will be used.
2. Auto SE exchanges the credit amount of US-$ 1,116,505 at the current exchange rate of US-$ 1.15 / € 1 into € 970,874 (US-$ 1,116,505 / 1.15). This euro amount is invested at 4 % for a year and yields € 1,009,709 including interest rate and repayments after a year (€ 970,874 x 1.04).

Since both financial transactions are equivalent, it follows that after a year the resulting respective capital amounts (US-$ 1,150,000 and € 1,009,709) must also be equivalent. This **equivalency in a year**, however, is only given for a specific exchange rate. This desired exchange rate is the forward exchange rate and arises from

$$US\text{-}\$\ 1,150,000\ /\ €\ 1,009,709 = \underline{\underline{US\text{-}\$\ 1.1389\ /\ €\ 1}}.$$

This forward rate is calculated from current capital markets information (current exchange rate, interest rates in both currencies). Since the calculated forward rate is not always exactly the same on foreign-exchange markets, the calculated forward rate is more precisely called the **implicit forward exchange rate**. In the following discussions, the implicit is equated with the actual forward exchange rate for simplicity. In

Figure 4.10, the calculation of the implicit forward exchange rate is shown graphically using a corresponding financial hedge.

Today:

Investment in Euro: €970,874 — x 1.04 → Interest payment and repayment in Euro: €1,009,709

Spot exchange rate: US-$1.15 / €1

Forward exchange rate: US-$1.1389 / €1

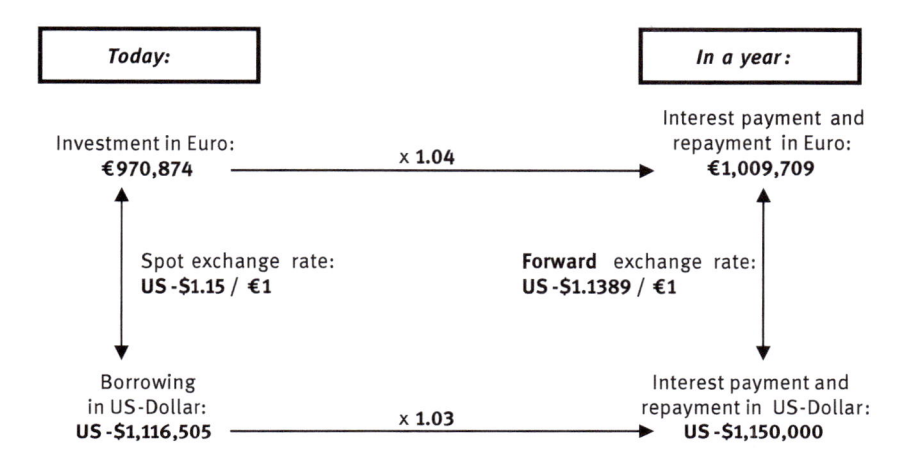

Borrowing in US-Dollar: US-$1,116,505 — x 1.03 → Interest payment and repayment in US-Dollar: US-$1,150,000

In a year:

Fig. 4.10: Calculation of the implicit forward exchange rate using a financial hedge

The implicit forward exchange rate can also be calculated with the help of the forward rate:

$$ForwardRate = Spotrate \cdot \frac{(1 + Interest_{Foreign})}{(1 + Interest_{Domestic})}$$

$$= 1.15 \cdot \frac{1.03}{1.04} = 1.1389.$$

The difference between the forward exchange rate and current spot exchange rate is called the **currency swap rate** and amounts to **–US-$ 0.0111** (US-$ 1.1389 – US-$ 1.1500). A negative currency swap rate is called **Deport** and a positive rate is called **Report.** The currency swap rate can also be calculated directly without using the financial hedge as follows:

$$Swaprate = \frac{Spotrate \cdot (Interest_{Foreign} - Interest_{Domestic}) \cdot Days}{36,000 + Interest_{Domestic} \cdot Days}$$

$$= \frac{1.15 \cdot (3-4) \cdot 360}{36,000 + 4 \cdot 360} = -0.0111$$

and without taking the maturity (here 360 days) into account

$$Swaprate = Spotrate \cdot \left[\frac{(1 + Interest_{Foreign})}{(1 + Interest_{Domestic})} - 1\right] = -0.0111.$$

If the domestic interest rate is higher than in the foreign currency, this results in a Deport (discount) on the current exchange rate at the forward exchange rate, because the investment is more lucrative in euro, and conversely for a Report (surcharge).

The effects of closing a forward exchange transaction, from the perspective of Auto SE, can be analyzed for various scenarios of the **actual exchange rates** in **one year** (which in reality never agree with the implicit forward exchange rate).

The following **scenarios** will be used:
1. US-$ 1.3000 / € 1,
2. US-$ 1.1389 / € 1,
3. US-$ 1.1000 / € 1.

The scenarios differentiate between whether or not Auto SE did or didn't sell a currency position of US-$ 1.15 mill. one year forward at US-$ 1.1389 / € 1. The effects are directly related to the originally calculated profit margin of € 3,000 per car, so to the total planned profit of € 150,000.

In **scenario 1**, Auto SE would have to take a reduction in the total profit of € 115,385 to € 34,615 (US-$ 1.15 mill. / 1.30 − 50 x € 17,000 = € 34,615) if it didn't complete the forward exchange transaction. If Auto SE had closed the forward exchange transaction, the profit margin could even have increased to € 159,746. The **forward exchange transaction**, therefore, would have been very **advantageous**.

In **scenario 2**, with a future exchange rate of 1.1389, which corresponds to the forward rate, the forward exchange transaction and no hedging together increase the profit margin by € 159,746. **No advantage** would have been realized.

In **scenario 3**, the result of not hedging would have been an increase in the total profit to € 195,455 (US-$ 1.15 mill. / 1.10 − 50 x € 17,000 = € 195,455). Hedging the forward exchange rate with a profit margin of only € 159,746 would have then been **detrimental**. This scenario is therefore also referred to as a so-called **swap rate risk**. The swap rate risk becomes crucial if a "better" currency swap rate actually results for the company (here –US-$ 0.0500 instead of –US-$ 0.0111) than was realized with the forward exchange transaction.

In the framework of risk control, the **control possibilities** of using a forward exchange transaction can be summarized using the scenarios as follows:

By closing a forward exchange transaction, the profit margin planned and calculated today from future foreign-currency positions can be hedged at a specific forward rate. If **increasing exchange rates** are expected or if the **security** of the **profit estimate** is in the foreground, then the forward exchange transaction is suitable for this. See Section 3.4.3 for the effect on the RoRaC in forward exchange transactions. If, however, decreasing exchange rates are also anticipated and additional profits are not to be sacrificed, then a forward exchange transaction is not appropriate due to the swap rate risk. In this case, the application of currency options is more expedient.

4.1.2.4 Currency options

Currency options certify the right to be able to buy (Call) or sell (Put) foreign exchange positions at a specific time in the future at a specific previously established exchange rate in return for payment of a fee (= option premium).

The mechanism for the purchase of a currency option can be illustrated by the following **example**:

A currency option entitles someone to sell (Put) one US-Dollar in one year at an exercise price of **US-$ 1.18 / € 1** in return for an option premium of € 0.01. The option writer therefore pays € 0.8475 for one US dollar in one year. The current spot exchange rate in turn amounts to US-$ 1.15 / € 1.

If Auto SE wants to hedge the future foreign exchange position of US-$ 1.15 mill. with the currency option, it must buy 1.15 mill. units of put options for € 11,500. Figure 4.11 represents the profit and loss profile resulting from the put option plus the foreign-currency position from the perspective of Auto SE.

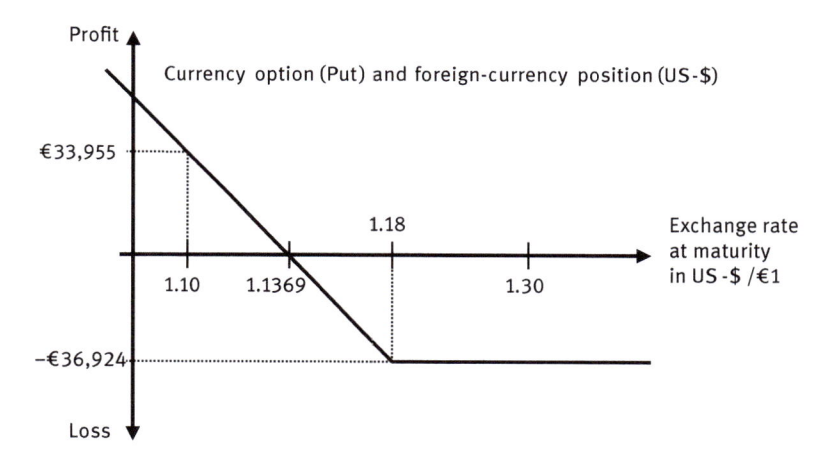

Fig. 4.11: Profit and loss profile of a currency option (put) and the associated foreign-currency position

The course of the curve in Figure 4.11 is exactly opposite that of the corresponding general representation in Section 3.4.2 of put options and the associated base position (see Figure 3.7).

This is due to the peculiarities of dealing with exchange rates, where a decreasing exchange rate can lead to an asset gain from the foreign-currency position (US-$ 1.15 mill.) and, conversely, a loss can arise from increasing rates (so, exactly the reverse of, for example, stocks). This is also clear from the following discussions of the above figure:

- If the exchange rate at maturity has fallen to **US-$ 1.10 / € 1**, then the currency position has increased by € 45,455 (US-$ 1.15 mill. / 1.10 – US-$ 1.15 mill. / 1.15) compared to the spot exchange rate of US-$ 1.15 / € 1. This asset gain is offset by a loss of € 11,500 from the payment of the option premium, so that an overall profit of **€ 33,955** results. Exercising the put option is not worth it, since the exchange rate at maturity lies under the exercise price of US-$ 1.18 / € 1.
- The profit of € 11,500 from the currency position for an exchange rate of **US-$ 1.1369 / € 1** at maturity equals the loss from the option premium, for an overall profit/loss of **€ 0**.
- Up to an exchange rate of **US-$ 1.18 / € 1** at maturity, the option is not exercised. For US-$ 1.18 / € 1 there is a total loss of **–€ 36,924** (–€ 25,424 from the currency position and –€ 11,500 from the option premium).
- For exchange rates of over US-$ 1.18 / € 1, a profit can be achieved by exercising the option, which can be used for a partial loss compensation of the currency position. Thus an exchange rate of e.g **US-$ 1.30 / € 1** delivers a loss from the currency position of –€ 115,385. If the put option is exercised, then US-$ 1.15 mill. can be bought for US-$ 1.30 / € 1 and immediately resold at the exercise price of US-$ 1.18 / € 1. A profit of € 89,961 (US-$ 1.15 mill. / 1.18 – US-$ 1.15 mill. / 1.30) will be the result. If the option premium is still deducted, this results in a total loss of **–€ 36,924**.

So if the future exchange rate climbs above US-$ 1.18 / € 1, then the total loss is always limited through the put option to –€ 36,924. By higher exchange rates, the increased losses of the currency position always exactly cancel out the increased profits from the option. Therefore, **losses** from increasing exchange rates (euro appreciation) can be **limited** for foreign-currency positions by purchasing currency options (Puts), **without** completely having to **sacrifice profits** in the case of sinking exchange rates (such as with forward exchange transactions). However, the profit is narrowed with decreased exchange rates due to the option premium. For the effect of currency options on the RoRaC, see Section 3.4.2.

Thus currency options are more suitable than forward transactions even if sinking exchange rates are also anticipated, in order to participate in potential profits, and if hedging the calculation is not the only priority. At the same time, it must be taken into account that the **option premium** payment **lowers** the **overall results** in every case, which is not so with the forward transaction.

In summary, it can be established that currency options are suitable for risk friendly companies which count on stronger exchange rate fluctuations. Forward exchange transactions are by contrast more appropriate for conservative business planning. Using the basics of exchange rate risk and the mechanism of exchange transactions, in the next step it is practical to describe the calculation of the VaR of foreign exchange positions.

4.1.2.5 VaR calculation of foreign exchange positions

Two peculiarities must be taken into account in calculating the **value at risk** of **foreign exchange positions**: the conversion of a foreign-currency position into domestic currency, and the calculation of the exchange rate volatility. Both will be illustrated using the above example.

The foreign exchange position for the amount of US-$ 1,150,000 in the above example is the risk position for which the associated value at risk should be calculated. It is assumed that this foreign exchange position is already available or coming in today and not only a year from now. This assumption is unproblematic, since with the help of the **forward exchange rate**, foreign exchange positions which flow in or out at different times can be made comparable in time.

A fundamental goal of the value at risk concept is the comparability of risks of different asset positions. To achieve comparability, all positions must therefore be determined in the same currency, namely in the domestic currency of the euro. So in the first step, the **foreign exchange position** must be converted with the current exchange rate into the corresponding **euro amount**. For the above assumed spot exchange rate of US-$ 1.15 / € 1 a risk position of **€ 1 mill.** thus results.

The year 2005 will be chosen for the observation period for the calculation of volatility. The following spot exchange rate was established for the first days of the year 2005:
- 3.1.2005: US-$ 1.3507 / € 1
- 4.1.2005: US-$ 1.3365 / € 1
- 5.1.2005: US-$ 1.3224 / € 1
- 6.1.2005: US-$ 1.3183 / € 1.

The **relative exchange rate changes** can be used to calculate the associated asset change in euro. The relative exchange rate changes from January 3 to January 4, 2005 amount to +1.051 % (–1 x [1.3365 – 1.3507] / 1.3507). Multiplication by minus one is required, since decreasing exchange rates cause an increase in assets and the reverse. This relative exchange rate change can be used to determine the associated asset change in euro. The asset amounts to € 851,410 (US-$ 1.15 mill. / 1.3507) on January 3, 2005. From that comes an asset change of **+€ 8,948** (US-$ 1.15 mill. / 1.3507). The calculation of the asset change on the dollar basis delivers the exact same result, namely

$$US\text{-}\$\ 1.15\ mill.\ x\ 1.051\,\% = \div US\text{-}\$\ 12{,}087 = \underline{+€\ 8{,}948}\ (US\text{-}\$\ 12{,}087 / 1.3507)$$

The relative exchange rate changes are therefore possible for calculating the asset changes in euro, irrespective of the form of the exchange rate quotation (price or quantity quotation) and the currency basis (US-$ or Euro). The **volatility** for the **relative exchange rate changes** for the year 2005 amount to **0.543 %**. Thus the calculation of the value at risk for the foreign-exchange position of US-$ 1.15 mill. for a current exchange rate of US-$ 1.15 / € 1 for a liquidation period of 10 days and a confidence level of 99 % is possible as follows:

Risk position: x Volatility.: x Liquidation period: x Level of confidence: = VaR:
€ 1 mill.   x 0.543 %   x $\sqrt{10}$ x 2.33   = **€ 40,009**.

The calculation of the **value at risk** for multiple foreign-exchange positions of different currencies, so-called **foreign currency portfolios**, follows a procedure similar to the one described in Section 2.3.3. The calculation of the **portfolio weightings** is based on the stocks of the various foreign-exchange positions of the entire portfolio, on a uniform euro basis. The conversion to euros is carried out using the current exchange rate. The portfolio volatility of the foreign currency portfolio is calculated using the correlations between the relative exchange rate changes of the various currencies. The value at risk for the foreign currency portfolio is then determined from these values using the general calculation method.

4.1.3 Stock price risk

The measurement and control of stock price risks does not have the same importance as interest rate risk and exchange rate risk. Measurement, control and analysis of stock price risk for investment portfolios as part of the investment assets represents a general application area of stock price risk, especially for non-banks. Here, larger stock packages are bought with the aim of building up a **strategic investment**. In this case, realizing stock price profit is not usually the focus, rather the right to have a voice in the firm and possibly an ongoing dividend payment. Here the minimization of stock price risk plays a larger role than achieving stock price gains.

Stock price risk is defined as the negative deviation from a planned target value (asset, profit) due to uncertain future developments of the stock prices.

In contrast to interest rate risk, the relative **stock price changes** (stock returns) can be converted directly into the corresponding **asset changes**. This is why the example calculations were carried out for two stocks (BMW and MAN) in Chapter 2. The methods and results represented there will be referred to in the following discussion of further possibilities for management of stock price risk. This includes in particular the distinction between **individual stock position** risks (volatility) and **stock portfolio** risks (taking into consideration the correlations between the individual stock returns through measurement of the covariance).

For further discussion it is still necessary to **distinguish** between **stock price risk** and **credit risk**. Stock price risk is understood to mean only the usual stock price fluctuations. High and sustained markdowns till the stock becomes worthless due to impending or occurring bankruptcy is classified as credit risk. For the measurement and control of a possible total loss of an equity stake through bankruptcy, the default risk instruments are needed (e. g. credit rating categories, see Section 4.2), which are fundamentally different from the stock price risk approaches. In contrast, instruments are needed for stock price risk which are more strongly oriented toward the dependency of stock prices on economic developments (so-called systematic risk) and not on company specific conditions, as is necessary in the case of default risk.

In the following discussions, **control** of **stock price risk** will be expanded beyond the second chapter in two different ways:
- Risk minimization is carried out based on **portfolio theory** through specific portfolios configurations.
- Risk management is carried out based on the so-called **CAPM**, taking into account the cyclical macroeconomic risk.

4.1.3.1 Portfolio theory

The portfolio VaR is calculated using the **basics** of **portfolio theory** (see Section 2.3.3). The size of the so-called diversification effect depends on the strength of the relation between the stock returns, measured through the correlation or the covariance. The VaR is smallest for a correlation of –1 and largest for +1. The correlation can nonetheless not be influenced, rather it is observed on the corresponding capital markets. For **active risk control** the company or portfolio investor can change the composition of the portfolio, i. e. the weighting of the individual **risk positions**. The example from Section 2.3.3 will be used again to represent risk control options based on portfolio theory.

The current weightings (w) of the risk positions for BMW and MAN respectively amount to

$$w_{BMW} = 45.12\,\%, w_{MAN} = 54.88\,\%.$$

The returns (r) and volatilities (s) add up to

$r_{BMW} = 0.042\,\%, r_{MAN} = 0.175\,\%, r_P = 0.115\,\%, s_{BMW} = 1.031\,\%, s_{MAN} = 1.386\,\%, s_P = 1.025\,\%.$

A typical representation in portfolio theory is the figure of the so-called transformation curve. The **transformation curve** maps the returns in relation to the related volatilities (risk) in a **return-risk diagram** based on the associated correlations. Figure 4.12 shows the transformation curves for the portfolio, consisting of BMW and MAN stocks, based on the observed correlations of $CR_{BMW,MAN} = 0.36$ as well as the two theoretical correlations of –1 and +1.

The points of the transformation curve represent a **specific portfolio weighting** of the two stocks. If the portfolio consists only of BMW stocks, then this again delivers the return and volatility of a single BMW stock as determined in Section 2.3.2 (likewise for a MAN stock). A correlation of +0.36 gives the already calculated portfolio return and volatility of $r_p = 0.115\,\%$ and $s_p = 1.025\,\%$ for BMW and MAN stocks.

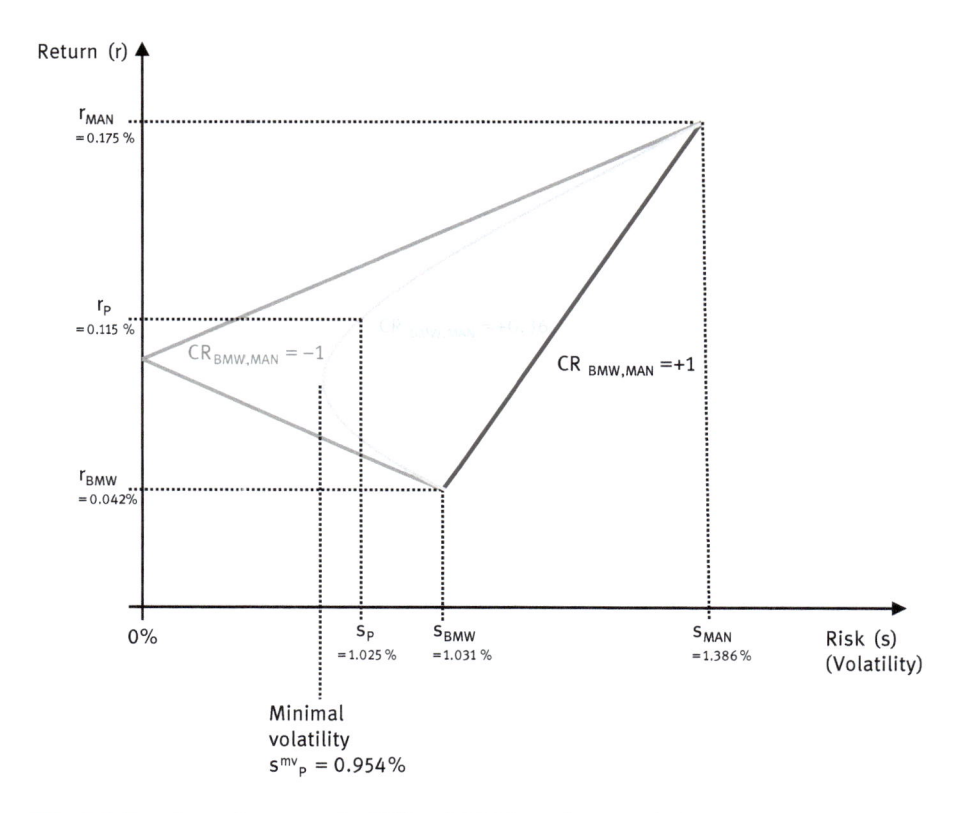

Fig. 4.12: Transformation curves for BMW and MAN for various correlations

For correlations that are clearly smaller than +1, the transformation curve indicates a possible portfolio combination, which generates e. g. the same risk for a smaller portfolio return. These are the points on the lower half of the transformation curve. These **portfolio combinations** are thus referred to as **inefficient**. From the perspective of active risk control, this directly results in the instruction to avoid this type of configuration. A better return-risk ratio can be achieved only by restructuring the existing stocks (i. e. a higher return for the same risk).

Another useful property becomes apparent from the course of the transformation curve. There exists in every case a portfolio combination where the **portfolio volatility** is **minimal**. This point lies at the transition between the inefficient and efficient areas and represents the first efficient portfolio. With a completely positive correlation (+1), there are no inefficient areas and the smallest portfolio risk is realized if investment is only in the stocks with the smallest individual risk (so, only invest in BMW, see Figure 4.12). The portfolio weighting with the minimal volatility, thus the portfolio with the smallest risk, is calculated through the first and second derivative of the portfolio volatility on the weighting (see References Section 4.5), as follows:

$$w_{BMW}^{mV} = \frac{s_{MAN}^2 - s_{BMW,MAN}}{s_{BMW}^2 + s_{MAN}^2 - 2 \cdot s_{BMW,MAN}}.$$

For a correlation of CR=+1, the above equation is not applied (or is not defined). In this case, the portfolio with the minimal volatility consists 100 % of stocks with the lowest individual volatilities. Inserting the values calculated for the variance, volatility and covariance in Section 2.3.3 into this equation results in:

$$w_{BMW}^{mV} = \frac{0.01386^2 - 0.00005158}{0.01031^2 + 0.01386^2 - 2 \cdot 0.00005158} = \underline{\mathbf{71.98\,\%}},$$

and thus for MAN a weighting of **28.02 %**. For this weighting, the portfolio volatility and return amounts to the minimal portfolio volatility **s$^{mv}_p$ = 0.954 %** and **r$^{mv}_p$ = 0.079 %**. The lower risk is thus again associated with a lower portfolio return. If the portfolio investor is focused exclusively on the lowest possible risk, then he gets the best results through the indicated minimization, the lower the correlation is. It is clear from Figure 4.12 that with a **"theoretical" correlation** of −1 the **portfolio risk** could even sink to **zero**. However, since a correlation of −1 cannot be observed empirically in practice, rather at best a correlation that approaches −1 (and this also very rarely), this special case will not be explored further here. A completely negative correlation of negative one is not conceivable, since the stock prices always depend also on some identical influencing factors (such as e. g. the Business Climate Index, GDP development and so on). If these general influencing factors deteriorate then most stock prices will typically also (to various degrees) decline and a completely negative correlation is then no longer possible.

Independently of a theoretical correlation of −1, however, the following **properties** for **active risk control** can be summarized from the above representations based on portfolio theory:

− If the focus is on risk reduction for the investor then the most favorable results can be achieved through a corresponding portfolio weighting, the **smaller** the **correlation** is or the nearer it lies to −1. This finding also appears for the portfolio's VaR calculation, where the VaR is smallest for a theoretical correlation of −1 (see Table 2.11). The selection of stocks for the portfolio is thus oriented to the observed correlations of the returns between the available stocks.

− In the next step, the stock portfolio must be investigated for **possible inefficiencies**. The range of inefficient configurations lies in the bottom half of the portfolio with the minimal volatility. From Figure 4.12 it is clear that in the example, this

range is above 71.98 % for a weighting of the BMW stocks. All portfolios with a weighting of the BMW stock above the weighting for the minimal portfolio volatility are thus inefficient. The BMW stock is the position with the smallest individual return. Generally, therefore, the inefficient range lies with the smallest individual returns for all weightings of the stock that lie above the minimum portfolio volatility weighting.
– Ultimately, a portfolio combination is chosen from within the efficient area which corresponds to the individual **risk attitude** of the investor. The risk-averse investor thus chooses the portfolio with the **minimum volatility** (see Section 3.3).

Possible individual risk approaches of companies or investors and the mapping (through the so-called utility functions) within portfolio theory will not be further explored in the framework of this book (see References in Section 4.5). Nonetheless, the **RoRaC concept** (see Section 2.6) presented in the context of risk analysis can be applied to the above example.

The yearly profit calculated in Section 2.6 consists of the dividend payment as well as the price return minus the interest rate for a risk-free investment and amounts to € 36.08 for BMW and € 192.60 for MAN. The result is a total profit for the **original portfolio** in the amount of € 228.68. The portfolio VaR projected on one year amounts to € 313.34. If the total profit is divided by the VaR this delivers a **RoRaC** of **0.7299** (see Table 2.19). Likewise, for the portfolio with the minimum volatility corresponding to the new stock, a total profit can be identified in the amount of € 57.56 for BMW and € 98.34 for MAN. The total portfolio profit then amounts to € 155.90. Using the minimum portfolio volatility results in a VaR of still only € 57.63, and € 291.58 for a year. For the **portfolio** with the **minimum variance**, the **RoRaC** amounts to **0.5347**!

The risk has indeed fallen through the minimization of the volatility, but at the same time the profit has fallen much more sharply through the restructuring, which as a result leads to a **worsened profit-risk ratio** (RoRaC, see Section 2.6). An investor bent exclusively on risk reduction would nonetheless choose the portfolio with the minimum risk. A risk-taking investor who was focused on achieving profits would only invest in MAN stocks, since this would provide the highest RoRaC. Risk analysis with the help of the RoRaC thus delivers in the framework of portfolio theory only an additional decision criterion (risk minimization) in relation to the individual risk attitude of the investor (company).

The calculation of the portfolio VaR in Section 2.3.3, and in particular for the above explanations about risk reduction based on portfolio theory, must fulfill three elementary assumptions:
– The investor considers only **a period**, at the beginning of which he invests a specific amount in stocks (€ 820.00) which he then resells after a period at an uncertain price. This assumption can be considered fulfilled if the period is based on the same period (e. g. one year) as the calculations in the framework of the risk analysis.

- These stocks are **arbitrarily divisible**, i.e. any possible portfolio combination (w_{BMW}, w_{MAN}) is feasible. In the above example, this premise is unrealistic. However, whole stocks are not included in the example for the sake of computational simplicity. In business practice, portfolios have such a high volume or number of stocks that the assumption for the calculation can usually be seen as fulfilled.
- The expected **returns** and **associated volatilities** must be assumed to be **constant**. This assumption or problem in the case of non-fulfillment has already been discussed in Section 2.2.1 in connection with the various options for calculating volatility. If the volatilities change, the calculations must be renewed and as a result a portfolio with the desired properties can be achieved through restructuring. The incidental transaction costs for this must then be taken into account accordingly in the risk analysis, especially in the RoRaC. To this end, the benefits of the portfolio restructuring and the related costs should be balanced out.

4.1.3.2 Capital Asset Pricing Model (CAPM)

Another approach to actively control stock portfolio risk is based on the so-called **Capital Asset Pricing Model**. In the framework of the CAPM the **overall risk** of a stock is divided into **systematic risk** and **unsystematic risk**. The systematic risk of a stock is defined as the **economically conditioned** threat of stock price fluctuations. Unsystematic risk is **company specific risk** which can lead to fluctuations of the stock prices. In the CAPM it is assumed that unsystematic risk can be diversified away through a suitable portfolio configuration and it is therefore not taken into account. Systematic risk is measured through the **beta factor**.

In the CAPM it is assumed that the systematic risk of a stock can be measured through **correlation** of the **stock return** (r_i) with the return on the so-called **market portfolio** (r_M). The market portfolio (M) represents a fictive portfolio which contains all conceivable market investments. Due to its high level of diversification, the market portfolio M is not meant to refer to unsystematic risk, and thus reflects only economically conditioned risk. The **DAX** is usually used to represent the market portfolio in Germany. The beta factor ($ß_i$) is measured by the covariance ($s_{i,M}$) between the stock return i and the market portfolio return M, and is divided by the market portfolio variance (s^2_M) for reasons of comparability:

$$ß_i = \frac{s_{i,M}}{s^2_M}.$$

The calculation of the beta factor in the CAPM corresponds to the construction of the beta factor for determining the component value at risk in Section 2.3.3. The only difference regarding the component value at risk is the use of the stock portfolio itself instead of the market portfolio. A stock that is completely uncorrelated with the market has the beta factor of ß$_i$ = 0 and the market portfolio itself has the beta factor

$$\beta_M = \frac{\sigma_{M,M}}{\sigma^2_M} = 1.$$

The **central statement** of the **CAPM** is this: the expected return of a stock r_i is made up of both the return on risk-free investments (r_{rf}) (e. g. federal bonds) and a **risk premium** for the **systematic risk**!

The difference between the market portfolio return (r_M) and the return on the risk-free investments (r_{rf}), multiplied by the beta factor (ß$_i$), represents the risk premium for the systematic risk. The central equation for the CAPM can be represented as follows:

$$r_i = r_{rf} + (r_M - r_{rf}) \cdot \beta_i.$$

The higher the beta factor is, the greater the risk premium is for the systematic risk and with it the expected stock return (r_i). The amount of the risk premium therefore depends **linearly** on the beta factor.

The **CAPM** will be illustrated using the **example** of the BMW and MAN stocks, expanded by the DAX as a representative for the market portfolio. To do this, the relative daily changes to the DAX for the observation period of 2005 are also used. The average (daily) market portfolio return amounts to:

$$r_{DAX} = \underline{\mathbf{0.093\,\%}}$$

and the associated variance of the DAX amounts to

$$s^2_{DAX} = \underline{\mathbf{0.00005831}}.$$

The covariances between the stock returns and the DAX returns for the BMW and MAN stocks can be calculated analogously to the procedure in Section 2.3.3 and amount to

$$s_{BMW,DAX} = 0.00004522 \text{ or } s_{MAN,DAX} = 0.00006196.$$

The calculation of the beta factor then gives

$$\beta_{BMW,DAX} = \underline{\mathbf{0.776}},$$
$$\beta_{MAN,DAX} = \underline{\mathbf{1.063}}.$$

The beta factor is supplemented by the additional DAX in order to distinguish this beta factor from the beta factors for calculating the Component Value at Risk (CoVaR). The beta factors for determining the CoVaR do not refer to the DAX but rather to the portfolio consisting of BMW and MAN stocks.

For the **risk-free return**, the basis will be an interest rate of 3% per annum. For suitable comparability, the daily DAX return must be projected onto a year and gives r_{DAX} = **23.81% p. a.** From that, the expected returns for BMW (r_{BMW}) and MAN (r_{MAN}) can now be calculated from the above CAPM base equation:

$$r_{BMW} = \underline{19.15\% \ p.\ a.},$$
$$r_{MAN} = \underline{25.12\% \ p.\ a.}$$

The linear relationship between the expected stock returns (r_i) and the associated beta factor ($ß_i$) is frequently shown in the literature through the Security Market Line. The yield is thus shown as a function of the beta factor. Figure 4.13 represents the corresponding Security Market Line for the above example.

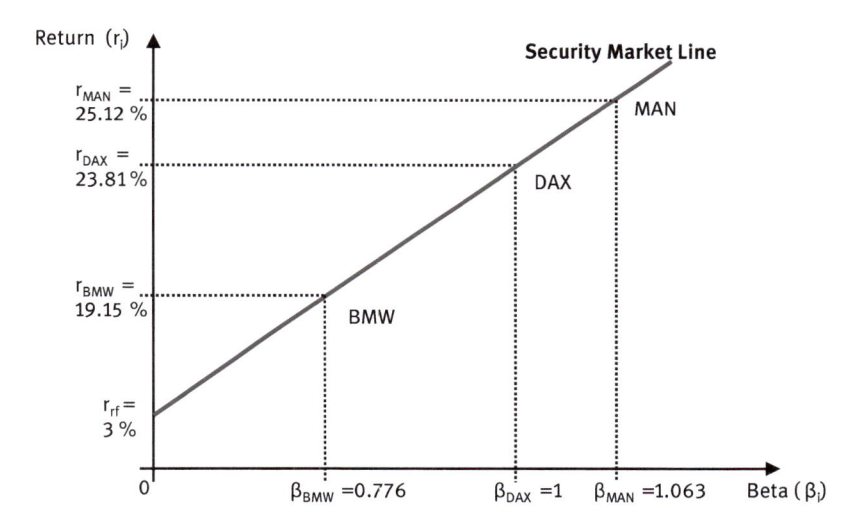

Fig. 4.13: Security Market Line based on the CAPM

The higher correlation (measured through the covariance) between the MAN stock return and the DAX return compared to BMW leads to a **higher beta factor**. The systematic risk is thus larger for MAN than for BMW, which is expressed in a higher risk premium. MAN is thus exposed to stronger economic risk (measured through the DAX) than BMW. Due to the higher risk premium, the expected return for the MAN stock is also correspondingly higher. This tendency can also be observed already in the portfolio theory or VaR calculation.

Nonetheless, the stock returns calculated from the historical data cannot agree with those from the CAPM. With the **CAPM**, the calculation is done through the DAX (for the mapping of systematic risk) on a totally **different data basis** and also a totally different **economic concept**. So the amount of the risk premium depends not only the beta factor but also on the difference between the DAX return and the risk-free interest rate. Neither quantity, however, has an influence on the calculation of the equity return in the context of portfolio theory. The greater this difference is, the peakier the course of the market security line in Figure 4.13.

For **active risk control**, the findings from the CAPM can be applied using the beta factor in order to carry out a stock portfolio risk assessment corresponding to the investor's individual risk attitudes based on economic developments. A risk-averse investor who wants to be exposed to the smallest possible economic risk chooses stocks with a very small beta factor. Risk-taking investors, whose focus is on higher returns, choose stocks with a higher beta factor and expect a correspondingly higher return. Due to the linear relationship between the risk as measured through the beta factor and the corresponding return, applying the RoRaC calculations leads to no further analytical results (in contrast to the portfolio theory in the above example).

For the application of the CAPM in the framework of active risk management, similar assumptions must be made as with portfolio theory. The most important **premises** for practical application are as follows:
- The central assumption with regard to measurement of systematic risk is the function of the **DAX** to adequately **represent** the **economic risk.** However, the composition of the DAX is primarily based on the sufficient size of the respective companies. The necessary size for inclusion in the DAX is determined by, among other things, stock market capitalization (number of stocks times the stock price) and not, for example, industry affiliation. As a result, certain industries can be overrepresented in the DAX (e. g. banks, car companies) and the requirement of complete diversification of unsystematic (company specific) risk is not fulfilled. Conversely, this means that the DAX does not only represent systematic risk.
- The **risk-free interest rate** is **constant.** In capital market practice, however, the risk-free interest rate changes constantly. This means that the risk premium also changes constantly and with it the investor's assessment of the risk content. In relation to the amount of the risk premium, today's changes to the risk-free interest rate are nonetheless relatively small and negligible.
- **Constancy** is also assumed for the **beta factor**, which is never fulfilled in reality. The covariances between stocks and market portfolio, as well as the market portfolio variance, can change. The principle of equivalence is used for this assumption, as already explained for the portfolio theory assumptions. There must be a balance between the costs of a possible restructuring and the associated benefits.

For the application of **stock options** and **stock futures**, the general explanations in Sections 3.4.2 and 3.4.3 can be transferred without further ado. The **respective stock** evaluated at the current price (mark to market) can be used as the **basis**. Special features like those for interest rate risk (conversion by the modified duration) or for exchange rate risk (conversion between various currencies) are not given for risk measurement and analysis of stocks.

4.1.4 Real estate price risk

Real estate price risk plays a smaller role for companies than investments in fixed interest securities or stocks. Nonetheless an approach is needed in the framework of business wide risk management. A substantive analysis of real estate price risk first requires a distinction regarding the application of risk measurements methods between:
- Real estate which is predominantly kept for **own use**, especially for operating activities. This primarily entails risks through extraordinary wear and tear and external damage. For risk measurement, risk analysis and risk control, the methods and instruments in the framework of operating risks (see Section 5.1) are applicable.
- In the case of real estate acquired as a **capital investment**, the focus is not on own use but rather performance and possible returns (e. g. through rental income). The control instruments applied to market price risks can be transferred over here and are the focus of the following discussions.

Real estate price risk is defined as the negative deviation from a planned target value (asset, profit) of real estate investments due to uncertain future developments in the real estate markets.

The following **important characteristics** of this type of risk must be taken into account in the transfer of methods and instruments of risk management from market price risks to real estate price risk:
- Real estate possesses compared to e. g. stocks some considerable serious **peculiarities** based on structural features of **real estate objects** and on the respective region. These characteristics are crucial for pricing the real estate. **Capital market theoretical models** such as e. g. portfolio theory or the CAPM are **not directly applicable** to the management of real estate capital investments.
- The approach to real estate price risk was in the past notable for conservative behavior by investors (e. g. in contrast to investment banking). This behavior by real estate investors was especially characterized by a **lack of transparency** about the development of real estate-related risk and the control of real estate portfolios. Thus the **introduction** of the **KonTraG**, in which the obligation to disclose all real estate risks is required by law, led to especially **large** and **rapid changes** in handling real estate price risks.
- In the **past**, up to the beginning of the 1990s, the real estate markets, especially in Germany, were characterized in nearly all segments of the real estate market by a **continuous price increase**. Because of this, **development** of risk-management **instruments** was **strongly neglected** in theory and practice up until the slump in the real estate market in the 90s (in contrast to the other market price risks).
- Numerous bankruptcies of reputable real estate firms and proprietary business failures by banks in the area of real estate, and especially the financial crisis (see

Section 4.4), led in the past not only to considerable business losses but also much damage to the economy. As a result, parts of the **real estate market** have been in a crisis for some time.
- **Buying** and **selling real estate** is for legal reasons to some extent very complicated and especially takes much longer to wind up than other financial positions (e. g. stocks). This must be adequately taken into account through the choice of liquidation period when calculating the VaR.
- Decisions about real estate investments are nearly always oriented towards the real estate object and the region. Consideration of macroeconomic framework conditions and factors is neglected and leads to economically undesirable **disturbances** in the **real estate market**.

These peculiarities of the real estate market lead to a correspondingly necessary consideration of real estate, which basically can be described by the following **characteristics** of **risk management** of **real estate investment**:
- Investment decisions for real estate investments have been mainly on the basis of rent estimates (based on planned rental income). **Risk considerations** were at best dealt with **intuitively** based on the location and the utilization concept. In the past, quantification of the risk, for example, through the VaR concept, did not take place.
- Investment and **risk control** does **not** exist since, on the one hand, the necessity for it has not been seen so far and, on the other hand, there is little room for maneuver following an investment decision about large real estate investments.
- Even though due to the special nature of the real estate market there are not many risk control instruments (such as e. g. derivatives) or they are not applicable, at least the **RoRaC concept** could be transferred into the risk analysis of **real estate investments**.

For the **application** of the **VaR concept** to a **real estate** object X (e. g. commercial real estate with 3,000 m^2 effective floor area), in condition Z, in region Y (e. g. the greater Munich area), the weekly price developments in the real estate market in the last five years (e. g. weekly real estate section of the major daily newspapers) for similar objects in region Y can be used (this also corresponds to roughly 250 observations, as in the above examples of interest rates and stocks). From observations of the relative changes in the real estate prices, the associated VaR can be calculated based on e. g. a liquidation period of six months. The evaluation of the real estate (risk position) is carried out with the complete purchase price, since a daily mark to market evaluation is not possible (once the real estate is bought, it can no longer be evaluated on the market due to its uniqueness).

The **profit** is settled up by the planned yearly lease as well as the expected price increase projected onto a year (analogously to stock price), minus the risk-free interest rate. If the annual profit projection is divided by the annual VaR projection, the result is the corresponding RoRaC for real estate object X. Using the VaR and the **RoRaC**, the **various real estate investments** within a real estate portfolio might be **compared** with each other for possible risk measurement and control.

The most important market price risks, their VaR calculation and management approaches are thus presented. The second main category within financial economic risks is default risk, which will be explored in the following section.

4.2 Default risk

The concept of default risk is differentiated in theory and practice. In the subsequent discussion, the following **broader concept** of **default risk** is used in contrast to the **narrower concept** of **credit risk**:

Default risk is defined, on the one hand, as the complete or partial default on **interest** and **principal payments** (**repayments**) in a credit transaction. On the other hand, insolvency-related losses of other assets such as e. g. strategic shareholdings or acquired corporate bonds are also included in default risk. The distinction from market price risk (in particular stock price risk and interest rate risk) is based on the severity of the loss: default risk involves a greater or more complete price or value loss resulting from insolvency. A market price risk, in contrast, is discussed when market-driven (cyclical) fluctuations are to be observed.

There are several reasons for choosing a broader definition for default risk compared to the concept of credit risk:
- The general definition of default risk also comprises the handling of default risks for non-banks. These include in particular the trade receivables from **deliveries and services** to business customers. Commercial credits are becoming increasingly important and in the following discussions the distinction in particular from traditional bank credit transactions will also be highlighted, along with the resulting specific problems.
- Although credit risk plays a central role for banks, the **treatment** of **credit transaction characteristics** for banks will **not be the focus** of the following remarks. Therefore a general definition in this context is not only appropriate but even necessary.
- Within the framework of defining default risk, the focus is on representing **fundamental methods** and **instruments** which can also be used by non-banks.
- A number of developments, methods and principles of credit risk management for banks (e. g. Basel II/III, Rating procedures) are also relevant from the **perspective** of **non-banks** as **borrowers**. Thus the application should not be restricted to banks alone.
- The various market risks have already been **delineated** and classified according to the criteria of which **instruments** are appropriate for measurement and

control. This principle should also be applied to default risk, i. e. instruments which can be used not only in the banking sector but also used for non-banks can serve as delineation criteria.

4.2.1 Measurement of individual transaction default risk

As with various stocks that belong to one combined stock portfolio, there is also such a differentiation with default risk. In the case of individual transaction default risk, only **one borrower** or **one borrower unit** will be considered. With overall transaction default risk, by contrast, the issue is measurement, analysis and control of **credit portfolios,** i. e. it involves at least two borrowing entities that are independent from each other. With credit portfolios, the covariances or correlations between the various loans or borrowers are again considered. Consideration of correlations plays an important role primarily for banks (through application of specific credit portfolio models, which will not be discussed here). The discussion of credit portfolios will therefore be limited to statements which may also be potentially meaningful for non-banks. In this case, non-banks can also combine several borrowers in one credit portfolio to which trade credits are granted. The question of how useful it is to **consider correlations** in the case of **non-banks** will be discussed.

The **measurement** of **individual transaction default risk** results from two influencing factors, which in turn depend on other parameters.

Default risk generally results from multiplying the **probability of default** by **the amount at risk of default**.

This definition of default risk measurement requires yet another definition of further default risk parameters, which the explanations in the framework of **Basel II/III** also use. Under the Basel II/III concept, the risk-differentiated allocation of credit and the necessary equity coverage by banks is newly regulated (see Section 4.4.3).

The probability of default (default rate) indicates the **borrower-specific** probability of default. The amount of this **default probability** depends on
- the credit rating of the borrower,
- the reference period,
- industry specific developments and so on.

When a default has actually occured must be defined ahead of time and handled in various ways. Possible events for the definition of a default event are, for example, interest and principal repayments being overdue by days, using collateral or opening insolvency proceedings.

The default-threatened amount depends on the features of the credit and consists of the repayment rate in the case of insolvency and the loan amount in the case of default (credit exposure).

The insolvency repayment rate is usually referred to as the **recovery rate (RR)** in literature and practice, and indicates what percent the indebted borrower can still pay to the lender in the case of bankruptcy. This rate primarily depends on
- the nature and value of the collateral provided,
- the utilization costs,
- the possible guarantees and
- the position of the lender in the insolvency process.

In the framework of Basel II, the so-called **loss given default (LGD)** is always used instead of the recovery rate. The LGD indeed contains the same contents but is used computationally as the complement of the recovery rate. A recovery rate of 40% means that 40% of the open credit amount will be paid back to the lender in an emergency situation. A recovery rate of 40% corresponds to an LGD of 60% according to Basel II.

The last component of measuring the default risk is, finally, the **credit equivalent** (or Credit Exposure (**CE**)). In the statements on Basel II, the credit equivalent is called the **Exposure at Default (EaD)**. The credit exposure indicates the amount of outstanding credit at the time of default. The credit exposure depends primarily on
- the planned repayment conditions or
- the estimated utilization of the granted lines of credit.

The so-called **expected loss (EL)** of an individual borrower can be calculated using these default risk parameters (in Basel II referred to as risk parameters) by multiplying them. To illustrate, the following example takes two credits as a basis, credit A (with a rating classification of A) and credit B (rating classification of B):

The Probability of Default for A amounts to 2% (B 3%), the recovery rate for both is 40% (Loss Given Default = 60%) and the credit equivalent is € 200,000 for A and € 100,000 € for B. The expected loss then amounts to:

Expected Loss	=	PD	x	(1 – Rec. Rate)	x	Exposure at Default		
EL (A):	=	2%	x	(100% – 40%)	x	€ 200,000	=	**€ 2,400.00**,
EL (B):	=	3%	x	(100% – 40%)	x	€ 100,000	=	**€ 1,800.00**.

This expected loss represents a simplified measurement of the individual transaction default risk. If there is only one single loan then it is immediately clear that the **actual possible damage** cannot match up with the expected loss. If the borrower doesn't default, then the actual loss is € 0. If he does default, the actual loss is not € 2,400 but rather € 120,000. If an unlimited number of borrowers with small credit amounts is assumed, then the expected loss can be taken as the average loss over all the loans (the so-called **granularity principle**, see Section 3.4.1).

Comparable considerations are also employed for other risks such as e. g. stock price risk with the expected (average) stock price returns, in order to measure the risk from an expected return in the form of the VaR. Thus in the case of credit risk, the expected loss is also used as a starting figure for a risk measurement that is comparable to the VaR. To this end, the section on calculating the risk-adjusted lending rates (see Section 4.2.3) will include some **further reflections** on **default risk** measurement.

4.2.2 Analysis of individual transaction default risk

The **creditworthiness** of an **individual borrower** stands at the center of the analysis of the individual transaction default risk, i. e. the financial ability to repay the interest and principle to the lender. The level of the **probability of default** for measuring the default risk also depends directly on the creditworthiness. The following major categories of instruments, among others, are available for analyzing the borrower:
- procedures for balance sheet and income statement analysis,
- rating procedures,
- mathematical statistical procedures.

The traditional procedures for **balance sheet** and **income statement** analysis (also credit report) consist primarily of key indicators, with which various groups of balance sheet positions and/or income statement positions are compared. Some of the most important key indicators of balance sheet analysis in the context of testing creditworthiness is, for example, cash flow profitability, degree of liquidity, equity ratio and so on. The crucial disadvantage of all balance sheet and income statement key indicators consists in the orientation towards the past. Since the balance sheet and income statement rests on historical data, this problem cannot be computationally remedied, but rather only expanded through additional evaluations of the future by the lender.

If quantitative and qualitative characteristics are to be incorporated together into one credit assessment, this occurs through the so-called **rating procedures**. The foundation of rating procedures is risk measurement based on scoring models (utility analysis), which were already discussed with examples in Section 2.5. Rating procedures have the advantage that, along with the quantifiable key indicators from the balance sheet and income statements, the lender can also take into account **qualitative evaluations** about the future ability of the borrower to meet his obligations.

Nonetheless, a **considerable disadvantage** must also be accepted. Different lenders can arrive at different assessments of the borrower's credit rating due to the potentially different implementation options of a scale from e. g. 1 to 10. The weaknesses of rating procedures also emerged in the wake of the financial credit crisis (see

Section 4.4). Nonetheless, rating procedures for judging default risk have prevailed and, in the opinion of the author, will continue to be the decisive instrument for evaluating creditworthiness. Consideration of important **borrower-specific characteristics** that are not quantitatively measurable is only possible using rating procedures. A very simplified schema for a rating procedure is represented in Figure 4.14.

Criteria:	Weights in %: Criteria group:	Weights in %: Individual criteria:	Individual criteria in model:	Points: 0 1 2 3 4 5 6 7 8 9 10
Business risks:	50			
– Products		30	15	8
– Technology		20	10	7
– Marketing		10	5	4
– Management		40	20	7
		100		
Financial risks:	50			
– Profit situation		50	25	8
– Assets situtation		30	15	3
– Financial situation		20	10	6
		100		
Sum:	100		100	Weighted points: **6.55**

Computing the sum of weighted points:

8 x 0.15 + 7 x 0.1 + 4 x 0.05 + 7 x 0.2 + 8 x 0.25 + 3 x 0.15 + 6 x 0.1
= **6.55** (Maximum: 10.00 points)

Fig. 4.14: Example rating

In credit industry practice, the catalogs of **individual assessment criteria** are very **much more comprehensive**. A correspondingly detailed representation will be omitted here since the fundamental principles are the same. The central weaknesses are once again clear from the schema in Figure 4.14. Of two different lenders, for example, one could give 7 points in the management category and the other, based on his subjective assessment, could give only 6 points. Credit institutes try to remedy the central weaknesses of rating procedures by defining **working guidelines** which specify in the greatest possible **detail** how many points to give for every single assessment criteria. The result of the rating procedure forms the central basis for further methods of measuring and controlling default risk.

Rating procedures also represent an important foundation for **non-banks**. On the one hand, for a bank the borrowing costs (as will be shown later) of the borrowed capital depend on the rating. On the other hand, non-banks also have to orient themselves to market credit conditions in allocating trade credit, which in turn depends largely on the respective rating of the recipient (borrower).

The third group of instruments for assessing default risk are the mathematical and statistical procedures, which includes primarily **discriminant analysis, cluster analysis** and **artificial neural networks**. The main goal of these procedures is to install the most objectively verifiable methods possible, which distinguish clearly between good and bad (i. e. those to be rejected) borrowers. Since such procedures can only be practically used in large volume credit businesses like banks or for large credit portfolios, these procedures will not be further discussed here.

The rating procedure or **classification** of a borrower into a **rating class** corresponding to his credit rating forms the basis for determining probabilities of default. Thus the following rating classes are constructed in literature and practice (for example, as with Moody's):

AAA, AA, A, BBB, BB, B, CCC.

These are frequently provided with further gradations ("+" or "−") or modifications ("AAa"). Here the rating classification AAA stands for the best credit rating, i. e. a borrower with this credit rating would normally have a default probability of 0 %. The rating classification CCC stands for a borrower with a high threat of insolvency, i. e. for example a default probability of 24 % (chosen arbitrarily here) within a year. The rating categories in between are corresponding gradations.

There are three fundamental possibilities for ranking a borrower and determining the associated default risks:

1. The lender **carries out** his **own ranking** according to a specific rating scheme and, based on historical observations, determines the corresponding default probabilities. For the above example, the lender would, for example, award the best rating category of AAA for point values between 9 and 10, the second best rating of AA for point values between 8 and 9, and so on. In the next step, the default probability is calculated using the mean value, based on historical defaults in the respective ranking. The associated standard deviation of the average default probability, which is necessary for ongoing risk measurement, can be determined at the same time.
2. Lenders can fall back on the default probabilities of **external rating agencies**. The main ones to be mentioned are Standard&Poor's, Moody's Investor Service and Fitch Ratings. If the borrowers are already rated by external rating agencies (which is usually the case for large companies and banks listed on the exchange) this approach is unproblematic. If there is no external rating, then the default probabilities can be determined through a so-called rating-mapping. In that case, internal rating classifications are transferred to an appropriate external rating classification (e. g. 9–10 points from the internal rating above would be assigned to a AAA rating from Standard & Poor's) and the associated default probability is used from the external rating.

3. Corporate bonds listed on the stock exchange are compared with default risk free bonds (e. g. government bonds). The difference between the effective interest rates forms the so-called **credit spread**. The credit spread then becomes the basis for trying to draw conclusions about the default probability. Since in Germany only very few company bonds are quoted on the exchange (in contrast to e. g. the USA or in relation to government bonds), this possibility will not be further explored.

For the application of external ratings, the cumulative default probabilities for selected example credit periods for the observation period of 1981 to 1998 are shown in Table 4.5.

Tab. 4.5: Cumulative probabilities of default (%) according to Standard&Poor's

Rating class:	1 year period:	5 years period:	10 years period:
AAA:	0.00 %	0.17 %	1.00 %
AA:	0.00 %	0.27 %	0.96 %
A:	0.04 %	0.56 %	2.06 %
BBB:	0.24 %	2.19 %	5.03 %
BB:	1.01 %	12.38 %	23.69 %
B:	5.45 %	28.38 %	42.24 %
CCC:	23.69 %	54.25 %	60.91 %

The significantly higher default probability for loans with a period of 5 or 10 years rests on the surrounding economic context, which within the longer period poses a greater threat of insolvency, since insolvency-causing factors have a longer time to work.

Which possibility for determining the default probability is to be used should be made dependent upon the respective interests and the **available historical data**.

Credit institutes that want to map the particular structure of their borrowers (of the credit portfolio) and have sufficient historical default rates available will use the first option, especially when there are only few external ratings available for the credit customer.

Conversely, the **use of external ratings** is practical when there is no historical rating data available (e. g. when introducing a new rating procedure, with nonbanks). The introduction and use of rating procedures is far too complex in relation, especially, to the actual goal of granting supplier and commercial loans. With commercial loans in particular the focus is not on achieving a profit margin by granting a loan, but rather unbureaucratic bridging until the goods are sold. This is intended to promote sales and not lending. Nonetheless, market-oriented and risk-adjusted lending rates are necessary also for commercial loans. The determination of default probabilities necessary for that is then only practically possible with the second option (external ratings).

By analyzing the credit rating of the borrower using a rating procedure and the default probabilities (expected, average) derived from that, as well as the associated standard deviations of the default probabilities, the risk-adjusted lending rate can be calculated in the next step.

4.2.3 Risk-adjusted lending rates

There is a great difference between calculating the risk-adjusted lending rate and the return for market price risks. While with stocks the average stock return is derived from the capital market data and is not made explicit by the stock purchaser (except through active portfolio management), with loans this is not only possible but necessary! The possible credit **default risk** for a loan must be **adequately covered** by the **credit conditions**. The level of the expected and also the unexpected default risk must be represented by calculating a corresponding risk premium in the loan interest rate.

When this is not done, the so-called **adverse selection effect** frequently occurs. This says that in the case of a flat rate risk premium for borrowers with good and bad credit ratings, borrowers with good credit ratings pay the lender risk premiums that are too high and borrowers with bad credit ratings pay premiums that are too low. As a result, borrowers with a good credit rating leave (because they pay too much interest) and thus more bad borrowers come (because they pay too little interest). This is also precisely the reason for Basel II. While Basel I only required a flat equity coverage (requirement) of 8 % for both good and bad credit ratings, Basel II provides for a risk differentiation (see Section 4.4.3).

In order to be able to carry out risk differentiation in the form of a risk premium within the lending rate, the individual **components** of the **lending rate** will first be represented. The lending rate usually is made up of the following components:
1. Refinancing costs,
2. Operating costs,
3. Standard risk costs,
4. Equity capital costs,
5. Profit margin.

There are two options for granting a loan. On the one hand the money for the loan is already available as liquid funds. In this case, by the **opportunity principle**, the calculation of the lending rate assumes that the lender, instead of granting a loan, could invest the loan sum in a similar way with regard to amount and maturity in some other opportunity interest rate. Thus the interest rate of a risk-free investment with regard to the default risk, e. g. government bonds, can be selected. In the second case, which is the norm for banks, the lender must procure the money for lending at a specific **refinancing rate** in order to pass it on to the borrower. This refinancing rate will be based on the same maturity as the credit and also of course the same amount on the money and capital markets. This principle (which also rests on the so-called market interest rate method) is also called **structure-congruent refinancing** on the money and capital markets. Determining the refinancing rate is unproblematic on the money and capital markets at the time the credit is granted. For the following example calculations, the simplest assumption is that a possible refinancing interest rate and a potential opportunity rate correspond to the risk-free interest rate of government bonds.

The **operating costs** include one-off and ongoing administrative costs associated with the granting of the loan, such as e. g. checking the loan application, monitoring current interest and principle payments, handling a non-performing loan and so on. The amount of the costs is determined through internal accounting or controlling of a firm (lender) based on the causation principle according to the processor-oriented standard individual cost calculation, and is likewise relatively unproblematic.

The **standard-risk costs** are a fundamental part of the risk premium of a risk-adjusted lending rate. The standard-risk costs reflect the **expected loss** of a loan and cover the part of the default risk which is already expected on average by the lender when the loan is taken out. In the above example of the two loans A and B, the expected loss amounts to € 2,400 for A and € 1,800 for B. If the expected loss is transferred to, for example, stock price risks, then these correspond to the expected stock returns. The expected stock returns, however, do not match the actual risk but rather only the VaR based on the standard deviation. This is also exactly what is done with credit risk and leads to an unexpected loss.

The **equity capital costs** are based on the **unexpected loss** of the loan, since the economic equity capital serves as a buffer for unexpected loss which would have to be called upon in an emergency. The unexpected loss represents the potential for damages beyond the expected loss, which corresponds to the concept of the VaR for market risks. The VaR concept cannot be directly transferred to measurement of default risk, since relative changes are considered with market price risks, and with credit risk the loss is measured in monetary units. For this reason the unexpected loss is also measured in monetary units for credit risk and is thus referred to as **Credit Value at Risk (CVaR)**. If the Credit Value at Risk is added to the expected loss, then the result is the corresponding quantile, analogous to the VaR concept. This relation is shown in Figure 4.15 for a confidence level of 99 %.

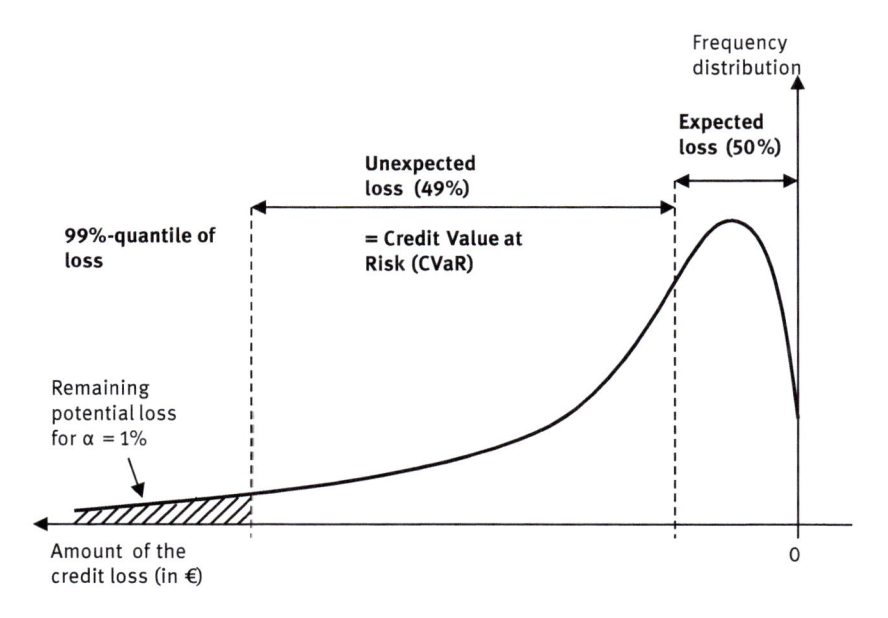

Fig. 4.15: Measurement and distribution of default risk

What stands out first in Figure 4.15 is that the loss distribution is not symmetrical but rather **left skewed**. This is based on the fact that a credit with a high probability will not default at all or will lose only a very small amount. Very large defaults, by contrast, happen very seldom.

The **calculation** of the **unexpected loss** or Credit Value at Risk can be done using the parameter for calculating the expected loss (see Section 4.2.1). In that case, the loss rate (Loss Given Default [LGD]) is factored in instead of the recovery rate for reasons of computational simplicity. For calculating the unexpected loss, the standard deviation of the loss rate (s_{LGD}) is needed on the one hand, and the volatility of the default probability (s_{PD}) on the other.

Determining the **standard deviation** of the **Loss Given Default** is based primarily on the type of collateral. For an open credit (i.e. no collateral) the loss will certainly occur and the **standard deviation is zero**. The standard deviation should be determined according to the type of collateral, based on sufficiently long historical values (e.g. chattel mortgage, guarantee and so on).

For determining the **standard deviation** of the **default probability** (PD) it is assumed that default probabilities follow a binomial distribution. This distribution assumption is plausible, since only two conditions are considered: the default occurs or the loan does not default. On the condition of this assumption, the standard deviation of the default probability (s_{PD}) can be calculated as follows:

$$s_{PD} = \sqrt{PD \cdot (1 - PD)}$$

For the above example of the two loans A and B, the resulting standard deviations of the default probabilities are:

$$s_{PD}^A = \sqrt{PD_A \cdot (1 - PD_A)} = \sqrt{2\% \cdot 98\%} = 14.00\%,$$

$$s_{PD}^B = \sqrt{PD_B \cdot (1 - PD_B)} = \sqrt{3\% \cdot 97\%} = 17.06\%.$$

The unexpected loss, and thus the Credit Value at Risk (CVaR), can now be calculated as follows, using the standard deviations with help from the **credit equivalent** (credit exposure (CE), Exposure at Default [EaD]) for a confidence probability of 99 %:

$$CVaR = CE \cdot \sqrt{PD \cdot s_{LGD}^2 + LGD^2 \cdot s_{PD}^2}.$$

In calculating the CVaR for credits A and B, a 20 % standard deviation of the loss rate (LGD) is assumed in each case (which roughly corresponds to the dimensions from some empirical research, e. g. Moody's). The calculation of the CVaR for A and B then gives:

$$CVaR_A = CE_A \cdot \sqrt{2\% \cdot 20\%^2 + 60\%^2 \cdot 14\%^2} = €\,200{,}000 \cdot \sqrt{0.007856} = \underline{€\,17{,}726.82},$$

$$CVaR_B = CE_B \cdot \sqrt{3\% \cdot 20\%^2 + 60\%^2 \cdot 17.06\%^2} = €\,100{,}000 \cdot \sqrt{0.011676} = \underline{€\,10{,}805.55}.$$

This Credit VaR, which is equated with the unexpected loss, must be converted into the associated **equity costs** in the next step. The lender must hold equity capital (economic) for the amount of the Credit VaR. This equity capital, nonetheless, is not freely available, but must return interest at the rate required by the capital investors. There are various approaches to determining this **required return on equity**. These different variations will not be explored further here (the Capital Asset Pricing Model [CAPM] represents a common approach). For the example, a required return on equity of 10 % is assumed. However, since the equity can in every case invest at risk-free interest rate, the risk-free interest rate must still be deducted from the required equity return. Subject to acceptance, the **risk-free interest rate** amounts to 3 %. From these particulars the equity costs for A and B can now be determined as follows:

*Equity costs$_A$ = (10 % – 3 %) x CVaR$_A$ = 7 % x € 17,726.82 = **€ 1,240.88**,*
*Equity costs$_B$ = (10 % – 3 %) x CVaR$_B$ = 7 % x € 10,805.55 = **€ 756.39**.*

After determining the equity costs, the **profit margin** is finally determined. Loan profit margins play an important role of credit institutions, since banks typically intend to make a profit with loans. By contrast, merchandise loans primarily further sales to merchandise buyers (=borrower). Consequently the profit margin plays no particular role. The consideration of a profit margin greater than zero would not change the risk adjustment of the interest rate. For this reason, the specific features of determining profit margins for banks in the framework of bank lending will be omitted. A profit margin is zero will be assumed for the above example.

If **operating costs** are assumed to be € 2,000 for A or € 1,000 for B, and the **risk-free refinancing rate** is 3 %, then the **complete risk-adjusted lending rate** can now be represented using its individual components. The individual components for loans A and B are summarized in Table 4.6 in absolute euro amounts and percentages.

Tab. 4.6: Risk-adjusted lending rate and its components

	Absolute (€):		Relative: (%):	
Component:	Credit A:	Credit B:	Credit A:	Credit B:
Credit exposure:	€ 200,000.00	€ 100,000.00	100.00 %	100.00 %
Refinancing:	€ 6,000.00	€ 3,000.00	3.00 %	3.00 %
Operating costs:	€ 2,000.00	€ 1,000.00	1.00 %	1.00 %
Standard risk costs: (Expected loss)	€ 2,400.00	€ 1,800.00	1.20 %	1.80 %
Equity costs: (Unexpected loss):	€ 1,240.88 (€ 17,726.82)	€ 756.39 (€ 10,805.55)	0.62 % (8.86 %)	0.76 % (10.81 %)
Profit margin:	€ 0.00	€ 0.00	0.00 %	0.00 %
Complete lending rate:	**€ 11,640.88**	**€ 6,556.39**	**5.82 %**	**6.56 %**
Customer interest rate:	€ 12,000.00	€ 6,750.00	6.00 %	6.75 %
Profit: (Customer rate – refinancing costs – operating costs)	€ 4,000.00	€ 2,750.00	2.00 %	2.75 %
Total risk: (expected + unexpected loss)	€ 20,126.82	€ 12,605.55	10.06 %	12.61 %
RoRaC:	0.199	0.218	0.199	0.218

In Table 4.6 the **difference** between the **expected loss** and the **unexpected loss** is once again especially clear. Because of the skew to the left, the unexpected loss is very much higher than the expected loss. While the expected loss must be transferred directly into the lending rate as standard costs, the unexpected loss only has to consider the costs for provision of corresponding equity in the lending rate.

The advantage between credits A and B can be assessed with the **RoRaC** in the framework of risk analysis. For this purpose, it must first be defined which components of a loan are associated with profit and which are risk components. If, for example, the standard risk costs are taken into account in the profit, these components may not also be included (doubled) in the risk as expected loss. If the RoRaC is calculated on the basis of expected and unexpected loss, then only the refinancing and operating costs are taken into account in determining the profit (counters of RoRaC). The standard-risk costs and the equity costs are reflected in the risk (denominator of RoRaC). For determining the RoRaC for loans A and B in Table 4.6, a customer interest rate will be assumed of 6 % p. a. for A and 6.75 % p. a. for B. The RoRaC of loan A is slightly smaller than that of loan B. Loan B is therefore more advantageous, because the higher credit risk with B is overcompensated by the customer interest rate (profit).

The risk-adjusted lending rate is not only an important control factor for banks. The risk-adjusted lending rate is also an important **lower limit** for non-banks in structuring the **conditions** of a **loan** in the framework of, for example, trade credits or merchandise credits. With trade and merchandise credits, collateral in the form of assessment of the standard deviation of the loss rate must also be adequately taken into account if recovery of goods provided as security comes into effect. In the next step, measurement of default risk and the resulting risk-adjusted lending rate create the basis for management of individual transaction default risk.

4.2.4 Control of individual transaction default risk

One possibility for **risk control** in the framework of **risk provision** consists in **increasing** the **equity** and thus increasing the risk buffer for potential defaults. The **equity costs** are **already taken into account** in the risk-adjusted lending rates, so that an increase in equity is only necessary if the existing equity is no longer sufficient to cover all possible unexpected losses. Since the equity capital is nonetheless not available for unexpected loan defaults, but rather for other risks, increasing the equity is appropriate only as a sharply restricted control instrument. In particular, ordinary equity increases are also usually only used to finance long-term investments and not to cover new risks (see Section 3.1).

Traditional risk management of individual transaction default risk is carried out in the framework of **risk provision** through collateral. Among the most important **types** of **collateral**, including in the non-banking sector, are
- the guarantee,
- the chattel mortgage,
- the assignment for security,
- the reservation of ownership,
- the mortgage.

A description of the **functioning** of various types of collateral will be omitted here and referred to the relevant bank management literature. The application of the reservation of ownership is important in the framework of granting trade credit by non-banks. Thus the liquidated goods remain in the possession of the lender until the borrower has paid for the goods. In this case the power of disposition over the goods is transferred from the lender to the borrower in spite of the reservation of ownership.

The requirement for collateral affects the calculation of the risk-adjusted lending rate. Thus the **loss rate** (LGD) is **lowered** by **additional collateral** (or the recovery rate is raised), through which the expected and unexpected loss likewise decrease! A decreased loss leads to a lower lending rate. For the credit relationship between lender and borrower, the result is the following **three** potential **effects** on the profit/risk ratio.

- If the lender, based on his contractual position, can demand additional collateral without having to factor this into the lending rate, then the calculated lending rate will decrease. The difference to the actual agreed lending rate represents an additional profit margin for the lender. In other words: the **profit/risk ratio** has **improved** for the lender.
- If the borrower can demand additional collateral that he can pass on in full through a lowered lending rate, then the lender's **profit/risk ratio** does **not change** but the lender's claimed economic equity or its costs will be reduced.
- If the borrower finds himself in a good enough negotiating position that he accepts additional collateral only if this is taken into account by the lender over and above the calculated lending rate, this has the following effect on the lender. A potential available profit margin is narrowed or the calculated lending rate is undercut. In every case his **profit/risk ratio** is **worsened**. Whether the lender should transact such a loan should depend on other possible factors. This includes, in particular, a potentially smaller equity requirement while maintaining the business relationship with the borrower (e. g. especially in the framework of trade credit).

Risk control through risk avoidance is carried out in business practice for default risk primarily through the **limit system**. This can include application of various types of limits which have already been generally introduced in Section 3.2. For this reason, the special features of credit risk limitation will only be briefly discussed.

As with price risks, limitation through pure **volume limits** is not suitable since the actual risk content of the loan is not taken into account. Although in the past, especially for banks, such volume limits were used for control, the perception has prevailed that a risk limitation related to rating classes is more meaningful. The following two variations are possible:

- A **limit** that depends on the rating of each **borrower** (e. g. credit customers with a rating of AAA have a maximum credit volume of € 5 mill., AA: maximum of € 3 mill.).
- A **limit** that depends on the **authorised persons** of the lender.

Likewise, such limits should in turn be made dependent on the credit rating of the borrower (e. g. a loan officer can approve a maximum of € 200,000 credit volume to a credit customer with a AAA rating; the head of the credit department can approve a maximum of € 1 mill. for a credit customer with a AAA rating).

The author's perspective is that **limiting** credit on the basis of the **Credit VaR** is most appropriate, since the credit risk is measured and considered directly in monetary units (and not indirectly through rating classes). Furthermore, the related utilization of the available economic equity can be directly compared and controlled through a CVaR-based limit system. Apart from that, such a limit system can developed using a one-to-one transfer of the VaR limit system discussed in Section 3.2 (especially Figure 3.2).

The **risk distribution** (diversification) of the default risk is carried out primarily by **control** of the **credit portfolio** (see Section 4.2.5), which plays an important role mainly for banks. The distribution of individual credits can take place in the framework of the so-called **syndicated loans**. In this case, individual lending exposures whose volumes are too large and therefore too risky for an individual lender are spread over several lenders (syndicate banks). Since syndicated loans are irrelevant for non-banks, a detailed representation will be omitted here.

A **risk transfer** of the individual default risk can be carried out through **credit insurance**. The credit insurer agrees a previously specified claim for the loss (default of borrower) and in return receives an insurance premium from the lender. In the framework of calculating the lending rate, taking out credit insurance functions in principle like collateral. The decreased (or completely avoided) default risk is set against reduced profit through payment of the insurance premium. In general, it is not possible to describe how the lenders **profit/risk ratio** is **changed** by this. It depends on the conditions of the credit insurers (for the general functioning of insurance, see Section 3.4.1). In Germany there are various credit insurers, who usually offer insurance for specific goals and the promotion of concrete projects. The most important credit insurers are, among others:
– **Euler Hermes** ensures its customers against loss through insolvency of their buyers on the national and international markets. Political risks are also covered.
– **Coface** conducts global trade credit and export credit insurance.
– **Atradius** is a special credit insurance for capital goods, which covers claims arising from the manufacture and delivery of mobile investment goods with a term of up to 36 months.

For **risk compensation** of default risk through **derivatives**, a general definition of credit derivatives is first required:

Credit derivatives transfer the credit risk with respect to a third party (borrower, debtor) from the beneficiary (lender, creditor) to the guarantor, who promises the beneficiary financial compensation in the credit event of a reference instrument and in return receives a premium from the beneficiary.

Credit derivatives in the framework of default risk management are currently only used by a few large German banks, who can participate in the **global credit derivative markets** because of their size and expertise. For this reason, credit derivatives will not be explored further. However, a clear trend is appearing that increasing numbers of companies and institutions are falling back on the instrument of credit derivatives. Therefore, only the most important features and principles of credit derivatives will be represented in the following overview.

A credit derivative represents a **forward transaction** without **interference** in the original **contractual obligation**. This is the crucial difference to guarantees, warranties and credit insurance, for which the default risk compensation is coupled to the original obligation by either personal or assets (**accessoriness**). Thus the personal guarantee is only valid for the original liability. The guarantee refers also to deliveries and services.

Even if the basic principle of credit derivatives correspond to the derivatives for market price risks, credit derivatives must nonetheless be differentiated from these. Figure 4.16 gives an overview of classification and delineation of credit derivatives within risk transfer and risk compensation.

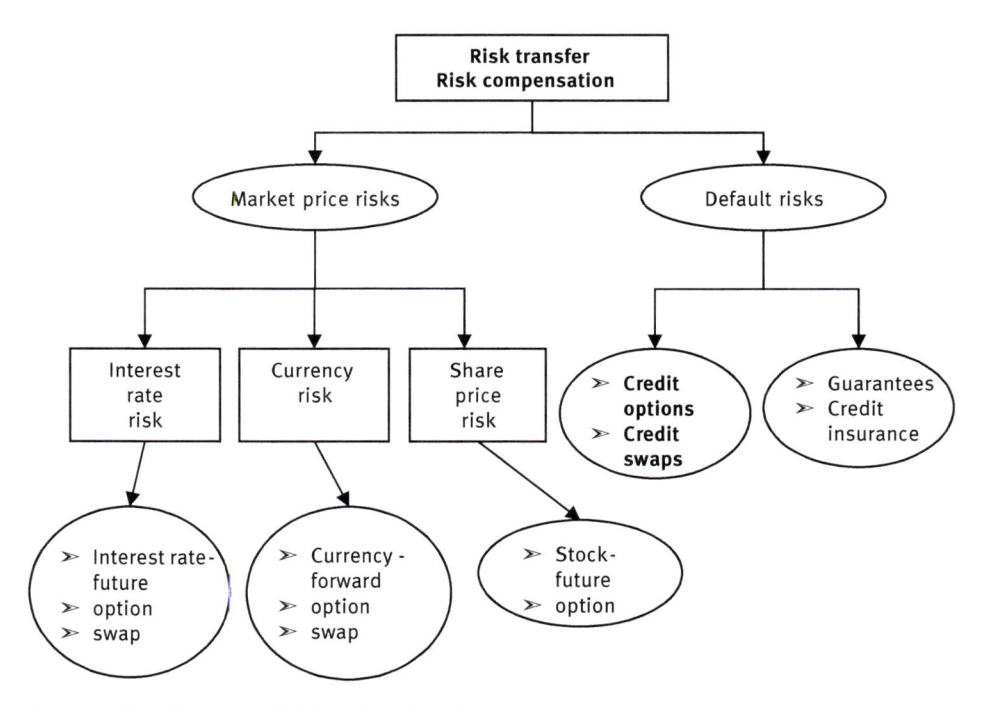

Fig. 4.16: Classification and delineation of credit derivatives

For distinguishing the various basic forms of credit derivatives, the different **contractual elements** of **credit derivatives** will first be discussed.
- The **reference instrument** corresponds to the base position of a derivative. The reference instrument is used to measure when the debtor default occurs. Borrower-issued reference bonds or credit claim are often used as reference instruments. However, for example, the constitution or the liquidity of the borrower can also be used as reference instruments.
- The **credit event** determines the conditions of the borrower's loss and when the seller of the credit derivative has to compensate the purchaser. The credit event can be defined as e. g. a shortfall by the reference bond from a specified market price, a specified time delay in interest or principal payments due on the loan or an insolvency application on the part of the borrower.
- The **compensation** establishes how much and in what form the guarantor has to fulfill the beneficiary claim in the case of a credit event. Usually, the reference value (bond, credit claim) is transferred against a previously fixed payment or there is a cash settlement.
- The **premium** represents the fee the guarantor takes in return for accepting the credit risk. The premium is usually paid in basis points, with reference to the nominal volume of the derivative.
- The **nominal volume** of the credit derivative is usually oriented to the nominal volume of the associated loan.
- The **maturity** of the credit derivative is likewise usually based on the credit period of the loan or the maturity of the bond.

A fundamental distinction within credit derivatives is the differentiation between credit options and credit swaps.

With **credit options**, the beneficiary pays the guarantor the premium only once at the beginning.

In the context of **credit swaps**, by contrast, the premium is paid yearly until the end of the maturity. Based on options, there are the following types, among others:
- The **credit default option** is the traditional credit option, which corresponds to the above general definition of a credit derivative.
- With the **credit spread option**, a credit event is not specified in the traditional sense, but rather the reference instrument is defined by a spread between financial securities that have default risk exposure and a risk-free instrument (e. g. EURIBOR). If this spread widens during the maturity (i. e. the default risk of the risk-exposed financials increases), then the guarantor has to pay this spread increase to the beneficiary.
- The **sovereign risk option** is not based on the default risk of a single borrower, but on the so-called country risk (see Section 4.2.6).

With credit swaps there are, among others, the following traditional characteristics:

The **credit default swap** is the most important and most common form of credit derivative. The credit default swap corresponds to the credit default option of the general definition of the credit derivative and is represented schematically in Figure 4.17.

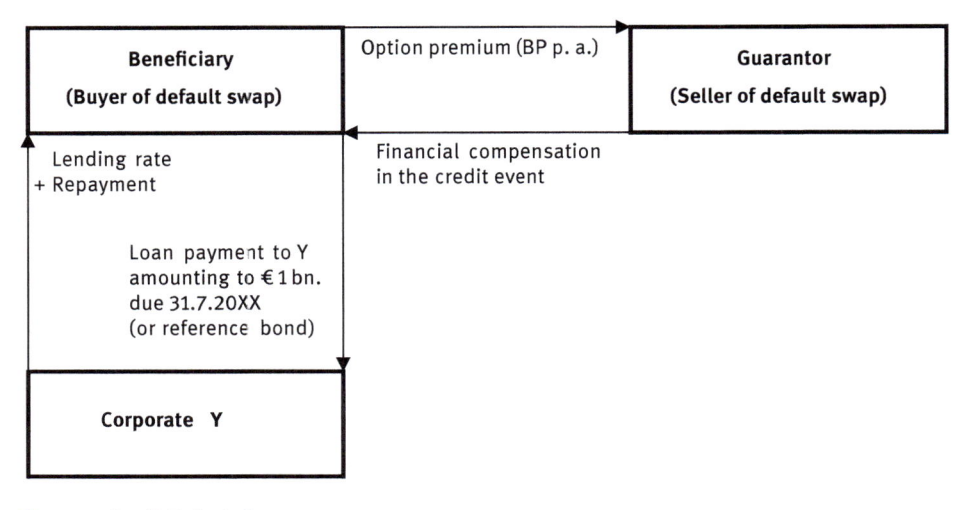

```
┌─────────────────────────┐   Option premium (BP p. a.)   ┌─────────────────────────┐
│       Beneficiary       │ ────────────────────────────▶ │        Guarantor        │
│  (Buyer of default swap)│                               │ (Seller of default swap)│
└─────────────────────────┘                               └─────────────────────────┘
    ▲                         Financial compensation
    │ Lending rate            in the credit event
    │ + Repayment        ◀────────────────────────
    │
    │ Loan payment to Y
    │ amounting to €1 bn.
    │ due 31.7.20XX
    │ (or reference bond)
    ▼
┌─────────────────────────┐
│       Corporate Y       │
└─────────────────────────┘
```

Fig. 4.17: Credit Default Swap

With the **total return swap**, the guarantor takes over not only the default risk but also at the same time the interest rate risk. The functioning of a total return swap is shown in Figure 4.18.

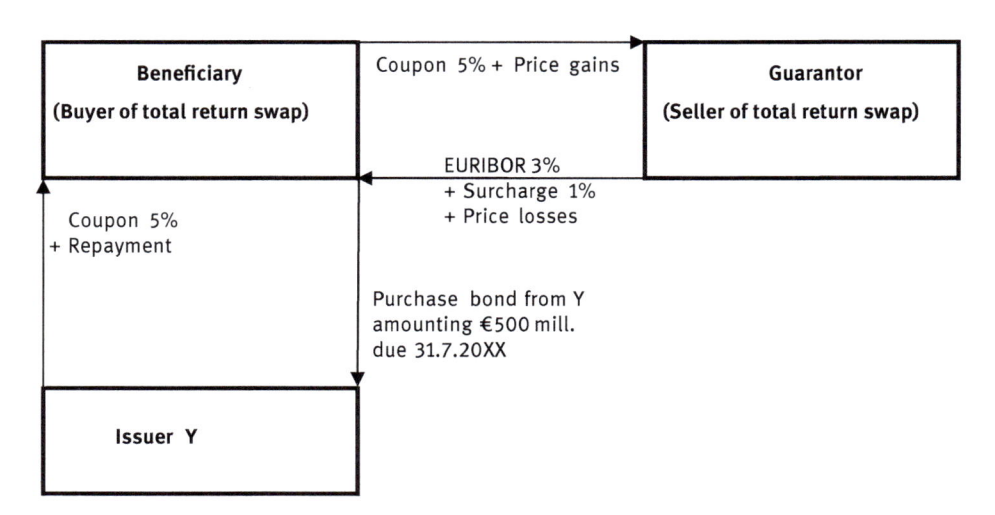

```
┌─────────────────────────────┐   Coupon 5% + Price gains  ┌──────────────────────────────┐
│        Beneficiary          │ ─────────────────────────▶ │         Guarantor            │
│ (Buyer of total return swap)│                            │ (Seller of total return swap)│
└─────────────────────────────┘                            └──────────────────────────────┘
    ▲                              EURIBOR 3%
    │                              + Surcharge 1%
    │ Coupon 5%                    + Price losses
    │ + Repayment             ◀────────────────────────
    │
    │ Purchase bond from Y
    │ amounting €500 mill.
    │ due 31.7.20XX
    ▼
┌─────────────────────────────┐
│          Issuer Y           │
└─────────────────────────────┘
```

Fig. 4.18: Total Return Swap

A **basket credit default swap** refers to not just a single borrower but rather to an established credit portfolio consisting of several borrowers (see Section 4.2.5).

In the case of the **total return swap** shown in Figure 4.18, the beneficiary acquires in the first step a bond from issuer Y. The bond is fixed with a current interest rate of fixed 5 % p. a. and a repayment due at maturity. With the purchase of the bond and without a total return swap, the beneficiary incurs a price loss if the interest rates increase, and a potential total loss if e. g. the issuer Y becomes insolvent. If the interest rates fall, the beneficiary can only re-invest the distributed coupon interest at a lower interest rate. By transacting a total return swap, he passes the coupon interest rate of 5 % and possible price gains from falling interest rates on to the guarantor. In return, the beneficiary receives from the guarantor the EURIBOR and a premium of 1 % plus the potential price loss from increased interest rates or the default risk of the issuer Y! In receiving the EURIBOR, the beneficiary has no re-investment risk from falling interest rates and at the same time through the refund of the potential price loss also has no more price risk from climbing interest rates or the default of the issuer Y. The beneficiary has, therefore, simultaneously offset the interest rate risk and the default risk through the total return swap.

There are yet further **applications** of **credit derivatives** for the management of default risk.
- Credit derivatives can be used to **hedge new loans** against taking on additional risk. This is especially important when the equity for covering additional default risks is no longer sufficient, but for business policy reasons a new loan (e. g. trade credit to increase sales) is desired.
- In the same way that new loans can be hedged, **reduction of existing credit risks** is also possible through credit derivatives, if the risk has increased due to recent downgrading of the credit rating. In this case the credit is indeed not liquidated, but at the same time the income from the credit is reduced by the premium payment.
- With credit derivatives a credit portfolio can be **optimized** from **income** and **risk perspectives** (see also Section 4.2.5).
- Credit derivatives can also be used to **reduce** so-called **cluster risks**. This involves credit portfolios whose loans were predominantly to borrowers who are all in the same industry.
- Finally, credit derivatives can be used to **take on credit risks** for the purpose of speculation, diversification or arbitrage without concluding equity-burdening credit transactions. This is achieved by purchasing credit derivatives and is not a typical application possibility in the framework of risk management.

The use of credit derivatives is nonetheless also afflicted with some **problems**:
- The **evaluation** of credit derivatives is difficult, in particular if the underlying reference instruments are not traded on the exchange.

- The **regulatory treatment** of credit derivatives for banks is still being discussed in theory and practice and is not yet closed.
- Credit derivatives played a not inconsiderable role in the **financial crisis** and can amplify crises. The consequences from the financial crisis and the regulation of credit derivatives is not completely discussed and settled.
- In the euro zone especially, the **market** for credit derivatives is **imperfect**, especially also for German companies. This manifests as inadequate market depth, a smaller liquidity in the market and too few rating categories of German businesses from independent rating agencies.

These principles and methods for controlling individual transaction default risk form the basis in the next step for treatment of the credit portfolio.

4.2.5 Measurement and management of credit portfolios

The **measurement** of **credit portfolio default risk** is, as already mentioned in the introductory comments above, primarily relevant for banks. For this purpose, banks use various so-called **credit portfolio models**, which will not be explored further here. A short overview, however, can also be interesting for non-banks.
- The **CreditMetrics** model from the American investment bank JP Morgan is based on the underlying concept of the so-called Merton model and microeconomic interrelationships between cause and effect. In this case, the default risk is measured via market values. Thus the values of active financial securities are used for risk-causing factors and the associated correlations are derived from stocks. The loss rates are assumed to be random and the solution procedures rely on simulations and analytical methods.
- The Swiss mega-bank Credit Suisse based their approach to their **CreditRisk+** model on an insurance model. In contrast to CreditMetrics, default losses and default rates are used for defining and measuring the credit risk instead of market values. The associated correlations are calculated on the basis of observed default rates. The loss rates are assumed to be constant and only analytical solution procedures are used.
- The credit portfolio model **CreditPortfolioView** from the McKinsey consultancy uses econometric macroeconomic models as a basis. The default risk is measured using market values and McKinsey's definition of default risk rests on macroeconomic influencing factors, from which the correlations are also derived. The loss rates are generated by a random process and the solution approaches are based on simulation procedures.

A central component of any credit portfolio observation is the **consideration** of the default risk **correlations** between the various borrowers in the credit portfolio.

Several empirical investigations have looked for typical credit correlations to measure. Certain correlations are also recognized in the framework of Basel II. A general statement about the size of credit correlations of course cannot be assumed, since these are also indeed always dependent on the specifics of a credit portfolio. In order to nonetheless consider correlations for the above example of credits A and B, for the example a correlation of 0,1 will be assumed between A and B (a value which lies roughly between the results from empirical research and the guidelines from Basel II).

The consideration of the correlation is again based on portfolio theory, as was already done for the VaR calculation of portfolios in Section 2.3.3 and for stock portfolios in Section 4.1.3. The unexpected loss (=Credit Value at Risk) of the portfolio (=CVaR$_P$) for n general different loans, **taking into account the correlation** k$_{i,j}$, is as follows:

$$CVaR_P = \sqrt{\sum_{i=1}^{n}\sum_{j=1}^{n} CVaR_i \cdot CVaR_j \cdot k_{i,j}}$$

In the above example, only n = 2 loans (credit A and credit B) are considered. In this case the general equation simplifies to

$$CVaR_P = \sqrt{CVaR_A^2 + CVaR_B^2 + 2 \cdot CVaR_A \cdot CVaR_B \cdot k_{A,B}}$$

If the correlation is set to a value of 0.1 and the values from Section 4.2.3 are used for the CVaR, then this delivers for the credit portfolio a CVaR of:

$$CVaR_P = \sqrt{17,726.82^2 + 10,805.55^2 + 2 \cdot 17,726.82 \cdot 10,805.55 \cdot 0.1} = \underline{\underline{€\,21,663.56}}.$$

Without considering the correlation between the default risk probabilities between A and B, the CVaR for the credit portfolio amounts to **€ 28,532.37** (€ 17,726.82 + € 10,805.55). By considering the correlation, the **diversification effect** of the credit portfolio then adds up to **€ 6,868.81**. (€ 28,532.37 – € 21,663.56). Considering possible correlations based on the orders of magnitude is thus also necessary in measuring the credit portfolio default risk.

The **analysis** of a **credit portfolio** is not limited to only the **measurement** of possible **correlations** and resulting portfolio compositions with the lowest possible correlations (to utilize the greatest possible diversification effect) but in **practice** a credit portfolio is often analyzed by so-called monitoring.

With **monitoring** of credit portfolios, the concentration risks (so-called cluster risks) are **analyzed** with reference to size classes, industries and regions. With credit portfolio monitoring, however, there is no assessment of the quality of the risk, i. e. whether a particular credit portfolio composition is good or bad. It is only the credit portfolio's structure that is described.

Credit portfolio management can, on the one hand, use **credit derivatives** (see Section 4.2.4) designed especially for specific standardized credit portfolios (e. g.

through a **Basket Credit Default Swap**). However, this control possibility is limited to banks.

The management possibilities for individual transaction default risk can also be applied to whole **industries**, **regions**, **risk classes** and **size classes**. These include, for example
- a per industry **limit** in order to avoid cluster risks,
- the application of **syndicate loans** for a specified size class above a certain size,
- taking out **credit insurances** for export loans.

The most important **control** and **analysis instrument** for credit portfolios is the RoRaC. Using the derivations in Section 2.6 and 4.2.3, the RoRaC for a loan is defined as follows:

$$\text{RoRaC Credit} = (\text{Profit margin} \times \text{Credit exposure}) / \text{VaR}$$

In this case the risk-free rate may not be taken into account for equity provision in terms of the opportunity costs, since this is already included in the refinancing costs. The **VaR** of a **loan** is composed of the expected loss and the unexpected loss (=Credit Value at Risk) together (see Figure 4.15 and Table 4.6). For the application of the RoRaC concept to the loans A and B above, please see the data and results in Table 4.6. The RoRaC for A and B as well as for the credit portfolio (respectively with and without the **diversification effect**) can be calculated as follows:

$RoRaC_A = (6.00\% - 4.00\%) \times €\,200{,}000 / (€\,2{,}400 + €\,17{,}726.82) = \underline{\mathbf{0.199}}$,
$RoRaC_B = (6.75\% - 4.00\%) \times €\,100{,}000 / (€\,1{,}800 + €\,10{,}805.55) = \underline{\mathbf{0.218}}$,
$RoRaC_P$ (without d.) $= (6.00\% - 4.00\%) \times €\,200{,}000 + (6.75\% - 4.00\%) \times €\,100{,}000$
$\qquad\qquad\qquad\qquad / (€\,4{,}200 + €\,28{,}532.37) = \underline{\mathbf{0.206}}$,
$RoRaC_P$ (with d.) $\;\;= (6.00\% - 4.00\%) \times €\,200{,}000 + (6.75\% - 4.00\%) \times €\,100{,}000$
$\qquad\qquad\qquad\qquad / (€\,4{,}200 + €\,21{,}663.56) = \underline{\mathbf{0.261}}$.

The analysis of the individual transaction default risk thus leads to the result that loan B is more advantageous for the lender then loan A. The control mechanism would then be a possible increase to the customer interest rates for borrower A. Without taking correlations into account, the credit portfolio RoRaC has to lie between the two individual RoRaC values for loans A and B (here with 0.206). Finally, the **credit portfolio RoRaC with** the **correlation** indicates how much the overall result can be improved by taking advantage of the diversification effect. Including the Component VaR in the RoRaC calculation is not easily possible due to the left skew (see Figure 4.15).

4.2.6 Country risk

Country risk is a special form of default risk. It arises through the issuance of government bonds by foreign countries or through international loans from domestic lenders to foreign borrowers.

Country risk is defined as the potential loss of interest and principal payments by a foreign state (for foreign bonds) or the unwillingness to provide the necessary foreign currency for payment of interest and principal payments.

If interest and principal payments on issued bonds are no longer paid abroad, then so-called **sovereign risk** is also referred to (differentiated as a component of country risk). Country risk has the following characteristics or **properties** compared with domestic default risk:

- Even if a foreign borrower is willing to meet the interest and repayment obligations, this is futile if the borrower's country restricts or terminates all foreign exchange payments abroad. This risk is known as **foreign-exchange transfer risk**.
- A foreign borrower can likewise no longer meet his obligations in the event of so-called political risk. **Political risks** include wars, revolutions, embargoes or confiscations.
- **Country risk overlaps** with the **credit rating** of foreign **borrowers**. If the credit rating of the foreign borrower is better than that of his country, then the higher country risk must be reflected in a credit rating surcharge or a higher risk premium for the foreign borrower.

As with individual transaction default risk, a classification of the respective countries into a so-called **country rating** is necessary for measuring the country risk. The country rating is based on the analysis of the country risk. The **country risk analysis** is basically subdivided into two areas.

International influencing factors the country risk refer to e. g. developments of world market prices, exchange rate changes, protectionist developments and the country's export diversification.

National influencing factors for country risk include e. g. the gross national product per capita, the production balance, the currency reserves in relation to imports, the interest-export rate, the currency requirement-currency revenue rate etc.

Measurement of country risk can take various approaches. The following **measurement methods** are the most commonly used:

- Based on **country ratings**, the default probabilities are estimated and these in turn serve to determine the expected loss from country risk. Country ratings are created by e. g. Institutional Investor, Moody's and Standard&Poor's.

- Another way of determining default risk probability is econometric methods of forecasting influencing factors based on **macroeconomic models** (similar to CreditPortfolioView, see Section 4.2.5 credit portfolio models).
- More recent approaches to measuring country risk are based on risk factors observable on the market. This group of measuring techniques includes approaches based on **option price theory** and the analysis of **capital market spreads**.

Regardless of the choice of measurement method, ultimately the default probability (PD) and the loss rate (LGD) as well as the associated volatilities must be specified. Together with the credit equivalent, the **expected** and **unexpected loss** of the **country risk** must be determined, analogously to the procedure for the individual credit and credit portfolios.

Using the above example from Section 4.2.1 to illustrate, assume that borrower A comes from country Y and the probability of country Y defaulting is

$$PD_Y = \mathbf{0.5\,\%}.$$

A variance of the default probability of

$S^2_{PDY} = (1 - 0.005) \times 0.005 = \mathbf{0.004975}$ or a standard deviation of $s_{PDY} = \mathbf{\underline{7.0534\,\%}}$ emerges. The **loss rate** based on the historical data amounts to

$$LGD_Y = \mathbf{40\,\%} \text{ with an associated } \textbf{volatility} \text{ of } s_{LGDY} = \mathbf{20\,\%}.$$

The **credit equivalent** is exactly as high as for borrower A without country risk. Without country risk, the expected loss for A in the above example amounts to (see Section 4.2.1; $PD_A = 2\,\%$, $s_{PDA} = 14\,\%$, $LGD_A = 60\,\%$, $s_{LGDA} = 20\,\%$, $CE_A = €\,200{,}000$):

$$EL\,(A): = 2\,\% \times 60\,\% \times €\,200{,}000 = \mathbf{\underline{€\,2{,}400.00}}.$$

The **expected loss** for the **country risk** of country Y for borrower A likewise amounts to:

$$EL\,(Y): = 0.5\,\% \times 40\,\% \times €\,200{,}000 = \mathbf{\underline{€\,400.00}}.$$

The calculation of the Credit VaR (unexpected loss) without country risk adds up to (see the calculation of risk-adjusted lending rates in Section 4.2.3):

$$CVaR_A = CE_A \cdot \sqrt{2\,\% \cdot 20\,\%^2 + 60\,\%^2 \cdot 14\,\%^2} = €\,200{,}000 \cdot \sqrt{0.007856} = \mathbf{\underline{€\,17{,}726.82}}.$$

Likewise, the calculation of the **credit VaR** (unexpected loss) for the **country risk** of Y for borrower A adds up to:

$$CVaR_Y = CE_Y \cdot \sqrt{0.5\% \cdot 20\%^2 + 40\%^2 \cdot 0.004975} = €\,200{,}000 \cdot \sqrt{0.000996}$$
$$= \underline{\underline{€\,6{,}311.89\,€}}\,.$$

If the country risk is handled separately from the credit rating risk of the individual borrower, then no further calculations or considerations are necessary. All previous descriptions can then be transferred to country risk on a one-to-one basis.

However, if the borrower's default risk and country risk are to be merged, then this can be done by simply adding up the calculated losses (or cost components of the lending rate). In this case, however, the **interaction** between **country risk** and **borrower** is neglected in terms of probability.

Consideration of the interaction between country risk and credit rating risk leads to the following possible constellations:
1. The country risk becomes central, but the borrower does not default and remains ready and willing to make payments.
2. Both the country and borrower default.
3. The country doesn't default but the borrower is unable to make payments.

Statistical independence is assumed between the country risk and the borrower default, so the default probabilities can be determined probabilistically by simply multiplying the three different possibilities by the respective probabilities of occurrence, as follows:
1. PD = 0.5% x (100% – 2%)   = **0.49%**,
2. PD = 0.5% x 2%   = **0.01%**,
3. PD = (100% – 0.5%) x 2%   = **1.99%**.

To calculate the expected loss for the three possibilities, the respective LGDs are still necessary. In cases 1 and 3, the respective LGDs correspond to the country or the borrower. In the second case, the calculation of the loss rate is based on the assumption that the loss rate of the borrower is applied first (60%) and the loss rate of the country risk (40%) is then applied to the remaining 40%. The result is the following loss rate:
1. LGD = **40%**,
2. LGD = 60% + (40% x 40%) = **76%**,
3. LGD = **60%**.

Based on the default probabilities and the loss rates, the following expected losses result:
1. EL: = 0.49% x 40% x € 200,000 €   =   **€ 392.00**,
2. EL: = 0.01% x 76% x € 200,000 €   =   **€ 15.20**,
3. EL: = 1.99% x 60% x € 200,000 €   = **= € 2,388.00**.

If the expected loss amounts are added up for all three possibilities, this delivers an expected loss for the borrower's country risk and credit rating risk combined:

$$EL\ (Y+A) = €\ 392 + €\ 15.20 + €\ 2{,}388 = \underline{\mathbf{€\ 2{,}795.20}}.$$

The consideration of the probabilistic interactions thus leads only to a very slight downwards deviation compared to the simple addition (€ 2,400 + € 400 = € 2,800). For consideration of the interactions with the CVaR, the standard deviations of the loss rates are still necessary. In the first and third cases these are assumed to amount to 20 %. The second case is likewise based on a simplified standard deviation of 20 %. The standard deviation of the default probability results from the above calculated default probabilities (PD) as follows:

1. s_{PD} = **6.983 %**,
2. s_{PD} = **1.000 %**,
3. s_{PD} = **13.966 %**.

From that comes the following CVaR:

1. $CVaR = CE \cdot \sqrt{0.49\%\cdot 20\%^2 + 40\%^2 \cdot 6.983\%^2} = €\ 200{,}000 \cdot \sqrt{0.000976}$
   = **€ 6,248.20**,
2. $CVaR = CE \cdot \sqrt{0.01\%\cdot 20\%^2 + 76\%^2 \cdot 1.000\%^2} = €\ 200{,}000 \cdot \sqrt{0.000062}$
   = **€ 1,574.80**,
3. $CVaR = CE \cdot \sqrt{1.99\%\cdot 20\%^2 + 60\%^2 \cdot 13.966\%^2} = €\ 200{,}000 \cdot \sqrt{0.007817}$
   = **€ 17,682.76**.

Summing the **CVaR** of the three different possibilities gives a total CVaR of **€ 25,505.76**. The simple addition of the CVaR from the borrower's country risk and credit rating risk delivers a value of € 24,038.71. Taking the interaction into account therefore leads to a higher CVaR, based on consideration of the unexpected loss in the second case (country and borrower default), which in the simplified case is omitted.

Management of **country risk** can be carried out using the same instruments as those used for individual transaction default risk and for credit portfolios. Indeed, management of country risk for **government guarantees**, **export loan insurance** etc. is especially important for the promotion of German exports. In particular, these instruments can lead to a **lower loss rate** for the country risk compared to the credit rating risk of an individual borrower.

With country risk, the most important features of default risk have finally been described. The new laws and regulations (e. g. Basel III) which have arisen after the financial crisis play an important role for all forms of default risk. Section 4.4 will discuss the financial crisis and, for example, Basel III in detail.

4.3 Liquidity risks

Liquidity risks can occur in various modalities and arise especially from various business roots. First a **general** business **definition** of liquidity risk is necessary.

4.3 Liquidity risks

> **Liquidity risk** is defined as the possible damages that arise when a company **cannot** always meet its **financial obligations** (= *injury* to **financial equilibrium**).

Another way of looking at liquidity risk consists of the **cash flow-related** representation. In that case, future payouts are provided with a negative sign and deposits are given a positive sign. The sum of these payouts and deposits (so-called cash flow) should at no point in the future be negative, since this could signify damage to financial equilibrium. In that case, possible borrowing to increase the deposits would have to be already taken into account.

The **damage** from not fulfilling the financial obligations can take on varying proportions. On the one hand, the company can incur **late fees**, **court costs** etc. due to delayed payments to creditors of the company. On the other hand, the company can at the end face **insolvency**.

While late fees or court costs are relatively easy to consider in so far as the profits of the originating position are correspondingly smaller, **measuring** the **damage** from **insolvency** is fundamentally more difficult. In a first step, it could be assumed that insolvency signifies the greatest possible loss for a company and thus the company's entire equity would have to be made available for the liquidity risk. It is obvious that this approach is not an objective, since the equity cannot just provide coverage for the liquidity risk but rather must be available for many other key company risks. Protecting liquidity is thus also a strictly observed **secondary condition** of the company's operating activities and not a primary goal.

For the measurement of liquidity risk it is therefore necessary to break a potential insolvency-triggering overall liquidity risk down into its **individual** causative **components**. In a second step, the proportional liquidity risk can then first be measured and controlled for the individual components, insofar as this is possible. If the measurement of liquidity risk individual components is not possible or not meaningful, then the proportional liquidity risk must be assigned to the area, product or other position which originally caused the proportional liquidity risk and be accounted for accordingly there. Liquidity risks generally don't arise in isolation from other risks.

The breakdown of the overall liquidity risk in the following section is based for convenience on the different types of liquidity risk, which in literature and practice are often dealt with in the form of cross sector classification.

4.3.1 Types of liquidity risk

In order to classify different liquidity risks, it is first useful to create a rough subdivision into market liquidity and company liquidity.

Market liquidity is defined as the ability of market participants to make liquid funds available for the purchase of goods, financial, services and so on. A liquid market means the objects traded on this market can be sold at any time at a fair market price. Conversely, illiquid markets lead to the situation that selling is often only possible at a considerable markdown compared to the fair market price. An individual company cannot usually influence market liquidity.

Company liquidity basically corresponds to the general definition of liquidity, namely that the company can meet its financial obligations at any time. Company liquidity can be substantially controlled by the company itself. **Market liquidity** also **influences company liquidity**. So insufficient market liquidity can negatively affect company liquidity when asset positions are sold at a markdown and the planned market price is not achieved. In the following discussions, the focus is on company liquidity. Market liquidity will be considered only to the extent that it directly affects company liquidity.

The treatment of liquidity risk has so far only played an important role for banks due to legal requirements. A breakdown of various liquidity risks for non-banks is rather rare. The following will discuss the various liquidity risks for banks to the extent that they can also be applied to non-banks. The various **types** of company **liquidity risk** can first be subdivided into active and liability liquidity risks, for banks as well as for non-banks. The following types belong to **active liquidity risks**:
- asset liquidation risks,
- deadline risks,
- investment and business risks.

Asset liquidation risk is tightly bound up with market liquidity. It consists in the danger that assets can only be resold at a markdown due to insufficient liquidity in the corresponding market. The markdown when selling can lead to a smaller than planned deposit and as a result the liquidity is negatively affected or threatened. The asset liquidation risk is therefore to be considered in measuring the risk of the respective asset position.

Deadline risks are defined as **delayed interest** and **principal payments** by the company's borrowers. Deadline risks therefore arise when the loan is taken out, for example, in the case of trade receivables (active position). If the borrower pays late, then a liquidity risk can arise for the lender. If the interest and principal are not paid by the borrower at all then there is a default risk. In terms of risk, this is shown by the expected loss and the Credit VaR (see Section 4.2.3). The delayed interest and principal payment is so tightly bound up with default risk that is sensible to consider the possibility of delayed payments in the default risk. So with credit derivatives, for example, delayed interest and principal payments are also defined as potential credit events and lead to financial compensation by the guarantor (see Section 4.2.4).

Investment and business risks relate to future planned cash flow from investments or due to sales through operational business activities. Investment decisions are primarily made using planned future returns (cash flows). If these planned returns don't occur, then there may be a threat to liquidity. Accounting for the insecurity of future returns when making investment decisions is considered using appropriate investment calculation methods, which will not be further discussed here (see References in Section 4.5). The investment decision itself does not solve the problem of possible later liquidity difficulties, since every investment alternative is afflicted with the problem of uncertain returns.

The uncertainty of investment returns is primarily due to the uncertainty regarding the **revenues** which are to be generated by the investment. Most other future investment expenditures (e. g. for materials, wages, electricity, maintenance etc.) are relatively certain. The risk of uncertain future revenues is captured and measured by the **sales risk** (see Section 5.2)

The liability-side liquidity risks consist primarily of refinancing risks, which can be further subdivided into
- substitution risks,
- prolongation risks and
- financing costs risks.

Substitution risk is the danger that a business **cannot replace** obligations due (liabilities) with required new liabilities (loans) and this could jeopardize the liquidity.

Prolongation risk is related to the same issues as substitution risk. It consists in the danger that loans are **not extended**. Prolongation risk refers primarily to the credit lines granted by banks to business checking accounts. If these credit lines are shortened or completely deleted then this can lead to payment difficulties for the company.

Financing-cost risk consists in the danger that due to a **downgrading of company's credit rating**, the lender will demand a higher debt capital interest rate, and the increased interest rates could impair the company's liquidity.

Liability liquidity risks are all based on the company's credit rating, i. e. therefore on the **rating classification** by the **lender**. If the company's credit rating doesn't degrade then usually there is also no liability liquidity risk. Consideration of the liability liquidity risks should therefore be based on the company's credit rating in the VaR concept.

4.3.2 Measurement of the liquidity risks

Measurement of the **liquidity risks** as a **whole**, so the measurement of the company-wide liquidity risks through a VaR, is **not possible** for the following reasons:
- A business-wide liquidity risk is composed of **different liquidity risks** whose treatment as described above requires various instruments and approaches.
- The liquidity of the company is not traded as an asset position on a market and, above all, the **liquidity cannot** be assessed in **monetary units**. There are indeed instruments with which the liquidity status can be judged and also to some extent

managed (e. g. so-called liquidity ratios), but an assessment such as with stocks, bonds etc. is not possible.
- The **liquidity status** is constantly **changing** due to the numerous influencing factors (market size, company activities, economic influences). This considerably hampers the evaluation of whether a condition has worsened in the risk sense or not. In other words: while, for example, the future cash flow of a bond can be fixed and the bond can be assigned a fixed value, the company's cash flow constantly changes.
- The **liquidity risk** can only settle down in an extreme case: **insolvency**. There are only two states with regard to business-wide liquidity. Either the company can meet its payment obligations or not. This hinders, as with the default risk, the application of a VaR concept.

In spite of the stated difficulties of measuring the liquidation risk, there are some approaches which at least measure certain types of liquidity risk based on the VaR concept, which are presented below.

The liquidity risk plays an especially important role in the banking area. For this reason, the considerations of liquidity risk are much more advanced, especially in the banking industry literature and practice. Thus the concept of so-called Liquidity at Risk (LaR) was developed for measuring and controlling banking liquidity risk.

Liquidity at Risk (LaR) in the framework of short-term bank liquidity management is defined as the level of net outpayments that, for a previously fixed confidence level, is not exceeded.

Transferring the Liquidity at Risk to **non-bank** company-wide liquidity risk is not easily possible, from the author's perspective. For this reason, this concept will not be further explored here (see References Section 4.5).

The **measurement** of **asset liquidation risk** is based on the price-volume function for the asset (e. g. bond, stocks, currency position), which is observable on the market. The price-volume function describes the relationship between the offered or requested quantity of the asset and the resulting price. In that case, there is a distinction between the bid and ask prices. The **bid price** is the price at which the asset is demanded and the **ask price** is the price at which the asset is offered. With increasing quantity demand for the same offer, the bidding price goes up and the asking price goes down (and conversely). The difference between bid and offer prices (the so-called bid-ask spread) is an **indicator** for the **market liquidity** of the asset. The greater the bid-ask spread, the lower the market liquidity. Thus if a company wants to sell an asset on the market, then it usually must accept some amount of markdown from the average exchange rate. This discount is a measure for the market liquidity risk and can be calculated as follows:

The bid-ask spread is first calculated as a percentage by subtracting the offered quantity's associated asking price from the bidding price and dividing by the average price (= average of bid and ask price). Using this relative bid-ask spread (BAS), the asset position's **liquidity-adjusted VaR (LVaR)** can be calculated by adding a liquidity risk surcharge (L) to the normal market risk VaR:

$$LVaR = VaR + L = VaR + \tfrac{1}{2} \times \text{Risk position} (= RP) \times BAS \times \sqrt{T}.$$

In this case, RP is the amount of the risk position. The **calculation** of the liquidity adjusted VaR will be illustrated using the **example** of the **BMW stock** from the second chapter again). The evaluation price of the BMW stock corresponds to the average price and amounts to € 37 per BMW stock. The volatility of the BMW stock return amounts to 1.031 %, the liquidation period is 10 days and the risk position adds up to € 370 (10 stocks). The resulting VaR for the BMW stock amounts to € 28.11 (see Section 2.3.2). For a more practical application it will now be assumed that the investor wants to sell not 10 stocks but 100,000 BMW stocks on the exchange. For such volumes, with a bid price of € 37.15 and an ask price of € 36.85, an average price of € 37 is observed. The daily relative bid-ask spread amounts then to 0.81 % ([€ 37.15 – € 36.85] / € 37). The result for the liquidity-adjusted VaR is:

$$LVaR_{BMW} = €\,3{,}700{,}000 \times 1.031\% \times \sqrt{10} \times 2.33 + \tfrac{1}{2} \times €\,3{,}700{,}000 \times 0.81\% \times \sqrt{10}$$
$$= €\,281{,}071.18 + €\,47{,}386.73 = \underline{\mathbf{€\,328{,}457.91}}.$$

The liquidity risk surcharge in this case is not inconsiderable, amounting to 16.89 % of the market risk VaR. The amount and relevance of this surcharge is primarily determined by the relative bid-ask spread. The literature about the theory of liquidity risk presents even more general approaches to calculating the liquidity risk surcharge L, taking into account the confidence level and volatility for fluctuating (not constant) bid-ask spreads (see Section 4.5).

The **measurement** of **liquidity risk,** which is triggered by **deadline risks,** is, as indicated above, tightly coupled with the default risk. It is also a good idea to levy another surcharge on the VaR for the default risk, which takes into account the damage that arises through delayed interest and principal payments. In the case that the interest and principal payments are not made at all, the expected loss and the credit VaR are calculated. The question arises of how an appropriate surcharge for liquidity risk can be calculated. To the knowledge of the author, the literature at this point so far offers no suggestions and discussions.

A **surcharge** for the **deadline risk** has to be oriented to four factors:
- the amount of the interest and principal payments,
- the average period of a delay,
- the probability of a delay,
- the interest rate used for assessing the damage caused by the delay.

The **amount** of the **interest payments** and **repayments** arise out of the credit conditions. Since in the event of a delay not all interest payments may be affected (because in that case it would be a default), it would also be appropriate to consider the full repayment and a one- time interest payment.

The average **period** of the **delay** would have to be determined using historical data from default threatened loans where a delay but still no complete default took place. One can also use reminder periods and loan collection deadlines as orientation measures.

The **probability** of a **delay** is, **analogously** to the determination of default probability (PD), established using past observations of delays for the various rating classes.

The risk-free refinancing interest rate can conveniently be used as the **interest rate** for measuring **damages due to delay**, since at least this interest rate would have to be paid by the company to bridge liquidity shortages. However, higher interest rates can also be used when it is established that these are payable by the company.

The **Liquidity-adjusted Credit VaR** (LCVaR) can then be calculated as follows :

$$LCVaR = CVaR + L = CVaR + \text{repayment} \times (1 + \text{loan interest rate}) \times (\text{period of delay [days]} / 360) \times \text{refinancing interest rate} \times \text{probability of delay}.$$

To illustrate the above example of loan A (see Section 4.2.2), an average delay of 120 days will be assumed. The risk-free refinancing interest rate is 3 % and the loan interest rate (customer interest rate) is 6 %. The CVaR amounts to € 17,726.82. The probability of a delay will be assumed to be 5 %. The liquidity-adjusted credit VaR then amounts to

$$LCVaR = CVaR + L = CVaR + € 200{,}000 \times (1.06) \times (120/360) \times 3\% \times 5\%$$
$$= € 17{,}726.82 + € 106.00 = \underline{\mathbf{€\ 17{,}832.82}}.$$

Although the surcharge for the liquidity risk is very small in relation to the credit VaR, this can be understood in an economically plausible way. The Credit VaR represents the loss of the entire loan amount or a portion thereof, while the liquidity surcharge only represents the damage from a delayed payment. Furthermore, it must not be overlooked here that the calculated surcharge for the liquidity risk for loan A represents only a small component of the overall business-wide liquidity risk. Only the sum of all liquidity surcharges can be used for purposes of comparison with the VaR of other types of risk.

The **measurement of liability liquidity risks** is characterized by the fact that it is not about asset values and their risk assessment but rather about the ability to absorb or maintain debt. This ability depends primarily on the company's credit rating. The credit rating is assessed and at the same time also measured by the lender using rating classes. For considering the own credit rating in the framework of the

VaR concept in the context of risk measurement, the following approach is often suggested in the literature:

The **default probabilities** published by external rating agencies are used to set the **confidence level** for the **VaR** calculation. In Table 4.7 are extracts from Moody's published default probabilities, and the respective associated number of standard deviations based on the normal distribution, for calculation of the VaR (for number of standard deviations see Section 2.3.1).

Assume a company measures the entire risk based on the VaR for a confidence level of e. g. 99.93 % (corresponding to an alpha quantile of 0.07 %), which corresponds to 3.19 standard deviations. If the VaR of the entire company calculated for 3.19 standard deviations is **completely covered** by the equity capital, then this corresponds to a rating classification in the A3 class and thus a corresponding credit rating for the company (see Table 4.7). The liability liquidity risk then in turn depends on the credit rating of the company. In this manner, the liability liquidity risk can be indirectly considered through the VaR calculation by choosing a confidence level which corresponds to the sought credit rating and is at least as good as the company's current credit rating.

Tab. 4.7: Default probabilities as a function of rating class and number of standard deviations

Rating class (Moody's):	Probability of Default (1 year):	Number of standard deviations:
Aaa:	0.01 %	3.72
A1:	0.05 %	3.29
A2:	0.06 %	3.24
A3:	0.07 %	3.19
Ba1:	1.25 %	2.24
Ba2:	1.79 %	2.10
Ba3:	3.96 %	1.76
B1:	6.14 %	1.54
B2:	8.31 %	1.38
B3:	15.08 %	1.03

If the desired credit rating is not reached because the existing equity doesn't cover the entire VaR based on the necessary confidence level, then conversely the credit rating can be construed according to the existing equity capital in order to initiate corresponding measures for liquidity risk management. Possible measures for controlling liquidity risk will be discussed in the following Section 4.3.3.

4.3.3 Control of liquidity risks

From the discussions of liquidity risk above it is already clear that the "traditional control instruments" described in the third chapter cannot be applied. The basis for liquidity risk management is **financial planning**. Financial planning is an umbrella term which can be divided into numerous variations, especially according to the criteria of maturity and instruments. Financial planning content is a component of practically every textbook on the subject of corporate finance. There is, however, no unified description and approach to financial planning in the practice and literature, since financial planning is usually adjusted to the particular needs and peculiarities of the company. For this reason, the most important components and instruments of financial planning will be presented in the following insofar as they can be generally applied to the management of liquidity risk. For a deeper discussion of the topic of financial planning, see the literature references (see Section 4.5).

In the first step, financial planning should be differentiated into liquidity planning and long-term financial planning (= capital commitment planning and requirement planning). In the framework of liquidity planning, there is further differentiation between daily liquidity disposition and short-term financial planning.

Within the framework of the **daily liquidity position**, the company cash flows are planned and controlled on a daily basis for a planning horizon or forecasting period of from one week to a month. In this case, for example, cash funds are invested or absorbed in the short term based on of the planning principles of so-called cash management models. Because it is short-term, subjective forecasting and experience are used more frequently than objective, statistical forecasting methods. The primary goal of daily liquidity disposition is minimizing the interest rate cost.

In **short-term financial planning**, the cash flows are controlled and planned using a planning unit of a week or month towards a planning horizon of a year. Short-term financial planning focuses on the comparison between income and outgo within the planning unit time period. In that case, the cash flows are differentiated into normal business payments (e. g. sales revenues), extraordinary payments (e. g. distributed profits) and payments in the context of the credit plan (e. g. borrowing, interest payments and principal payments). Different forecasting methods (pragmatic, extrapolating, causal forecasting procedures) are then used for planning the different cash flows. Short-term financial planning, for example, is the link between daily liquidity disposition and long-term financial planning. Thus short-term financial planning delivers disposition assistance for the daily liquidity position, while at the same time the short-term financial planning forecasts rely on information from the long-term financial planning.

Long-term financial planning operates with balance sheets as a planning unit rather than with cash flows. Thus a time period of 3 to 5 years is planned. The goal of long-term financial planning consists primarily in securing long-term financial equilibrium and the best possible capital structure. The planning is basically carried out using the balance sheet and income statement. So, for example, long-term and permanent liquidity ratios (the ratio of liquid funds to short-term liabilities) greater than one are pursued, and budgeted balance sheets are generated on the basis of projected and planned revenue developments or planned investments.

The **control of liability liquidity risks** can take place at three points:
- **Increasing** the **equity capital** to cover the liquidity risks. As already described above, an increase in capital equity is usually motivated primarily by new comprehensive investments rather than risk coverage. For this reason, this approach is less suitable for active management.
- **Decreasing** the **risk positions** and thus also decreasing the overall VaR. In individual cases, each risk position must be examined separately to establish whether a decrease is possible or whether other business factors speak against a reduction (e. g. strategic investments). Such a review is tightly bound with risk analysis of the asset positions (see Section 2.6).
- The implementation of the consequences arising in the framework of Basel II/III (especially for small and medium-sized enterprises (SME), see Section 4.4.3) in the form of increased **transparency** and strengthened **communication** with the lenders. Establishing or improving efficient controlling can prevent the liquidity difficulties that may result from cancelled overdraft credits or possible limit reductions.

Managing and **avoiding deadline risks** can be done with functioning **receivable management**. This includes, among others
- careful credit rating checks or rating classification before lending,
- consistent payment monitoring and timely detection of a possible payment delay,
- permanent credit rating monitoring,
- timely reminder procedure when agreed payment deadlines are missed,
- rapid and timely receivable collection.

Concluding with liquidity risk measurement and control, all the basic financial risks can now be measured, analyzed and controlled. In the following section, the financial crisis and its effects on financial risk management will be explored in detail.

4.4 The financial crisis (since) 2008

The financial crisis is a very complex and extensive range of topics. A detailed scientific discussion of all facets or related disciplines would be far beyond the scope of this book and its objectives. Thus an overview will be attempted of the most important aspects of the financial crisis which are relevant in relation to financial risk management.

With regard to the question of what a financial crisis is, there are many different perspectives (depending on the scientific discipline). The question of when a financial crisis begins and when it ends can also have various answers. The term "financial crisis" is first defined as an umbrella term, which can be divided into the three subsections of banking, financial markets and states. One possible **definition** is the following:

A **financial crisis** is a collapse or sharp decline of one or more globally connected, systemically relevant banks (= **bank crisis**), financial markets (= **financial market** crisis), states or regions (=**government debt crisis** or euro crisis).

A collapse means a halt to trading activities, an insolvency of a bank or state. A sharp decline means no collapse yet, but a slump in trading activities which is too strong to be explained by economic cycles. A sharp decline of banks and states is based on the credit rating and means a reduction to one or two credit rating levels before insolvency.

The financial markets can be divided again into submarkets (credits markets, currency markets, money markets, and so on). The concept of systemically relevant banks is discussed more precisely in the appraisal (see Section 4.4.4). Banking can be further roughly subdivided into investment banking and retail banking.

The necessary action required before, during and after a financial crisis, as well as the relationship to risk management, arises from the dangers and causes of a financial crisis, which will be discussed in Section 4. 4. 1.

4.4.1 Dangers and causes of the financial crisis

The **dangers** of a financial crisis consist in the effects and the subsequent reactions. So, the danger of a collapse by a systemically relevant bank is that it can no longer repay its debts (e. g. individual savings, company deposits), which leads directly to a loss of trust. As a consequence of this possible loss of trust, private savers may consume less or companies may invest less. The result would be a negative effect on the real economy. A loss of trust among banks or financial market collapse can lead to reduced lending to private individuals and companies (a so-called credit crunch). These negative effects on the real economy can in turn lead to fewer jobs, a slump in business profits, reduced tax revenues etc. At the same time, more tax money is required for the necessary rescue measures (e. g. scrappage premiums to boost the automobile industry, rescue funds for banks and states). The state's increased financial need usually leads to a higher national debt, since a timely increase in tax revenues is not possible due to the crisis. A higher national debt has, in turn, negative effects on the state's room for maneuver (higher interest burden, lower credit rating).

If the necessary rescue measures don't have the desired effect, then a severe recession can result from
- a loss of savings,
- unplanned use of tax revenues,
- job losses,
- a slump in company profits and
- increased national debt.

The **causes** of the financial crisis are complex and interdependent or have mutually influenced each other. In the discussion of risk identification in Chapter 1.3, this complexity was also demonstrated and was dealt with there in the context of the causation principle and the control principle. Now, which risk caused the financial crisis? In order to answer this question, one must observe the respective businesses at the beginning of the crisis (2008). Between 2002 and 2006 there was a price explosion (real estate bubble) on the US-American real estate market. From 2007, the variable mortgage loans that had increasingly been granted to US households with dubious payment capacity (subprime) were no longer being repaid by the borrowers due to increased interest rates. This led to difficulties for the corresponding US real estate banks who, as a consequence, could no longer service their own debts (refinancing).

The results were insolvency and liquidity bottlenecks for US banks and also other globally operating commercial banks. These were likewise affected by asset backed securities (ABS) from the troubled US mortgage loans, i. e. securities for which US real estate loans or other credit guarantees are deposited or guaranteed as collateral. This in turn led to mistrust among the banks and caused liquidity bottlenecks on the money market (the market on which the banks mutually lend each other money). If one now applies the causation principles to the financial crisis, then the financial crisis was triggered by the **interest rate risk**. The interest rate risk in turn triggered other risks (liquidity risks, default risks). Thus it involves a **financial market and bank crisis**.

At the same time, an ongoing **national debt crisis** was triggered in the **Eurozone** in 2010 by, among other things, the banking crisis outlined above. **Ireland** suffered a collapse of the state budget because the banks had to be rescued by state capital subsidies. The cause of the Irish national debt crisis was thus a bank crisis of globally networked commercial banks. In **Greece** it came to a discrepancy between the fundamentals (high national debt, low debt sustainability due to low tax revenues) and the interest rate level of other euro countries. The creditors of Greek government bonds demanded higher risk premiums, which increased Greece's national debt even more. The result was, in turn, lower debt sustainability, which once again led to higher risk premiums. The cause of national debt crisis in Greece was therefore primarily a failure by Greek politicians (reform inability), which was accelerated by the interest rate markets and their players (rating agencies). In **Spain**, and in a weakened form also in **Portugal**, the cause was a real estate bubble, i. e. through a strong over-valuation (relative to the fundamental value) of real estate. The cause of the national debt crisis in Spain and Portugal was a failure of the real estate markets. The popping of the real estate bubble then led to the bank crisis and this (analogously to Ireland's national debt crisis) led to the national debt crisis in Spain and Portugal. In **Italy**, inherited liabilities and a lack of reforms to the Italian government led to a light national debt crisis or a downgrading of Italy's credit rating.

In order to consider and treat the individual causes of the financial crisis, these can be broken down into five **categories** (see Figure 4.21):
1. missing or insufficient **laws** and **regulations** as well as mistakes by the **regulatory authorities** (Basel II, burgeoning bonus payments, lack of shadow bank regulation, insufficient legal regulation of risk reporting, lack of facilities for the regulatory agencies),
2. **human error** (economic-sociological, -psychological and -ethical),
3. **failure** of **markets** or market institutions/market participants (mistaken evaluations by rating agencies, failure of confidence by market participants, misjudgment by market participants, lack of market liquidity and market regulation, uncovered short sales, high-frequency trading risks),
4. mistaken decisions by **politicians**, **government representatives** and **decision-makers** (flawed monetary and financial policy, lack of reforms, lack of legislation, inadequate control function in supervisory boards),
5. shortcomings in **risk management** (insufficient equity, faulty risk measurement).

A closer investigation of these categories makes it clear that the individual categories are linked to each other and mutually influence each other. Legislative policy failures directly affect the category of laws and regulations. Human error in the form of unchecked expectation of returns can also be directly reflected in risk management by ignoring the risks in high-return transactions. Deficient market regulation can lead to a failure of markets, in particular e. g. in high-frequency trading. These **interdependencies** have the consequence that global financial management is ever more interdisciplinary and complex. If one is looking for a solution approach to avoid future crises, then it comes to a mixture (interdisciplinarity) from the discipline of financial management and other disciplines like sociology, law, computer science, and economics. There are, however, also examples of a certain separation between the individual categories, where the solution approach can focus on individual disciplines. Thus a failure of politicians in supervisory capacities, defective measurement and risk management or a market failure that comes about e. g. by overvaluation of real estate can each be the sole trigger for possible crises. The next section will attempt to demonstrate an overview of the already implemented and the possible or planned solution approaches, using the various categories and taking into account the interactions between the categories.

4.4.2 Solution approaches to avoiding and redressing financial crises

There are two basic possibilities for representing possible solution approaches to financial crises:
1. The solution approaches are described according to **causal** categories (see above).
2. The classification is carried out according to the three different **types** of financial crisis (financial markets, banks, states).

A clear and precise representation is not possible with one way or the other. In the following, the causal basis will be used. This representation starts from the roots of crises and not from possible consequences (Ireland's national crisis was a result of the banking crisis).

4.4.2.1 Laws and regulations

Solution approaches for avoiding mistakes and deficiencies in **laws** and **regulations** and in **regulatory authorities** consists in the personnel and material reinforcement of the various regulatory authorities. This is already happened in Germany (for example, the BaFin) and in Europe (for example, with unified banking supervision (SSM)). If the regulatory authorities haven't the personnel and material in place to monitor compliance with the rules and regulations, new and revised rules and regulations do not offer adequate protection against new crises. On the other hand, solution approaches primarily consist in revision or development of new and existing laws and regulations. These include, among others
a) Basel III, CRD IV, CRR (Leverage Ratio, Liquidity Coverage Ratio, Net Stable Funding Ratio, Total Loss-Absorbing Capacity),
b) minimum Requirements for Risk Management (MaRisk),
c) comprehensive assessment (CA), consisting of stress testing and asset quality review (AQR),
d) banking unions, bills and regulations for banking and national insolvency (restructuring), deposit insurance,
e) risk reporting in accordance with IFRS, IAS, DRS, HGB, US-GAAP
f) financial Instruments Directive (MiFID II, MiFIR),
g) individual regulations and directives (e. g. high-frequency trading law, short selling regulation, rating agencies, Act on Ringfencing and Recovery and Resolution Planning for Credit Institutions, shadow banking regulation, regulation of salary and bonus payments).

With regard to a)
In **Basel III**, the required equity coverage for default risk (credit risk) is newly regulated for banks. Management of default risk is a basic pillar of risk management and

was already handled in detail in Section 4. 2. The leverage ratio is a further concept for measuring the equity capitalization of banks and is also related to risk analysis (see Section 2.6). Because of these close connections, the essential components of Basel III are discussed in more detail in section 4. 4. 3.

With regard to b)
The **MaRisk** (minimum requirements for risk management) contains the requirements for banks according to ICAAP (International Capital Adequacy Assesment Process) with regard to these core elements
– risk management and controlling processes,
– determination of risk bearing capacity (methods of risk measurement, stipulation of the risk coverage potential)

and with respect to the requirements of MaRisk in general, among others
– structural and procedural organization
– separation of functions,
– revision/auditing,
– documentation,
– resources.

The MaRisk is reflected in many areas of this book (e. g. the risk management requirements in Chapter 3, risk bearing capacity and risk measurement in Chapter 2 and risk controlling in Chapter 6).

With regard to c)
The **stress test** carried out in the framework of the **Comprehensive Assessment** by the ECB or the EBA (European Banking Authority which was established by the ECB) has a close connection to the stress test in Section 2.4. The other pillar of the Comprehensive Assessment consisting after in the **Asset Quality Review** (AQR), and involves the examination of bank assets, whether they have been properly and fully evaluated and balanced. The AQR is carried out by auditors engaged by the ECB. It is a prerequisite for the stress test and is closely connected with accounting standards such as e. g. IFRS and US GAAP.

The stress test, which was carried out for the first time in 2014 by the ECB and the EBA, was a reaction to the financial crisis. The 128 most important (systemically relevant) banks in the Eurozone were subjected to a stress test, which was meant to protect tax payers and savers against future losses. The basic stress test procedure has already been described in Section 2.4 and in particular the general weaknesses were also discussed. The particular characteristics of bank stress tests will be addressed in the following remarks.

The emphasis of the stress test was assets or investment portfolios (800 portfolios and 119,000 borrower) classified by the ECB as especially risky or non-transparent.

These are, among others, derivatives, shipping-, real estate- or government loans. In a first step, the quality of the assets up to December 31, 2013 was reviewed. This investigation extends to questions of where the identified risks are or whether the loans and collaterals are properly valued.

The actual stress test begins only in the second step. The **basic scenario** builds on the expected economic development in the Eurozone. In the basic scenario, the banks must meet a core capital ratio of at least eight percent at the end of the observed years 2014, 2015 and 2016.

In the **stress scenario**, an economic slump with increasing unemployment, a stock market crash and declining real estate prices is also assumed for the three years up to the end of 2016. Banks pass the scenario when they maintain a core capital ratio of at least 5.5 % under these conditions by the end of 2016.

Banks that don't pass these tests must close the capital gaps by reducing their assets or taking on new equity. If a credit institution doesn't achieve this, a politically appointed committee (from the EU commission, national supervisory authority and the ECB) decides on the **restructuring** of this bank. In this case, new capital is needed for processing or for maintaining parts of the bank that are still healthy, which comes from a rescue fund (restructuring fund) to be replenished by the banks themselves over the subsequent three years.

With regard to d)
The financial crisis had such far-reaching consequences, because, among other things, the effects of insolvency of an individual bank or an individual country were not foreseeable and thus not calculable. New and revised legislation for **country** and **bank insolvency** start at exactly this point. Bank insolvency legislation should regulate how the creditors are dealt with (in terms of debt relief) and how exactly a bank should be handled or restructured in case of insolvency. In particular, limitations to the possible repercussions of insolvency must be regulated. The planned European **bank union** consists of three pillars:
- common European bank supervision,
- a uniform bank processing mechanism and
- deposit insurance.

The above remarks on Comprehensive Assessment and Basel III (see Section 4.4.3) are components of **European banking supervision** (SSM).

The **uniform bank resolution mechanism** regulates the liability in the case of bank insolvency. Thus bank owners and creditors should be primarily liable in case of insolvency. If that's not enough, the resources should come out of a restructuring fund to which the banks themselves must contribute. In the next eight years, contributions in the amount of € 55 billion are planned. This bank levy is to be carried out at the national level by the Financial Market Stabilization Authority (FMSA), which also administers the Financial Market Stabilization Fund (SoFFin). The SoFFin is meant to support threatened German banks by granting silent participations until they can pay back the silent participations. The uniform bank resolution mechanism is intended to prevent the taxpayer from being liable for insolvent banks in future.

The establishment of so-called **bad banks** is in the same direction as the Financial Market Stabilization Fund. A bad bank is a separate credit institution for taking up derivatives, certificates and bad loans from distressed banks. The liability for the risks from the outsourced transactions now lies not with the respective distressed bank but with the bad bank and thus with the state or safety fund (SoFFin) as the owner of the bad bank. The bad bank liquidates the securities later in the hope that the economy and thus the prices will have recovered by then. In the best case, the state can even realize a profit through this. In the worst case, the state pays the failing bank too much for the outsourced positions and the prices don't recover. Then the losses are at the expense of the taxpayer. Bad banks also play a role in the solution approaches to market failure by restoring trust among market participants.

On July 2, 2014 the new European Deposit Guarantee Directive came into force and was implemented in German law on November 19, 2014. The new European **Deposit Guarantee Directive** consists altogether of the following rules:
- savings deposits are legally guaranteed up to € 100,000 per customer and per bank,
- in case of damage, savings depositors get their deposits back within seven working days,
- for especially vulnerable deposits (such as from the sale of private property) there is protection of up to € 500,000 for up to six months,
- all banks in the 28 EU states must be part of a prefinanced (ex ante) deposit guarantee scheme.

The deposit guarantee schemes of German banks and savings institutions, which often guarantee a higher level of protection then the European Deposit Guarantee Directive, remain and can be recognized by law. The European banking authority EBA is developing two guidelines based on the Deposit Guarantee Directive policy, which specify the methods for calculating the risk-oriented contributions to deposit guarantee schemes. The Deposit Guarantee Directive will be taken up again for solution approaches to market failure (see Section 4.3.3).

In the event of **state insolvency** it would also be necessary to regulate how claims are treated when the creditors do not agree with partial or complete waiving of their claims. The **European stability mechanism** (ESM) was established in the Eurozone to avoid state insolvency. The ESM is an international finance institution, and part of the Euro safety net. The function of the ESM is to support overextended member states of the Eurozone through emergency loans and guarantees in order to prevent their inability to pay.

With regard to e)
The standards for **financial reporting** regulate the scope and quality of reporting on risk management in the annual accounts. In Section 1.1, the legal framework conditions were named as a reason, among others, for risk management. These legal grounds include especially the regulation of financial reports in accordance with HGB (including the DRS (Deutscher Rechnungslegungs Standard – German Accounting Standard)), US GAAP (for US-American businesses on the US-American exchange), the IAS/IFRS (International Accounting Standards) and the IFRS (International Financial Reporting Standards). The treatment of this topic belongs primarily the business discipline of financial accounting and will be briefly described in Section 6.4 on external risk reporting. In the wake of the financial crisis, the **new Standard IFRS 9** was developed for all industries and the final version was published by the International Accounting Standards Board on April 24, 2014. The standard IFRS 9 "Financial Instruments" supersedes the IAS 39 "Financial Instruments: Recognition and Measurement" as of January 1, 2018, which the standard IFRS 7 also refers to and supplements. At the German level in particular the DRS 20 superseded the old DRS 5 for risk reporting, with effect from December 31, 2012.

The IFRS 9 contains changed standards for classifying and evaluating of financial assets, as well as a new risk provisioning model in which the **expected loss** is also taken into account. There will also be new rules for hedge accounting in the IFRS 9. With the IFRS 9, the balancing of financial instruments is based more on principles (e. g. no rigid effective limits) than on the extensive individual regulations of the previous IAS 39. As a result, there is more flexibility in the application, which is closer to economic risk management (e. g. through retroactive adjustment of the hedge relationships). However, this new standard will also affect products (for example, credit agreements), processes, organizational structures, IT systems and data requirements. It is especially worth emphasizing the relationship of the IFRS 9 to risk management. The new standard will result in greater harmony between **financial reporting** (in particular of financial hedge accounting) and **economic risk management**, in which from the banking perspective:
- the need for retrospective effective measurement falls away,
- by using flexible fair value options, banks can improve their credit risk management modelling and
- the basis risk from foreign currency transactions is clearly regulated.

Under certain conditions, industrial businesses are allowed to separate individual components of commodity risk for the purpose of hedge accounting, which in turn will improve economic risk modeling and reduce fluctuations in the profit and loss calculations.

With regard to f)
The **European Financial Instruments Directive** (MiFID) of 2004 was an important cornerstone for stronger integration of the common European financial market and part of the Financial Services Action Plan. It improved investor protection and regulation of financial intermediaries and liberalized exchange trading through so-called multilateral trading facility (MTF). The revised version of the European Financial Instruments Directive MiFID II came into force on July 3, 2014 and was supplemented by the financial market regulation MiFIR. The European securities and market authority ESMA will implement MiFID II and MiFIR by means of technical standards. MiFID II and MiFIR first come into use in European member states from January 3, 2017. The main content changes can be divided into the two major blocks of investor protection and market-related issues. The **market-related contents** of **MiFID II** are discussed in connection with the solution approaches to market failure (see Section 4.4.2.3).

With regard to g)
In addition to the above-mentioned laws and regulations, there are still **individual regulations** and directives for special problem areas of the financial crisis.

The **High-Frequency Trading Act** of May 7, 2013 (legislation for avoiding the dangers and abuses of high-frequency trading) counteracts the particular risks of high-frequency trading and closes supervisory gaps in the area of high-frequency traders without entirely prohibiting trading that uses algorithmic programs (=high-frequency trading). In recent years, electronic trading of financial instruments has become increasingly important due to technological developments and increased competition between financial centers through creation of new types of trading platforms. Certain traders use algorithmic trading programs in electronic trading which generate buy and sell signals in extremely short intervals, sometimes only split seconds, and arrange to hold the financial position for only very short periods. The use of these algorithmic high-frequency trading strategies has increased the speed and complexity of trading. It entails in addition a multitude of risks such as, for example, the overloading of the trading system through over-use in the case of a very high volume of orders. There is also the risk that algorithmic trading strategies react to other market events, which can likewise increase volatility. Finally, certain types of improper behavior can arise through high-frequency trading. The core of the High-Frequency Trading Act consists of a modification of the corresponding paragraphs of
- the Stock Exchange Act,
- the Banking Act,
- the Securities Trading Act,
- the Investment Act.

The modifications also have an influence on market failure (see Section 4.4.2.3).

Another individual regulation is the European **regulation on short selling** and certain aspects of credit default swaps from March 14, 2012. Short selling in times of considerable financial instability could substantially reinforce the downward spiral of stock prices and thus a possible crisis. The regulation refers to uncovered short selling of stocks and public debt securities which are traded on regulated markets and multilateral trading facility (MTF, see also European Markets in Financial Instruments Directive) within the European Union. The prohibitions against short-selling do not apply to derivatives nor to the sale of call options (see Section 3.4.2). The prohibition against uncovered short sales is closely linked to maximum loss (see Section 2.1.1).

In 2013 the EU parliament adopted stronger regulation of the **rating agencies**, which will be discussed in more detail with regard to market failure (4.4.2.3).

There is currently no regulation, directive or legislation for **regulating shadow banks**, but various plans are being discussed on different political and economic levels. A shadow bank is a financial institution that does business similar to banks without having a bank license or being a credit institution, such as e. g. hedge funds and private equity funds. However, subsidiaries of banks and firms that operate outside of bank balance sheets (so-called off-balance sheet transactions), like e. g. certain types of special-purpose vehicle, also fall under the term shadow banks.

If shadow banks take out large scale **loans from banks** and the repayments later become questionable, the creditor banks can then in turn get into trouble. This can intensify a financial crisis or loss of confidence in banks. Since the mid-1990s, the volume of transactions in the shadow banking system has increased rapidly and now amounts to ca. € 50 trillion globally and in the EU to € 25 trillion (estimate). Since shadow banks are not banks in the sense of the banking union and the national or international supervisory authorities, they don't fall under the regulations mentioned above such as e. g. Basel III. The role and influence that the shadow banks have on financial crises is a controversial discussion. There is, however, consensus that shadow banks were also a cause of the 2008 financial crisis and must be regulated. The following approaches or priorities are currently being discussed for the regulation of shadow banks:
- rules for money market funds with respect to their liquidity profiles (size of daily and weekly asset ratios),
- transparency of the shadow bank sector through collection of reliable and comprehensive data,
- issues of the location of shadow banks (e. g. Cayman Islands),
- regulations in connection with security loans and repurchase transactions,
- strengthening the supervisory regulations for transactions between banks and shadow banks and the
- creation of resolution instruments for shadow banks.

In the European Union, **bonus payments** for bank employees were **limited** for the first time with effect from January 1, 2014. This is meant to prevent the banking incentive structure from becoming distorted to the point that employee risk appetite becomes excessive and no longer compatible with the bank's risk capital (equity capital). Bonus payments may no longer exceed salary (maximum 1:1 relationship). Shareholders of the bank may allow bonus payments of double the fixed salary only as an exception. Future bonus legislation also provides incentives for longer-term and more sustainable remuneration options. In order to give bank employees incentive for long-term success planning, bonus payments exceeding the annual base salary must include at least 25 % deferment for five or more years and can only be repaid under certain conditions. The EU commission committed to check by the end of 2016 whether the bonus payment limit leads to a competitive disadvantage for European banks. Limiting bonus payments is part of a legislative package which translates the capital requirements for banks (Basel III see Section 4.4.3) negotiated by global banking oversight into EU law. The precursor on the German level is the Institutional Remuneration Directive (InstitutsVergV) which came into force on October 13, 2010 and which allowed supervisory assessment of salaries based on the specific situation (in particular the overall risk profile) of the institution. The close connection to risk management (overall risk profile) is also clear here.

Limitation of **salary payments** is currently taking place on the German level in the framework of the Financial Market Stabilization Fund Act (FMStFG). Thus institutions with at least 75 % direct or indirect involvement by the Financial Market Stabilization Fund (SoFFin) are not allowed to pay more than € 500,000 per year salary to board members and employees. Variable salaries (bonus payments) are not permitted.

The **Act on Ringfencing and Recovery and Resolution Planning for Credit Institutions** ("Separate Banking Act") is intended to stabilize the European banking system. It came into effect on August 13, 2013 and comprises three regulatory areas
- restructuring and resolution plans in cases of threatened insolvency,
- separation of risk areas from deposit transactions and
- rules for penalizing bank and insurance executive boards in the case of breaches of risk management duty.

The Separate Banking Act as an article of law is part of the German Banking Act (KWG) and the Insurance Supervision Act (VAG). The initial problem for the Separate Banking Act was the danger triggered by the financial crisis that savers would lose their deposits due to risky investment banking transactions by banks. The separation between investment banking or risk-area transactions and deposit transactions is intended to protect savers. The second point was therefore the original impulse for the Separate Banking Act, which also inspired the name. The first point begins from the same position as the second pillar of the banking union (uniform bank resolution mechanism). One part of the Separate Banking Act can therefore be seen as the German precursor to the second pillar of the banking union. The third point of the Separate Banking Act regulates penal measures for gross breaches of duty against risk management standards, which may lead to total bankruptcy of a bank or insurance company. Violations of basic risk-management obligations are punishable by up to five years in prison if the credit institution's stock or the insurance company's ability to fulfill insurance contracts is subsequently jeopardized (VAG). This third pillar goes in the same direction as the KonTraG (see Section 1.1) from April 27, 1998, but nonetheless represents a significant tightening of obligations and a stricter sanctioning of management misconduct.

In Figure 4.19 the most important laws and regulations for the causes and solution approaches to the financial crisis are represented in overview.

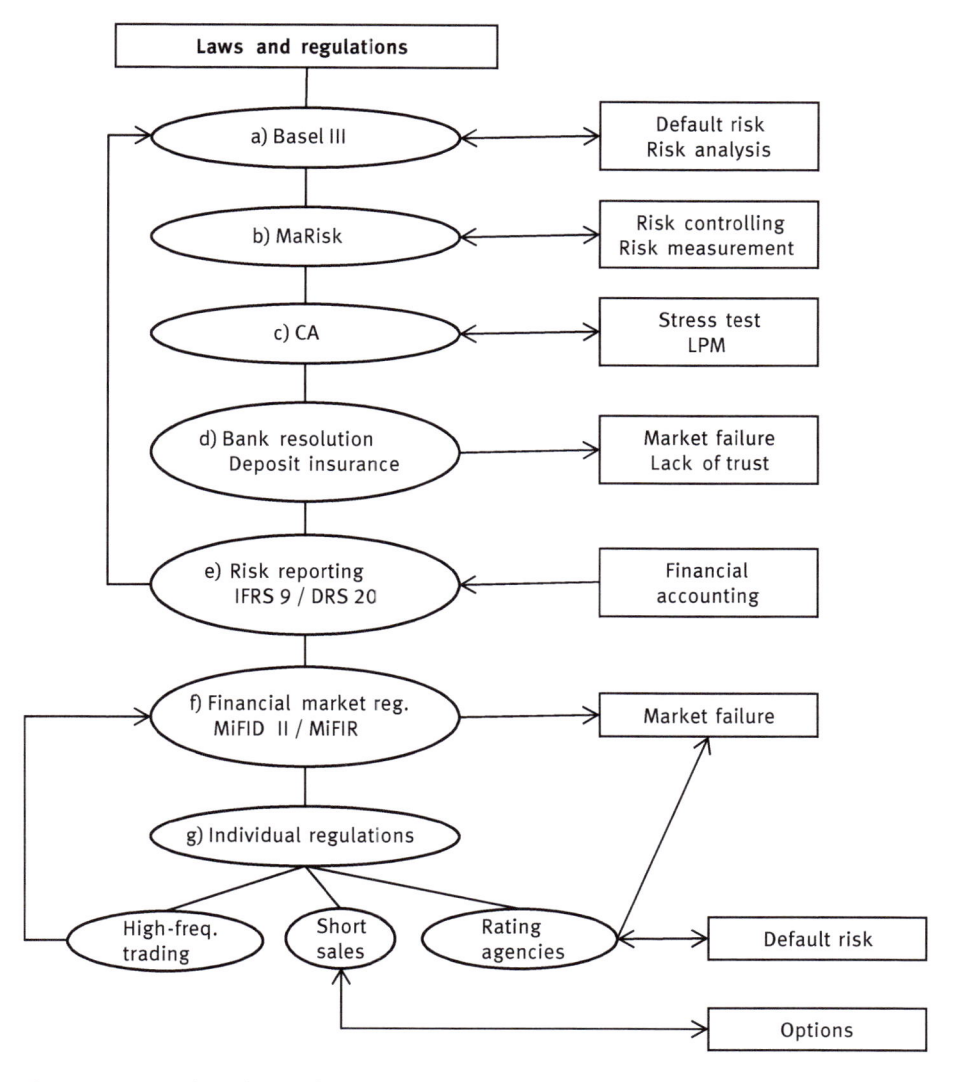

Fig. 4.19: Laws and regulations for the causes and solution approaches to the financial crisis

4.4.2.2 Human misconduct

Another cause of financial crises is in the area of **human misconduct**. This misconduct primarily is manifested in an unreflecting pursuit of ever greater returns or revenues (bonus payments, salaries). Through exaggerated profit-seeking (sociologists also speak of "greed" under certain conditions), some bank decision-makers and financial market players can experience motivation to develop new products with ever higher returns while circumventing legal standards, regulations and risk management. However, it is also human misconduct when decision-makers and controllers consent to certain transactions without further investigation or against their better knowledge (e. g. because of time pressure). This area of causation also includes misconduct by politicians. There is also a connection here to the capping of bonus payments, mentioned above, in order to limit excessive pursuit of returns.

The disciplines of sociology (economic sociology), psychology (business psychology) and ethics (business ethics) offer the solution approach for this causal category. The extravagant and mindless profit-seeking (in a few extreme cases it can be also be called "greed") is triggered or supported by incentives. Incentive systems are the subject of the following disciplines:
– **Economic sociology** concerns itself with the sociological analysis of economic anomalies (e. g. unreflected pursuit of returns) in the social context.
– **Business psychology** is concerned with subjective experience and people's behavior in the economic environment as well as social contexts. As a subcategory of applied psychology, business psychology transfers psychological insights to economic questions (e. g. the causes of exaggerated profit-seeking).
– **Business ethics** is concerned with applying ethical principles such as humanity, solidarity and responsibility to the area of economic activity. The justification of business ethical norms comes from the effects of economic activities on other people and the environment, with reference to social justice and sustainability.
– **Behavioral economics** as a sub category of business sciences is concerned with human behavior and incentive systems in the economic context.

A direct connection to the risk management methods described in this book is not readily apparent. For more detailed discussion, please see the relevant literature from the disciplines mentioned above. Nonetheless, it can also be understood as a task of risk management to check incentive systems in order to avoid potential misconduct through short-term behavioral incentives.

4.4.2.3 Market failure

One causal category of financial crises is the **failure** of **markets** or of market institutions and market participants. It should first be clarified what is meant by market

failure. There is a broad range of definitions, each of which depends on the economic perspective. The spread ranges from a distinctly economically liberal position, which holds that free markets cannot fail, to the position that free markets don't work at all and must be fully steered and planned by the state (planned economy). Economics deals with, among other things, the functioning of markets. In the following remarks, market failure should be understood as a complete collapse of markets and extreme, non-cyclical market fluctuations upwards and downwards (even with extreme market fluctuations upwards, losses can occur for certain derivatives). Extreme market fluctuations can be triggered by particular economic and socio-political events as well as by particular (i. e. deviating from normal "every day business") products and market participant activities. A further distinction can be made between a failure of the pricing process or the market participant, and bad decisions or judgments by market institutions. **Examples** of a **pricing process** failure or a bad decision by a **market participant** could be:
- self-fulfilling crises (e. g. Greece),
- false assessment by market participants (e. g. real estate bubbles),
- lack of trust among market participants (e. g. banks on the money market),
- lack of market liquidity,
- technical failures in processing market orders (e. g. IT-based order processing),
- price formation in high-frequency trading and
- the trading of products that reinforce market fluctuations (e. g. uncovered short selling).

Examples of bad decisions by **market institutions** can be:
- mistaken judgments by rating agencies (e. g. Moody's, Standard&Poor's, Fitch Ratings) and
- lack of (technical) market regulation by market supervisory authorities (e. g. ESMA).

Solution approaches for these examples are related to some of the solution approaches described above for the other causal categories. Different rules and regulations impinge on the financial markets. Thus uncovered short selling is forbidden and high-frequency trading is regulated in Germany (see above 4.4.2.1 g)). The high-frequency trading act also affects the technical processing of orders. Whether high-frequency trading has an inflationary effect on the real economy (e. g. on grain prices) is controversially debated in various studies. The **European financial market guidelines** MiFID II and MiFIR are important interventions in the European financial markets. The market-related contents of MiFID II and MiFIR include
- broadening of trading transparency (pre-and post-trade transparency for almost all instruments, products and derivatives (MiFID II)),
- Europe-wide regulation of high-frequency trading (MiFID II),

- innovations to the market microstructure (limiting the ratio of orders to executed transactions for every trading center (MiFID II)),
- the general obligation to keep records of all services, activities and transactions (MiFID II),
- access to central counterparties, trading centers and benchmarks (MiFIR),
- the trading obligation for OTC derivatives (MiFIR).

European financial market guidelines are primarily meant to reduce or eliminate risks on the technical side of the European financial markets. Risks coming from financial market failures can also frequently have **psychological** or **sociological causes**. Lack of trust between market participants, self-fulfilling crises and overvaluing by market participants are examples of this. Economic measures such as, for example
- liquidity subsidies by the ECB to restore confidence among banks,
- ending the ECB's expansionary monetary policy in order to avoid asset bubbles,
- establishing security funds, bad banks (e. g. deposit guarantee funds, restructuring funds, SoFFin for restoring trust in ailing market participants),
- stricter regulation of rating agencies in order to avoid self-fulfilling crises,

support the functioning or avoid the failure of finance markets. Nonetheless, the so-called psychology of the market and the business psychology (see above) which have themselves helped to cause the self-fulfilling crises and asset bubbles must also be taken into account.

Rating agencies have a considerable influence on financial markets or investors. In the case of the Greek crisis, the rating agencies downgraded the Greece's country rating (see Section 4.2.6). As a result, the risk premiums for Greek government bonds rose. Due to the increased risk premiums, Greece had to achieve a higher debt service. As a result the creditors feared that Greece could no longer completely accomplish its debt service. Due to these creditor fears, the rating agencies lowered the Greece's country rating again, thus in turn increasing the debt service again. Because of its experience with the Greek state crisis, the EU parliament adopted stricter regulations of rating agencies, consisting of the key points:
- allows unsolicited country ratings only at certain times,
- offers investors the opportunity to sue rating agencies for gross negligence and
- breaks through the dominant market position of the three largest rating agencies.

Previous efforts to install a European rating agency have so far failed. However, even in the USA, where the three largest rating agencies have their headquarters, the fee regulations for rating agencies have been redesigned. This is meant to reduce the dependency of rating agencies on their clients (banks and firms that have commissioned a credit rating from the rating agencies).

The market supervisory authority should be well-equipped in terms of both personnel and material resources in order to be able to monitor the financial markets thoroughly and independently.

The market failure causes and solution approaches described above are currently also discussed in relation to the topic of European **capital market union**. The intended goal of the capital market union is to make the European capital market more efficient, more competitive and more diverse. At the same time, the European capital market should be more resistant to shocks and crises. In particular, the market supervisory authority (ESMA) and the European Financial Market Directive (MiFID II, MiFIR) form the first components of this capital market union. As further components of the capital market union, the following are being discussed:
- finalization of the single financial market, and in particular of the securities sector, through a suitable prospectus standard, transparency of securitization and a sufficient liquidity,
- better European capital market financing, especially for SMEs through lower capital costs, better information acquisition on the capital markets and more venture capital financing,
- harmonization of tax regulations, insolvency law and accounting in the EU.

The **connection** of rating agencies to **risk management** and in particular the fundamental problems of rating procedures are dealt with in Sections 2.5 (qualitative risk measurement), 4.2.4 (analysis of individual transaction default risk) and 4.2.6 (country risk). A general relation between market failure and risk management consists in the measurement of volatility (Section 2.2.1). Volatility can be better and more reliably assessed (and thus also the VaR, see Section 2.3) if it is not subject to strong fluctuations triggered by any form of market failure. In other words: the distribution of the past changes in return strongly deviates from the normal distribution in the case of market failures. In particular, the so-called fat tails (see Section 2.3.7) are observable during market failures and crises. In Figure 4.20, market failure as a cause of the financial crisis, the solution approaches, and their respective relationships, are presented in overview.

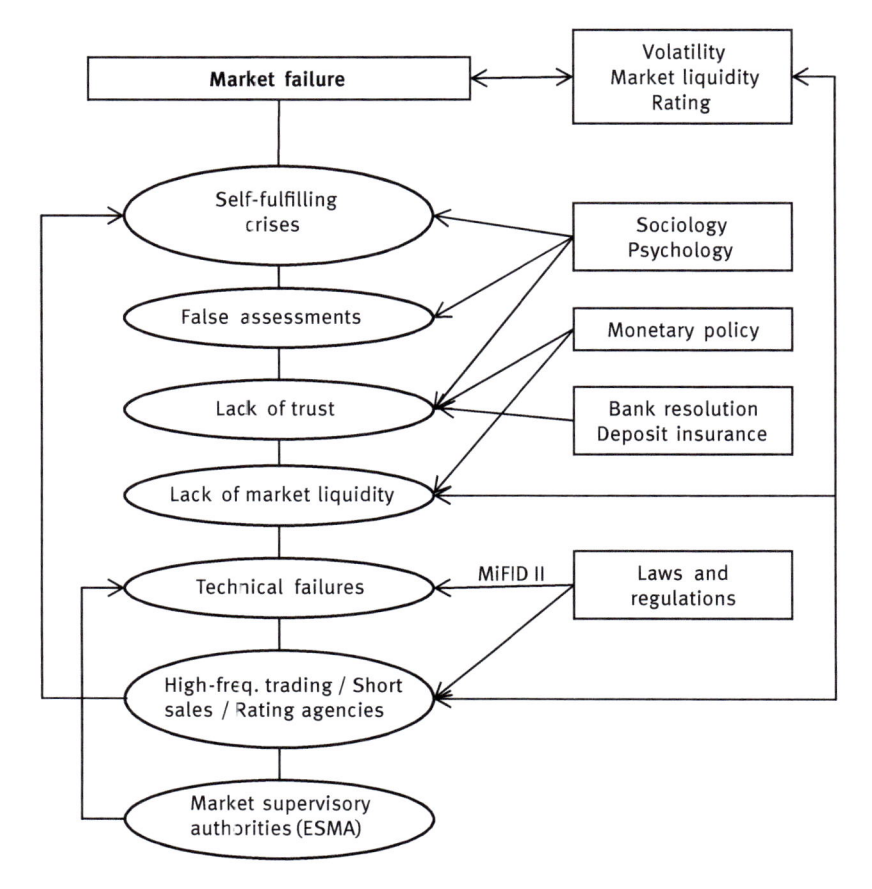

Fig. 4.20: Market failure for the cause and solution approach to the financial crisis

4.4.2.4 Mistaken decisions by politicians and regulators

Possible **mistaken decisions** by **politicians** or **government representatives** and other decision-makers as a cause of the financial crisis can next be sorted again into the different categories of:
- mistakes in monetary and fiscal policy,
- lack of reforms regarding the need for new frameworks for the national real economy,
- missing legislation for regulating banks and lack of implementation of new laws at the EU level (e. g. the regulation of shadow banks),
- no exercise of control functions in enterprises and institutions that are partly owned by the state.

Monetary policy decisions are primarily concerned with decisions of national central banks and globally with decisions of European and US American central banks (ECB, FED). The decision-makers of central banks are, at least formally, independent of politics and government in their decisions. Nonetheless, politicians and government representatives have indirect influence on central banks and their monetary policies. So, for example, the directors of the ECB appointed the Council of Europe, which represents the governments of the EU member states. Mistaken decisions by the central banks have a considerable influence on the emergence, avoidance and resolution of financial crises. The primary goal of monetary policy is to maintain price stability, i. e. to combat inflationary or deflationary tendencies. The effects of the financial crisis are, among others, a lower overall economic demand (see above Section 4.4.1). The central bank can counteract this through an expansionary monetary policy, i. e. by decreasing (monetary policy) key interest rates.

An **expansionary monetary policy** can **stimulate** investment and exports by lowering interest rates (through depreciation of the domestic currency) and thus boost overall economic demand. Since there is usually no inflationary pressure in a recession, this can be an effective instrument even while preserving the primary objective of price stability. At the beginning of a banking crisis, the monetary policy instrument of direct liquidity grant from the central banks to the commercial banks on the money markets (interbank market) is available. The goal of this instrument is to restore trust among the banks on the money market in order to ensure sufficient liquidity among the banks on the money market and avoid a so-called credit crunch.

However, the impact of an expansionary monetary policy can also have **undesirable side effects**. Thus the additional liquid funds or lowered interest rates may not be passed on by the banks in the form of loans to companies, but rather put into other types of investments, in particular liquid investments such as German government bonds. In addition, there is a limit to how much interest rates can be lowered. When key interest rates sit close to zero % over a long period of time, the stimulus effect of the expansionary monetary policy may sharply diminish, and other incentive mechanisms must be put in place by the central bank in order to further boost the overall economic demand. This can be done, for example, through negative deposit rates at the ECB. If these negative or near-zero deposit rates are passed on by commercial banks to their customers, including bank costs, this then leads to further burdens on the economy instead of promoting investment. However, the ECB can also buy financial securities, e. g. government bonds, on the market, which likewise expands the money supply. In that case, the central banks have a significant balance sheet extension, which is bound up with potential negative effects again later. An example of the undesirable side effects of an expansionary monetary policy is the prolonged recession in Japan in the 1990s.

Another undesirable side effect of an expansionary money policy is that the additional liquid funds are not used for loans to companies for investment but rather put into financial assets (stocks, property funds). This can lead to a strong overvaluation of financial assets, the so-called bubble formation, which can in turn trigger a new financial crisis when the **bubble bursts**. Finally, low interest rates have a negative impact on willingness to save and capital formation in private households.

There is a tight relationship between **monetary policy** and **risk management**. Interest rate levels and, in particular, changes in interest rate, affect a company's success and risks. Management of interest change risks is discussed in detail in Section 4.1.1. Figure 4.3 illustrates another side effect of low interest rates due to an expansionary monetary policy. The present value function follows a very steep course when interest rates sit close to zero (in comparison to high interest rates). This means that the present value of financial securities is sharply altered by interest rate changes. If the ECB raises the interest rate again because of e. g. inflationary tendencies, the result is a great interest change risk for all interest-dependent assets, linked to the danger of severe negative effects on company earnings.

Fiscal policy is, next to monetary policy, the second economic policy starting point in order to stabilize the economy as a whole in or after a crisis. In contrast to monetary policy, fiscal policy measures are the direct responsibility of politicians and government representatives. In the framework of fiscal policy, government spending can be directly increased by the state buying more goods and services (e. g. investment in transport infrastructure, scrappage premiums). This strengthens overall economic demand. However, state revenue and at the same time taxes can also be lowered. That allows more income to remain in private households and companies, which they can use for enhanced consumer demands. Both measures have a negative effect on the national budget: the national debt increases. An increasing national debt is, in turn, a possible cause for a national crisis. National debt that increased during a recession can be reduced again by surpluses from an economic boom. However, this requires corresponding institutionally or constitutionally embedded budgetary rules. It is difficult for politicians to convey to the people why surpluses from good times should be used to compensate deficits from the recession. There is no discernible direct connection from fiscal policy to risk management. For this reason, please refer to the relevant economic and finance literature for more detailed representation of possible instruments and effects of fiscal policy.

A fundamental prerequisite for reducing government debt through e. g. tax revenues at cyclical highs are favorable **framework conditions** for the overall real economy. By contrast to monetary policy, government representatives and politicians are directly responsible for that. Framework conditions include, among other things
- a seamless and functioning tax collection system or tax administration,
- a modern transport infrastructure,
- favorable employment market conditions,
- efficient and capable public administrations,
- comprehensive and modern educational systems.

In Greece, Italy and partially in Portugal, missing framework conditions were a cause of the national crisis with the results already described above. The creation of favorable framework conditions is basically arranged by national politicians and depends on the party affiliation as well as the political design processes. The question of what portion of its budget a state invests in the respective types of framework conditions and what impact this will have is very broad and complex. Since no direct connection to risk management is visible, please refer again to the relevant, comprehensive economic literature.

A central area where politicians and governments influence financial crises is through **legislation** on the national and international (EU) level. So, laws for regulating banks and financial markets can be designed and accelerated but also delayed by governments. The close connection to the above-mentioned solution approaches through rules and regulations is obvious here. As a rule, politicians deal with the content of laws before deciding whether or not to pass them.

There a problem arises: for that they need a large measure of bank specific expertise. Bank specific expertise, on the other hand, is the exception, possessed only by politicians with the corresponding professional background. There are various possibilities for achieving the expertise necessary for evaluating legislative proposals:
- information provided by own specialized authorities and ministries (e. g. the Ministry of Finance, Parliament's scientific service),
- consultation with interest groups (e. g. the banking association),
- commissioning of expert opinions (e. g. through specialized law firms, corporate consultancies),
- surveys of independent experts (e. g. expert panels, professors, economic institutes).

It is up to politicians to decide which of these possibilities they will use and to what extent. In the past, politicians have often made decisions in the context of **focusing events** (for example, a 100-year flood). In such cases, politicians have **trusted their sources** and that has played a central role in their decisions. The various sources of information take different interests into account. So, for example the German Banking Association will have a legitimate interest in representing its banking regulation requirements from its own perspective, differently than e. g. the BaFin (Federal Agency for Financial Services Supervision). As a result, the content of the final legislation is frequently a technical and political compromise solution due to the political decision-making process (e. g. Basel III, see Section 4.4.3).

Another possibility for politicians to intervene in financial crises is the exercise of **control functions** in businesses and institutions that have state participation (e. g. German KfW, IKB, Landesbank). The control function is usually governed by law or regulation. The difficulty for politicians is similar to that of passing specialist laws (legislation), as mentioned above. Either they have the necessary expertise due to their professional backgrounds or they delegate representatives with appropriate

expertise to the regulatory bodies. The following requirements should be met for effective control:
- the politician is independent of or has no conflict of interest in the supervised companies/institutions,
- sufficient available time,
- social competence and
- professional suitability to exercise control.

It is currently being discussed how these requirements can best be fulfilled in practice, for example, through limiting the number of control mandates. The same applies to the control of private companies by supervisory boards.

4.4.2.5 Risk management

Deficiencies in business **risk management** as the possible cause of financial crises, as well as the question of whether crises can be avoided through risk management, are the central concern of this book. During and after the financial crisis, it was apparent that companies (in particular banks) with thorough and consistent risk management coped with the financial crisis relatively well. However, due to the multiple influencing factors, "good" risk management cannot be the sole and all-encompassing protection against the impact of financial crises. It is nonetheless an important pillar. The "best methods" of risk management are no use when these are circumvented because of unreflected return expectations or other human misconduct. The connections between financial crises and risk management are explored in more detail in the respective sections (e. g. risk analysis, liquidity risks). An overview of the most important links between financial crises and risk management will be summarized here.

Risk management:		Financial crisis:
Reasons for risk management (1.1)	⇔	New laws/regulations
Maximum loss (2.1.1), options (3.4.2)	⇔	Uncovered short selling
LPM (2.3.6), stress test (2.4)	⇔	Banking union, stress test
Risk analysis (2.6)	⇔	Sufficient equity coverage
Interest rate risk (4.1.1)	⇔	Monetary policy
Default risk (4.2, 4.4.3)	⇔	Bank insolvencies, Basel III
Country risk (4.2.6)	⇔	Rule of rating agencies
Liquidity risks (4.3)	⇔	Crisis of confidence among banks
Risk controlling	⇔	MaRisk

To conclude, the most important causes and solution approaches of the financial crisis as well as their relationships are shown in overview in Figure 4.21.

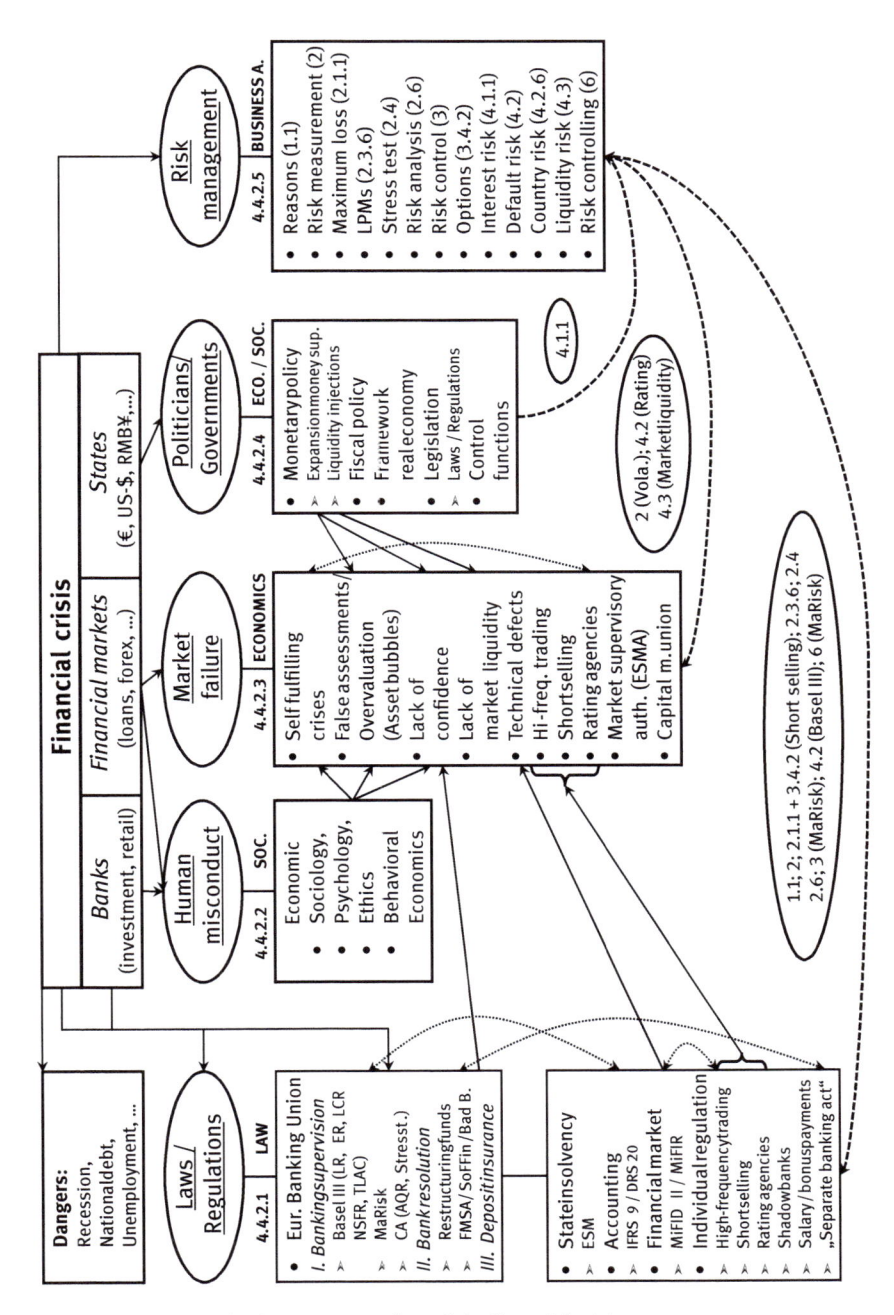

Fig. 4.21: Causes and solution approaches of the financial crisis

The various categories of crisis causes are shown in ovals in Figure 4.21 (4.4.2.1 – 4.4.2.5). Underneath the different cause categories, the associated possible solution approaches and causes are shown in the rectangles. The various (main) solution approaches are marked with a dot, and possible examples or subtopics are marked underneath with a triangular arrow. The dotted arrows indicate links between various approaches within a category. The solid arrows sketch links and effects between solution approaches from different categories. Finally, the thick dashed arrows show the relationships between the various categories (4.4.2.1 – 4.4.2.4) and risk management (4.4.2.5). For better clarity, not all conceivable relationships are represented by arrows, but only the most important and previously described connections. So, for example, the link between the cause categories of 4.4.2.4 legislation and 4.4.2.1 laws/regulations is not explicitly represented (since this connection is obvious).

4.4.3 Basel III

As already mentioned in 4.4.2.1 a), Basel III describes an important regulation for bank equity coverage in relation to default risk. Hidden in the term **Basel III** on the one hand is the founding of the **Basel committee on Banking Supervision** (BCBS) (by the Bank for International Settlements (BIS)) in the year 1975. The goal of this foundation was the avoidance of worldwide financial crises through appropriate recommendations for national banking supervision. On the other hand, a recommendation was already made in 1988 in the framework of **Basel I** and also broadly implemented in national law that every bank must hold 8 % of issued loans in equity capital. In other words: the maximum amount a bank can lend cannot be more than 12.5 times its own equity capital. This recommendation or national requirement did indeed lead to stabilization of the financial system, but there was no individual risk differentiation. The lack of risk differentiation causes **regulatory arbitrage** from good to bad credits, already described above in Section 4.2.3 under the term "Adverse Selection Effect". Avoiding this regulatory arbitrage is one of the main goals of **Basel II**. **Basel II** basically consists of **three pillars**:
1. minimum capital requirements,
2. supervisory review procedures and
3. disclosure of default risks and operational risks.

The heart of Basel II is the **minimum capital requirement pillar**, which deals with the actual risk differentiation. Organizational implementation of the other two pillars is only relevant for banks and will not be discussed further here.

Basel II provides three different approaches for risk differentiation:
- the standard approach,
- the basic IRB approach and
- the advanced IRB approach.

The **standard approach** provides for a equity coverage, as with Basel I, of 8 %. Where possible, the use of external ratings is permitted, with the additional possibility of reducing the risk weightings and thereby lowering the equity coverage or capital costs. Table 4.8 shows the risk weightings on the basis of Standard & Poor's. So there exists the possibility to set a risk weighting of 50 % for a non-bank with a Standard&Poor's of A+ and thus only be required to have a 4 % capital deposit. By doing so, the equity costs are halved. With the standard approach, only financial collateral is taken into account by reducing the risk weighting, and the maturity (M) is not considered.

Tab. 4.8: Risk weightings on the basis of Standard&Poor's

Rating class:	AAA AA-	A+ A-	BBB+ BBB-	BB+ BB-	B+ B-	Worse than B-	Not assessed
States	0 %	20 %	50 %	100 %	100 %	150 %	100 %
Banks	20 %	50 %	100 %	100 %	100 %	150 %	100 %
Non-Banks	20 %	50 %	100 %	100 %	150 %	150 %	100 %

The IRB approach (IRB = Internal Ratings Based) generally provides for the use of **internal bank ratings**. With the **basic IRB approach**, only the default probabilities (PD) are internally determined. The other risk parameters (Loss Given Default (LGD), Exposure at Default (EaD), Maturity (M)) are set by the banking supervisory authority.

With the **advanced IRB approach**, by contrast, all the risk parameters are internally assessed or calculated.

Using the bank supervisory **risk weighting function**, the associated risk weighting is then calculated from the risk parameters, in the same way as the standard approach, and the equity coverage or equity costs per credit are determined from this. Parts of the **VaR** of the credit are also included in the bank supervisory risk weighting function (see Section 4.2.3).

The IRB approach must be approved by the banking supervisory authority. Thus banks only apply the IRB approach if costs for the credit rating assessment or equity costs results are lower compared to the standard approach. In comparing the standard approach with the IRB approach, taking the **VaR** into account makes it clear that the IRB approach is better for modeling or supporting the necessary equity coverage and credit risk management. Most banks apply the standard approach. The advanced IRB approach is only applied to a few special banks.

However, the 2008 financial crisis exposed significant weaknesses in Basel II's banking regulation. The term **Basel III** refers to a new framework with amended equity and liquidity requirements, which was published in 2010 and subsequently discussed in detail. In the European Union, Basel III was implemented on January 1,

2014 through a new version of the Capital Requirements Directive or Regulation (**CRD IV or CRR**), with comprehensive transitional provisions.

The financial crisis showed that some banks had too little high-quality equity capital. The focus of Basel III is therefore on the so-called **core capital** (also called **tier 1**). **Common equity** will therefore consist exclusively of the subscribed capital and the open reserves. Hybrid core capital instruments (e. g. Mezzanine capital) are only allowed as tier 1 elements on a limited basis. The Basel committee formulated 14 criteria for common equity. The most important ones include the unlimited transfer and the most subordinated claim in case of liquidation. **Non-common equity** includes, among others, silent participations, treasury stocks, adjustments from currency conversion, non-cumulative preference stocks, and special items for general banking risks. There are also regulatory criteria for recognizing non-common equity.

So long as the supervisory criteria are met, **supplementary capital** (so-called **tier 2**) consists of, among other things, profit participation rights, long-term liabilities, unrealized profits, other valuation adjustments, cumulative preference stocks, minority interests.

Third-ranking funds (so-called **tier 3**) are subordinated liabilities with a term of 2 to 5 years. Third-ranking funds are completely abolished by Basel III.

The **total capital ratio** (total equity coverage) stays at 8 %. In the context of Basel III, total capital refers to the total equity component and not, as in the financial sector, the sum of equity capital and borrowed capital. From January 1, 2019, after a transition phase, the combination will be reset to the following values. The common equity must amount to a minimum of 4.5 % (previously 2 %), the non-common equity to at least 1.5 % (previously 2 %) and the supplementary capital can be up to 2 % (previously 4 %). In addition, the banks must build a **capital conservation buffer** consisting of only common equity of 2.5 % by 2019. So the banks must show common equity of 7 % by 2019. The capital conservation buffer is meant to represent a capital reserve for economic or financial stress phases, which can also be mined in such phases. The Basel committee also developed a capital buffer which is dependent on the economic cycle and which is intended to slow down cyclical overheating and excessive credit growth. This **anti-cyclical capital buffer** consists of common equity or other capital (which fully absorbs a loss) and is meant to lie between 0 % and 2.5 % according to national macroeconomic conditions. The **risk-weighted assets** are used to calculate the ratios (so-called equity ratio). The risk weightings are determined using the standard approach or the IRB approach according to Basel II (see above). The transitional phase is intended to enable banks to implement the Basel III reforms without jeopardizing their lending to the rest of the economy. In Figure 4.22, the various capital requirements are compared according to Basel II and Basel III.

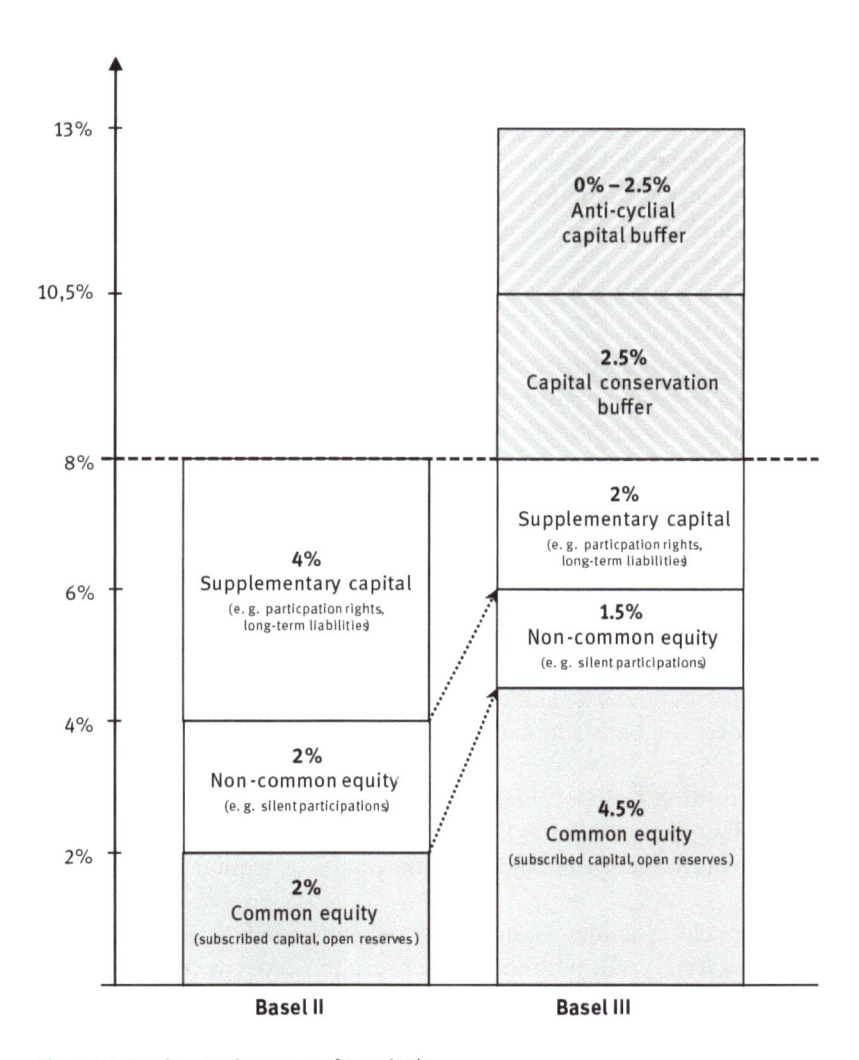

Fig. 4.22: Equity requirements of Basel II/III

The Basel committee introduced a so-called leverage ratio. The **leverage ratio** is the ratio of total regulatory core capital to the unweighted (not risk-based) balance sheet total. The concrete arrangement of this leverage ratio has not yet been finalized. At the moment, a leverage ratio of at least 3 % is planned, which is intended to be introduced as binding from 2018. From 2015, the leverage ratio is to be published in the framework of disclosure (pillar 3 of Basel II). It is meant to supplement or reinforce the risk-weighted equity standards (pillar 1) mentioned above. The leverage ratio is supposed to limit destabilizing debt build-up in the banking system in order to avoid destabilizing processes from forced asset sales during crisis periods.

These destabilizing processes manifest through (strongly) decreased market prices and corresponding losses of value which can cause bank equity to melt away. Due to the lower equity, the banks can grant fewer loans and must eventually sell more assets, which in a recession can exacerbate crises for the real economy.

With Basel III the capital requirements for the **counterparty risk** were also changed. This is intended to reduce the losses that occur in derivative transactions due to deterioration in creditworthiness of counterparties. Such a downgrading is expressed, on the one hand, in increased credit-related value adjustments of the outstanding derivative transactions (Credit Value Adjustment (CVA)). On the other hand, banks are supposed to transact their business increasingly through central counterparties. In this way, the counterparty risk is reduced but not completely avoided. Banks must deposit equity to cover their credit risk towards central counterparties.

The **liquidity coverage ratio** (LCR) is a minimum liquidity ratio introduced in the wake of Basel III to assess the short-term liquidity risk of credit institutions. The LCR is the ratio of the portfolio as a top tier asset to the total net outflow of the next 30 days. The LCR is determined through application of a Basel III stipulated stress scenario (to be distinguished from the banking stress test described above). The LCR must amount to 100 % or more in order to meet the standard. The standard is meant to ensure that the liquidity requirements of credit institutions are covered even under extremely unfavorable conditions for at least 30 calendar days. Thus the liquidity coverage ratio should cover the bank's liquidity risk. Liquidity risks were dealt with in Section 4.3.

The **net stable funding ratio** is a long-term oriented refinancing standard with the goal of avoiding long-term structural liquidity mismatches. The NSFR is the ratio of the actual to the required stable refinancing, and should be greater than or equal to one.

Finally, the Financial Stability Board (FSB) recommended a so-called **total loss-absorbing capacity** (TLAC). With this loss absorption capacity, the 30 largest banks worldwide should have a TLAC of 16 % to 20 % of their risk-weighted assets and 6 % of their unweighted assets. The TLAC consists of equity capital as well as other elements such as e. g. bonds which can be converted into equity capital by the bank. The TLAC thus represents a kind of combination of leverage and equity ratio as well as of core capital plus supplementary capital, in accordance with Basel II/III.

From these very brief descriptions of Basel II and Basel III, some **consequences** and **action recommendations** can be derived for default risk management from the perspective of lenders as well as borrowers.

A **best** possible **negotiating position** for credit negotiations is achieved from the borrower's point of view when an **external rating** can be provided. Since in this case the rating is public, the borrower also knows roughly the lender's equity capital costs, which improves the borrower's negotiating position. With internal ratings, by contrast, this is not the case. In Europe, however, external ratings are only available for large companies, so internal ratings mainly basically come into use for small and medium-sized enterprises.

The demands of **lenders** have especially changed for the **small- and medium-sized** enterprises, for which there are no external ratings. Some potential consequences for SMEs from Basel II/III are the following:
- The increased equity requirements for banks by Basel III can lead to an increase in capital costs and thus to a **cost increase** in loans. If the higher value equity (core capital) cannot be provided, then this can also lead to a credit shortage.
- **Transparency** towards lenders regarding economic situation, financial standing, future sustainability of the product etc. should be **increased**.
- **Regular communication** with lenders should be seen as an opportunity (e. g. to improve image and also rating). This also includes taking a downgrading of the rating as advance warning and accordingly working with the lender to seek out a solution.
- **Efficient controlling and risk management** wins additional importance through Basel II/III. Through a better controlling system and better risk management, lenders can be given additional and more precise information for the rating classification. A more favorable rating classification leads to more favorable financing conditions. The cost savings of more favorable financing conditions can in turn be used towards further measures to improve the rating.
- The borrower's **annual account** is a central element of the credit assessment (or rating) and gained renewed importance through Basel III. The annual statement can under some circumstances be optimized to a rating classification using approach and valuation options (although the International Accounting Standards Board is always working on reducing the corresponding leeway). This can lead to an improvement of the rating without actually having to increase the equity.
- SMEs, which do not profit from a differentiated risk assessment because Basel II/III worsens the credit conditions for these companies, should try to exploit the **new possibilities** for **equity capital** and **borrowed capital financing** (e. g. strengthened internal financing, mezzanine financing, Asset Backed Securities (ABS), credit groups).

Although the points represented above refer to borrowers, consequences and recommendations for lenders and default risk management can now be derived from them by implication, as follows
- Bank loans through non-banks, especially in the form of goods and delivery loans, can increase **information requirements** from their **borrowers**, since in the framework of Basel II/III these already have to satisfy higher information requirements than banks do.

- Since the **credit conditions** for banks have become more **transparent** through Basel II/III, non-banks must also follow this transparency. So now borrowers with a good rating can also demand improved credit conditions from non-banks.
- Due to the increased transparency, lenders have more potential to get relevant **information** for **calculating** the **risk-adjusted lending rate**. This relates in particular to necessary historical default rates, loss rates and the associated volatilities.

It is clear that Basel II/III increased the risk management requirements for banks. Here the focus is on the borrower's differentiated credit rating assessment (Basel II) and higher quality requirements for equity coverage. These requirements also inevitably strengthen communication between borrower and lender, both quantitatively and qualitatively.

4.4.4 Appraisal and outlook

The described solution approaches tend in the right direction. A sometimes strong presence in all the media provides for a more or less pronounced sensitivity in large portions of the population regarding the topic of the financial crisis. In the meanwhile, there is also comprehensive literature on the financial crisis and its presence takes up a lot of room on the Internet as well. In many financial markets, downturns caused by the financial crisis could be repaired again. There are also numerous examples where the prices clearly show higher listings (e. g. the German DAX) than before the crisis. Whether the previous solution approaches are sufficient to avoid future financial crises is doubtful, since the **positive developments** can also be set against numerous critical issues which will be considered more closely below.

The adopted or planned rules and regulations are **not globally harmonized**. In the EU alone there are ca. 100 special rules for banks on the national level. Basel II was not ratified in the USA and there are national exemptions for implementation of Basel III (CRD IV, CRR) on the EU level as well. However, there is not only a lack of harmonization on the state level, but also on the level of the various rules and regulations. So there are sometimes considerable differences in risk reporting on the level of
- the bank supervisory board (Basel II/III),
- the financial statement (IFRS 9/DRS 20) and
- the business risk management (Value at Risk).

The results of the lacking harmonization are so-called **regulatory arbitrage** and distorted competition. Thus banks can shift their transactions to countries or regions which are less regulated and thereby also lower the cost of their transactions and products. There are further examples of this problem of regulatory arbitrage, such as the tax deductibility of the bank levy in the restructuring funds, the discussions about a planned financial transaction tax (capital transfer tax on financial transactions) or the various deposit protection systems in the EU.

Two results also come directly from this regulatory arbitrage. Eurozone banks fear a **competitive disadvantage**, particularly against US-American banks, due to overly strict regulations or other financial burdens from the EU. Global harmonization would also lower the costs of expensive double (for supervisory and IFRS) record-keeping for banks. This would relieve banks, especially in times of an expansionary monetary policy with lower interest rates and a corresponding margin pressure, without the regulatory goals having to suffer qualitatively or quantitatively.

Potential harmonization (of tax laws and insolvency laws, see Section 4.4.2.3) will also be pursued through the planned and currently discussed **capital market union**. With the capital market union, however, there is in turn the danger that in promoting the European capital markets, certain developments (e. g. crowdfunding, lending to SMEs by shadow banks) are not sufficiently regulated. These developments could, in turn, trigger or reinforce new crises.

The reasons for the lack of harmonization are complex but can be summarized into two core points. On the one hand, there are **national economic interests** which are perceived and pursued by government representatives and politicians in the harmonization negotiations (e. g. Great Britain with the trading venue London, Netherland, Cayman Islands). On the other hand, global **financial transactions** are so **complex** and so incomprehensible to the layman that it is difficult to communicate to the wider population why, for example, it can be necessary to prohibit (worldwide) uncovered short selling.

The central negative aspect with regard to adopted and planned regulations consists in the arrangement of the **contents** and the applied **methods**. The contents of adopted rules and regulations refer almost without exception to the financial crisis since 2008. They represent necessary corrections and improvements from the **ex post** perspective. Indeed, the most fundamental mistakes of the financial crisis are retroactively refurbished in the rules and regulations (in particular at German level), but there are no basic **ex ante** position guidelines proposed for substantively avoiding or lessening the risk of future financial crises.

This can be illustrated by two examples (stress test, Basel III). The bank stress test already refers to the mentioned **deficiency** in Section 2.4.

First, there are the **arbitrary assumptions** of the **stress scenario** (e. g. 15 % decline in property prices in Germany compared to assumption of 5 % decline in property prices in Spain). In such cases there should be some attempt to do justice to the peculiarities of various countries and regions of the EU. This fundamental flaw of stress tests could be remedied, for example, with the concept of the lower partial moments (see Section 2.3.6). Second, the scenario (e. g. 15 % decline in property prices) is no longer a future stress for a bank when it has been tested in the present for whether there is sufficient equity capital to cover the case. This methodological flaw of stress tests can only be remedied by a fundamental change of methodology.

The third flaw lies in the role of the ECB, that is, the institution conducting the stress tests. From a monetary policy perspective, the ECB has an interest in banks granting more loans in a weak economic cycle. In its role as banking supervision, the ECB has an interest in reducing bad debt for commercial banks. Stress tests are useful despite the mentioned defects, since they force banks to deal with their risk assets and to test and adjust their risk and business policy if necessary. Whether stress tests alone can prevent bank insolvency or even financial crises is doubtful because of the mentioned shortcomings.

Basel III displays serious, scientific methodological defects. The financial crisis showed that some banks were quantitatively and/or qualitatively ill equipped with equity capital, which was a primary cause of the financial crisis. According to Basel III, the **total capital ratio** remains at **8 %!** Only the core capital ratio will be increased in the coming years. The quality of the equity capital was adjusted, but not the quantity. There are economists who call for a necessary adjustment of equity capital in relation to the overall unweighted bank assets up to 20 %–30 %. These demands may be unrealistic in the short and medium term. What is crucial is a equity coverage that represents the risk content of the assets as well as possible (see Section 2.6 and 4.2). With the IRB approach, this tends to occur through the VaR influencing factors. However, the banks only apply the IRB approach when it is more favorable for them (e. g. if the risk weighting is smaller than with the standard approach). Only with a rating worse than B- or for non-banks worse than B+ does the 150 % risk weighting (=12 % capital deposit) have to be applied according to the standard approach. Thus the application of the IRB approach is declining for banks. An obligation to apply an IRB approach that maps the risk as adequately as possible would be necessary.

Finally, the application of the **leverage ratio** shows a further methodological weakness of Basel III. It is meant to put the brakes on banking debt. That is necessary when banks have no requirement for a equity coverage for specific positions according to the standard or IRB approach. This is done, for example, for government bonds with a rating better than AA. As a result, however, the risk content is not correctly represented, which could be observed in the Eurozone in the financial crisis. If the risk is adequately represented and corresponding equity is deposited, then the debt will automatically be limited and a leverage ratio would not be necessary.

Along with these business critical aspects, there are also still legal problems to be solved for avoiding future crises. These include, among others, the worldwide legal regulation of **state** and **bank insolvencies**.

The grounds for the weaknesses described above essentially lie in two central areas. On the one hand, the regulatory enterprise is implemented on the political as well as the national level. The regulations must therefore also be comprehensible to the layman. For this reason, many regulations are in their approach necessarily **political compromise solutions**. On the other hand, regulations must also be both **achievable** and **reasonable** in **business.** A good example of that is the standard and IRB approach according to Basel II. The IRB approach goes in the right direction for business, but is bound up with a great deal more expense than the standard approach. The same goes for the stress test. The application of, for example, lower partial moments would have been commercially very expensive and the possible results also very difficult to make comprehensible to the wider population. The currently used stress test was relatively easy to convey: banks passed the test assuming certain crisis scenarios, or they didn't.

In addition to the weaknesses described above for the rules and regulations, there are other difficulties which were brought out by the financial crisis. For one thing, this includes the question of when exactly a financial crisis can be spoken of (see the definition of a financial crisis above) and tightly linked to that, the question of which **banks** are **systemically relevant**. Possible criteria for delineating the system relevance of banks are the size, connectivity, global business activity, substitutability and complexity. The size of the bank plays an important role (with respect to the danger of a financial crisis), but it is doubtful whether many smaller banks produce a more stable financial system. It is precisely because of their international diversification that globally acting banks are not just part of the problem, but also by all means part of the solution. These examples illustrate the problem of an effective definition of the term "systemically relevant banks".

On the other hand, the financial crisis showed its strong effects on the real economy and revealed the problem of how to separate the financial sector from the real economy, or if separation is necessary. The Separate Banking Act represents an approach to separating investment banking from standardized retail banking. There are, however, also many examples of how specific investment banking transactions have a not only useful but also necessary function for the real economy. One example is the hedging of the exchange rate through forward exchange transactions for cost planning of e. g. automobile manufacturers operating globally. For such offers to be available to the real economy, however, there must also be counterparties who speculate on a contrary market development and then potentially have no more reference to the real economy. Thus all financial products must be tested for their functionality and necessity for the real economy. The positive diversification effect also speaks against separation of investment banking and standardized retail banking (investment banking profits can absorb customer transaction losses and vice versa).

Finally, **sociological** and **psychological** causes of the financial crisis can only be partly remedied through laws and regulations. The various **incentive systems** are also a good example of that after the financial crisis. It is currently difficult to identify approaches to prevention (in the form of laws, regulations) or other sanctioning mechanisms of such causal triggers of financial crises.

Possible **mistaken decisions** by **politicians** can only be remedied in limited ways because of their free mandate. It is difficult to identify and prove mistaken decisions as such. Formal regulations can be set in force (limitations of the control mandate, disclosure of ancillary activities, etc.). How much a politician incorporates the material in order to avoid a mistaken decision must be left to him or brought about by public pressure.

For a closing **view**, the critical aspects and open problems of the financial crisis are summarized in the following:
- lack of harmonization of laws and regulations, competitive distortion, regulatory arbitrage,
- contents, methods (ex post perspective, Basel III, leverage ratio, stress test, regulations for state and bank insolvency),
- national (economic) interests,
- complexity of financial transactions (derivatives),
- political enforceability, business feasibility (bank profitability),
- systemic relevance (bank size),
- relationship with the real economy (forward exchange transactions),
- sociological and psychological causes (unreflected return expectations),
- mistaken decisions by politicians or decision-makers.

For **avoiding future crises**, a great deal depends on how intensively the effort is pursued on the economic and political level to achieve global harmonization of rules and regulations with the right contents and methods. The success of these efforts will largely depend on
- **willingness** of national political and economic stakeholders **to compromise** on content,
- **transparency** of the economic relationships around the financial crisis and financial products for the general public,
- reduction of the **complexity** of those financial transactions which don't serve the real economy and
- possible sociological and psychological solution approaches to avoiding certain **incentive systems**.

In other words: there is a globally networked financial world with full technical potential as well as the related advantages and disadvantages, but the necessary globalized rules to govern it are not there yet. The financial crisis has now shown the necessity for these globalized rules. The same problem also shows up in similar form with other crises, e. g. for one thing with climate risk (market failure of the emission trading system), and the efforts at the world climate summits to achieve globally binding standards regarding production of ecologically harmful substances. For another thing, the problem comes up around increasing digitalization and the (still) lacking regulation of data protection and copyright. But also, the thus far fruitless and strenuous battles around tax oases are an expression of a globalized, digitized world without the necessary global regulations.

In the next chapter, the other large and significant risk category of **operating risks** will be dealt with.

4.5 References

Beike, Rolf/Schlütz, Johannes: "Finanznachrichten lesen – verstehen – nutzen: Ein Wegweiser durch Kursnotierungen und Marktberichte", Schäffer Poeschel, 5. Auflage, 2010,
Brett, Michael: "How to Read the Financial Pages", Random House Business Books, 5th ed., 2003

give a very good overview and insight into the **various forms of securities** (stocks, bonds, funds, derivatives, etc.) and a description of virtually all important **stock exchange issues** relevant to financial risks.

The books of

Alexander, Carol Alexander, Carol: "Market Risk Analysis: Volume I: Quantitative Methods in Finance", Wiley, 2008,
Heidorn, Thomas: "Finanzmathematik in der Bankpraxis – Vom Zins zur Option", Gabler, 5. Auflage, 2006,
Hull, John C.: "Options, Futures, and Other Derivatives", Prentice Hall, 8th Edition, 2011,
Schierenbeck, Henner: "Ertragsorientiertes Bankmanagement", Band I, 8. Auflage, 2003

show how to calculate zero coupon rates from coupon rates using the so-called **bootstrap method**, among others.

Consideration of partial years (fractional maturities) can be also be looked up in

Kruschwitz, Lutz: "Finanzmathematik – Lehrbuch der Zins-, Renten-, Tilgungs-, Kurs- und Renditerechnung", Oldenbourg, München, 5. Auflage, 2010

and the English work

Richardson, Clarence H./Miller, Isaiah Leslie: "Financial Mathematics", Ulan Press, 2012

along with the above-mentioned works from *Heidorn*.

The application of duration and convexity for **non-parallel shifts** in the interest rate structure is treated in detail in

Wolke, Thomas: "Duration & Convexity", Dissertation, FU Berlin, 1996

and more generally in

Kruschwitz, Lutz/Wolke, Thomas: "Duration und Convexity", in WiSt Heft 8, S. 382–387, August 1994.

or in English

Hull; John C.: "Risk Management and Financial Institutions", Wiley, Hoboken, New Jersey, 4th ed., p. 189–191, 2015.

The construction of **portfolios** with long durations and a **modified duration** of null, as well as the properties of duration and convexity in relation to e. g. interest rates, are also described. **Another approach** to dealing with the non-parallel shift in the interest rate structure can be found in

Löffler, Andreas/Wolke, Thomas: "Variance Minimizing Strategy and Duration", working paper HU Berlin, 1996.

A detailed treatment of the various bond portfolio **immunization strategies** can be found in

Wondrak, Bernhard: "Management von Zinsänderungschancen und -risiken", Physica-Verlag, 1986

or the English work

Zündel, Caroline: "Yield curve shifts and the selection of immunization strategies: Importance of Duration and Convexity in the selection process Portfolio immunization against interest rate risks", Akademikerverlag, 2016

The above-mentioned works from *Heidorn* and *Hull* suitably describe and evaluate **interest rate swaps, interest rate options** and **interest rate futures.**
The works of

Blattner, Peter: "Internationale Finanzierung: Internationale Finanzmärkte und Unternehmensfinanzierung", Oldenbourg Wissenschaftsverlag, München, 1997,
Sperber, Herbert/Sprink, Joachim: "Internationale Wirtschaft und Finanzen", Oldenbourg, München, 2. Auflage, 2012

and the English works

Butler, Kirt C.: "Multinational Finance – Evaluating the Opportunities, Costs, and Risks of Multinational Operations", Wiley Finance, 6th ed., 2016,
Eitemann, David K./Stonehill, Arthur I./Moffett Michael H.: "Multinational Business Finance", Pearson, 14th ed., 2016,
Shapiro, Alan: "Multinational Financial Management", Wiley, 10th ed., 2013

provide a suitable exploration of **exchange rate risk**.
A detailed treatment of **portfolio theory** and the **CAPM** e. g. for deriving the minimal variance portfolio weightings and considering the utility functions for stocks can be found in, among others,

Elton, Edwin J./Gruber, Martin J./Brown, Stephen J./Goetzmann, William N.: "Modern Portfolio Theory and Investment Analysis", Wiley, 9th Edition, 2014,
Markowitz, Harry M.: "Portfolio Selection", Journal of Finance 7, no. 1 (March 1952), p. 77–91, 1952,
Sharpe, William F.: "Capital Asset prices: A Theory of Market Equilibrium under Conditions of Risk", Journal of Finance 19, no. 2 (September 1964), p. 425–442, 1964

and

Kruschwitz, Lutz: "Finanzierung und Investition", Oldenbourg Wissenschaftsverlag, München, 6. Auflage, 2010.

A successful overview and understandable description of the **measurement, analysis** and **control instruments** for **default risk** can be found in

Hull; John C.: "Risk Management and Financial Institutions", Wiley, Hoboken, New Jersey, 4th ed. p. 383–459, 2015,
Jorion, Philippe: "Financial Risk Manager Handbook", Wiley, Hoboken, New Jersey, 6th edition, p. 449–610, 2011,
Saunders, Anthony/Allen, Linda: "Credit Risk Management In and Out of the Financial Crisis: New Approaches to Value at Risk and Other Paradigms", Wiley Finance, 3rd ed., 2010,
Schulte, Michael/Horsch, Andreas: "Wertorientierte Banksteuerung II: Risikomanagement", Frankfurt School Verlag, 4. Auflage, 2010.
Schmeisser, Wilhelm/Mauksch, Carola: "Kalkulation des Risikos im Kreditzins nach Basel II", in: Finanz Betrieb, Heft 5, 2005, S. 296–310

undertakes a calculation of the **risk-adjusted lending rate** using a numerical example.

For an explanatory note on risk adjusted lending rate see also

Basel Committee on Banking Supervision: "An Explanatory Note on the Basel II IRB Risk Weight Functions", Bank for International Settlements, Basel, 2005,

There is also a general representation of this theme without numerical examples in

Oehler, Andreas/Unser, Matthias: "Finanzwirtschaftliches Risikomanagement", Springer, Berlin, 2. Auflage, 2013.

Rating classifications and the associated **default probabilities** as well as further useful information around this theme are available for free from **Standard&Poor's** and **Moody's** on the Internet at

http://www.standardandpoors.com

http://www.moodys.com

The theme of **credit derivatives** is dealt with in detail in

Burghof, Hans-Peter/Henke, Sabine/Rudolph, Bernd u. a. (Hrsg.): "Kreditderivate. Handbuch für die Bank- und Anlagepraxis", Schäffer Poeschel, 2. Auflage, 2005
Hull, John C.: "Options, Futures, and Other Derivatives", Prentice Hall, 8th Edition, p. 547–570, 2011.
Servigny, Arnaud de/Renault, Olivier: "Measuring and Managing Credit Risk", MCGraw-Hill, 2004,
McNeil, Alexander J./Frey, Rüdiger/Embrechts, Paul: "Quantitative Risk Management – Concepts, Techniques and Tools", Princeton University Press, Princeton and Oxford, p. 425–475, 2015

is a suitable exploration of the topic of **default risk measurement and control**, especially of **credit portfolios**.

Application and documentation of the **credit portfolio model CreditMetrics** can be found under

www.msci.com.

The book from

Gundlach, Matthias/Lehrbass, Frank: "CreditRisk+ in the Banking Industry", Springer Finance, 2004

is, along with the above-mentioned works from *Jorion (Handbook)* and *McNeil*, suitable for the **CreditRisk+** model.

For a detailed **comparison** of various **credit portfolio models,** the articles of

Crouhy, Michel/Galai, Dan/Mark, Robert: "A comparative analysis of current credit risk models", in: Journal of Banking & Finance, issue 24, 2000, p. 59–117, 2000

and

Gordy, Michael B.: "A comparative anatomy of credit risk models", in: Journal of Banking & Finance, issue 24, 2000, p. 119–149, 2000.

are especially good.

For a descriptive and lucid representation of the most important **analysis** and **control possibilities** for **country risk**, the above-mentioned work of *Schulte/Horsch* is helpful.

Dresel, Tanja: "Die Quantifizierung von Länderrisiken mit Hilfe von Kapitalmarktspreads", in: Johanning, Lutz/Rudolph, Bernd: "Handbuch Risikomanagement", Band I, Uhlenbruch, S. 579–609, 2000,
Du, Wenxin/Schreger, Jesse: "Local Currency Sovereign Risk", in: Journal of Finance 71, no. 3 (June 2016), p. 1027–1070, 2016

deliver an approach to **measurement** of **country risk** using capital market spreads.

For the subject of **country risk** see also

Kühlmann, Torsten M./Haas, Hans-Dieter (Hrsg.): "Internationales Risikomanagement –
   Auslandserfolg durch grenzüberschreitende Netzwerke", Oldenbourg Verlag, München, 2009,
Shapiro, Alan: "Multinational Financial Management", Wiley, 10th ed., 2013,
Toksöz, Mina: "Guide to Country Risk: How to identify, manage and mitigate the risks of doing
   business across borders", The Economist, 2014

as well as

Wolke, Thomas: "Bewertung von Staatsanleihen", in: WISU, Heft 5/12, S. 671–674, 2012

or in English

Wolke, Thomas: "The Functioning of Government Bonds – The Example of Greece and Vietnam", in
   Economic Development Review, January 2011, S. 31–36, 2011

for **country risk** in the context of the evaluation of bonds.

A general approach to calculation of a liquidity premium for **market liquidity** in the framework of **liquidity risk** is represented in

Bangia, Anil/Diebold, Frank/Schuermann, Til: "Liquidity on the Outside", in: Risk, Issue 12, p. 68–73,
   1999,
Hull, John C.: "Risk Management and Financial Institutions", Wiley, Hoboken, New Jersey, 4th ed. p.
   499–524, 2015.

The concept of **liquidity at risk** for banks was developed by

Zeranski, Stefan: "Liquidity at Risk zur Steuerung des liquiditätsmäßig-finanziellen Bereichs von
   Kreditinstituten", Verlag der Gesellschaft für Unternehmensrechnung und Controlling m. b. H.,
   2005,

Detailed descriptions of **financial planning** as a means **controlling liquidity risk** can be found in numerous standard textbooks. The works of

Brealey, Richard A./Myers Stewart C./Allen, Franklin: "Principles of corporate finance", McGraw Hill
   Education, 12th ed., p. 732–812, 2016,
Perridon, Louis/Steiner, Manfred/Rathgeber, Andreas W.: "Finanzwirtschaft der Unternehmung",
   Vahlen, 17. Auflage, S. 719–768, 2016

and

Wolke, Thomas: "Finanz- und Investitionsmanagement im Krankenhaus", MWV, Berlin, 2010

are mentioned here as representative.

Meanwhile, there is a great deal of literature on the topic of the **financial crisis**. The following references represent only a small selection on particular aspects (e. g. Basel III) of the financial crisis.

The **daily press** provides an initial general entry into the current events around the impact of the financial crisis and the multitude of new and altered laws and regulations as well as the respective media presence.

The text of the **laws** and **regulations** and an overview of the financial crisis, as well as a good summary of the very long legal texts, were gathered on the **Internet**:

www.bafin.de (Federal Financial Supervisory Authority, laws at German level),
www.bis.org (Bank for International Settlements (BIS), original texts of Basel II/III),
www.bundesbank.de (German Central Bank, bank crisis, Basel II/III),
www.bundesfinanzministerium.de (Federal Ministry of Finance, Basel II/III)
www.bundesgesetzblatt.de (Original texts of all German laws),
http://ec.europa.eu/finance/bank (European Commission, e. g. regarding the Deposit Guarantee Schemes).

For a good introduction to the complex topic of the financial crisis and the **monetary** and **fiscal policy** options, compare:

Brunetti, Aymo.: "Wirtschaftskrise ohne Ende – US-Immobilienkrise Globale Finanzkrise Europäische Schuldenkrise", hep, Bern, 3. Auflage, 2012,
Financial Crisis Inquiry Commission: "The Financial Crisis Inquiry Report", Official Government Edition, 2011

A scientifically solid, detailed description of the **commercial dealings** which triggered the financial crisis, and the consequences, is provided in

Rudolph, Bernd: "Lehren aus den Ursachen und dem Verlauf der internationalen Finanzkrise", in: zfbf 60, S. 713–741, November 2008,
Brunnermeier, Markus K.: "Deciphering the Liquidity and Credit Crunch 2007–2008", Journal of Economic Perspectives, no. 23, p. 77–100, 2009.

The two anthologies

Ebke, Werner. F./ Seagon, Christoper/Blatz, Michael (Hrsg.): "Internationale Finanzkrise – Erfahrungen, Lehren, Handlungsbedarf", Nomos, Baden Baden, 2012

and

Kadelbach, Stefan.: "Nach der Finanzkrise – Rechtliche Rahmenbedingungen einer neuen Ordnung", Nomos, Baden Baden, 2012.

are suitable on the topic of the financial crisis from a (German) **legal** perspective.

For comparison, the **background** of the financial crisis from a business perspective can be found in the anthology from

Elschen, Rainer/Lieven, Theo (Hrsg.): "Der Werdegang der Krise – Von der Subprime- zur Systemkrise", Gabler, Wiesbaden, 2009,
Hull, John C.: "Risk Management and Financial Institutions", Wiley, Hoboken, New Jersey, 4th ed. p. 121–136, 2015.

For a perspective on the financial crisis from a former **investment banker**, compare

Balz, Enno.: "Finanzmarktregulierung nach der Finanzmarktkrise – Vorschläge für eine Neuordnung der internationalen Finanzarchitektur", Hans Böckler Stiftung, Düsseldorf, 2011,
Smith, Greg: "Why I Left Goldman Sachs: A Wall Street Story", Grand Central Publishing, New York, Boston, 2012.

A suitable anthology for an **economic** perspective on the financial crisis is

Gup, Benton E.: "The financial and Economic Crisis: An International Perspective", Edward Elgar Publishing, 2010,
Kromphardt, Jürgen (Hrsg.): "Die aktuelle Finanz- und Wirtschaftskrise und ihre Überwindung", Metropolis, Marburg, 2013.

For a scientific, comprehensive and deep description of many **banking themes** and **banking rules** or regulations as well as the impact of the financial crisis on banks, compare

Hartmann-Wendels, Thomas/Pfingsten, Andreas/Weber, Martin: "Bankbetriebslehre", Springer Gabler, Berlin Heidelberg, 6. Auflage, 2015,
Hull, John C.: "Risk Management and Financial Institutions", Wiley, Hoboken, New Jersey, 4th ed. p. 353–371, 2015.

On the topic of the **IFRS 9** and risk management, see

Bernhardt, Thomas/Erlinger, Daniel/Unterrainer, Lukas: IFRS9: The New Rules for Hedge Accounting from the Risk Management's Perspective", Oxford Journal of Finance and Risk Perspectives, no. 53, p. 1–14, 2016,
Menk, Michael T./Warkentin, Sergej.: "IFRS 9 im Spannungsfeld von Risikomanagement und Aufsicht, in: Die Bank, Heft 9/14, S. 14–19, 2014.

On the subject of **stress testing**, a brief overview is offered by:

Hennersdorf, Angela/Fehr, Mark: "Die zehn wichtigsten Fragen zum Stresstest", in: Die Wirtschaftswoche, Heft 43, S. 64–66, 20. 10. 2014

or for a more detailed work see

Dent, Kieran/Westwood, Ben: "Stress Testing of Banks: An Introduction", Bank of England Quarterly Bulletin, 3rd Quarter, Vol. 56, Issue 3, p. 130–143, 2016.

For the problem of **self-fulfilling crises**, compare

Dullien, Sebastian/Schwarzer, Daniela: "Umgang mit Staatsbankrotten in der Eurozone", SWP-Studie, Berlin, Juli 2010

or for an empirical test

De Grauwe, Paul/Ji, Yuemei: "Self-Fulfilling Crises in the Eurozone: An Empirical Test", CEPS Working Document no. 366, June 2012.

For the **evaluation** of **bonds** in connection with the Greek national debt crisis, see

Wolke, Thomas: "Bewertung von Staatsanleihen", in: WISU, Heft 5/12, S. 671–674, 2012

and in English

Wolke, Thomas: "The Functioning of Government Bonds – The Example of Greece and Vietnam", in Economic Development Review, January 2011, S. 31–36, 2011.

On the topic of **Basel III**, see also

Klauck, Kai-Oliver/Stegmann Claus: "Basel III – Vom regulatorischen Rahmen zu einer risikoadäquaten Gesamtbanksteuerung", Schäffer-Poeschel, Stuttgart, 2012,
Barfield, Richard: "Practitioner's Guide to Basel III and beyond", London Sweet & Maxwell, 2011.

See

Ferretti, Paola: "New Perspectives on the Bank-Firm Relationship : lending, management and the impact of Basel III", Cham Palgrave Macmillan, 2016,
Müller, Stefan/Brackschulze, Kai/Mayer-Friedrich, Matija D.: "Finanzierung mittelständischer Unternehmen nach Basel III – Selbstrating, Risikocontrolling und Finanzierungsalternativen", S. 24 ff., C. H. Beck, Franz Vahlen, München, 2. Auflage, 2011

and

Ehrmann, Harald: "Risikomanagement in Unternehmen – Mit Basel III, S. 233 ff., Kiehl, Herne, 2. Auflage, 2012.

for the **consequences** and **action recommendations** for borrowers (corporates, SME) from **Basel II/III**.

Regarding the problem of the concept of **systemically relevant banks**, compare

Weistroffer, Christian: "Systemisch relevante Finanzinstitute", in: Deutsche Bank Research, 3. 11. 2011,
Elliott, Douglas J./Litan, Robert E.: "Identifying and Regulating Systemically Important Financial Institutions: The Risks of Under and Over Identification and Regulation", Brookings Working Paper, January 2011.

On the issue of **leverage ratio** and equity ratio (risk weighted equity ratio), see

Bank for International Settlements: "Basel III Leverage Ratio Framework and Disclosure Requirements", January 2014,
Hull, John C.: "Risk Management and Financial Institutions", Wiley, Hoboken, New Jersey, 4th ed. p. 360–361, 2015,
Schäfer, Dorothea: "Banken: Leverage Ratio ist das bessere Risikomaß", in: DIW Wochenbericht, S. 11–17, Heft Nr. 46, 2011.

Concerning the problem of **greed** from a **sociological perspective**, compare

Mennell, Stephen: "What Economists forgot (and what Wall Street and the City never learned): A Sociological Perspective on the Crisis in Economics", in: History of the Human Sciences, Vol. 27(3), p. 20–37, 2014,
Neckel, Sighard: "Der Gefühlskapitalismus der Banken: Vom Ende der Gier als ‚ruhiger Leidenschaft'", in: Leviathan, Heft 1 März 2011, S. 39–53, 2011.

4.6 Technical appendix

The **present value** (PV) of an interest position with a non-flat interest rate structure is as follows:

$$PV = \sum_{t=1}^{T} z_t \cdot (1 + i_t)^{-t}$$

with
z_t: cash flow at time point (year) t,
i_t: capital market interest rate (zero coupon interest rate) for maturity t,
T: maturity of the interest position (e. g. 10 years).

In the literature the so-called **discount factor** is also frequently applied, as follows:
$q^{-t} = (1+i_t)^{-t}$.

In order to determine present value changes dependent on interest rate changes, the **first derivative** of the **present value function** using the **interest rates** is generated as follows:

$$\frac{\partial PV}{\partial i_t} = -1 \cdot \sum_{t=1}^{T} t \cdot z_t \cdot (1 + i_t)^{-t-1}$$

The modified duration (D^{mod}) is defined and calculated as follows using the first derivative:

$$D^{\text{mod}} = -\frac{\partial PV}{\partial i_t} \cdot \frac{1}{PV} = \frac{\sum_{t=1}^{T} t \cdot z_t \cdot (1+i_t)^{-t-1}}{\sum_{t=1}^{T} z_t \cdot (1+i_t)^{-t}}$$

From the definition of the modified duration one can **estimate** a possible **present value change** for sufficiently small **interest rate changes** Δi, as follows:

$$\Delta PV \approx -D_{\text{mod}} \cdot PV \cdot \Delta i \text{ or for a relative present value change}$$

$$\frac{\Delta PV}{PV} \approx -D_{\text{mod}} \cdot \Delta i$$

In that case, a **parallel shift** in the interest rate structure is implied, i. e. all maturity dependent interest rates i_t change by the same amount Δi.

The **convexity** is calculated using

$$C = \frac{\partial^2 PV}{\partial i_t^2} \cdot \frac{1}{PV} = \frac{\sum_{t=1}^{T} t \cdot (t+1) \cdot z_t \cdot (1+i_t)^{-t-2}}{\sum_{t=1}^{T} z_t \cdot (1+i_t)^{-t}}$$

That allows the following **improved** formula for estimating a **present value change** to be derived on the basis of a **Taylor expansion:**

$$\Delta PV \approx -D^{\text{mod}} \cdot PV \cdot \Delta i + \frac{1}{2} C \cdot PV \cdot \Delta i^2 \text{ or for a relative present value change}$$

$$\frac{\Delta PV}{PV} \approx -D^{\text{mod}} \cdot \Delta i + \frac{1}{2} C \cdot \Delta i^2$$

The following can be used to calculate the **portfolio weighting** w_i of a portfolio (P) interest position i:

$$w_i = \frac{PV_i}{PV_P} \text{ and}$$

$$\sum_{i=1}^{N} w_i = 1 \text{ or } \sum_{i=1}^{N} w_i \cdot PV_P = PV_P$$

for a portfolio P which consists of a total of N interest positions. The modified **duration** and **convexity** of the **portfolio** P can be calculated using the portfolio weighting with the help of

$$D_P^{\text{mod}} = \sum_{i=1}^{N} w_i \cdot D_i^{\text{mod}} \text{ and } C_P = \sum_{i=1}^{N} w_i \cdot C_i$$

The formula for the **Macaulay-Duration** is:

$$D^{Mac} = \frac{\sum_{t=1}^{T} t \cdot z_t \cdot (1+i_t)^{-t}}{\sum_{t=1}^{T} z_t \cdot (1+i_t)^{-t}}$$

For the **immunization** of the **end value** of a portfolio consisting of two interest rate positions A and B using the **Macaulay-Duration**, the following applies:

$$w_A \cdot D_A^{Mac} + w_B \cdot D_B^{Mac} = Ph \text{ and } w_A + w_B = 1,$$

where **Ph** is the investor's intended **planning horizon** for the immunization. If the second equation is solved using $w_B = 1 - w_A$ and plugged into the first equation, then this gives the **portfolio weighting** for the **immunization** of the **end value**:

$$w_A \cdot D_A^{Mac} + (1 - w_A) \cdot D_B^{Mac} = Ph \Leftrightarrow w_A \cdot D_A^{Mac} + D_B^{Mac} - w_A \cdot D_B^{Mac} = Ph$$

$$\Leftrightarrow w_A \cdot (D_A^{Mac} - D_B^{Mac}) = Ph - D_B^{Mac} \Leftrightarrow w_A = \frac{Ph - D_B^{Mac}}{D_A^{Mac} - D_B^{Mac}}.$$

The **implicit forward exchange rate** can be calculated directly using the forward rate, as follows

$$FR = K \cdot \frac{(1+z_A)}{(1+z_I)}, \text{ or}$$

the calculation of the swap rate (Sw) for a currency forward transactions, as follows

$$Sw = \frac{K \cdot (z_A - z_I) \cdot T}{360 + z_I \cdot T}$$

with

K: current exchange rate (spot rate),
z_A, z_I: interest rate for investments and loans in foreign currency (A) or domestic currency (I),
T: maturity of currency forward transaction in days.

The calculation of the portfolio weighting w^{mV}_A for the portfolio (consisting of two stocks A and B) with the **minimal volatility** under the condition $s_A \times s_B \neq s_{A,B}$ is as follows:

$$w_A^{mV} = \frac{s_B^2 - s_{A,B}}{s_A^2 + s_B^2 - 2 \cdot s_{A,B}}$$

with

$s_{A,B}$: covariance between returns A and B,
s_A, s_B: Standard deviation of returns A or B.

The following is used for the calculation of the **Credit VaR**:

$$s_{PD} = \sqrt{PD \cdot (1 - PD)} \text{ und}$$

$$CVaR = CE \cdot \sqrt{PD \cdot s_{LGD}^2 + LGD^2 \cdot s_{PD}^2}$$

with

PD: probability of default,
s_{PD}: standard deviation of probability of default,
CE: credit equivalent (amount of outstanding credit, exposure at default),
LGD: loss given default,
s_{LGD}: standard deviation of loss given default.

5 Performance risks

Performance risks arise primarily through the business **process** of **creating goods** and **services** and **utilizing** them on the markets. Real economic processes thus stand in the foreground, even if performance risks can lead to economic and especially liquidity risks.

It is expedient to divide performance risks into operational risks and sales/procurement risks. **Operational risks** arise mainly in connection with the service creation process or transaction processes, and can therefore be assigned primarily to the business functional area of **production**. **Sales risks** are central when planned revenues are not achieved and are thus assigned to **distribution**. **Procurement risks** result from losses based on higher prices for e. g. raw materials, supplies and operating materials, which can be assigned to the functional area of **procurement**.

5.1 Operational risks

Operational risks are also known in literature and practice as operating or operational risks. In the following discussions, operational risks will be used. Based on Basel II, the following definition of operational risk can first be proposed:

Operational risks are defined as the danger of losses resulting from inadequacy or failure of internal persons, processes and systems or external events. This definition includes legal risks but not strategic or reputational risks.

The focus of this definition is on the causes of operational risks, why damage cases arise, and breaks down the sources of loss according to persons, processes, systems and external events. Therefore, operational risks will first be subdivided into **internal operational risks**, which include risks based on failure of persons, processes and systems. Risks based on external events will be counted as **external operational risks**. A corresponding subdivision of the operational risks with some examples is represented graphically in Figure 5.1.

```
                           ┌──────────────────┐
                           │ Operational risks │
                           └──────────────────┘
                    ┌──────────────┴──────────────┐
                    ▼                             ▼
         ╭───────────────────╮         ╭───────────────────╮
         │ Internal operational │      │ External operational │
         │    risks (5.1.1 )    │      │    risks (5.1.2 )    │
         ╰───────────────────╯         ╰───────────────────╯
```

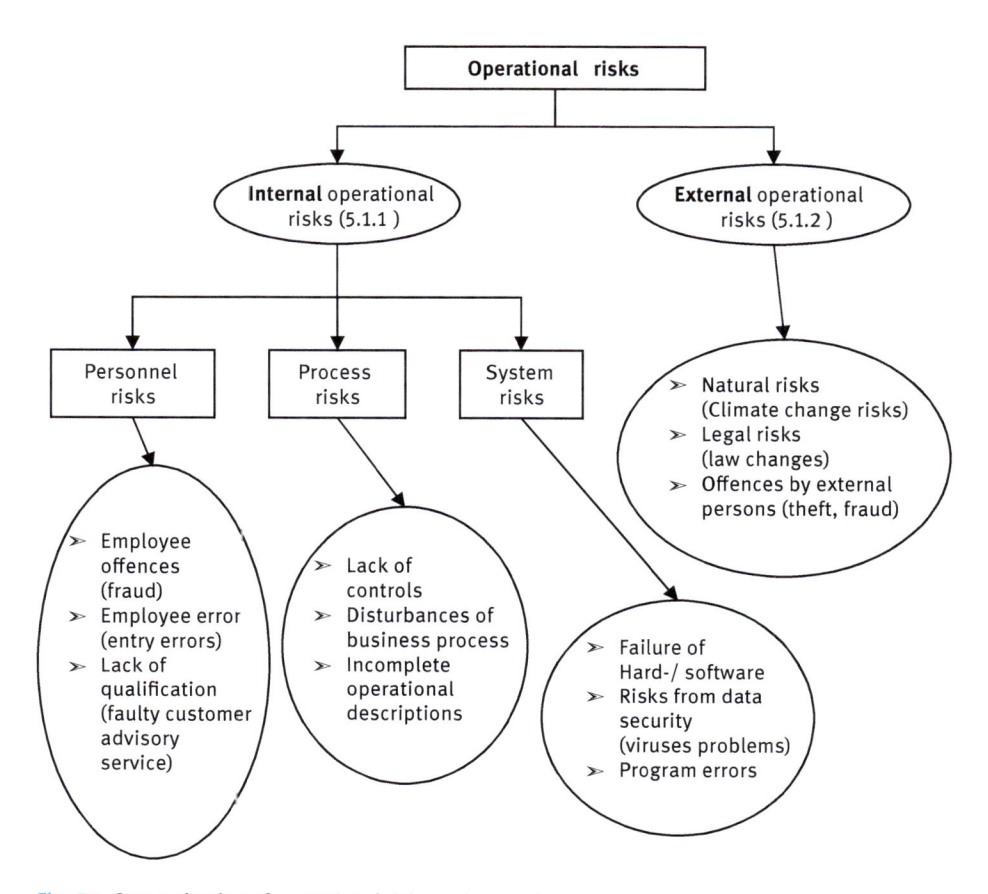

Personnel risks | Process risks | System risks

- Natural risks (Climate change risks)
- Legal risks (law changes)
- Offences by external persons (theft, fraud)

- Employee offences (fraud)
- Employee error (entry errors)
- Lack of qualification (faulty customer advisory service)

- Lack of controls
- Disturbances of business process
- Incomplete operational descriptions

- Failure of Hard-/ software
- Risks from data security (viruses problems)
- Program errors

Fig. 5.1: Categorization of operational risks and examples

5.1.1 Measurement of operational risks

The measurement of operational risks has the following **characteristics** and **problems** compared to e. g. the measurement of market price and default risks:
- While causes of market price risk and default risk are located outside of firms, the typical operational risk is triggered by the **company's internal processes**. Consequently, operational risks are **strongly** stamped by the **specific business**.
- There is usually **no** external **historical data** available for measuring operational risk, as there usually is for stocks, interest rates and currencies.
- Operational risks **cannot** be directly assigned to a **source of income**. With default risk, for example, the measured default risk can correspond directly to the lending rate. With stocks, the average price returns and the dividends can

be related to the VaR. There is only limited potential to control operational risks using a profit/risk ratio.
– Operational risk is very multifaceted and can therefore have very **different causal origins** which can require different respective measurement approaches.
– The **treatment** and **measurement** of operational risks is only just **beginning** in literature and business practice. In particular, the measurement methodologies are not yet so well-developed as they are for market price risks.

Measuring operational risks primarily deals with the problem of identifying the damage amount and its probability of occurrence. There are two fundamentally **different approaches** that can be applied to solving this problem:
– The so-called **top-down approach** uses data from the entire company to measure risk. In this case, every risk not assigned to market and default risk is assigned to operational risk. The **operational risk** is in this sense regarded as a **residual figure**. In the second step, those profit components which can be assigned from asset positions as credits, stocks, bonds, currency positions are subtracted from the total company profit. The remaining company profits are used to measure the operational risk, by calculating their volatility as a measure of the operational risk. This approach is indeed easy to implement and data collection is also unproblematic but up against that are also a crucial disadvantage. This type of operational risk measurement is not **cause related**. Thus the profit can, for example, also decline based on changes in macroeconomic influencing factors unrelated to potential operational risks. In that case, control of operational risk using the measurement results is not possible. Since this approach has not prevailed in literature and practice due to the so-called central weaknesses, the top-down approach will not be discussed further.
– With the **bottom-up approach**, the object is to capture the operational risks and measure them where they arise. This capture can be oriented on business sectors, organizational entities or operational processes. This procedure is indeed difficult to realize, but has the advantage of **risk measurements that are more closely related to the causes** and thus offer a better basis for building more effective operational risk control. Furthermore, the assignment of operational risks to specific company products or services is only potentially meaningful through the bottom-up approach. This assignment then in turn allows consideration of the pricing of different company products or services. In the literature there is likewise a clear tendency towards the bottom up approach, which is the foundation for the operational risk calculation methods described in the following sections.

There are numerous possibilities and variations for measuring operational risk. The most important **categories** of **measurement methods** include

- comparison with other similar companies in the **same industry** (peer group),
- calculating the **volatility** of the **company profits** after subtracting the credit, stock, bond and currency position profits,
- procedures in compliance with **Basel II**,
- **scoring models** at the process and/or business sector level,
- **statistical actuarial models**.

Comparison with other companies usually fails due to the unavailability of company information about operational risks, and poor transferability. The derivation from stock price risk or volatility of company profits shows the weaknesses discussed above within the top-down approach regarding the lack of reference to causation. The business indicator approach or standard approach in the framework of Basel II also belongs to the top-down approach methodology. Scoring models do correspond to the bottom-up approach, but are nonetheless unsuitable for a calculation that corresponds to the VaR concept and that doesn't include likelihoods of occurrence. Finally, the **statistical actuarial models** are the most frequently applied in the **literature** and will therefore be described in more detail below for the calculation of operational risk.

The value at risk concept is the basis for applying the statistical and actuarial model. However, transferring the VaR concept to the calculation of market price risks is less suitable for application to operating risk. A symmetrical normal distribution assumption, which can at least be approximated for market price risks, does not apply to operating risk. The principles of credit value at risk in the framework of default risk can nonetheless at least be transferred to the operational risk approach, since the following parallels between default risk and operational risk do exist:
- With business as well as with default risk, the losses are necessarily measured in **monetary units** and not as percentage changes (in contrast to market price risks).
- Both types of risk focus **exclusively** on a possible **loss**. Profits are not included in the distribution function (in contrast to market price risk, where earnings increases are indeed also represented in the distribution function, see Section 2.3.2).
- With both types of risk, smaller losses occur with a higher probability and higher losses occur with a much lower probability. Thus the associated distribution function has a **left skew** (see Section 4.2.3).
- Finally, due to the mentioned characteristics, both are subdivided into **expected** and **unexpected loss**.

For these reasons, it makes sense to apply the default risk methods to operational risk as well. With credit risk, two parameters play a fundamental role: the default probability and the credit equivalent multiplied by the loss ratio. Transferred to operational risk, the loss frequency and the loss amount map the corresponding items from operating risk to default risk.

Modeling the **distribution** of the **loss frequency** serves to generate the likelihood of occurrence of an operational risk within the given observation period. In that case, the observation period corresponds to the applied liquidation period in the framework of market price risk (see Section 2.3.2 or 4.1). For operational risk, the basis of the observation period is usually taken to be a year. In the traditional models of actuarial mathematics, the Poisson distribution with the parameter λ or the negative binomial distribution are used for modeling the loss figure.

For the **distribution** of the **loss amount** (analogously to the credit equivalent and the loss ratio with default risk), an adaptation of various continuous distributions is often assumed. Empirical research has shown that the log-normal distribution and the Weibull distribution are well-suited for this (since these are good at modeling the left skew). The formal description of these parametric distributions will be omitted here and referred to the statistical and business literature (see Section 5.3). The adaptation is problematic when only brief historical data is available, since the estimate of the distribution parameters is then very imprecise.

In the next step, data for the loss frequency and loss amount must be **collected**. The following procedures can be used for this purpose:
- A so-called **loss database** is used for the historical data. The loss database collects information about the amount and timing of losses that actually occurred, broken down by organizational entities and processes. The data collected in the loss database is based on information from, for example, internal auditing, accounting, the legal department or quality management. Since operational risks have not been a focus of risk management for very long, in business practice there is often no loss database that contains a sufficiently long history.
- The collection of **external data** represents an alternative to the internal company loss database. In this case, loss data from comparable companies is procured and adapted or transferred as well as possible to the company's own specific circumstances. Often, however, this is exactly where the difficulty lies. Obtaining external data about operational risk is also generally problematic, since no company is obliged to publicize data about operational risk.
- A further possibility for collecting loss data, when no data exist for specific loss possibilities, is **expert estimates**. In that case, experts are interviewed about their estimate of loss amounts and likelihoods of occurrence for specifically constructed scenarios.

In the end, the loss frequency and amount distributions are **aggregated** in a **total loss distribution** using the collected data. For that, a formal analytic aggregation can be done using the estimated distribution parameters from the historical data (see References Section 5.3). In this case, there are nonetheless analytical representations of the aggregate total loss distribution only for particular combinations of distributions. For simple data constellations, however, **full enumeration** has contended with aggregation of distributions in business practice and literature recently.

With full enumeration, a combined loss distribution is generated by forming **all** possible **combinations** of **loss numbers** and **amounts** for the available historical data. In that case it must be assumed that the distributions of the number and the amount are **statistically independent** of each other. The combination of number and amount is done separately for every operational risk type (separated according to organizational entity, working process). This procedure will be illustrated in the following example.

Table 5.1 shows the observed losses from **hardware failure** listed in the internal company loss database for the last 10 months in **business sector** xy:

Tab. 5.1: Example of observed losses from hardware failure

Month:	Losses (damages):
1	–€ 10,000
2	–€ 20,000
3	–.–
4	–€ 30.000
5	–€ 20,000; –€ 10,000
6	–€ 20,000; –€ 10,000
7	–€ 20,000
8	–.–
9	–€ 20,000
10	–€ 10,000

Two distributions can now be derived using the losses from the loss database shown in Table 5.1. First, the **loss number distribution** will be calculated. In two of the 10 months there was no loss, i. e. the frequency of a loss number of zero amounted to 20 %. Analogously, a loss number of one had a frequency of 60 % and two losses occurred with a frequency of 20 % (month 5 and 6).

The **distribution of the loss amount** (without considering months 3 and 8, in which the loss amount was null) can be constructed in the same way. A loss in the amount of –€ 10,000 occurred 4 times in a total of 10, so with a frequency of 40 %. A loss of –€ 20,000 occurred with a frequency of 50 % and damages of –€ 30,000 with a frequency of 10 %. The distributions of the loss number and loss amount are summarized in overview in Table 5.2.

Tab. 5.2: Distributions of the loss number and loss amount for an example of operational risk

Distribution of the loss number:		Distribution of the loss severity:	
Loss number:	Frequency:	Loss severity:	Frequency:
0	20 %	−€ 10,000	40 %
1	60 %	−€ 20,000	50 %
2	20 %	−€ 30,000	10 %

The **expected total loss** can be calculated from the two distributions. The **expected loss number** of one (0 x 0.2 + 1 x 0.6 + 2 x 0.2) can be **multiplied** by the expected loss amount of −€ 17,000 (−€ 10,000 x 0.4 + −€ 20,000 x 0.5 + −€ 30,000 x 0.1) and gives **−€ 17,000**. This value is helpful for the purpose of possible further analysis.

In the next step, the aggregated total loss distribution can be determined from the distributions of the loss number and the loss amount by
− forming **all** possible **combinations** of loss number and loss amount,
− assuming stochastic independence between the loss number and the loss amount and
− using the observed **frequencies** as appropriate **estimators** for the respective **probability of occurrence**.

All possible combinations and the associated probabilities, as well as the resulting total losses with their respective probability of occurrence, are shown in overview in Table 5.3.

Tab. 5.3: Aggregation of loss number and loss amount distribution

Loss number:	Prob. loss number:	1. Loss severity:	2. Loss severity:	Prob. 1. Loss amount:	Prob. 2. Loss amount:	Total loss severity:	Total probability:
0	20 %	---	---	---	---	€ 0	20.0 %
1	60 %	−€ 10,000	---	40 %	---	−€ 10,000	24.0 %
1	60 %	−€ 20,000	---	50 %	---	−€ 20,000	30.0 %
1	60 %	−€ 30,000	---	10 %	---	−€ 30,000	6.0 %
2	20 %	−€ 10,000	−€ 10,000	40 %	40 %	−€ 20,000	3.2 %
2	20 %	−€ 10,000	−€ 20,000	40 %	50 %	−€ 30,000	4.0 %
2	20 %	−€ 10,000	−€ 30,000	40 %	10 %	−€ 40,000	0.8 %
2	20 %	−€ 20,000	−€ 10,000	50 %	40 %	−€ 30,000	4.0 %

Tab. 5.3 (continued)

Loss number:	Prob. loss number:	1. Loss severity:	2. Loss severity:	Prob. 1. Loss amount:	Prob. 2. Loss amount:	Total loss severity:	Total probability:
2	20 %	−€ 20,000	−€ 20,000	50 %	50 %	−€ 40,000	5.0 %
2	20 %	−€ 20,000	−€ 30,000	50 %	10 %	−€ 50,000	1.0 %
2	20 %	−€ 30,000	−€ 10,000	10 %	40 %	−€ 40,000	0.8 %
2	20 %	−€ 30,000	−€ 20,000	10 %	50 %	−€ 50,000	1.0 %
2	20 %	−€ 30,000	−€ 30,000	10 %	10 %	−€ 60,000	0.2 %

The total loss amount is made up of the sums of loss amounts 1. and 2. together. The associated total probability comes from multiplying the associated probabilities (e. g. loss 1. of −€ 10,000 + loss 2. of −€ 10,000 gives a total loss of −€ 20,000 with a total probability of 3.2 %). The results from Table 5.3 can now be represented more clearly by capturing the total losses that are identical and adding up the associated probabilities. Table 5.4 shows the combined total loss distribution and additionally the **cumulative probabilities**.

Tab. 5.4: Total loss distribution and cumulative probabilities for an example of operational risk

Total loss amounts:	Total probabilities:	Cumulative probabilities:
€ 0	20.00 %	20.00 %
−€ 10,000	24.00 %	44.00 %
−€ 20,000	33.20 %	77.20 %
−€ 30,000	14.00 %	91.20 %
−€ 40,000	6.60 %	97.80 %
−€ 50,000	2.00 %	99.80 %
−€ 60,000	0.20 %	100.00 %

The aggregation of the loss number and loss amount distribution into the total loss distribution is shown graphically in Figure 5.2.

5.1 Operational risks — 257

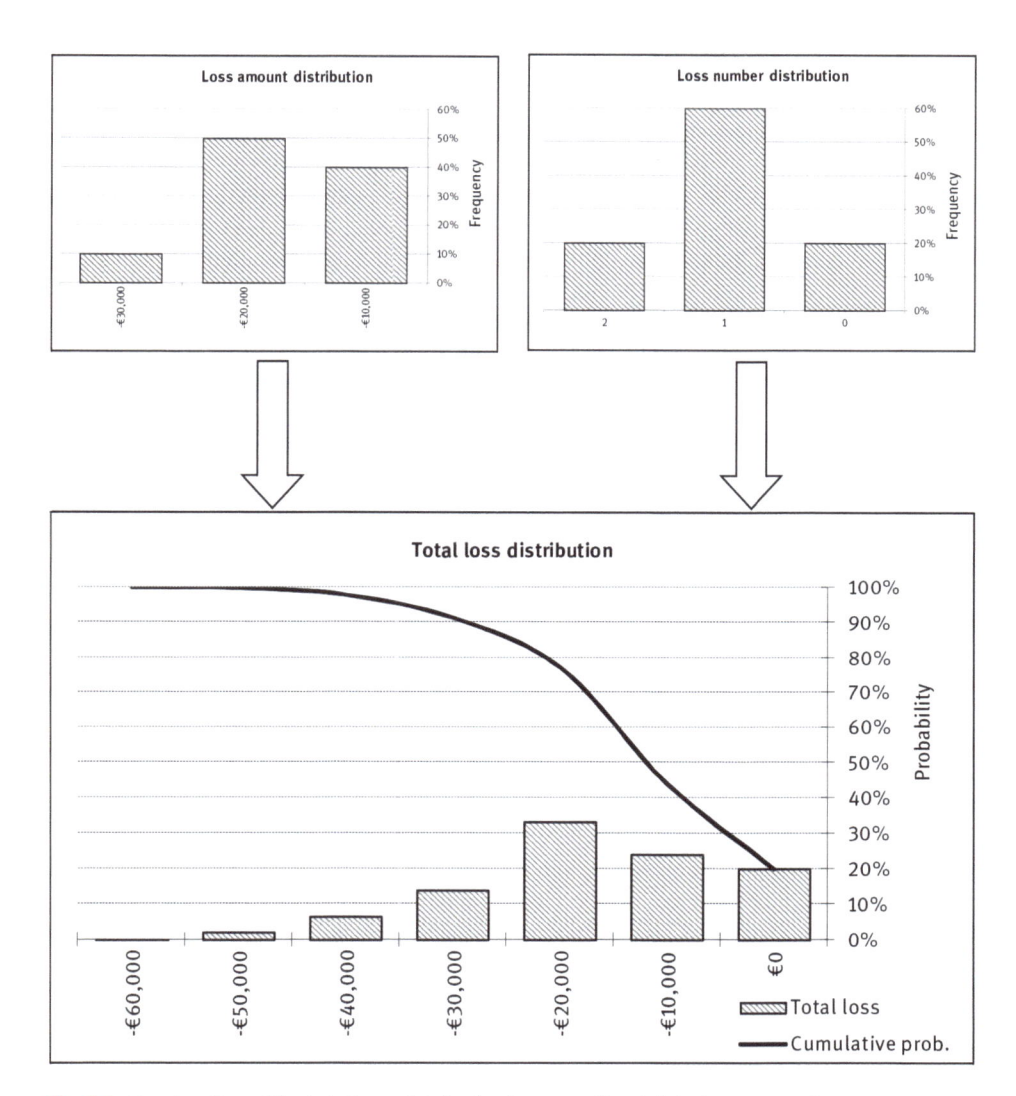

Fig. 5.2: Construction of the total loss distribution for operational risks in an example

Finally, the **Value at Risk** of the **operational risk** can be read from the cumulative probabilities of the total loss distribution in Table 5.4. For a confidence level of 97.80 %, the VaR amounts to **€ 40,000** and for a confidence level of 99.80 % it amounts to **€ 50,000**. If the VaR for a confidence level of e. g. exactly 99.0 % is required, then the VaR can be calculated using a **linear interpolation** as follows (for a detailed description of linear interpolation see the Technical appendix in Section 5.4):

$$-€\,40{,}000 + (0.99 - 0.978)/(0.998 - 0.978) \times (-€\,50{,}000 - (-)€\,40{,}000) = -€\,46{,}000$$

Indeed, the linear interpolation represents a simplification of the actual non-linear distribution function, but this margin of error will be ignored here.

Analogously to default risk, the Operational Value at Risk is defined as the difference between the Value at Risk and the expected loss. The expected total lost was already calculated above with −€ 17,000, which gives an **Operational Value at Risk** of **−€ 29,000** (−€ 46,000 − (−)€ 17,000). The **time period**, or, in analogy with market price risks, the liquidation period, corresponds in that case to a time period of **one month**, since this corresponds to the time periods of the observed losses in the loss database.

The **aggregation** of the individual **types of operational risk** and organizational entities takes place the same way in the second step. For this purpose, the number of all losses and their respective amounts from throughout the company are likewise combined through full enumeration. The associated Value at Risk of the operational risk is calculated for the defined confidence levels using the thus generated aggregated distribution function of the company-wide total losses.

In spite of the clarity of the procedure of the demonstrated approach to determining the total losses through full enumeration, a final **grave disadvantage** of this method cannot remain unremarked. In the above example, only a maximum of two losses for every observed month was assumed and only three possible forms of the loss severity assumed. With more than three possible losses, constellating all combinations is very much more laborious. For a number of e. g. up to six losses per time period and five different forms of possible loss severity, a total of 19,531 combination possibilities would have to be manually taken into account, which would make the procedure no longer practical. For this, a computer-based Monte Carlo (see Section 2.3.4) simulation would then be more expedient.

After measuring the operational risks with the Operational Value at Risk based on the various organizational entities or working processes, the question arises how the measured **risks** can be **analyzed** and **managed**.

The **analysis** of **operational risks**, as it was generally represented in Section 2.6 based on the RoRaC concept, is not possible, since operational risks cannot be directly assigned to profits. Because of this, an analysis of operational risks is only possible in a company-wide total context or analysis and will be carried out there (see Section 6.3). In the framework of **risk control** of **operational risks**, what stands in the foreground is the decision about which operational risks should be avoided through internal measures and when to transfer a risk to a third party (e. g. to an insurance). Potential measures for **risk avoidance** and **risk transfer** can be discussed independently of risk analysis. For this it is nonetheless appropriate to distinguish the possible measures according to their causes and risk types, which will be undertaken in the following two sections.

5.1.2 Internal operational risks

All risks based on **business transactions within** the **company** can generally be counted as internal operational risks. Business operations are conducted by people, processes and systems, which can form the basis for subdividing the operational risks. For the control of internal operational risks, structural and procedural organizational measures are the first thing to be considered, carried out by the company itself (in contrast to external risks, see Section 5.1.3). Simply preventing internal operational risk would then in consequence be ceasing operations and thus also mean foregoing chances or profits, which would not be the goal of business activities.

5.1.2.1 Personnel risks

Personnel risks can generally be defined as risks of loss based on **human misconduct**.

This delineation of personnel risks does not, however sufficiently cover all personnel risks in relation to their causes. In particular, losses due to lack of qualification and motivation cannot be directly considered as misconduct. Also, losses due to
- a bad working climate,
- a wrong understanding of management,
- missing communication and so on

can be assigned to personnel risk without having to interpret them nonetheless as misconduct. In addition, **personal failure** due to e. g. illness or accident is assigned to personnel risk.

Measures for avoiding personnel risk include primarily personnel **training measures** and the recruitment of very good personnel. However, **organizational measures** (e. g. tuning internal working processes) or a code of conduct for employees can also be used for prevention.

For **shifting** personnel risks, there is, for example, (binding) **professional liability insurance** and insurance against internal fraud.

5.1.2.2 Process risks

Process risks include damages or losses from disruptions of the course of business which do not rest primarily on IT risks or personnel risks. These are chiefly disruptions to the course of business due to
- lack of controls,
- incomplete operational descriptions and
- flaws in the operational structure or procedure.

The most infamous example in economic practice was the 1995 case of **Barings Bank** (in the person of Nick Leeson) with damages of US-$ 1.2 bill. due to a lack of control mechanisms in the working processes. But also, mistakes when hiring Nick Leeson can be primarily assigned to personnel risk. This demonstrates the problem that various operational risks cannot always be clearly delineated from each other.

For process risks the following **organizational structural and procedural measures**, among others, are available for **avoiding risk**:
- separation of control and executive functions,
- clear assignment of tasks, competencies, and responsibilities,
- formal foundations in the form of standards and policies.

5.1.2.3 System risks (IT risks)

The terms of system risk and IT risks are used synonymously. The term system risk will be used below, which generally includes all possible damages due to
- lack of **available data** (loss and/or manipulation of data),
- **unavailability** of IT systems (networks, **Hardware**) and applications (software) as well as
- noncompliance with **legal requirements** in relation to the IT systems that are in place.

Nonetheless, this does not yet cover all system risks, by far. Due to the complexity and rapid technical development, a more detailed representation will be omitted. Some **current** especially relevant system risks can, however, still be mentioned:
- risks from inadequate data security (viruses),
- data input mistakes from employees and
- inadequate control and plausibility checks for large databases.

The **management** of **system risks** can be roughly subdivided into the following bundles of measures:
- IT **security** (firewall, data encryption),
- IT **infrastructure** measures (e. g. new investments in the hardware area),
- **organizational** measures (IT training for employees, rules for access rights, improvement of network structures, elimination of isolated applications).

5.1.3 External operational risks

External operational risks are notable for the fact that they **cannot** be directly **influenced** by companies, or only **very slightly**. This is especially visible in risk management instruments, where risk transfer by taking out insurance plays a much greater role than internal company measures (trainings, organizational measures). External risks can basically be subdivided into legal and natural risks.

5.1.3.1 Legal risks

Legal risks include risks from the alteration of laws (e. g. tax law changes). But also, legal risks include the potential obligation to pay fines or penalties because of private legal agreements. Also, however, compensation claims from concluded contracts (e. g. in the framework of product liability), violations of legal requirements as well as fraud and crimes by third parties can be assigned to legal risks.

There are three **instruments** for the **management** of legal risk:
- the **internal legal department**,
- **external legal consultants**,
- **legal insurance**.

Which instrument is respectively most appropriate depends on the characteristics of the company and the industry, which cannot all be described here. Basically, an internal legal department is sensible when the company is above a certain size or for industry-specific characteristics (e. g. banks). For small and medium-sized enterprises, legal consultants in combination with legal insurance proportional to the cost-benefit ratio is frequently more suitable than an internal legal department. Nonetheless, this cannot be generalized to all industries.

5.1.3.2 Natural risks

Natural risks include damage and losses from, for example
- **fire,**
- **bad weather,**
- **earthquakes,**
- **floods** etc.

The most important instrument for **managing natural risks** is **insurance**. Next, technical **risk avoidance** measures such as, for example
- smoke alarms,
- water protection systems,
- weather early warning systems, and so on

can be put into place.

The types of operational risk described here represent only an overview of all the possible operational risks. The characteristics and manifestations of operational risk depend very heavily on the respective industry specifics. All operational risks, nonetheless, demonstrate a central similarity with regard to their measurement: the left skew of the loss distribution, which arises because losses can only be realized in monetary units (in contrast to market price risks). It is exactly this skew to the left that distinguishes operational risks from procurement and sales risks, which will be dealt with in Section 5.2.

A particular feature of natural risks are climate change risks, which will be discussed in Section 5.1.4.

5.1.4 Management of climate change risks

Climate change and the **related risks** have gained **new importance** in the last 20 years. On the one hand, considerable damages from extreme weather events (hurricanes, floods, heat waves and droughts) have occurred. On the other hand, there has been ever more coverage of climate change in media. The not very successful climate summit, the publishing of the Stern reports in 2006 and the parallels to the financial crisis (see Section 4.4.4) have led to more preoccupation with climate change in business risk management. That will be discussed in this section.

In the classification of risk types, climate change management belongs to external operational risk (Section 5.1.3). The listed natural risks include, among others, floods and storms, which can be connected to climate change and climate risks. The central **challenges** of climate change management include
– identification of climate risks,
– possible methods of measuring climate risks,
– possible methods of managing climate risks (e. g. insurances).

Furthermore, economic engagement with climate change and climate risk is extremely complex, multilayered and bound up with high uncertainty. This is a problem which also appeared in similar form in the causes and solution approaches of the financial crisis (see Section 4.4.4). Many companies have integrated climate change risks into their risk management or see a necessity to do so in the future.

A categorization of the risk types is useful for **identifying** climate risks (see Section 1.3). Types of **climate risk** can basically be subdivided into **four subcategories**:
I. **Natural physical climate risks** arise as a consequence of climate change through global warming or from extreme weather events. Examples are water shortages, heat waves or floods that can have a negative effect on production and procurement (e. g. scarcity of raw materials). Extreme weather events can cause damage to infrastructure (transport routes). This can, in turn, trigger risks in the area of logistics, in particular in distribution and procurement. Extreme weather events can also trigger direct risks in production and administration (e. g. storm damages, flood damages to facilities).

II. **Regulatory climate risks** include the results of state measures and regulations for weakening climate change. Examples are emissions regulations and energy conservation regulations, due to the unexpected or additional costs that arise from restructuring energy, transport and building systems (e. g. installing new filters, insulation).
III. **Reputational** and **competitive climate risks** primarily refer to changes in the sales market, in particular because of changing consumer behavior due to climate change. Thus the demand for products that are not climate friendly (e. g. refrigerators with bad energy efficiency, cars falsified emission values) can decrease unexpectedly. Demand can also unexpectedly collapse if a company or product brand suffers a loss of image due to climate change issues. Also, however, new more climate friendly competitors and technologies can pose a sales risk for companies with aging technologies.
IV. **Liability** and **litigation risks** include liability lawsuits based on emissions-related climate damages. Such lawsuits have very little chance of formal legal success, since a connection between e. g. auto emissions and later droughts can only be proved with very great difficulty. At the moment, this type of climate risk plays a subordinate role. Nonetheless, this type of risk will remain for the long-term.

With natural physical climate risks, climate change directly affects the operational risk in the form of natural risks within external operational risks. If climate risk affects the scarcity of raw materials, then the area of procurement risk (see Section 5.2.2) is also **indirectly** affected (through procurement prices). Damages to the transport infrastructure can also indirectly affect sales risk (see Section 5.2.2) through higher distribution costs. Regulatory climate risks indirectly affect various operational areas (e. g. production and administrative locations, logistic). In the area of external operational risks (see Figure 5.1), these are formally included in legal risks. Reputational and competitive climate risks indirectly influence sales and thus sales risk as well as procurement risk. Liability and litigation risks are, in turn, assigned to legal risks.

Climate change also affects **various business risks** in an indirect manner. With the risk types in Section 1.3, this problem (a business transaction triggers various types of risk) is treated with causal and management principles. According to the causal principle, the external operational risk (natural risks) here, which can be directly triggered by climate change, should be mentioned. The indirectly affected sales and procurement risk can only be managed or taken into account indirectly through a climate risk premium. The regulatory climate risk and liability risk are assigned to legal risk from the area of external operational risks, and can be covered using the operational risk measurement methods. Due to the impact of climate risk on various operational risk types, the capture, measurement and assignment of climate risk is difficult and complex. This is one reason why so far there are scarcely any quantitative methods for managing climate risk from a business perspective.

The **measurement** of **climate risk** is difficult because of the different risk types involved and because of the minimal penetration and treatment in business theory and practice. The possible approaches to measurement will be introduced in the following and the respective related problems will be demonstrated.

One approach to measuring the Value at Risk of climate risk is "**The Carbon Trust**" (Carbon Trust is an independent global organization for reducing carbon dioxide emissions). Here, however, the respective Value at Risk for the climate risk is only evaluated for entire industries with reference to the total market value (measured by FTSE-Index) of all companies in this industry (e. g. airlines 50 %, banks 1 %–2 %). This is an economic consideration. Conclusions for business economic methods for company-specific risk measurement cannot be derived from this, or only with difficulty.

For the measurement of natural physical climate risk and the legal risks from climate change, the methods described in **Section 5.1.1** for **measuring operational risks** can be applied. Specific problems arise in measuring climate risks. Climate risks can be especially hard to assign to an income source, and then only indirectly. Climate risks are company-specific in particular ways (especially climate risk related to competitiveness) and thus the collection of external data through comparison with other companies or industry values is not meaningful. Assigning climate risk according to origin is especially difficult, which leads to problems determining the amount of damage and the associated probability of occurrence. Calculating the Value at Risk based on a loss database is consequently very limited and only possible with simplified assumptions. There is still the possibility of expert estimates, which however are usually only undertaken for industries (see The Carbon Trust above) and does not do justice to company-specific features. Only in individual cases can expert estimates be called in for especially large firms. For small and medium-sized enterprises, this is not a sensible business possibility under cost-benefit aspects.

For the measurement of **reputational** and **competitive climate risks**, operational risk measurement methods cannot be applied, since here the climate risks impact indirectly on procurement or sales prices. Thus the methods for measuring price risks must be applied. Since climate risks only affect sales and procurement prices indirectly, the corresponding stock of price risk can also not be measured directly. One approach to mapping climate risks indirectly to price risks lies in determining the **risk premium** for climate risk.

The same principle used to determine market risk liquidity (see Section 4.3) could be used to determine this climate risk premium. The bid-ask spread is a possible indicator for market liquidity; this indicator gives the risk surcharge (risk premium) on the price risk of the respective asset values. Analogously, an indicator for the climate risk can now be found from which the risk premium can then be calculated for procurement or sales risks (see Sections 5.2.1 and 5.2.2). In this case, industry values, estimates or market values from emissions trading could be used. How a concrete calculation of these risk premiums might look is, according to current knowledge, not yet dealt with in the business research.

Because of the described difficulties with measuring climate risks, **risk control** (see Chapter 3) of **climate risks** is especially important.

With climate risk control, **transferring risk** by taking out corresponding damage insurance (see Section 3.4.1) and benefit exclusion due to *force majeure* play an important role. With regard to climate risks, there are in that case two special features. On the one hand, certain losses are not covered by insurance, since the amount of the loss is not calculable for insurance purposes (damages from nuclear power plants accidents) or the risk premium would be prohibitively high from the company's business perspective. In agriculture there is at the moment no climate risk insurance (e. g. against crop failure from drought) for similar reasons, but it is being currently discussed. On the other hand, the amount of the "correct" risk premium is difficult to calculate since the results of climate change usually have an indirect effect on business, and thus the cause-effect relationship is difficult to capture and calculate. Along with taking out insurance, climate-related losses like delivery delays or production stoppages can be shifted through contractual agreements with suppliers.

Risk provision includes the improvement of risk-bearing capacity though an increase in the equity capital, in order to be able to take on new risks (see Section 3.1). Such new risks include also climate impact risks. Additional equity capital must be deposited for the part of climate risks which cannot be covered by the value at risk of operational risks (or procurement and sales risks) and cannot be covered by risk control instruments. The amount of this additional equity capital buffer can be oriented towards, for example, the industry values of The Carbon Trust (see above), even if in that case the company-specific characteristics are not sufficiently considered.

Limits (see Section 3.2) are the primary measures taken for **risk avoidance** and **risk limitation** of financial positions. If these are transferred to climate risks, then they are measures of climate protection and of adaptation to climate impacts. This includes all personnel, technical and organizational measures for limiting the extent of losses (e. g. reinforcing dikes, stocking up on water supplies, etc.). Risk avoidance also includes the partial relinquishment of business dealings with unmanageable or insupportable climate risks.

Risk shifting (see Section 3.3) would include companies or parts of them being moved to regions in which the climate risks are smaller or almost nonexistent. An example would be moving to regions which are less liable to floods or droughts.

Risk diversification (see Section 3.3) is a theoretical management possibility with regard to climate risk, which is extremely difficult to implement in practice. A possible theoretical approach would be a goods production process which is subjected to various climate risks.

Finally, the use of weather derivatives would be a possibility in the framework of **risk compensation** (see Section 3.4.2).

The various control instruments can also be combined as desired in order to achieve better control effects (e. g. risks which cannot be transferred with insurance can be controled with risk shifting or relocation).

In summary, climate risks or climate change risks can basically be modeled using the instruments of business risk management or integrated into existing systems. In that case, special issues and problems arise that rest on
- the complexity,
- the indirect cause-effect relationship,
- the difficulties in measuring potential loss severitys and probabilities of occurrence and
- the problematic assignment to business risks and measurement methods of climate change risks.

Mastering climate change risks is nonetheless not a problem on the business level but, analogously to the financial crisis, a problem to be solved globally. This requires economic and sociopolitical stakeholders to negotiate and ratify global, appropriate compromise solutions for **adapting** (e. g. building higher dikes) and **avoidance** (e. g. reducing CO_2 emissions) climate change.

5.2 Procurement and sales risks

The treatment of procurement and sales risk shows clear differences, which were discussed above, compared to management of market price risks. Procurement and sales risks also show differences compared to operational risks when it comes to risk measurement. The following **properties** of procurement and sales risks can be regarded as important:
- For procurement and sales risk, there is usually **no historical** (daily) **market data** available. Determining the volatility of procurement and sales prices can then take place in two ways. Either through assessment based on internal company historical data (e. g. from accounting) or through expert estimates based on individual experience.
- In contrast to market price risks, there are **no current evaluations** of asset positions, but rather the risk exists in the negative deviation from future planned or target prices.
- Sales risks in particular are subject to risks that lie **far in the future** (e. g. 1 – 5 years).
- With operational risks (and also default risks) the highest possible loss is estimated with the VaR, provided that in the best case there is no loss (so, when no default or no business loss occurs). However, with operational risks, **no profit** can be realized. With sales risk, however, the starting point is **positive expected**

sales and the VaR measures the potential negative deviation from these expected sales.

The last feature is particularly necessary in order to **distinguish procurement** and **sales risks** from **operational risks**, since in each case different methods of VaR measurement and risk-control instruments are used. Thus business and default risks are based on a **left-skewed loss distribution** (see Section 4.1.5). By contrast, sales risks can be based on a **symmetrical distribution** around the expected sales.

5.2.1 Procurement risks

Procurement risks refer to necessary (and not self-produced) materials and immaterial goods and services (production factors) necessary to performance. Which goods are procured and how their risk can be measured and analyzed is specific to the company and industry.

A general definition of **procurement risk** includes all dangers of loss which can arise in the procurement of production factors up to their use in performance (service creation).

In the framework of this general definition, procurement risk distinguishes between the following **types** of **procurement risk**:
- Under **demand risk**, the loss is defined as (e. g. in the framework of contract manufacturing) necessary production factors that are unavailable and as a results profits disappear or valid compensation claims are made by the buyer (client).
- **Transport risk** encompasses all possible losses through the transport of production factors from suppliers to businesses (industrial company). This includes basically the destruction and damage of the production factors.
- If the procured production factors are destroyed or damaged in the warehouse, this would be assigned to **storage risk**.
- **Delivery risk** is identified as the risk that arises through failure of the delivery (delivery default risk), a delivery defects (delivery defects risk) or an unexpectedly higher price (delivery price risk).

This general definition and breakdown of procurement risk shows the disadvantage that there is no differentiation regarding the application of the VaR concept and the use of risk control instruments. Therefore, as already explained above, only **delivery price risk** will be dealt with in the following paragraphs in the framework of **procurement risk**, since for this the VaR concept can be applied in the sense of a symmetrical distribution around an expected delivery price. The other types of procurement risk will be assigned to operational risk, since they must be based on a left-skewed loss distribution. Thus, for example, transport risk can only give rise to loss but no profit or other advantage. With delivery price risk, by contrast, an advantage can occur if production factors can be acquired for a more favorable price than was expected (e. g. in case of decreasing commodity prices).

In order to apply the VaR concept to delivery price risk, it is first necessary to distinguish between the different **types** of **production factors** to be procured. Such differences are strongly company-and industry-dependent. A rough breakdown can be made into the following categories:

- **Raw materials** and **bulk goods** (e. g. crude oil, precious metals, grains etc.) that are traded on the **daily commodities exchange**. For these production factors the associated standard deviation can be easily calculated from historical data (by assuming the normal distribution). The VaR concept can thus be simply applied to the **raw material** and **commodities price risks**, analogously to the market price risks, with the help of the standard normal distribution.
- For **raw materials** and **commodities** that are not **traded daily on** the **exchange**, the standard deviation must be estimated based on the internal company historical procurement prices or on the basis of expert consultations.
- The procurement of **capital goods** (machines, buildings etc.) is subject to a procurement risk when the purchase price is not fixed. Since this is only plausible for special goods dependent on specific industries, this risk will be omitted in the following and a fixed purchase price will be assumed. Because of the long-term nature of capital goods, the risk of a fluctuating purchase price for future investments can also be ignored. Thus a future investment in, for example, 10 years is not taken into account for a company-wide risk representation that is based on a planning horizon of five years (see Section 6.3).
- For **trading companies**, the delivery price risk consists in the procurement of **manufactured goods**. For the estimate of the standard deviation, the same applies as for raw materials and commodities prices.
- Another important category is **recruitment**. The risk lies in the unexpected increase of future wages and salaries for personnel required for production. Future wage development is dependent on many factors, such as e. g. the inflation rate, macroeconomic development, demographic trends and so on. At this point only experts can do an estimate of the standard deviation, taking into account the influencing factors mentioned. This requires, nonetheless, a very complex and personnel-specific approach which will not be explored further here.

Raw materials and goods price risks for commodities that are traded daily on the exchange are summarized in the literature under the term **commodity price risks**, which will also be used here. Price risks of commodities that are traded daily on exchange are also often classified and treated as **market price risks**. This seems sensible and plausible, since for risk measurement the same methods as e. g. for stock price risk can be applied. The risk control instruments, especially to the forward transactions, are also very similar. Nevertheless, in this book, all commodity price

risks (whether traded on the exchange or not) will be assigned to **performance risks** for the following reasons:
- For many companies, procuring goods that are not traded daily on the exchanges stands in the foreground. For those commodities, the **methods** for **market price risks cannot be transferred** one to one.
- For company-wide representation, commodity price risk focuses on the **physical procurement** of raw materials and commodities, since the procurement is a prerequisite for production.
- In the framework of **company-wide risk measurement** and control, it is necessary to assign procurement risks together with sales risks to **Cash Flow at Risk** (see Section 5.2.3 and 6.3).
- Applying the VaR concept to procurement risks doesn't work for existing asset positions whose value could decrease, but rather only for the risk that procured **goods** could become **more expensive** in the future.

Commodity risk can be generally defined as follows:

Commodity price risk is the negative deviation from a planned target figure (asset, profit) by the operational business due to uncertain future developments of procurement prices.

Commodity price risks form the **central cause** of **company risk** due to uncertain future cash flow (see Section 5.2.3) and longer forecasting horizons (procurement, production and performance evaluation form a primary risk source for industrial companies compared to banks; with banks it is the finance positions).

Future **commodities price changes** and the related costs are tightly connected with **future exchange rates** and sales revenues. So, for example, an increasing US-$/€ exchange rate (Euro revaluation) leads to more favorable import prices of e. g. crude oil. At the same time, however, the export possibilities (see Section 4.1.2) worsen. Exchange rate risk is considered separately from procurement risk and they are only put back together in the company-wide risk aggregation (see Section 6.3).

Increased procurement prices likewise negatively influence the profit margin (if the increased procurement prices cannot be directly passed on to the sales prices). Nonetheless, a risk measurement based on the VaR concept can initially be carried out for procurement risks, which can then later be merged with the cash flow at risk.

This approach to risk measurement on a disaggregated basis and later company-wide aggregation displays a **fundamental advantage** over other frequently suggested concepts (based on a Monte Carlo simulation) in the literature. The results of an aggregated risk measurement or risk analysis can then be analyzed with reference to their occurrence and corresponding control measures can be initiated. Thus the respective **risk contributions** of the total **company-wide VaR** can be represented using the individual VaR from business, procurement and sales risks. Through that, targeted risk control is possible for the individually caused risk carriers, depending on their stock of the overall risk. This approach corresponds to the **bottom-up approach** already applied to operational risk. If, by contrast, the individual risk types are included in the total risk through a simulation without calculating the individual VaR, and only the VaR of the total risk is determined, then a quantitative analysis of the risk of the causal areas is not possible. The possibilities for analyzing the total risk based on the bottom-up approach will be described in detail in Chapter 6.

The basic application of the VaR concept to procurement risks will be illustrated using an example of **procurement** of **crude oil** for an industrial company.

For this purpose it will be assumed that a company plans the monthly **purchase** of **1000 barrels** of **crude oil**. Furthermore, an **expected procurement price** must be defined (which corresponds to market price risks of the current valuation of the asset position). In this case there are two conceivable approaches. On the one hand, the current crude oil price can be used as the future price. On the other hand, future target figures based on internal company forecasting are possible. The latter are, however, burdened with uncertainty and are also more difficult to determine. Using current prices as target figures also offers the advantage that this represents a plausible basis for cost-oriented pricing of the goods produced and sold. On January 2, 2006, the price for a barrel of crude oil (Europe Brent Spot Price FOB Dollars per Barrel) amounted to US-$ 58.34. At an exchange rate of US-$ 1.1826 / 1 € on January 2, 2006, this corresponds to € 49.33 per barrel. The resulting **risk position** is in the amount of **€ 49,330**.

The standard deviation of the historical crude oil prices will also be necessary for calculating the VaR. In this case an observation period of January 3, 2005 to December 30, 2005 will be chosen, in analogy with the calculation of the market price risks. Here, the crude oil prices based on US-$ are converted to euros at the daily trading exchange rates and the daily relative price changes are calculated for the crude oil prices in euros (this is necessary, since the VaR calculation is based on the euro, see Section 4.1.2). The **standard deviation** of the **daily relative price changes** of crude oil for this period amounts to $s_{Oil} = 2.0\%$, and a simplifying value of $r_{Oil} = 0\%$ will be assumed for the expected daily price changes (for this simplification see also Section 2.3.1).

The VaR is calculated analogously to the calculation of the market price risks (see Section 2.3.1 and 2.3.2), but with one fundamental **distinction**. In the case of market price risks, a decrease in market prices is seen as a loss. By contrast, in the case of procurement risks, a rise in prices means a loss or a risk.

Figure 5.3 graphically shows this relationship and the associated distribution values for a **confidence level** of **99 %** of the **idealized density function**.

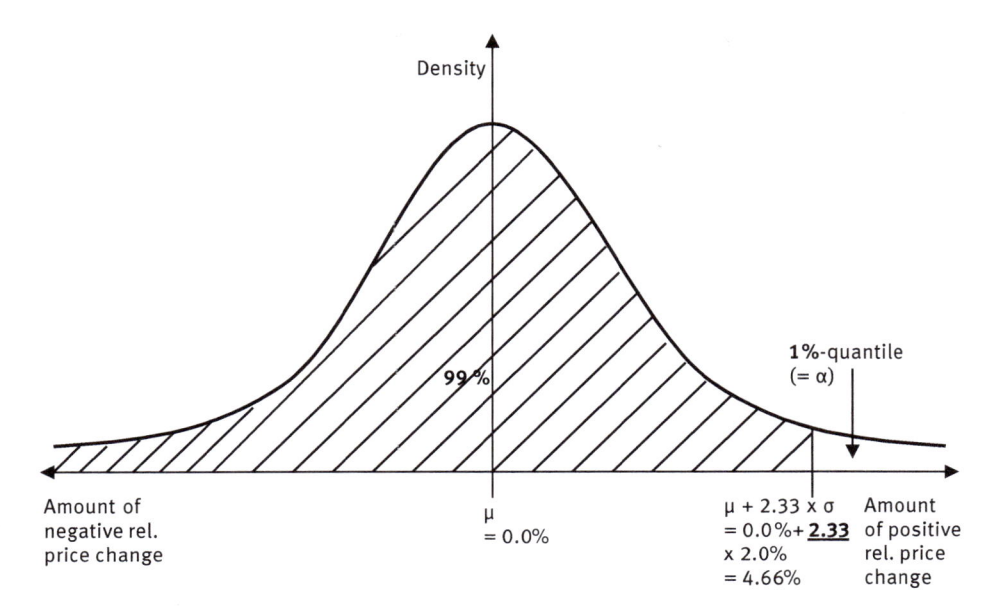

Density function figure with labels:
- Density (y-axis)
- Amount of negative rel. price change (left arrow)
- μ = 0.0%
- 99%
- 1%-quantile (= α)
- μ + 2.33 x σ = 0.0% + **2.33** x 2.0% = 4.66%
- Amount of positive rel. price change (right arrow)

Fig. 5.3: Density function and 1%-quantile for the procurement risk of crude oil

If the **liquidation period** (in the sense of a planning period) is defined as **20 trading days** because of the monthly procurement intervals, then the VaR for the procurement risk of crude oil can be calculated according to:

Risk position: x Volatility: x Liquidation period: x Level of confidence: =**VaR:**
€ 49,330   x 2.0%   x √20   x 2.33   = **€ 10,280.45**

This VaR is **interpreted** as follows:

A VaR of € 10,280.45 means that in the next 20 trading days, with a confidence level of 99%, the expected loss (or increased costs) through price increases for crude oil procurement will be less than or equal to € 10,280.45. In other words: a cost increase of more than € 10,280.45 through price increases for crude oil procurement will occur in the next 20 trading days with a probability of only 1%.

In this manner, the **VaR** can also be analogously calculated for **other forms** of **procurement risk**. The prerequisite for this is the determination through estimate or calculation of the standard deviation from historical data, under the assumption of a normal distribution as well as the ability to determine the risk position.

There are basically two instruments available for **control** of **procurement risks**:
- For hedging of raw materials and commodities prices that are traded on an exchange, **commodity futures** are usually available. Thus a company can buy a specific amount of a raw material at a specific price for a specific date in the future and is then protected against price increases in the future. The function-

ing and effects of risk control with commodity futures occurs through forward exchange transactions (see Section 4.1.2).
- The hedging or fixing of procurement prices for goods not traded on the exchanges can occur through long-term **supplier contracts**. It should, however, be taken into account that the supplier will generally only offer long-term price commitments with corresponding price surcharges. In this case the cost-benefit ratio must again be analyzed. In other words: Is the targeted risk reduction through supplier contracts worth it in relation to the increased procurement prices (which correspond to a diminished profit)?

The consideration of the procurement risks must next be merged with the sales risks. For this purpose, the necessary foundations for considering **sales risks** will first be represented. The procedure corresponds in that case to the above methods for procurement risk.

5.2.2 Sales risks

Sales risks relate to the sale of the company's products or services. As with procurement risk, sales risk is made up of various components and is, as with procurement risks, strongly company- and industry-dependent.

A general definition of **sales risk** includes all loss dangers that can occur in the sale of the products or after their production.

In the framework of this general definition of sales risk, the following **types** of **sales risk** can be distinguished:
- **Fulfillment risk** is defined as the loss when a contractually guaranteed product cannot produced or delivered.
- **Storage risk** includes all possible losses that occur when the produced products are damaged or destroyed in the sales warehouse.
- When the product is destroyed or damaged during transport to the customer, that is **transport risk**.
- **Purchasing risk** occurs when the customer does not fulfill his obligations (e. g. paying late or not at all = **payment risk**) or does not accept delivery of the purchased product.
- The primary element of sales risk is **selling risk**, which occurs when the product cannot be sold. Selling risk can be further subdivided: if no buyers are found (selling default risk) or if the products cannot be sold at the planned price (selling price risk). If the product cannot be sold to the extent of the planned quantities, that is called selling volume risk.

Analogously to procurement risk, applying the VaR concept requires clear assignment of the various types of sales risk. Fulfillment risk, storage risk, transport risk and purchasing risk belong to **operational risks**. Payment risk, as a subtype of purchasing risk, is assigned to **liquidity risk** (see Section 4.3). Payment risk represents a **default risk** when the products are sold by granting a supplier credit and the customer doesn't pay all (see Section 4.2).

The **selling risk** thus represents the core of sales risk, to which the VaR concept is applied. The selling risk is made up of a selling volume risk and a selling price risk together. The **revenues** therefore represent the **risk factor** of the selling risk. The revenues are defined as the price per item times the quantity sold. In this way, both components of selling risk are merged in the revenue risk factor. Revenues represent for most companies the central success factor. The application of the VaR concept therefore has a special importance. Thus various approaches to dealing with the revenues and their special characteristics will be discussed in the following remarks.

Applying the **VaR concept** to the **revenues** risk factor is not possible without further work. The VaR should not directly refer to the revenue risk factor, but rather must be broken down into its components of price and sales quantities, since both components can have different risk-related effects on the aggregated revenue amounts. The following **features** arise for the application of the VaR concept on revenues or price and sales volumes:

- The VaR calculation for the sales volume is not possible, since the VaR is defined in monetary units and not for an expression of quantity.
- The connection between price and quantity must be taken into account. This normally occurs in the form of a **price-sales function.** The involvement of such a price-sales (volume) function in the VaR concept is nonetheless not technically possible without further work (such a function is also especially difficult to determine or estimate).
- While the sales volume depends on exogenous factor among other things, such as e. g. consumer behavior, the price is determined by the company itself. For the price and sales volume, therefore, **various properties** of the **distribution** must be able to be considered.

Various methods and premises can be applied to consideration of these properties of revenues in the framework of the VaR concept. The methods can be divided into two groups. One group forms the **simulation procedures** and the other category forms the **analytical methods**.

An approach often used in the literature is the **Monte Carlo simulation**. In the first step, discrete probability distributions are estimated for the price and the sales volume. In the next step, evenly distributed random numbers are generated in the interval of zero to one. These random numbers are then mirrored in the distribution function of the underlying probability distribution.

If, for example, a sale of 1,000 pieces and a sale of 2,000 pieces with a respective probability of 50 % is assumed as the probability distribution of the sales volume, then for a random number between 0 and 0.5 a sale of 1,000 pieces is scheduled, and for random numbers between 0.5 and 1 a sale of 2,000 pieces is scheduled. The same is done for the price (e. g. a price of € 30 or € 40 with a probability of 50 %). From that, the revenue is calculated for every generated pair of random numbers by multiplying the assigned price by the associated sales volume. Every generated combination of sales volume and price is designated as a **scenario**. The procedure for five scenarios is shown as an example in Table 5.5.

Tab. 5.5: Monte Carlo simulation of revenues

Scenario:	Random number sales volume:	Assigned sales (pieces):	Random number price:	Assigned price:	Revenues:
1	0.3	1,000	0.6	€ 40	€ 40,000
2	0.2	1,000	0.8	€ 40	€ 40,000
3	0.9	2,000	0.4	€ 30	€ 60,000
4	0.7	2,000	0.3	€ 30	€ 60,000
5	0.4	1,000	0.2	€ 30	€ 30,000

The distribution function of the revenues can be determined using the simulated distribution of the revenues. A sales revenue of € 30,000 will occur with a probability of 20 %, a revenue of € 40,000 or € 60,000 with 40 % respectively. For the **distribution function** it follows that a revenue of at least € 30,000 will be achieved with a probability of 100 %. A revenue of at least € 40,000 will occur with a probability of 80 % and revenues of at least € 60,000 will occur with a probability of 40 %. From that, the associated revenue VaR can be calculated for the required confidence level using linear interpolation. For a confidence level of e. g. 90 %, the distribution function gives a value of € 35,000 (€ 40,000 + [90 %–80 %] / [100 %–80 %] x [€ 30,000 – € 40,000]; see Technical appendix Section 5.4). In order to calculate the VaR, an expected revenue is still necessary. The expected revenue for the generated distribution amounts to € 46,000 (€ 30,000 x 0.2 + € 40,000 x 0.4 + € 60,000 x 0.4). The difference gives a sales **revenue VaR** of **€ 11,000**. So the loss versus the expected revenue will be no greater than € 11,000, with a probability of 90 %.

This procedure has the following **advantages** or properties:
- The methodology seems plausible and easily comprehensible.
- Any number of factors and different distributions can be considered.
- In contrast to full enumeration, which is applied to measurement of operational risks (see Section 5.1.1), multiple influencing factors with numerous potential

forms can also be taken into account. In the above example, however, because of the few influencing factors (price, sales volume) and the minimal characteristics (two respectively), full enumeration would be much more precise.

These advantages are opposed nonetheless by serious **disadvantages**:
- Generating the distribution of revenues demands generating enough scenarios (e. g. 20,000) to get adequate precision, which **increases** the **computing power** required.
- It is not possible to **change** the **liquidation period** using the root function (e. g. for projecting from a month to a year). For the above example, a liquidation period can only be defined in advance, for which the simulation is then carried out.
- The **correlation** between the two generated random numbers for all scenarios is **random**. An explicit correlation of, for example, −0.5 cannot be mapped with the procedure described above (for a possible consideration of correlations in time series simulations, see References in Section 5.3).
- The crucial disadvantage consists in the approach of the simulation itself. Thus with different simulations and using different random number generators, different revenue distributions and therefore **different VaR** are generated. In the process, comparability is no longer guaranteed. So the amount of the VaR depends, for example, on the software (e. g. EXCEL) used. This limits transparency and precision.

If the disadvantages and advantages of a Monte Carlo simulation are summarized and compared, the following conclusion can be drawn for the **use of the method**. Monte Carlo simulation should only be used when an analytical calculation is not possible. Otherwise, analytical simulation methods are clearly superior with regard to comparability, transparency and, in particular, precision. For this reason, only the analytical solution approaches will be described.

In the framework of possible analytical methods for calculating the revenue VaR, various assumptions regarding the distribution of price and sales volume can be taken as a basis. Which of the following assumptions will be applied is dependent on the company and industry.

If the **price** and **sales volume** is based on a **normal distribution**, and a model **independence** assumed between the price and volume as well (i. e. a correlation of zero), then the expected value of the revenues can be determined by multiplying the expected value of the price by the expected value of the quantity. In the above example, the expected value of the price amounts to

r_p = € 30 x 0.5 + € 40 x 0.5 = **€ 35** *and the variance*
s_p^2 = (€ 30 − € 35)² x 0.5 + (€ 40 − € 35)² x 0.5 = **25 (€²)** *or the associated standard deviation*
s_p = **€ 5**.

Analogously, we get an amount of $r_Q =$ **1,500 pieces** and $s_Q^2 =$ **250,000 (€²)** or a standard deviation of $s_Q =$ **500 pieces**. From that comes an expected revenue value of $r_{QxP} =$ **€ 52,500** (in contrast to € 46,000 with the Monte Carlo simulation). The variance of the revenues is calculated according to

$$
\begin{aligned}
S_{QxP}^2 &= r_P^2 \times s_Q^2 + r_Q^2 \times s_P^2 + s_Q^2 \times s_P^2 \\
&= 35^2 \times 250{,}000 + 1{,}500^2 \times 25 + 250{,}000 \times 25 = \underline{\mathbf{368{,}750{,}000}}
\end{aligned}
$$

or the standard deviation of revenues s_{QxP} = **€ 19,202.86**.

The **liquidation period** and the **confidence level** must be defined in order to calculate the VaR. For the liquidation period it will be assumed that the estimate of the distribution is based on monthly statements. If the VaR is also calculated for a liquidation period of one month, then correcting the VaR using the root of the liquidation period is not necessary (or one). The confidence level will be set at 90 % in order to make it comparable with the example of the Monte Carlo simulation. If it is assumed for simplicity that the revenues in turn have a normal distribution, then the result is a value of 1,28 standard deviations (quantile). Since no percentage changes are determined, rather the revenue distribution is calculated in euros, then the revenue VaR can simply be calculated according to

VaR (revenues) = Volatility   x   Confidence level
                = € 19,202.86   x   1.28   = **€ 24,579.66**

This relationship is represented graphically in Figure 5.4 in the form of the idealized density function.

So, loss through diminished sales in one month will be at most € 24,579.66, with a probability of 90 %. Or, in other words: with a probability of 90 %, the revenues will not be less than € 27,920.34 (see Figure 5.4).

The assumption of independence between price and sales volume is not a business reality for many companies. A possible **connection** between **price** and **volume** can be considered by estimating the correlation. If a price decrease, for example, leads to an exactly proportional increase in the sales volume (and conversely a price increase leads to a sales slump), this can be taken into account through a **correlation coefficient** of **minus one**. On the other hand, if a price decrease only precipitates a tendency towards proportional increase of the sales volume, then this could be estimated through e. g. a correlation coefficient of −0.5. A correlation of −1 is used for this purpose in the example.

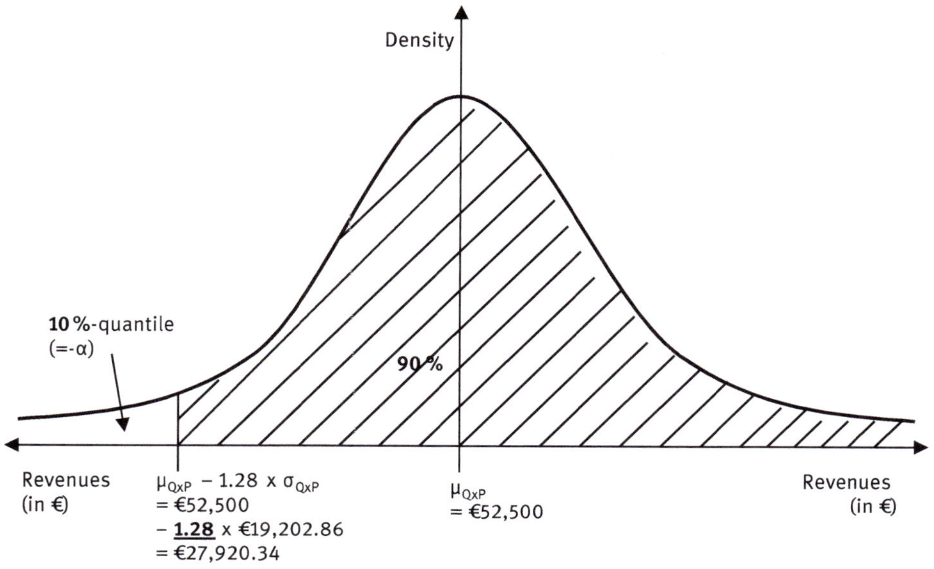
Density
10 %-quantile
(=-α)
90 %
Revenues
(in €)
μQxP – 1.28 x σQxP
= €52,500
– 1.28 x €19,202.86
= €27,920.34
μQxP
= €52,500
Revenues
(in €)

Fig. 5.4: Density function and 10 %-quantile for the sales risk as a function of the revenues

The expected value of the revenues then results from multiplication of the individual expected values plus the covariance between price and volume. In the next step, the correlation must therefore be converted into the associated covariance. This is done using the individual variances or standard deviations as follows (for an example see Section 2.3.3 and for the formal description see 2.8):

Covariance (price, volume) = Correlation x s_P *x* s_Q *= –1 x € 5 x 500 pcs. =* ***–€ 2,500***.

From that comes a **reduced expected value** of the **revenues** of r_{PxQ} = € 52,500 – € 2,500 = **€ 50,000**. Calculating the variance and thus also the **standard deviation** required by the VaR is not easy and transparent with regard to the covariance. A computational description will therefore be omitted and referred to the calculation formula in the Technical appendix (see Section 5.4). However, there are no fundamental changes in the VaR calculation compared to the explanations above. The calculation using the equations in the Technical appendix give a standard deviation of s_{PxQ} = **€ 10,606.60**.

Another approach to analytical calculation of the revenue VaR consists in the assumption of a **constant** (secure) **price** with a simultaneously **normally distributed sales volume.** This assumption is plausible from a business perspective when, for example, the company due to its competitive position can push through the planned sales price on the market and is also prepared to accept sales fluctuations. For the purposes of the above example it is assumed that the constant price corresponds to the expected price and thus amounts to P^{const} = € 35. In this case, the expected value and standard deviation can be determined simply by multiplying the expected value or the standard deviation of the sales volume by the constant price, and amounts to

$$r_{P \times Q} = P^{const} \times r_Q = € 35 \times 1{,}500 \text{ pcs.} = \underline{\mathbf{€\ 52{,}500}} \text{ and}$$
$$s_{P \times Q} = P^{const} \times s_Q = € 35 \times 500 \text{ pcs.} = \underline{\mathbf{€\ 17{,}500}}.$$

The VaR with an assumption of a constant price amounts to € 17,500 x 1.28 = **€ 22,400**.

The **various results** juxtaposed with the different assumptions and methods are summarized in Table 5.6.

Tab. 5.6: Results for different analytical methods of calculating the revenue VaR

Assumption:	r_P	s_P	R_Q	S_Q	$r_{P \times Q}$	$s_{P \times Q}$	VaR
Monte-Carlo simulation	€ 34	€ 4.90	1,400 pcs.	489.90 pcs.	€ 46,000	€ 12,000.00	€ 11,000.00
Price, volume n. d., independence	€ 35	€ 5.00	1,500 pcs.	500.00 pcs.	€ 52,500	€ 19,202.86	€ 24,579.66
Price, volume n. d., correlation = –1	€ 35	€ 5.00	1,500 pcs.	500.00 pcs.	€ 50,000	€ 10,606.60	€ 13,576.45
Price constant, volume n. d.	€ 35	€ 0.00	1,500 pcs.	500.00 pcs.	€ 52,500	€ 17,500.00	€ 22,400.00

The juxtaposition of the results demonstrates the **imprecision** and **lacking transparency** of the **Monte Carlo simulation** compared to the analytical approaches. Thus the lower VaR with the assumption of a constant sales price compared to the VaR with normally distributed prices can be explained by the standard deviation of zero. On the other hand, why the VaR is smaller with the Monte Carlo simulation than the standard deviation is not inexplicable. Also, with the Monte Carlo simulation, the multiplication of the expected price by the expected quantity (€ 34 x 1,400 pcs. = € 47,600) deviates from the simulated expected value of the revenues by € 46,000. The cause of this difference is not immediately apparent. On the other hand, the smaller expected revenues of € 50,000 with a correlation of minus one compared to the expected revenues of € 52,500 with independence is easily explained. The difference is based on taking into account the negative covariance between the price and sales volume.

Which assumptions or methods are chosen should depend on how well they reflect the business conditions and the available data and estimates.

For **control** sales risks, and especially **selling risks**, the following basic possibilities are available:

- Hedging or fixing of sales prices and/or sales volumes can be done through long-term **customer contracts**. As with procurement risk, however, it should be taken into account that the buyer in this case will expect a price surcharge from the company. The cost-benefit ratio should also be analyzed, to see whether the risk reduction through the customer contract is worth it in relation to the reduced sales price (or lower revenues).
- Another possibility to reduce sales risk is represented by increasing the supply power (and with it an improved competitive position) through formation of **sales associations**, insofar as that is legally permitted.
- Finally, the entire toolbox of marketing is still available. These include, for example, distribution, communication and pricing strategies. A more complete representation of these instruments falls into the area of marketing and therefore will not be undertaken in the framework of this book.

Thus the two most important main components of performance risk are covered and can now be merged in the next section, with the help of Cash Flow at Risk.

5.2.3 Cash Flow at Risk

Value at risk arose out of the need to manage market price risks. The idea, the concept of employing comprehensive measurement and management of all risks company-wide, is not possible in the form described so far. Rather, the concept must also be transferred to all performance risks. **Performance risks** are generally reflected one-to-one in the **cash flow** of a company. For this reason, an approach will be introduced to calculate the so-called "Cash Flow at Risk".

In sections 5.2.1 and 5.2.2, the two most important high-risk components of performance risk will be considered in light of the VaR concept. At the same time, however, not all factors of performance risk are considered and the individual components must still be merged. The following suitable **definition** of **cash flow** is necessary in order to transfer the VaR concept to performance risk.

Cash flow is defined as the sum of all **cash income** minus all **cash expenses** which stand in a direct relationship with the performance-related activities (usually operational transactions) of the company. The cash flow as so defined is therefore also called operational cash flow.

This definition of cash flow relies on the so-called **direct method** of determining the cash flow. With the **indirect method**, the annual net profit is corrected through the non-cash expenses and income. This procedure is nonetheless unsuitable for application of the VaR concept and analysis of the performance risks, since the actual risk-causing factors are not directly represented, but are rather contained in the annual net profit total figure.

The **calculation** of the **cash flow** by means of its individual elements is, again, company- and industry-dependent. A general possible calculation of the cash flow which comprehends its most important components can be seen as follows:

+ Revenues (sales)
− Material costs
− Wage costs
− Distribution and administrative costs
− Interest expense
− Tax expenses
= Cash Flow

The necessary considerations for modeling **revenues** are already set out above in Section 5.2.2. Revenues are usually in cash. Capitalized assets, therefore, are not to be taken into consideration. If deliveries and services are sold by granting a supplier credit and these trade receivables are not paid by the customers, then this is assigned to default risk or liquidity risk (see Section 4.2 and 4.3).

The **material costs** reflect the procurement risk (see Section 5.2.1) and is usually in cash. The procurement risk was already demonstrated above in the example of crude oil procurement. In business reality, however, it is exceptional if only one material is necessary for production (e. g. oil refinery). If different raw materials, supplies, operating materials and goods are needed, then the correlation of the procurement price between the different materials must be taken into account. This occurs analogously to calculating the portfolio VaR (see Section 2.3.3).

The **wage costs** refers to the cash wage and salary costs of producing goods and services. Wage costs can have a variable or fixed-cost character. The risk consists in unexpected wage increases, which with variable wage costs depends on the amount produced.

The **distribution and administrative costs** is similar to the wage costs, but the fixed-cost character prevails. Dependency on production or sales volume plays in this case a subordinate role (possible exceptions: sales commissions dependent on the sold volume). Along with the salaries for sales and administrative personnel, however, the cost of benefits in kind (e. g. IT system, office equipment) is also considered. The risk consists in unexpected salary increases and possible losses arising from benefits in kind that are required for sales and administration and not assignable to operational risk (e. g. unexpected price increases for the new IT system to be procured).

The **interest expense** refers only to financing of operating resources. This includes primarily raising credit through bank overdrafts for financing the procurement of production materials (raw materials, supplies, operating materials and goods employed). The risk is that the banks will demand higher interest rates on the borrowed capital. Interest expense from credits for financing investments and for improving liquidity etc. are assigned to financial risk (cash flow from financing activities) and especially to interest rate risk (see Section 4.1.1).

Similarly to interest expense, **tax expenses** is also differentiated by its connection to operational activities. Therefore the only tax expenses that will be considered is the one that arises in relation to the generated revenues. Tax payments for e. g. income from capital investments (interest income, price gains) must be assigned to the corresponding financial risk types or otherwise accounted for.

The cash flow at risk can be **defined** on the basis of the individual components of cash flow, as follows:

The **Cash Flow at Risk** is the maximum negative deviation from the expected future cash flow, for a specific confidence level, measured in monetary units.

This definition is based on the VaR concept. The application of the VaR concept to the cash flow at risk corresponds to the procedure for measuring the VaR of revenues in the framework of sales risk. Here also, there are again **various methods** available for calculating the cash flow at risk.

The literature often falls back upon the **Monte Carlo simulation**. This method will not be further discussed here because of the grave disadvantages demonstrated in the example in Section 5.2.2.

Analytical calculation stands at the center of the following explanations by means of example. It corresponds to the procedure for sales risk, however, it requires several modifications in order to take all the cash flow factors into account. One difference also consists in the addition of the individual risk factors instead of, as with the revenues, the multiplication of price and sales volume.

A further approach to calculating the cash flow at risk is the **replication** of the cash flow via **financial market instruments**. The central difficulty with that is finding plausible replication instruments. This approach is to that extent only suitable for very few companies and will therefore not be discussed.

The **multifactor analysis method** based on arbitrage pricing theory rests on determining the cash flow factors which are traded on the financial markets, like e. g. electricity prices, oil prices, raw materials prices. This procedure, however, is also only applicable to companies with specific products (e. g. airlines and kerosene price, car makers and metal price).

The **analytical calculation** of cash flow at risk will be represented in the following **example**. In the first step, the distribution and associated parameters (expected value and standard deviation) will be estimated or established for the individual components. As far as it is possible and meaningful, the VaR of the individual components will also be calculated for the later analysis.

A forecasting horizon of one month at a time will be defined for the **liquidation period** and the historical data collection will also take place at monthly intervals. In this way, a correction of the liquidation period by the root function is not necessary. A **confidence level** of 90 % (number of standard deviations = 1.28) will be applied.

The example from Section 5.2.2 will be used for the **revenues**. In that case, the variant with a constant price will be selected. The expected value of the revenues amounts to r_{PxQ} = € 52,500 and the standard deviation adds up to s_{PxQ} = € 17,500. With an assumption of a constant price, the VaR is VaR(PxQ) = **€ 22,400**.

The **material cost** will be demonstrated for the procurement of **crude oil** and **copper**. For the monthly production, 10 barrels of crude oil and 100 kg of copper are required.

The example from Section 5.2.1 will be used for the **crude oil**. The expected value of the relative daily price changes for crude oil amounts to r_{Oil} = 0 % and the standard deviation is s_{Oil} = 2 %. The price per barrel amounts to € 49.33. The value at risk in one month (price changes on daily basis) for the procured 10 barrels of crude oil comes to VaR (oil) = 10 x € 49.33 x $\sqrt{20}$ x 2.0 % x 1.28 = **€ 56.48**.

The price for **copper** amounts to € 8 per kg, with an expected value of r_{Co} = 0 % and a standard deviation of s_{Co} = 1 % for the daily price changes in the copper prices. The VaR for the procurement of copper then comes out to VaR (copper) = 100 x € 8 x $\sqrt{20}$ x 1.0 % x 1.28 = **€ 45.79**.

The **correlation** between the daily price changes of the oil and copper prices is +0.5. From that comes a covariance of 0.0001 (0.5 x 0.02 x 0.01). The expected value of the total material cost in euros results from the sum of the risk positions with an expected price change of 0 % in each case, so r_{Oil+Co} = **€ 1,293.30**. (€ 800.00 + € 493.30). The variance or standard deviation of oil and copper together can be calculated using the covariance according to

$$S_{Oil+Co}^2 = 800^2 \times 0.01^2 + 493.33^2 \times 0.02^2 + 2 \times 800 \times 493.30 \times 0.0001 = \underline{\mathbf{240.265956}} \text{ or}$$
$$S_{Oil+Co} = \mathbf{€\ 15.50}.$$

The algorithms applied here and in the following explanations for expected values and variances of combined random variables are formally represented in the Technical appendix (Section 5.4). The VaR of oil and copper together comes out to VaR (oil+copper) = **€ 88.73** (€ 15.50 x $\sqrt{20}$ x 1.28).

The **wage costs** are made up of a **variable** and a **fixed** component together. The expected fixed wage costs is r_{Wfix} = € 4,000 for one month and the associated standard deviation amounts to s_{Wfix} = € 300. The expected variable wage costs come to r_{Wvar} = € 3 per item and the associated standard deviation is s_{Wvar} = € 0.30. For the calculation of the total wage costs it will be assumed that the sold volume is identical to the produced volume. Then the total variable wage costs results from multiplying the variable wage costs per item by the sales volume. Since the sales volume again represents a random variable (with r_Q = 1,500 pcs. S_Q = 500 pcs., see Section 5.2.2), this again poses the problem of the difficulty in calculating the variance of the combined random variables. For this reason, a constant production volume of M^{const} = 1,500 items will be assumed for the expected sales volume, in order to simplify. Let there be a completely positive correlation of +1 between the fixed and variable wage components, and independence between the variable wage costs and sales volume. The total wage costs would then be

$R_{Wges} = r_{Wfix} + r_{Wvar} \times M^{const}$ = € 4,000 + € 3 x 1,500 pcs. = **€ 8,500**.
$S_{Wges}^2 = s_{Wfix}^2 + s_{Wvar}^2 \times M^{const2} + 2 \times M^{const} \times s_{Wfix,Wvar}$
  = € 300^2 + € 0.30^2 x $1,500^2$ + 2 x 1,500 x (+1) x € 300 x € 0.30 = **562,500** or
S_{Wges} = **€ 750**.

The VaR of the total wage costs thus adds up to VaR (wage) = € 750 x 1.28 = **€ 960**.

Similar assumptions hold for the **distribution and administrative costs**. However, it simplifies the example to only estimate a fixed component of r_{Adm} = € 2,000 and the associated standard deviation of s_{Adm} = € 100. This gives a VaR (administration) = € 100 x 1.28 = **€ 128**.

The **interest expense** is made up of two elements. On the one hand, from loans necessary for financing and on the other hand, from the interest to be paid to the bank. A constant credit amount of K^{const} = € 5,000 will be assumed for the loan. The interest rate demanded by the bank, which is immediately equated with the expected interest rates, amounts to i = 5 % p. a. The expected interest expense for a month then comes to

$$R_{Int} = € 5,000 \times 5\% \times 1/12 = \textbf{€ 20.83}.$$

The daily interest rates on the euro money markets for a period of a month are then used to determine the standard deviation. A standard deviation of 0.09 percentage points is the result for the observation period from January 3, 2005 to December 30, 2005. The associated standard deviation of the interest expense in euros then amounts to

$$S_{Int} = 0.09\% \times € 5,000 \times 1/12 = \textbf{€ 0.38}.$$

The associated VaR comes to VaR (interest) = € 0.38 x $\sqrt{20}$ x 1.28 = **€ 2.18**. The potentially increased interest expense due to possible interest rate increases is then for one month, with a confidence level of 90 %, not greater than € 2.18. In this case it is assumed that bank interest rate increases on the euro money market will be passed on to the customer (company) at the same level.

The **tax expenses** is also composed of two components. The average tax rate depends on the taxable income. The income to be taxed will be based on the revenues for simplicity. Thus the average tax rate for revenues up to € 30,000 amounts to 15 % p. a. For revenues between € 30,000 and € 52,500, the tax rate is 25 % p. a. and for revenues above € 52,500 the tax rate is 35 % p. a. The analytical link between the normally distributed revenues and these various tax rates is not possible without further work. For this purpose, the Monte Carlo simulation can again be usefully applied, however, it will be dispensed with here. For the sake of simplicity, the following remarks will be based on a constant average tax rate of $S^{const} = 25\%$ (independent of revenues). Then the result for one month is

$$r_{Tax} = €\ 52{,}500 \times 25\% \times 1/12 = \mathbf{€\ 1{,}093.75}\ and$$
$$s_{Tax}^2 = (25\% \times 1/12)^2 \times €\ 17{,}500^2 = \mathbf{132{,}921.007}\ with$$
$$s_{Tax} = \mathbf{€\ 364.58}.$$

The corresponding VaR amounts to VaR (tax) = € 364.58 x 1.28 = **€ 466.66**.

An overview of the parameters of the individual components and the associated VaR values are represented in Table 5.7.

Tab. 5.7: Expected values, standard deviations and value at risk values for individual components of cash flow

Component:	Expected value (μ,r):	Standard deviation (σ,s):	Value at Risk:
Revenues (PxQ):	€ 52,500.00	€ 17,500.00	€ 22,400.00
Material costs (oil + co):	€ 1,293.30	€ 15.50	€ 88.73
Wage costs (wag):	€ 8,500.00	€ 750.00	€ 960.00
Dist. and admin. costs (adm):	€ 2,000.00	€ 100.00	€ 128.00
Interest expense (int):	€ 20.83	€ 0.38	€ 2.18
Tax expenses (tax):	€ 1,093.75	€ 364.58	€ 466.66

In the next step, the individual components are merged into the cash flow at risk. For this purpose, the **components** are **joined up** in **pairs** by applying algorithms (see Section 5.4) to them, taking into account possible correlations between them.

The **gross profit** is defined by the revenues minus the cost of materials. In this case, a correlation of +0.3 is assumed. That means that an increase in the procurement price also leads in small measure to a higher sales price. This gives an expected value of

$$r_{Grp} = €\ 52{,}500 - €\ 1{,}293.30 = \mathbf{€\ 51{,}206.70}.$$

The calculation of the variance delivers

s_{Grp}^2 = € 17,500² + € 15.50² + 2 x (−1) x (+0.3) x € 17,500 x € 15.50 = **306,087,490.3** and
s_{Grp} = **€ 17,495.36**

The mixed term with the positive correlation coefficient must be subtracted from the sum of the squared individual variances. This follows computationally from the algorithms (see Section 5.4), since the procurement prices have a constant factor of a_{Oil+Co} = −1 after subtraction from the revenues. Or in other words: if procurement prices increase, it will have a risk-mitigating effect on the gross profit if there is a positive correlation with the sales prices (and analogously, the reverse with a negative correlation). The VaR amounts to VaR (grp) = € 17,495.36 x 1.28 = **€ 22,394.06**.

Next, the **wage** and **administrative costs** are combined, since both have a similar character. It is assumed that wages and salaries between administration and production are strongly positively correlated at +0.8. This then gives an expected value of

r_{W+A} = € 8,500 + € 2,000 = **€ 10,500**. The calculation of the variance delivers
s_{W+A}^2 = € 750² + € 100² + 2 x (+0.8) x € 750 x € 100 = **692,500** and
s_{W+A} = **€ 832.17** as the result.

The VaR comes to VaR (wag+adm) = € 832.17 x 1.28 = **€ 1,065.18**.

Finally, the interest and tax expenses are joined. Since both also have a financial character, the combined components are called the **financial cost** and independence is assumed between the two elements. The expected value adds up to

r_{Fin} = € 20.83 + € 1,093.75 = **€ 1,114.58**. The calculation of the variance delivers
s_{Fin}^2 = € 0.38² + € 364.58² = **132,921.151** and
s_{Fin} = **€ 364.58 €** as the result.

The VaR amounts to VaR (fin) = € 364.58 x 1.28 = **€ 466.66**. The risk of the interest expense is thus so tiny that it has a very small influence on the overall risk.

In the last step, the combined components are condensed into **cash flow**. For this purpose, independence is assumed between all components, which gives an expected cash flow value of

r_{CF} = € 51,206.70 − € 10,500 − € 1,114.58 = **€ 39,592.12**.

The variance of cash flow amounts to

s_{CF}^2 = € 17,495.36² + € 832.17² + € 364.58² = **306,913,047** and
s_{CF} = **€ 17,518.93**.

In that case, it is possible to calculate the **cash flow at risk** (CFaR) in the amount of CFaR = € 17,518.93 x 1.28 = **€ 22,424.23**. This result of the cash flow at risk should be interpreted as follows:

The expected cash flow of € 39,612.57 will be reduced by a maximum of € 22,424.23 in a month, with a confidence level of 90 %. Or to put it another way: with a confidence level of 90 %, the cash flow will not be lower than € 17,188.34 in a month.

The findings of the assembled components and the cash flow are summarized as overall results in overview in Table 5.8.

Tab. 5.8: Expected values, standard deviations, and value at risk values for the assembled components of the cash flow

Ass. components:	Expected value (μ,r):	Standard deviation (σ,s):	Value at Risk:
Gross profit (grp):	€ 51,206.70	€ 17,495.36	€ 22,394.06
Wage and administrative costs (wag+adm):	€ 10,500.00	€ 832.17	€ 1,065.18
Financial cost (fin):	€ 1,114.58	€ 364.58	€ 466.66
Cash Flow (CF):	**€ 39,592.12**	**€ 17,518.93**	**€ 22,424.23**

The analytical method introduced in the above example for calculating the cash flow at risk possesses three important **properties** and **assumptions** which are significant for transfer and application of the concept to other company-specific, industry-specific or business situations:
– In the case of an economically necessary **multiplicative combining** of individual components (e. g. revenues and tax expenses), a simplifying constant was assumed for one of the components in the example (e. g. price and tax rate). In the process it is assumed that the respective components pose no risk in obvious contradiction to the actual objective. Resolving this conflict is either possible through very complex analytical solution approaches (see Technical appendix 5.4) or by using simulation methods (e. g. Monte Carlo simulation) which have, however, considerable disadvantages.
– In the example, the distribution parameters of the desired target size (component) are first calculated and the value at risk is determined based on them. More explanatory power and a more precise risk analysis would be possible if the **merging** of the individual components were directly or **exclusively** based on the **VaR concept** and the associated correlations. A possible approach to realizing this will be represented in Chapter 6.

– For a meaningful result from the cash flow at risk, it is especially important to observe the applied **planning horizon**. In the example, a planning horizon of one month is used. In that case it is necessary to obtain monthly figures through division of per annum figures by twelve (e. g. interest rates and tax rates). In calculating the value at risk, when applying daily historical price data to the calculation of the standard deviation, the planning horizon of one month must be accounted for through multiplication by the root of the number of trading days (in the example a month is equivalent to 20 trading days for simplicity's sake). An analogous correction by the root function must be performed if the expected value and standard deviation are estimated from internal company data and these are not available in monthly intervals.

The **control** of the **cash flow at risk** is carried out by means of its individual components. The control possibilities for procurement and sales risk are represented in Sections 5.2.1 and 5.2.2. For management of the other components, the measures described in Section 5.1 in the framework of operational risk are partially applicable. However, what is crucial for the control of cash flow at risk are the individual risk components in relation to the cash flow at risk, measured through the respective individual VaR. Such an analysis is, nonetheless, only appropriate and meaningful if the financial risks are also included. In this case, a **company-wide concept** for encompassing all risks based on the VaR is necessary. This is central to the discussions in the sixth chapter.

5.3 References

A good insight into a risk-management structure for operational risks according to the **bottom-up approach** is shown by

Peccia, Tony: "Designing an operational framework from a bottom-up perspective", in: Alexander, Carol: "Mastering Risk Volume 2", Pearson, 2001.

A good **overview** of the various **methods** of **measuring operational risk** can be found in

Beeck, Helmut/Kaiser, Thomas: "Quantifizierung von Operational Risk mit Value– at–Risk", in: Johanning, Lutz/Rudolph, Bernd: "Handbuch Risikomanagement", Band I, Uhlenbruch, S. 633–653, 2000,

Hull, John C.: "Risk Management and Financial Institutions", Wiley, Hoboken, New Jersey, 4th ed. p. 479–496, 2015,

Good, comprehensible **examples** of the **calculation** of the **operational value at risk** using **full enumeration** is given firstly in

Hölscher, Reinhold/Kalnöfer, Christian/Bonn, Rainer: "Die Bewertung operationeller Risiken in
    Kreditinstituten", in: Finanz-Betrieb, Heft 7–8, S. 490–504, 2005,
Jorion, Philippe: "Financial Risk Manager Handbook", Wiley, Hoboken, New Jersey, 6th edition, p.
    557–560, 2011

and the interested reader will also find a checkable example in the work from *Jorion* (see Section 2.7).

For a **praxis-oriented representation** of numerous variants of operational risks, as well as analysis and control in practice,

Keitsch, Detlef: "Risikomanagement", Schaeffer-Poeschel, Stuttgart, 2004.

gives a detailed description using **surveys**.

For an approach to **analytical calculation** of the **operational value at risk** compare

Baesch, Anja: "Analytische Berechnung des OpVaR", in: Zeitschrift für das gesamte Kreditwesen, S.
    1284–1286, 2004

or for operational risk:

Brunel, Vivien: "Operational Risk Modelled Analytically", Risk 27, no. 7 (July 2014), p. 55–59, 2014,
Bank for International Settlements: "Operational Risk – Supervisory Guidelines for the advanced
    Measurement Approaches", June 2011,

For a very detailed representation of **general procurement and sales risks** and their control possibilities

Rogler, Silvia: "Risikomanagement im Industriebetrieb", DVU, 2002,

or for the **procurement risk of commodities**

Poitras, Geoffrey: "Commodity Risk Management", Routledge, New York, 2013.

is especially well-suited. However, it does not refer to application of the VaR concept, but is rather primarily **descriptive explanations** of risk policy measures.

For a deeper exploration of the calculation of **cash flow at risk** using examples based on the **Monte Carlo simulation**, the following works are suitable:

Bartram, Söhnke M.: "Verfahren zur Schätzung finanzwirtschaftlicher Exposures von Nichtbanken",
    in: Johanning, Lutz/Rudolph, Bernd: "Handbuch Risikomanagement", Band II, Uhlenbruch, S.
    1267–1294, 2000,

Bühler, Wolfgang: "Risikocontrolling in Industrieunternehmen", in: Börsig, Clemens/Coenenberg, Adolf G. (Hrsg.): "Controlling und Rechnungswesen im internationalen Wettbewerb", Stuttgart, S. 205–233, 1998

or for a short presentation of cash flow at risk

Damodaran, Aswath: "Strategic Risk Taking – A Framework for Risk Management", Pearson Education, New Jersey, p. 224–225, 2008.

In these essays, the cash flow at risk is only simulated in dependency on interest rates, currency exchange rates and raw materials prices. Consideration of **sales risk** in the framework of simulation can also be found in

Hager, Peter: "Corporate Risk Management-Cash Flow at Risk und Value at Risk", Band 3, Bankakademie Verlag, 2004

and using investment risk in

Kremers, Markus: "Risikoübernahme in Industrieunternehmen – Der Value-at Risk als Steuerungsgröße für das industrielle Risikomanagement, dargestellt am Beispiel des Investitionsrisikos", in: Hölscher, Reinhold (Hrsg.): Schriftenreihe Finanzmanagement, Bd. 7, Sternenfels, Berlin, 2002,

based on the Monte Carlo simulation in

Haney, Mark H.: "Teaching the concept of Investment Risk through Spreadsheet Monte Carlo Simulations", in: Journal of the Academy of Business Education, Winter 2016, Vol. 17, p. 236–256, 2016

as well as in

Wolf, Klaus/Runzheimer, Bodo: "Risikomanagement und KonTraG. Konzeption und Implementierung", Gabler Verlag, Wiesbaden, 5. Auflage, S. 65–79, 2009

For a more **detailed methodological** representation of the **Monte Carlo simulation** see

Deutsch, Hans-Peter: Monte-Carlo-Simulation in der Finanzwelt", in: Johanning, Lutz/Rudolph, Bernd: "Handbuch Risikomanagement", Band II, Uhlenbruch, S. 1267–1294, 2000,
Brandimarte, Paolo: "Handbook in Monte Carlo Simulation: Applications in Financial Engineering, Risk Management, and Economics". Wiley, 2014.

The various **fundamental approaches** to calculating the **cash flow at risk** are represented in overview in the work of *Diggelmann* (see Section 2.7).

For a detailed discussion of **climate change** and the resulting climate risks, compare:

Stern, Nicholas: "The Economics of Climate Change – The Stern Review", Cambridge University Press, 2007.

For an overview of **climate risk management** in companies, see also

Mahammadzadeh, Mohammad: "Risikomanagement: Bewältigung von Klimarisiken in Unternehmen – Bedeutung und Möglichkeiten", in: uwf 19, S. 101–108, 2011,
Kumarasiri, Jayanthi/Gunasekarage, Abeyratna: "Risk Regulation, Community Pressure and the Use of Management Accounting in Managing Climate Change Risk: Australian Evidence", in: Accounting and Risk, The British Accounting Review, January 2017, 49 (1), p. 25–38, 2017.

For a **detailed** insight into climate risk issues in companies, compare the frequently cited work of

Hasenmüller, Philipp: "Unternehmensrisiko Klimawandel – Risiken managen und Chancen strategisch nutzen", Gabler, Wiesbaden, 2009

or the Englisch work

Hansjürgens, Bernd/Antes, Ralf (Editors): "Economics and Management of Climate Change – Risks, Mitigation and Adaptation", Springer, New York, 2008.

For **classification** of climate risks and various risk types, compare

Onischka, Mathias: "Definition von Klimarisiken und Systematisierung in Risikokaskaden", Diskussionspaper des Projektes Mainstreaming von Klimarisiken und -chancen im Finanzsektor, Wuppertal Institut für Klima, Energie, Umwelt, 2009,
Arnell, Nigel: "A Short Guide to Climate Change Risk", Routledge, New York, 2016.

For an **industry-specific approach** to value at risk of climate risks, compare

Carbon Trust: "Brand value at risk from climate change", London, 2005.

5.4 Technical appendix

With **linear interpolation** it is assumed that the growth of the function values corresponds proporticnally to the growth of the independent variables. If the given value of the independent variable x lies between the available values of x_1 and x_2 with the associated function values y_1 und y_2, the desired function value y is

$$y = y_1 + \frac{(x - x_1)}{(x_2 - x_1)} \cdot (y_2 - y_1).$$

For the **sum** of **n random independent variables**, each of which is multiplied by a constant a_i, gives the following results

$$E\left(\sum_{i=1}^{n} a_i \cdot X_i\right) = \sum_{i=1}^{n} a_i \cdot E(X_i),$$

$$V\left(\sum_{i=1}^{n} a_i \cdot X_i\right) = \sum_{i=1}^{n} a_i^2 \cdot V(X_i).$$

If there is **no independence** then the following generally applies to the variance (no effect on the calculation of the expected value):

$$V\left(\sum_{i=1}^{n} a_i \cdot X_i\right) = \sum_{i=1}^{n} a_i^2 \cdot V(X_i) + 2 \cdot \sum_{i<j}^{n} \sum_{j=1}^{n} a_i \cdot a_j \cdot Cov(X_i, X_j) \text{ or}$$

$$V\left(\sum_{i=1}^{n} a_i \cdot X_i\right) = \sum_{i=1}^{n} a_i^2 \cdot V(X_i) + 2 \cdot \sum_{i<j}^{n} \sum_{j=1}^{n} a_i \cdot a_j \cdot k(X_i, X_j) \cdot s(X_i) \cdot s(X_j).$$

With **multiplication of two random variables** X and Y, expected value and variance with **independence** can be calculated as follows:

$$E(X \cdot Y) = E(X) \cdot E(Y),$$
$$V(X \cdot Y) = E(X)^2 \cdot V(Y) + E(Y)^2 \cdot V(X) + V(X) \cdot V(Y).$$

Generally speaking, the expected value of the product of two random variables (so, with dependency) can be found according to

$$E(X \cdot Y) = E(X) \cdot E(Y) + Cov(X, Y).$$

The calculation of the variance of the product of two random variables as a function of a specific covariance (or correlation) can be calculated as follows:

$$V(X \cdot Y) = E(X)^2 \cdot V(Y) + E(Y)^2 \cdot V(X) + V(X) \cdot V(Y)$$
$$+ 2 \cdot E(X) \cdot E(Y) \cdot Cov(X, Y) + Cov(X, Y)^2.$$

For the **product** of **n random variables**, each of which is multiplied by a constant a_i, expected value with **independence** gives the following result:

$$E\left(\prod_{i=1}^{n} a_i \cdot X_i\right) = \prod_{i=1}^{n} a_i \cdot E(X_i)$$

6 Risk controlling

With measurement and control of the most important financial and performance risks, the groundwork is laid for merging the risks together into a company-wide overall concept. To this end, various preliminary considerations are necessary with regard to the **organization** of risk management in a company. Several **definitions** and delineations for a total concept are also required as a basis for constructing a quantitative risk management. Finally, some aspects of accounting which are helpful for internal and external **risks reporting** will be integrated into risk management in the following sections.

6.1 Duties of risk controlling

The terms risk controlling and risk management are often distinguished from each other in the literature. In Section 1.1, the **term risk management** is defined as the measurement and control of all company-wide business risks. The further explanations in this book are conceptually oriented to the **process** of risk management (see Section 1.2).

Then it is time to have a look at **risk controlling** as an **element** of **risk management**. The general functioning of risk controlling consists in supporting the company leadership through **planning, control** and **information**. The **coordination function** is of even more particular significance for risk controlling.

Risk analysis (see Section 2.6) of all individual company risks and the overall risk forms the basis for the **planning** of company risks. In the process, the objective is to bring future company targets into harmony with planned risks. Risk controlling thus fulfills a supporting function for corporate management. The planning of the "classic" company targets such as e. g. capital returns, sales, costs and so on is complemented by the related risks. As a result, classical company planning is qualitatively improved through consideration of possible future risks by supplementing or replacing the targeted return on equity with targets that are in some way shaped by the RoRaC.

The **control function** of risk controlling is tied in the first step to capturing the current situation, that is, the representation of all risks forms the basis of control. In the next step, the originally planned risks (target situation) are calibrated with the current situation and possible deviations are analyzed. This includes, for example, the unexpected increase in the VaR of existing shareholdings, which was caused by e. g. increased volatilities. A typical control function of risk control is represented by **backtesting** (see Section 2.3.5). How reliably the applied VaR calculation methods predicted the actual losses that occurred in the past is retroactively examined.

Risk controlling fulfills the **information function** through reports to corporate management as well as to **individual business units** and **organizational units**.

Risk aggregation stands in the foreground of reports to company management. The **external risk reporting** in the annual report (see Section 6.4) is also tightly linked to management reporting. Therefore, coordination with the external accounting system is necessary. In contrast, information delivered to individual organizational units is based on relevant supplemental information (e. g. special features of risk measurement of individual business sectors) and in particular communication about methods and parameters to be used (e. g. level of confidence). This part of the information function is tightly bound up with the coordination function.

An important task of risk control is represented by the **coordination** of **risk measurement** and **control** between
- the individual business sectors,
- the administrative organizational units (in particular accounting and investor relations),
- corporate management and
- external persons and institutions (shareholders, creditors, suppliers).

Coordination by risk controlling must **ensure** that
- standardized risk measurement methods (based on Value at Risk concept) are applied,
- comparable time periods (e. g. one month or one year) of risk measurement are used as the basis,
- comparability and transparency with regard to estimating the parameters for the distribution of the risk factors is ensured (e. g. in selecting the historical time periods or applicable forecasting procedures if there is no historical data),
- a consistent evaluation of the asset positions by current market values is carried out and
- the same confidence level is used throughout the company.

The respective **profit-** and **risk-aggregation** must also be coordinated on the various company levels. This includes
- definition of limits for individual business units based on the VaR (see Section 3.2),
- preparation of a standard overall risk position by offsetting equal risk factors in different organizational units, the so-called netting.
- assigning of network effects through correlations, based on the Component VaR (see Section 2.3.3),
- distribution of the profits to the individual business units and organizational units in connection with accounting for the targeted determination of the profit-risk ratios by risk controlling and
- coordination by risk controlling of which risk information is to be delivered to which target audience.

The described tasks and functions form the basis for the structural and procedural integration of risk controlling and risk management in the overall organization of a company, which will be described in the following section.

6.2 Organization of risk controlling and risk management

The organizationally structured anchoring and integration of risk controlling and risk management into company procedural processes must be carried out with the objective of **distributing tasks** to and **determining competencies** and responsibilities for centralized and decentralized units. This also includes the questions of how risk causing and risk controlling organizational units are embedded or networked structurally and procedurally in companies. At the center of task delegation, therefore, is the aggregation of individual risks and profits into company-wide targets.

There are two fundamental approaches available for solving this main task: The **integration solution**, which delegates the tasks to decentralized organizational units, and the **separation concept**, which concentrates the tasks in a centralized organizational unit (staff department).

Both approaches have advantages and disadvantages. With the **integration solution**, there is the advantage that risk causes and risk controls lie organizationally close to one another. This requires less coordination cost (between risk causing and risk controlling units), and the necessary risk-specific expertise, for example, with regard to sales risk, stands in close relationship with the duties of risk controlling. The crucial **disadvantage** of the integration solution consists in the missing perception of the typical central duties of risk controlling. These include primarily the coordinative duties of risk control listed above and the actual controlling function with regard to the incurred risks.

The **separation concept** has the **advantage** of being able to implement coordinated duties better. This, however, also requires a corresponding risk controlling authority over the risk-causing decentralized organizational units. From the company's perspective, the separation concept offers the advantage that only one contact person (the central risk controlling) is necessary and not several decentralized organizational units, as with the integration solution. The **disadvantage** of the separation concept lies in the danger that risk controlling is not accepted due to its distance from the risk-causing organizational units. Thus the possibility does exist that a decentralized risk-causing unit will consider the risk methods prescribed by risk controlling to be inappropriate on technical grounds due to specific characteristics of certain risk types.

In a comparison of the respective advantages and disadvantages, it is evident that for **small- and medium-sized** enterprises the advantages of the integration solution predominate, since the corporate management can more easily take on the coordinative duties themselves, and the advantage of the closeness between expertise and control prevails. For **larger businesses**, the assumption of coordinative tasks by company leadership is no longer possible because the scope and complexity are too great. Likewise, the number of contact partners for the decentralized units would be too high. Also, the control function would lose effectiveness with many risk-causing organizational units. The disadvantage of lack of acceptance by decentralized units towards a central risk control nonetheless also remains in large companies. In business practice, a **mixture** of **integration solution** and **separation concept** has prevailed and can be traced in the organizational charts of many companies. Here, elements of integration solution still prevail in small companies, while fulfillment of the duties by a central risk control stands in the foreground for large companies. A statement that generally applies to all sizes of company cannot be derived from this. Basically, however, the traditional risk measurement and risk control tasks of risk management should rather be taken over by decentralized organizational units, while the coordinated duties should be fulfilled by a central risk control department. This approach will, therefore, form the basis for the following remarks on a concept for organizing risk controlling and risk management.

For a suitable **organizational structure** that takes into account the fundamentals mentioned above, the criteria for delineating the organizational units must first be established. **Risk types** (see Section 1.2) and the associated risk factors are the most important criterion for delineation according to risk-causing units. This criterion follows the **causation principle**, i. e., risks are measured and controlled in those organizational units in which they occur. Afterwards, basic organizational differentiation into business units would have to be undertaken, which would trigger either financial or performance risks.

The measurement and control of **financial risks** (see chapter 4) should therefore be amalgamated into "**financial management**". The financial management unit could then be subdivided by means of risk factors into, for example, the sub-units of "interest rate management", "foreign currency management", "stock management", "real estate management", "credit management", "liquidity management". A "financial management" organizational unit is often observable in business practice in larger companies (although also frequently under other names or classifications). In smaller companies, the duties of financial management are usually taken on by corporate management or accounting.

The organizational consideration of **performance risks** is carried out using the Cash Flow at Risk and its respective components (risk factors). The causes of performance risks are conveniently differentiated using the company's products and services. As a rule, this differentiation occurs in theory and practice by dividing the overall business into **business sectors**. With numerous or very complex products, the individual business sectors are further subdivided into **business units** or business groups.

The organizational structure according to the **causation principle** is, nonetheless, in some cases **not** always **clear-cut**. This can be especially well demonstrated by the example of liquidity risk. If products are sold on target, then the sales revenue is assigned to performance risks as the corresponding business sector. If the customer defaults, i. e. the claims are not settled by the customer when due, the default risk is central and at the same time there is a liquidity loss. Although the cause of all risks lies in the company's performance activities, a treatment of default risk and of liquidity risk with the corresponding financial instruments and methods is necessary and must be assigned to the area of financial management. Assigning risks according to the possibilities of risk measurement and risk control can therefore be called the **control principle**. The various risk types can be unproblematically assigned to an organizational unit when the risk can be clearly assigned according to the causation principle as well as the control principle.

This **difficulty** of risk assignment according to organizational units can be demonstrated, along with the examples in Section 1.2, by two further **examples**. If a business buys a foreign-currency bond with the repayment in a foreign currency (e. g. US-$), then the treatment of the related exchange rate risk clearly is assigned to financial management, since both the cause (buy of the foreign-currency bond) as well as the control possibility (e. g. conclusion of a forward exchange transaction) are assignable to financial management. The control of the default and interest rate risk of the foreign-currency bond would likewise have to be assigned to financial management. On the other hand, if a company product is sold in a foreign currency (e. g. by export to the USA), then an exchange rate risk also arises through the future returns in US dollars. According to the causation principle, this exchange rate risk would have to be assigned to the corresponding business sector (distribution, sales), and according to the control principal it would have to be assigned to financial management.

If a clear assignment according to both principles is not possible, then precedence should be granted to the control principal in the framework of **company-wide risk control**. Thus a business unit cannot be made responsible for losses from a foreign-exchange position if it has no potential or skills for controlling that. The foreign-exchange position and related (price-) profits then have to be assigned to financial management (foreign exchange management), and the financial management must in turn establish a binding exchange rate for the business unit for calculating sales prices, so that the business unit has no more exchange rate risk. At the same time, this procedure represents a mandatory requirement for **organizational procedural** involvement of risk controlling and risk management in the overall business.

The **unclear assignment** of risks to organizational units is company- and industry-dependent. For this reason, some general cases of an unclear assignment are explained in the following remarks:
- **Procurement risk** of **raw materials** which are traded daily on the exchanges and for which financial market risk control instruments are available are caused by business units (or triggered by goods production), but are assigned to financial management for technical control reasons.

– The increase in interest expense from overdraft facilities is caused by the financing of equipment, so, the business unit. Due to the control of **interest change risk**, it is assigned to financial management (interest rate management).
– The risk of a potentially higher **tax expenses** is caused by the (successful) activities of the business unit, through higher revenues which may trigger higher tax rates. The handling of the tax expenses (or tax risk), however, must take place in accounting, since only here can all the influencing factors of the ultimate average tax rate be directed or information about it can be merged.

This list can be considerably supplemented by specific companies and industries.

In light of the above remarks, it is necessary to merge all business units and central (staff) departments structurally and procedurally. In the business literature and in practice this usually is carried out using corresponding **organigrams**. In that case, nonetheless, the structural and procedural risks are not only considered, but also, for a profit-risk oriented company control, the **profits** are assigned to different units according to the risk distribution (by control and causation principle). To produce an example organigram, assume the following units and business sectors:
– corporate management,
– financial management (interest rate, foreign exchange, stocks, credit and liquidity management),
– risk controlling,
– accounting,
– personnel,
– central administration (EDP, organization, board office, facility management, and so on)
– business sector A (consisting of units A1 and A2) and
– business sector B (consisting of units B1 and B2).

These units will be organizationally assigned to the previously covered risk types or risk factors. That gives the following **functions**, **tasks** and **risk allocations** for the different units:

The **corporate management** decides and plans the company-wide risk attitude, the sought after RoRaC values and the coverage of all risks by the equity capital as a risk-bearing capacity.

In **financial management**, all financial risks from financial activities are measured and managed. Additionally, it manages the financial risks from performance activity and delivers the risk-free prices and evaluation rates to the business sectors in the framework of **internal service charges**.

Risk controlling takes over the functions and duties described in Section 6.1.

The **accounting department** has basically two duties to fulfill, besides its original tasks of financial statements as well as managerial accounting to support risk management. On the one hand, it calculates the **tax expenses** with consideration of all tax-relevant influencing factors, in order to provide a planned average tax rate for calculating the cash flow of the business sectors. On the other hand, accounting must **distribute profits** or expenses and income to the various organizational units as proportionally as possible to their degree of risk causation, since it is a necessary prerequisite for RoRaC- based company management.

The central **personnel department** applies itself to the management of personnel risk. This includes planning **personnel costs** to support the business sectors in calculating the cash flow, as well as carrying out measures for reducing personnel-related internal **operational risks** (in coordination with the business sectors; see also Section 5.1.2).

The focus of **central administration** is the measurement and control of **process** and systemic risks as well as **external operational risks** (see Section 5.1.2 and 5.1.3), insofar as these are not directly assigned to business sectors according to the causation principle. Typical application examples are the central EDP, the organizational establishment of work processes, the protection of buildings and facilities against external operational risks and so on.

For **business sectors**, risk management of sales and procurement risks and control based on **cash flow at risk** are in the foreground. But also, the **operational risks** that are caused by the business sectors through procurement, service provision and sales, are captured and managed here.

The **structural** and **procedural organigram** shown in Figure 6.1 can be derived as an example from these fundamental considerations and conclusions.

The links with arrows represent **processes** which ensure specified functions and communication paths of risk controlling and management. The dashed connecting lines without arrows form the **structural linkages** between the organizational units that are necessary from the perspective of risk management.

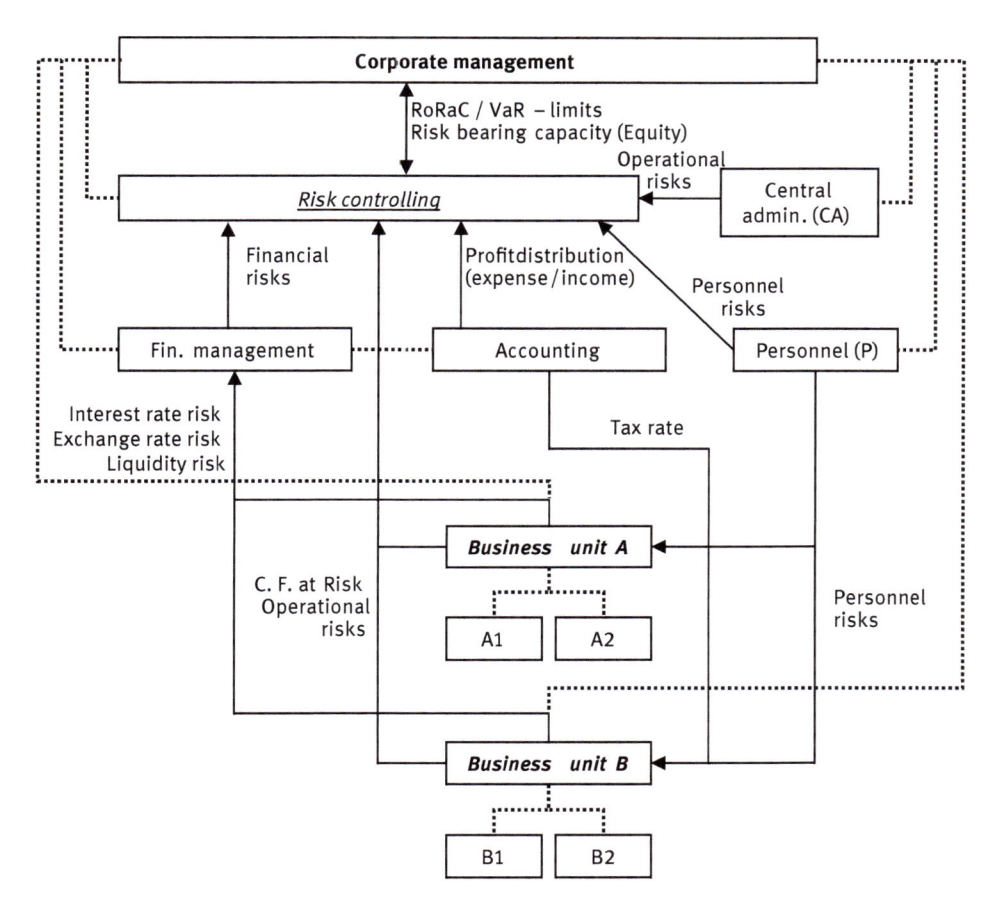

Fig. 6.1: Structural and procedural diagram for risk controlling and risk management

The described structural and procedural connection of the organizational units is not yet sufficient for a sound and meaningful risk report to corporate management. The various **risk types** or their risk factors must be allocated for the different possible **aggregation levels,** right up to the company management. Along with the allocation of risks to the various aggregation levels and units, the associated **profits** must also be subdivided proportionately. From the risk and profit allocations, it is finally possible to report to the company management for the individual organizational units and for the different aggregated levels on:
- the realized RoRaC values,
- the possible limits based on the VaR and
- the risk-bearing capacity of the equity.

Tab. 6.1: Scheme for the risk aggregation of risk types and organizational units based on the VaR (in € mill.)

Risks: (in € mill.)	Business unit A:	Business unit B:	Financial management (FM):	Central admin. (CA):	Personal (P):	A+B:	ZV+P:	Overall:
Interest rate risk:	–	–	125	–	–	–	–	125
Foreign exchange risk:	–	–	65	–	–	–	–	65
Stock price risk:	–	–	20	–	–	–	–	20
Default risk:	–	–	150	–	–	–	–	150
Liquidity risk:	–	–	15	–	–	–	–	15
Σ Financial risks:	–	–	375	–	–	–	–	375
Sales risk: (revenues)	1,250	1,300	–	–	–	2,550	–	2,550
Procurement risk: (material cost)	120	140	–	–	–	260	–	260
Wage risk: (wage costs)	70	80	5	35	5	150	40	195
Administrative costs:	6	9	3	23	9	15	32	50
Interest expense:	5	6	–	–	–	11	–	11
Tax expenses:	35	40	15	–	–	75	–	90
Cash Flow at Risk:	*1,486*	*1,575*	*23*	*58*	*14*	*3,061*	*72*	*3,156*
Personnel risks:	14	18	5	8	3	32	11	48
Systemic risks:	2	2	12	57	8	4	65	81
Process risks:	1	1	3	15	6	2	21	26
External risks:	3	4	–	3	2	7	5	12
Σ Operational risks:	20	25	20	83	19	45	102	167
Σ Performance risks:	1,506	1,600	43	141	33	3,106	174	3,323
Overall risk:	**1,506**	**1,600**	**418**	**141**	**33**	**3,106**	**174**	**3,698**

A possible scheme for an **example profit and risk aggregation** for the various risk types and organizational units, which would do justice to the demands of corporate management regarding the three points mentioned above, would be extremely complex and could not be summarized in a figure. For this reason, the scheme shown in Table 6.1 is in the first step based only on the **VaR values** for the organizational units described in Figure 6.1. The VaR values (respectively in mill. € for a liquidation period of one year and a confidence level of 99%) of the individual risk types and organizational units are randomly chosen and only meant to illustrate the fundamental principles of the aggregation. A completely positive correlation was assumed for the aggregation for the sake of simplicity. Through that, the VaR values can be merged across all aggregation levels by simple **addition**. This indeed does not model the business reality properly, but it is at least a cautious risk assessment, since the overall risk cannot be larger than the sum of the individual risks. The exact calculation of the diversification effect through the aggregation is carried out individually in Section 6.3.

For the sake of clarity, the organizational units of **corporate management**, **accounting** and **risk control** are not listed in the aggregation in Figure 6.1, since these do not directly cause risk themselves, but rather perform risk reporting as their basic functions. The necessary wage and administration cost or the risks which increase unexpectedly for these units are contained in the "central administration" unit (=CA).

The composition and **structure** of Table 6.1 depend on the selection of the aggregation levels. These are industry-and company-specific or result from corporate management's requirements from the risk report. Generally, the aggregation scheme can be distinguished on a horizontal and a vertical level.

The merging according to organizational units occurs on the **horizontal aggregation** level. In Table 6.1, the business units A and B are aggregated into one overall business, just as the central administration and personnel are merged into a central unit. Ultimately, all units are merged into a company-wide overall position on the highest aggregation level. Other aggregation levels can also be selected depending on the requirements, but this would not change the fundamental principles or the computational methods of the aggregation, so they will be omitted here.

The aggregation according to risk types forms the **vertical aggregation level**. In Table 6.1, the risk types are combined into financial risks, Cash Flow at Risk, operational risks and finally into performance risks. In the last line, all risks are aggregated into the overall risk of each organizational unit. The individual risks can also be merged into other aggregation levels according to necessity (e. g. in the literature, interest change risk is often merged with default risk). Another design possibility for the aggregation of risk types consists in classifying the risk types according to their respective **risk factors** (e. g. subdividing the interest change risk in the interest rates according to maturities, stock price risk according to different stock prices, procurement risk according to different raw materials). This description offers in particular the advantage of representing the risk aggregation more transparently across the individual organizational units (for details see Section 6.3). This is omitted in Table 6.1 for greater transparency, without fundamentally changing anything about the aggregation. The sum of all aggregated risk types ultimately corresponds to the sum of the risks across all the aggregated organizational units. In the above example, the overall risk (= the total VaR) of the company comes to **€ 3,698,000**.

Based on the structural and procedural embedding of risk controlling and risk management, the technical implementation requires the various risks and profits to be **computationally** distributed or aggregated. The various approaches for a company-wide distribution or aggregation will be represented in the following section.

6.3 Company-wide profit and risk aggregation

Along with the organizational structure and procedure, risk controlling must determine the VaR values and profits suitably for the individual organizational units and risk types, for inclusion in the risk report to corporate management on RoRaC and risk-bearing capacity. In order to aggregate specific groups of risk types and organizational units, particular scope or **diversification effects** must be computationally mapped as realistically as possible. To this end, various approaches are discussed in the literature, in particular with regard to the merging of interest change risks and credit risks. However, these approaches are suitable primarily for application within banks under certain conditions (see Literature references Section 6.5). In the following, an approach will be described which is generally appropriate with reference to transparency and comprehensibility for an aggregation like the one shown in Table 6.1.

The **aggregation** of **profits** across the various units and risk types is relatively unproblematic, since determination of profit is based on plan values (or expected values); this requires no assumption of uncertainty since uncertainty of profits is of course already mapped directly by the VaR. **Constant profit figures** can be merged through simple **addition**. The allocation of profit to individual organizational units, by contrast, is significantly more difficult to arrange. This issue is comprehensively dealt with in the framework of managerial accounting and will therefore not be further explored here (for corresponding literature see Section 6.5). The profits will be assigned where they are caused (causation principle) for the rest of this discussion. Organizational units that make no profits because of their functions will only be allocated attributable expenses. If the expenses are higher than the attributable income, then these are computationally taken into account by a negative sign and with the converse, by a positive sign.

Risk aggregation across the various **organizational units** is unproblematic for **identical risk factors** (e. g. crude oil price within procurement risk), since risks of the same risk factor are completely positively correlated and thus their VaR values can be added up. With **different risk factors** (e. g. crude oil and copper; see Section 5.2.3), the aggregation is carried out using the associated correlation based on the portfolio VaR (see Section 2.3.3).

On the other hand, **risk aggregation** across various **risk types** (e. g. financial risks vs. operational risks) is not so easily possible. Determining the correlation between various risk categories is usually not empirically calculable from historical data, since the data collections have either no comparable time series or no comparable time intervals. Also, the available data are often incompatible with each other because of different units (e. g. percentage change versus number of losses in a year). It is only within the same risk type that the calculation and consideration of correlations is unproblematic (e. g. between the interest rates for different maturities within interest change risk; see Section 4.1). Consequently, risk aggregation for most risk categories requires the **estimation** of **correlation coefficients** because of plausibility considerations about the business contexts of the risks.

In Section 5.2.3 the issue of aggregating various risk components of the cash flow is solved using an approach based on the **algorithms** for the **correlation** of **two random variables**. At the same time, the individual components are combined respectively in pairs into a new random variable and the parameters of the combined random variable are calculated using algorithms. The VaR of both aggregated risks is then determined using the standard deviation of the aggregated risks. This procedure is adequate or plausible in business terms, and comprehensible for determining the cash flow at risk. However, with regard to the application of this concept to company-wide risk aggregation across various risk categories, this procedure has the following fundamental disadvantages:

- The aggregation is carried out on the basis of the **distribution parameters** (standard deviation). For a transparent and more business-oriented risk report, an aggregation based on VaR values is more comprehensible.
- The simultaneous linkage is only ever possible **in pairs** meaningful and necessary exactly from a business perspective.
- A **grave disadvantage** of this procedure is closely related to the pair-wise aggregation. If, for example, three risk types A (e. g. revenues), B (e. g. material costs) and C (wage costs) are to be aggregated into a performance indicator, then with a pair-wise link, A and B are first merged pair-wise into a gross profit (A-B) under consideration of the correlation between revenues and material cost. Afterwards, the gross profit is merged with the wage costs into a performance indicator (A-B-C). In the process, the correlation between the gross profit and the wage costs is computationally accounted for. It would be reasonable for a business to possibly need to take account of the correlation between revenues (A) and wage costs (C) (thoroughly reasonable in business terms, since workers can also demand higher wages in the presence of increasing revenues), and in this case it could not be captured! Thus, with pair-wise aggregation, not all necessary correlations can always be adequately **considered**.

The two previously mentioned disadvantages can be avoided if one of three special cases is assumed between the merged risks(for the technical derivation and depiction of these contexts, see Section 2.8):

- There is **no correlation** between all risks (correlation coefficient = 0). In this case, the VaR of the aggregated figures is simply calculated by the root of the sum of the squared individual VaR values. The same goes for the calculation of the volatility of the aggregated figures from the individual standard deviations. This

assumption was, for example, also used for calculating the cash flow at risk (see Section 5.2.3 and in particular Table 5.7 and 5.8).
- A **completely positive correlation** (correlation coefficient = +1) is assumed. In this case, the VaR of the individual risks can be added up to the desired overall risk. This procedure can, for example, be meaningfully applied when aggregating across organizational units with identical risk factors.
- There is a completely **negative correlation** (correlation coefficient = –1). A typical sphere of application for this aggregation assumption is in the financial area, when the so-called long and short positions have the same risk factors. So, for example, a business obtains a US-$-position of 1 mill. through export revenues (=**long position**) and at the same time requires 4 mill. US-$ in the procurement area for the purchase of crude oil (=**short position**). If the VaR amounts to € 25,000 for 1 mill. US-$ and the VaR amounts to € 100,000 for the position of 4 mill. US-$, then the VaR for both positions result from the absolute difference between both individual VaR. The VaR for both positions together corresponds to the amount of € 100,000 minus € 25,000, which gives a VaR of € 75,000.

However, these special cases cover only a small portion of business practices. In many cases, a weak negative or positive correlation can be observed. It is thus necessary to take into account **every** possible **correlation in absolute terms**. At the same time, the three crucial disadvantages of pair-wise aggregation must be eliminated and **all** necessary **correlations** between and among multiple individual risk factors must be **taken into account**. However, this is not possible using the previously introduced approaches without further work. One solution approach consists in broadening the calculation of the portfolio VaR for only two risk positions (see Section 2.3.3) to any number of risk positions using general portfolio theory. A clear and computationally simple, workable representation of the VaR calculation for more than two risk factors is not possible in the form discussed thus far. The Technical appendix (Section 6.6) can be referred to for a precisely formal description. The basic principle, however, can be demonstrated using an **example** for **three risk factors**. To this end, we will fall back on the example of the Cash Flow at Risk calculation, using the aggregation of gross profit (grp), wage and administration cost (wag+adm) and financial cost (fin).

The calculation is carried out based on the distribution values and VaR (see Table 5.8) calculated in Section 5.2.3. Additionally, a correlation between gross profit and wage costs of $CR_{Grp,W+A} = +0.7$, a correlation between gross profit and financial cost of $CR_{Grp,Fin} = +0.2$ as well as a correlation between wage costs and financial cost in the amount of $CR_{W+A,Fin} = +0.1$ is taken into account. The variance of the cash flow (s_{CF}^2) under consideration of these correlations is then

$$s_{CF}^2 = s_{Grp}^2 + s_{W+A}^2 + s_{Fin}^2$$

$$+ 2 \cdot (-1 \cdot k_{Grp,W+A} \cdot s_{Grp} \cdot s_{W+A} + -1 \cdot k_{Grp,Fin} \cdot s_{Grp} \cdot s_{Fin} + k_{W+A,Fin} \cdot s_{W+A} \cdot s_{Fin}).$$

6.3 Company-wide profit and risk aggregation

The Cash Flow at Risk is then

$$CFaR = \sqrt{s_{CF}^2} \cdot \alpha$$

If a value of **null** is assumed for **all correlations** between the components, then the second mixed term in the above equation is null. The CFaR resulting from the example calculation in Section 5.2.3 (see Table 5.8) again comes to **€ 22,424.23**.

For the **various correlations of null** mentioned above, the CFaR is calculated as follows:

$$s_{CF}^2 = (€\ 17{,}495.36)^2 + (€\ 832.17)^2 + (€\ 364.58)^2$$
$$+\ 2 \times (-1 \times 0.7 \times €\ 17{,}495.36 \times €\ 832.17 + -1 \times 0.2 \times €\ 17{,}495.36 \times €\ 364.58$$
$$+\ 0.1 \times €\ 832.17 \times €\ 364.58)$$
$$=\ +\ €\ 306{,}913{,}047.01^2 - €\ 22{,}873{,}464.06^2 = \underline{€\ 284{,}039{,}582.96^2}.$$

The standard deviation of the cash flow amounts to s_{CF} = € 16,853.47. By taking the positive correlations into account, the CFaR amounts to **€ 21,572.45**. The CFaR thus decreased through consideration of positive correlations, since the wage and administrative costs as well as the financial cost was subtracted (multiplication by factor –1) from the gross profit. Because of that, with positive correlations the cost has a risk mitigating effect on the gross profit and thus also a risk mitigating effect on the cash flow (analogously to determination of the standard deviation for the gross profit in Section 5.2.3).

In the next step, this principle can be transferred to the company-wide risk aggregation using the example in Table 6.1. For later analysis of the aggregated values based on the RoRaC concept, it is still expedient to calculate the respective **Components VaR** values. The approaches described in Section 2.3.3 for determining the Component VaR are only suitable when the beta factors can be calculated from historical data. This is nonetheless not possible for all risks, in particular when the correlations have to be estimated. The Component VaR can also be calculated in a different way, if the data listed in the above example is the only available data (for a formal description of the calculation, see Section 6.6). For the above example, the Component VaR can be determined as follows:

In the first step, the associated beta factors are determined for the individual components. The beta factor for the gross profit ($ß_{Grp}$) is then calculated as

$$ß_{Grp} = (s_{Grp}^2 + s_{Grp,W+A} + s_{Grp,Fin})/s_{CF}^2$$
$$= (306{,}087{,}621.5 + -10{,}191{,}379.61 + -1{,}275{,}691.67) / 284{,}039{,}582.96$$
$$= \underline{1.03725}$$

Analogously, the resulting wage costs is $ß_{Wag,Adm}$ = **–0.03334** and the financial cost is $ß_{Fin}$ = **–0.00392**.

Multiplying the beta factors by the cash flow at risk gives the following Component VaR values:

$$CoVaR_{Grp} = €\ 21{,}572.45 \times 1.03725 = \mathbf{\underline{€\ 22{,}376.06}}\ (VaR_{Grp} = €\ 22{,}394.06),$$
$$CoVaR_{Wag+Adm} = €\ 21{,}572.45 \times -0.03334 = \mathbf{\underline{-€\ 719.12}}\ (VaR_{Wag+Adm} = €\ 1{,}065.18)\ \text{and}$$
$$CoVaR_{Fin} = €\ 21{,}572.45 \times -0.00392 = \mathbf{\underline{-€\ 84.49}}\ (VaR_{Fin} = €\ 466.66).$$

The sum of the individual Component VaR values again gives precisely the cash flow at risk of € 21,572.45. Putting the Component VaR next to the VaR from the individual risk positions illustrates the **diversification effect**. The **diversification effect** is illustrated by setting the Component VaR next to the VaR from the individual risk positions. The diversification effect can be seen to have the strongest impact on the wage and administration costs (168 % based on the individual VaR). The relative diversification effect amounts to 118 % for the financial cost and only 0.08 % for the gross profit. The proportional diversification effect is so small for the gross profit because the VaR for the gross profit is so great in relation to both of the other VaR values (see Section 2.3.3 regarding the influence of the portfolio weighting on the CoVaR). This also explains the **negative Component VaR values**, which are computationally necessary in order to explain the overall diversification effect.

With that, the **foundations** for a **company-wide aggregation** of risks and profits as well as the resulting analysis based on the RoRaC concepts are available. For application to the example in Table 6.1, the next step requires information about the correlations between the individual risk types and the standard deviations of the individual risk positions. It is convenient to divide the various risk categories (financial risks, cash flow risks, operational risks) in table format. The standard deviations are given in € mill. on the diagonal of the individual table sections, and the correlations are given in the lower half. Since the correlation value e. g. in the interest change risk row and the exchange rate risk column is identical to the value in the interest change risk column and the exchange rate risk row, they are not shown above the diagonals.

The respective **beta factor** of the individual risks is given in the row with the sum of the individual risk types. Its calculation is carried out analogously to the procedure described above using the example of the aggregation into Cash Flow at Risk. The respective **standard deviation** for the sum of the risks, taking account of the associated correlation, is then given in the column with the sum of the risks. For calculating the standard deviation of the sum of all performance risks, a correlation of +0.7 is assumed between cash flow and operational risks. For determining the standard deviation of the company-wide overall risk, a correlation of +0.1 is assumed between the performance and financial risks. Based on the calculations in Table 6.2, the company-wide overall aggregation is now possible for the individual risks across all organizational units according to the individual risk types. In addition, the **profits**, the respective **Component VaR values** based on the beta factors calculated in Table 6.2 and the resulting **equity utilization** and **RoRaC values** based on the Component VaR are given in Table 6.3. Equity in the amount of € 3 bn. is assumed for calculating the equity utilization.

Tab. 6.2: Correlations and standard deviations (in € mill.) of the individual risk groups

	Interest rate risk:	Foreign exchange risk:	Stock price risk:	Default risk:	Liquidity risk:	Σ Financial risks:
Interest rate risk:	53.65					
Foreign exchange risk:	−0.8	27.9				
Stock price risk:	−0.3	0.7	8.58			
Default risk:	0.6	0.2	−0.1	64.38		
Liquidity risk:	0.3	−0.4	−0.3	0.8	6.44	
Σ Fin. risks (ß):	0.33724	0.0033	0.003	0.621	0.035	**105.01**
	Revenues:	Procurement cost:	Wage costs:	Administrative costs:	Interest expense:	Tax expenses:	Σ Cash flow:
Revenues:	1.094.42						
Procurement cost:	0.7	111.59					
Wage costs:	0.2	0.2	83.69				
Administrative expense:	0.6	0.7	0.6	21.46			
Interest expense:	−0.2	0.1	0.2	0.2	4.72		
Tax expenses:	0.3	−0.1	−0.2	−0.3	−0.8	38.63	
Σ Cash flow (ß):	1.10450	−0.07224	−0.01	−0.01	0.001	−0.01	**983.43**
	Personnel risks:	Systemic risks:	Process risks:	External risks:	Σ Operational risks:	Σ Performance risks:	Overall risk:
Personnel risks:	20.60						
Systemic risks:	0.1	34.76					
Process risks:	0.8	0.8	11.16				
External risks:	0	0	0	5.15			
Σ Operational risks (ß):	0.23320	0.54545	0.212	0.009	**53.99**		
Σ Performance risks:						1.021.95	
Overall risk:							**1.037.73**

Table 6.3 represents the end point of the results of the **risk management process**. On the one hand, corporate management is informed by these results about the company-wide risk situation and, on the other hand, decisions regarding the first steps of the process are reviewed (see Section 1.2). These include, for example:
- renewed risk identification for considering further risks,
- introducing new risk indicators (because the ones previously applied are not meaningful enough),
- establishing new limits based on the VaR in the framework of risk management and so on.

The **interpretation** of the results in Table 6.3 can be carried out incrementally.

Tab. 6.3: Company-wide profits, VaR, Component VaR (in € mill.), RoRaC and equity utilization

Risks:	Profits:	Individual VaR:	Component VaR:	RoRaC:	Equity utilization:
Interest rate risk:	80	125	82.51	0.9695	2.75 %
Foreign exchange risk:	0.6	65	0.80	0.7537	0.03 %
Stock price risk:	0.5	20	0.69	0.7205	0.02 %
Default risk:	135	150	152.05	0.8878	5.07 %
Liquidity risk:	−8	15	8.62	−0.9284	0.29 %
Σ Financial risks:	*208.1*	*375*	*244.67*	*0.8505*	*8.16 %*
Revenues:	1,500	2,550	2,530.86	0.5927	84.36 %
Procurement cost:	−130	260	−165.54	0.7853	−5.52 %
Wage costs:	−40	195	−21.17	1.8892	−0.71 %
Administrative costs:	−24	50	−25.79	0.9307	−0.86 %
Interest expense:	−2	11	2.47	−0.8103	0.08 %
Tax expenses:	−20	90	−29.43	0.6796	−0.98 %
Cash Flow at Risk:	**1,284**	**3,156**	**2,291.39**	**0.5604**	**76.38 %**
Personnel risks:	0	48	29.34	0.0000	0.98 %
Systemic risks:	0	81	68.62	0.0000	2.29 %
Process risks:	0	26	26.70	0.0000	0.89 %
External risks:	0	12	1.14	0.0000	0.04 %
Σ Operational risks:	*0*	*167*	*125.81*	*0.0000*	*4.19 %*
Σ Performance risks:	*1,284*	*3,323*	*2,381.00*	*0.5392*	*79.37 %*
Overall risk:	*1,492*	*3,698*	*2,418.00*	*0.6171*	*80.60 %*

In the first step, the **profits** are set against the risk types. The profits are aggregated into the company-wide overall profit (in the amount of € 1,492 mill.) through addition across the various organizational units. To get a more detailed profit analysis, the presentation should be listed separately by the different units as in Table 6.1 (which was omitted here for clarity). Determining the profit must be done with a view to the desired risk analysis based on the RoRaC concept, according to the following **criteria**:
- The profit determination must be carried out for the time frame of the **liquidation period**, which is also the time period of the VaR calculation.
- The **allocation** of **profits** to individual risk types should be carried out according to the **causation principle**, since for corporate management the cause of profits and risks stands in the foreground of the risk report (in contrast to risk control in the framework of risk management; see Chapter 3).
- Earnings are only referred to where they also **arise**. There should be no distribution of the earnings, since this would make the risk analysis of the interpretation content much more difficult.
- Profits are determined as **fixed target values**. For the planned profits, in particular, no uncertainty is assumed. The uncertainty of potential profits is indeed taken into account precisely by the value at risk and would then be captured twice.
- The **operational risks** should not be assigned any income or expenses, since these do not correspond to the character of operational risks. Possible expenses from e. g. personnel risks are captured by wage costs in the framework of cash flow. Income are captured within the organizational units where they also arise. These are usually not identical with the organizational units in which the operational risks can occur.
- The income for **financial risks** includes primarily the expected price gains, dividends, interest on credit balances, coupon payments and so on.

A **profit analysis** according to these criteria based on Table 6.3 paints a picture that is typical for non-banks, where performance activities generate ca. 80 % of the total company profits, while only 20 % is generated from the financial activities.

The second column of Table 6.3 shows the individual VaR, which are aggregated based on an always completely positive correlation across the units. The aggregation is thus carried out by summation and therefore corresponds exactly to the values in the last column of Table 6.1. These individual VaR in fact have no application in further risk analysis, but they help interpret the **diversification effects** and possible VaR-based **limitations** where the diversification effect may only be considered on the aggregate level (see Figure 3.2).

The diversification effect is especially high with foreign-exchange risks, stock-price risks, wage risks and with the expense positions of the cash flow. The reason for this is the somewhat strong **negative correlations** to the other respective risk factors from the same risk categories, and the above-mentioned risk mitigating effect of positively correlated expense positions on revenues for the cash flow at risk. A juxtaposition of the aggregated individual VaR with the Component VaR shows from the orders of magnitude that the diversification effects must be taken into account. Direct addition of all risks, which is somewhat customary in business practice, would form a misleading picture of the company-wide risk situation.

In the third step, the calculated Component Value at Risk values are used to calculate the **RoRaC** for the individual risk types. The RoRaC (see Section 2.6) arises from the ratio of profit to component value at risk. The different organizational units and risk categories can be meaningfully compared with each other using the RoRaC (the comparison between the organizational units will be omitted for the sake of clarity). This shows that the financial management activities are more successful than the operating business activities (cash flow at risk). In other words: in financial management, higher income are generated with the same risks, or the same income with smaller risks.

At this point, however, the **limited significance** of corporate management based on the RoRaC is simultaneously also clear: If control were to be carried out based only on the RoRaC, then the entire operating business would have to be terminated and fully diverted into pure financial activities. For non-banks, nonetheless, this would be clear mismanagement, since their main objective consists in achieving profits from operating activities, and indeed equity is also made available to non-banks for these activities (and not for typical banking activities). Nonetheless, the RoRaC can be used in order to analyze where it can be improved and where, for example, the associated VaR is too high (or profits too low).

In the last step, the **equity utilization** (last column) is determined by dividing the component value at risk by the overall equity in the amount of € 3 bn. Ultimately, the information about the equity cost basically fulfills the following functions:

- Information about **risk-bearing capacity** and thus in particular about creditworthiness can be provided to investors using the equity utilization. So, for example, a measurement of all risks based on a confidence level of 99 % (2.33 standard deviations) and full coverage of the measured risks by equity means a Ba1 classification from Moody's (see Section 4.3.2 and in particular Table 4.7).
- The total equity utilization of 80.60 % indicates how large the buffer (here 19.40 %) is for future potential **crisis times**.
- An effective **limitation** can be carried out on the VaR basis using the equity utilization. This is how high equity utilization (e. g. sales risks) in particular can be subject to more targeted and efficient control through limits. On the other hand, it could be that due to low equity utilization, advanced risk limitation measures would not justify the concomitant effort (e. g. with foreign exchange risks, stock risks, liquidity risks, interest expense and external risks).

The representation in Table 6.3 can only display some **aspects** of a detailed **risk report**. In business practice, these aspects must be adapted to company- and industry-specific characteristics. These include primarily the structural and procedural particulars of the company as well as consideration of special risk types (e. g. company-specific operational risks). For this reason, the next section will discuss some important aspects of **external risk reporting** (in management report or annual report) which are mandatory for all companies.

Finally, in the seventh chapter a **case study** will demonstrate the implementation of the overall risk management process for a general example, in order to illustrate the interaction of the individual components of the process and their interconnection with each other.

6.4 The external risk report

The commercial code is the essential foundation of the external risk report for German companies. The commercial code (HGB) was explicitly expanded with the introduction of the KonTraG (see Section 1.1). This expansion includes, among other things, the scope of the risk report (§§ 289, 315 HGB). So, for example, in § 315 HGB the following points are specified regarding the group management report:
– the group's **risk management goals** and **methods**,
– the methods for hedging all important types of transactions in the framework of hedge accounting,
– the price change, default and liquidity risks,
– the risks from cash flow fluctuations.

In relation to this expansion of the HGB, the German Accounting Standard Committee (DRSC) issued a design for the risk report (**German Accounting Standard** (DRS) **No. 5** of 29 may 2001) which forms the basis for producing an external risk report (see Literature references Section 6.5).

The **DRS 20** version "Group Management Report" replaced the DRS 5 as of December 31, 2012. The DRS 20 formulates risks as the potential for **negative future developments** of the company's financial situation, which must occur in the group management report. An abstract formulation is consciously chosen here in order to satisfy the individual risk reporting requirements of the various companies and industries. A message that is essentially covered by the concept of this book.

A disclosure requirement is intended for **existential risks** and **risk concentrations** as well as the expected consequences of their occurrence. A specific risk categorization is not prescribed as compulsory, but the individual risks must be summarized in a suitable form (e. g. by segments, risk types). The relative significance of the risks (see Section 2.6) should instead be emphasized by developing a ranking of similar risk categories. Some characteristics will be mentioned for methods of **quantifying risks**. These include the recognition and reliability of the methods, the economic justifiability and the quantification of decision-relevant information for the audience of the group management report. According to DRS 20, the risk report primarily extends to quantifying **financial risks** and legal risks (e. g. fines). In contrast to DRS 5, there is an obligation to quantify of risks if these are also reported to management within the framework of **internal risk control**. The individual risks are combined into an overall picture of the risk situation, in such a way that consideration of diversification effects and risk-bearing capacity (see Section 2.6) can also be addressed.

The **forecasting period** (which in the previous explanations in this book corresponds to the liquidation period) is based on a time frame appropriate to the respective risk. The forecasting period for reporting existential risks must amount to at least one year. A description of the **interdependencies** (correlations) between the individual risks is desirable, and required if the risks cannot otherwise be accurately estimated. Risks may **not be balanced** against **opportunities**. Information about **possible opportunities** occur in the forecasting report or can be integrated into the risk report. Further statements should be made regarding the **strategy**, **process** and **organization** of the risk management system. Furthermore, all fundamental essential changes to the risk management system compared to the previous year are to be described and explained.

As a result of the DRS 20, the following points can be stipulated in this book, in comparison with previous statements:

- **Quantification** using the methods suggested in this book, in particular for performance risks, goes far beyond the requirements of the DRS 20.
- Some **definitions** and descriptions in this book strongly coincide with the corresponding descriptions of the DRS 20. This is particularly so for the points about individual risks, about not offsetting risks by opportunities and about no company-or industry-specific definitions of risks, opportunities, risk categories.
- The methods and applications introduced in this book fully cover the requirements formulated in the DRS 20 regarding the measurement of **relevant individual risks** (see Section 2.6).
- The risk management **standards** aspired to by the DRS 20 but not yet made a compulsory requirement are also fully covered by the instruments and methods in this book (e. g. risk reporting in a closed form; see Table 6.3).

For accounting periods from January 1, 2007, the rules of the standard **IFRS 7** apply to all industries. With these regulations, the recipients of annual reports are put in a better position to judge the financial instruments for the company's situation. It is intended to improve representation of the type and extent of risk. To this end, qualitative as well as **quantitative information** about market price risks, credit risks and liquidity risks must be provided. More features and requirements arising from the IFRS 7 are:

- disclosure of risk relevant information which concerns the **balance sheet**, the **income statement** and other information,
- expansion of the risk report, above all for **industrial and trading companies**,

- great challenges relating to **data acquisition** for the quantitative risk report, in particular for industrial and trading companies,
- expansion of the information about **credit risks**,
- implementation of an **internal risk report** which differentiates between financial and non-financial risks,
- showing the **effects** of market price risks on the **equity** and the profit and loss statement.

In the wake of the financial crisis, the **new Standard IFRS 9** was developed for all industries, and the final version was published by the International Accounting Standards Board on April 24, 2014. The Standard IFRS 9 "Financial Instruments" replaced the IAS 39 "Financial Instruments: recognition and measurement" on January 1, 2018, which was also based on the IFRS 7 and expanded it (to content of IFRS 9 see Section 4.4.2.1e)).

With these explanations of the most important aspects of external risk reporting, the remarks on risk controlling are concluded. In the seventh and last chapter, the most important aspects of risk control will be demonstrated yet again using a case study.

6.5 References

For a comprehensive description of the functions and duties of risk controlling, the work of *Bloss/Ernst/Häcker/Sörensen* mentioned in Section 1.4 is recommended. Likewise, the work of

Diederichs, Marc: "Risikomanagement und Risikocontrolling", Vahlen, München, 3. Auflage, 2012.

is suitable for a detailed representation on the topic of risk controlling and in particular on **internal risk reporting**.

The explanations from *Dowd* (see Section 2.7) and *Kremers* (see Section 5.3) are suitable for discussion and partly also for deeper exploration of the keywords **equity**, **risk-bearing capacity** and **risk capital**, as well as

Eisele, Burkhard: "Value-at-Risk-basiertes Risikomanagement in Banken", Deutscher Universitätsverlag, Wiesbaden, 2004,
Saita, Francesco: "Value at Risk and Bank Capital Management : Risk Adjusted Performances, Capital Management and Capital Allocation Decision Making", Academic Press Advanced Finance Series, Amsterdam, 2007.

for banking examples. Especially appropriate for non-banks are

Damodaran, Aswath: "Strategic Risk Taking – A Framework for Risk Management", Pearson Education, New Jersey, 2008,

Hölscher, Reinhold: "Von der Versicherung zur integrativen Risikobewältigung: Die Konzeption eines modernen Risikomanagements", in: Hölscher, Reinhold/Elfgen, Ralph (Hrsg.): "Herausforderung Risikomanagement-Identifikation, Bewertung und Steuerung industrieller Risiken", Gabler, Wiesbaden, S. 3–31, 2002

and

Schierenbeck, Henner/Lister, Michael: "Risikomanagement im Rahmen der wertorientierten Unternehmenssteuerung", in: Hölscher, Reinhold/Elfgen, Ralph (Hrsg.): "Herausforderung Risikomanagement-Identifikation, Bewertung und Steuerung industrieller Risiken", Gabler, Wiesbaden, S. 181–203, 2002.

For the **integration** or aggregation of **interest change risks** and **default risks**, see

Barthel, Hans-Ulrich: "Ansätze zur integrierten Betrachtung von Zins- und Bonitätsänderungsrisiken", in: Eller, Roland u. a. (Hrsg.): "Handbuch Gesamtbanksteuerung Integration von Markt-, Kredit- und operationalen Risiken", Schäffer-Poeschel, Stuttgart, S. 3–24, 2001,

Bellini, Tiziano: "Stress Testing and Risk Integration in Banks: A Statistical Framework and Practical Software Guide (in Matlab and R)", Elsevier, London, p. 235–264, 2016,

Cech, Christian/Fortin, Ines: "Messung der Abhängigkeitsstruktur zwischen Markt- und Kreditrisiko", in: Wirtschaft und Management, S. 65–70, November 2005,

McNeil, Alexander J./Frey, Rüdiger/Embrechts, Paul: "Quantitative Risk Management – Concepts, Techniques and Tools", Princeton University Press, Princeton and Oxford, p. 275–314, 2015,

Spellmann, Frank/Unser, Matthias: "Zinsänderungsrisiko und Bonitätsänderungsrisiko integriert betrachtet – ein Überblick über den Stand der Literatur", in: Oehler, Andreas (Hrsg.): "Credit Risk und Value-at-Risk Alternativen", Schäffer-Poeschel, S. 260–279, 1998.

The works of

Deimel, Klaus/Isemann, Rainer/Müller, Stefan: "Kosten- und Erlösrechnung", Pearson Studium, 2006,

Hoitsch, Hans-Jörg: "Kosten- und Erlösrechnung", Springer, Berlin, Heidelberg, 2004,

Horngren, Charles T./Datar, Srikant M./Rajan, Madhav: "Cost Accounting – A Managerial Emphasis", Global Edition, Pearson Education Limited, 15th ed., 2015

and

Schweitzer, Marcell/Küpper, Hans-Ullrich: "Systeme der Kosten- und Erlösrechnung", Vahlen, München, 10. Auflage, 2011.

can be drawn upon for distribution and aggregation of profit or the cost and revenue accounting system necessary for this.

The version of the **DRS-20** from the *German Accounting Standard Committee* (DRSC) for **external risk reporting** in the **group management report,** as well as further information on risk reporting, can be found at the original Internet source under

www.drsc.de.

The version of **IFRS9** from the *International Accounting Standards Board* (IASB) can be found at the Internet under

www.ifrs.org.

6.6 Technical appendix

For the **variance** of a **portfolio** (s^2_P) with a random number of N risk positions, the **matrix notation** is:

$$s_P^2 = \vec{1}' \cdot \Sigma \cdot \vec{1}$$

In this case, 1 is the (transposed) **unity vector** and Σ is the **variance-covariance matrix** in monetary units (€) of the following form:

$$s_P^2 = (1, 1, \ldots, 1) \cdot \begin{pmatrix} s_1^2 & s_{1,2} & s_{1,3} & \cdots & s_{1,N} \\ \cdot & s_2^2 & & & \cdot \\ \cdot & & \cdot & & \cdot \\ \cdot & & & \cdot & \cdot \\ s_{N,1} & s_{N,2} & s_{N,3} & \cdots & s_N^2 \end{pmatrix} \cdot \begin{pmatrix} 1 \\ \cdot \\ \cdot \\ \cdot \\ 1 \end{pmatrix},$$

which can also be put into the form

$$s_P^2 = \sum_{i=1}^{N} s_i^2 + 2 \cdot \sum_{i=1}^{N}\sum_{j<i}^{N} s_{i,j}.$$

If the co-variances between two risk positions are not available, but only the associated **correlations** ($k_{i,j}$); co-variances ($s_{i,j}$) can be determined according to

$$s_{i,j} = k_{i,j} \cdot s_i \cdot s_j.$$

Finally

$$Va R_P = \alpha \cdot \sqrt{s_P^2}$$

can be used for the portfolio Value at Risk (VaR_P).

The **beta factors** can be calculated in the form of beta vectors (ß) for N risk positions, as follows

$$\vec{\beta} = \begin{pmatrix} \beta_1 \\ \cdot \\ \cdot \\ \cdot \\ \beta_N \end{pmatrix} = \frac{\begin{pmatrix} s_1^2 & s_{1,2} & s_{1,3} & \cdots & s_{1,N} \\ \cdot & s_2^2 & & & \cdot \\ \cdot & & \cdot & & \cdot \\ \cdot & & & \cdot & \cdot \\ s_{N,1} & s_{N,2} & s_{N,3} & \cdots & s_N^2 \end{pmatrix} \begin{pmatrix} 1 \\ \cdot \\ \cdot \\ \cdot \\ 1 \end{pmatrix}}{s_P^2}.$$

If the variances and covariances are available as relative changes (or squared relative changes) rather than as monetary units (€), then the **weightings** (w) must be taken into account, which contains the associated relative i-th portfolio weighting (w_i) for the respective i-th risk position. The beta factors can then be calculated according to

$$\vec{\beta} = \begin{pmatrix} \beta_1 \\ \cdot \\ \cdot \\ \cdot \\ \beta_N \end{pmatrix} = \frac{\begin{pmatrix} w_1 \cdot s_1^2 & w_1 \cdot s_{1,2} & w_1 \cdot s_{1,3} & \cdots & w_1 \cdot s_{1,N} \\ \cdot & w_2 \cdot s_2^2 & & & \cdot \\ \cdot & & \cdot & & \cdot \\ \cdot & & & \cdot & \cdot \\ w_N \cdot s_{N,1} & w_N \cdot s_{N,2} & w_N \cdot s_{N,3} & \cdots & w_N \cdot s_N^2 \end{pmatrix} \begin{pmatrix} w_1 \\ \cdot \\ \cdot \\ \cdot \\ w_N \end{pmatrix}}{s_P^2}.$$

The **Component Value at Risk** of the i-th risk position ($CoVaR_i$) is calculated by multiplying the associated beta factors (β_i) by the portfolio Value at Risk (VaR_P):

$$CoVaR_i = \beta_i \times VaR_P.$$

7 Profit-risk-based company management using a case study

Numerical examples were constructed in the previous chapters in order to demonstrate the various calculations of the value at risk and for the various instruments for risk control. These examples were primarily based on the premise of representing specific facts as clearly and simply as possible. As a result, the example calculations from various chapters are not always compatible with each other or are not always built on each other. In order to better represent the relationships between these various methods and in particular the interactions of the various risk types up to the company-wide profit and risk aggregation, a company case study is described in the following discussion. In contrast to some of the previous examples, this case study is also meant to reflect realistic magnitudes of the asset positions of an industrial company. The close link to the balance sheet and income statement (under HGB) in equally realistic magnitudes represents another aspect of the case study.

7.1 Description of the case study

An example company called **Bsp AG** will be used as the basis for the case study (any similarity with a real, existing company is unintentional and entirely coincidental). Bsp AG is a large German **electrical appliance manufacturer** which aims to get some of its revenues through export of its products to the US dollar zone. Bsp AG shows the following **balance sheet** and **income statement** (using the cost-of-sales method) for the year 01 in € mill.:

Tab. 7.1: Balance sheet and income statement of Bsp AG in € mill. for the year 01

Assets:		Liabilities:	
Land and buildings:	2,000	Stock capital:	3,000
Equipment:	1,000	Reserves:	4,000
Tangible fixed assets:	*3,000*	*Equity:*	*7,000*
Shareholdings:	1,500	Provisions:	200
Bonds:	2,000	Bonds issued:	500
Financial assets:	*3,500*	Liabilities to banks:	200
Non-current assets:	6,500	Trade accounts payable:	100
Inventories:	500	*Borrowed capital:*	*1,000*
Trade accounts receivable:	700		

Tab. 7.1 (continued)

Assets:		Liabilities:	
Foreign currency receivables:	100		
Liquid funds:	200		
Current assets:	1,500		
Balance sheet total:	**8,000**	**Balance sheet total:**	**8,000**

Tab. 7.2: Income statement of Bsp AG in € mill. for the year 01

Sales revenues:	2,000.0
Production costs:	−1,000.0
Gross profit:	*1,000.0*
Selling and administrative costss:	−100.0
Operating result:	*900.0*
Income from shareholdings:	25.0
Income from bonds:	70.0
Other interest and similar income:	52.0
Depreciations of financial assets:	−50.0
Interest expense:	−70.0
Financial result:	*27.0*
Result of ordinary business activity:	*927.0*
Tax:	−185.4
Annual net profit:	**741.6**

The information from the balance sheet and income statement is vastly insufficient for a risk assessment. Much more detailed information will be necessary, which can be gotten from internal accounting or, for external investors, can usually be extracted from the appendix to the annual report. First, the required information is specified for the individual **assets**:

The **tangible fixed assets** (equipment, land and buildings) are reserved exclusively for the company's **own use** and are completely utilized for manufacturing the electrical appliances.

The **financial assets** consist of **shareholdings** and **fixed-interest federal bonds**. The strategic shareholding consists of two **stocks A1** and **A2**, for which the following information exists at the beginning of year 02:

7.1 Description of the case study

	A1:	A2:
Valuation price at the beginning of 02:	€ 25	€ 20
Numbers:	20 mill. pcs.	50 mill. pcs.
Expected dividend per stock for 02:	€ 0.50	€ 0.30
Volatility (for daily changes):	0.40 %	0.15 %

The expected relative stock price returns (μ) for the year 02 amount to 0.00 %. The face value of both stocks amounts to € 1.00 per stock respectively. The correlation between the returns of both stocks amounts to +0.5. The daily relative bid-ask spread for measurement of the liquidity risk amounts to 0.1 % for both stocks. Both stocks or the issuing companies have the best credit rating and therefore have no default risk (i.e. probability of default = 0.00 %).

For the **fixed-interest federal bonds F1 and F2** the following information is available:

	F1:	F2:
Nominal volume:	€ 1 bn.	€ 1 bn.
Coupon interest rate (%):	3 %	4 %
Maturity (years):	3	5

The face value per bond amounts to € 1,000. Both bonds are redeemed at face value on the maturity date and the coupons are paid out once yearly on January 1 retroactively (in arrears) for the previous year. The daily relative bid-ask spread for both bonds amounts to 0.080 %. The expected relative rate change or present value change (μ) for calculating possible gains for the year 02 is 0.00 %.

The following **bond yields** (zero bond rates, discounting rates) are available for calculating both bonds and their associated **volatilities** for the daily bond yield changes for the year 01:

Maturity:	1 Year:	2 Years:	3 Years:	4 Years:	5 Years:
Interest rate:	2.500 %	2.700 %	3.000 %	3.500 %	4.000 %
Volatility:	0.020 %	0.025 %	0.030 %	0.035 %	0.040 %

The term-dependent interest rates all fluctuate independently of one another, i.e. all **correlation coefficients** between the interest rates are null.

The following additional information is available for the individual positions of the **current assets**:

The **inventory** consists primarily of two raw materials which are required for production. These are copper for the wiring and steel for producing the housings of the electrical appliances. More precise details about **procurement risks** are in the income statement information. The inventory level itself (and not the procurement) is subject to the **operating risk** (e. g. theft).

The **deliveries and services receivables** consist of two borrower groups K1 and K2, for which the following data are available (observed for a time period of **one year**):

	K1:	K2:
Credit equivalent (exposure):	€ 200 mill.	€ 500 mill.
Rating classification:	AA	A
Interest income (interest rate % p. a.):	6.00 %	7.00 %
Probability of Default (PD):	0.50 %	1.00 %
Loss Given Default (LGD):	40.00 %	50.00 %
Volatility of LGD:	15.00 %	20.00 %
Operating costs:	€ 200,000	€ 500,000

The correlation coefficient between the default probabilities of K1 and K2 amounts to +0.50. For the assessment or comparison of the risk-adjusted credit rates with the actual received interest rates (of 6 % or 7 %), a profit margin of € 0.00 is assumed as the base. The receivables are not subject to **country risk**. The time period of a possible **delay** in the interest and redemption payments is on average 60 days for group K1 and 120 days for group K2. The probability of a payment delay amounts to 2 % for group K1 and 5 % for group K2.

The **foreign currency receivables** involve a foreign exchange position exclusively in US-$ mill. Observed over a year, the income and expenses in US-$ balance out in such a way that on average a foreign-exchange position of US-$ 125 mill. can be assumed. The rate for the calculation of the foreign-exchange position at the beginning of year 02 amounts to US-$/€ 1.25 (which corresponds to the € 100 mill. in the balance sheet). For the interest rate on the foreign currency receivables in US-$, an interest rate of 3.0 % p. a. is used. The volatility based on the daily changes of the US-$/€ exchange rate is 0.50 %. The daily relative bid-ask spread for the foreign-exchange positions amounts to 0.05 %.

The **liquid funds** (in the form of bank demand deposits) bear a constant interest rate of 1 % p. a. A default risk (e. g. of the bank where the deposits are held) or an interest change risk (with reference to the interest rate of 1 %) does not exist.

The following information is available for the individual **liability positions**:

The **equity** is available without restriction for risk coverage. The risk-bearing capacity can therefore be verified by the entire equity. To this end, the company-wide

VaR is set against the amount of the balance sheet equity. The (risk adjusted) **equity return** claimed by the shareholders comes to 10 % p. a.

The following data can be given for the **borrowed capital**: for the liabilities from issued bonds and with credit institutions, the interest change risks are regarded as negligible because of the long-term fixed interest rate. In the position of liabilities towards credit institutions, the **bank overdrafts** are € 100 mill., which are used entirely as operating loans. The average interest rate on the outside capital amounts to 10 % p. a. The rating classification of "AAa" is required from the external rating agencies in order to obtain borrowed capital or renew it when necessary (**passive liquidity risks**). This classification corresponds to a default probability of 1 %.

For the individual positions of the **income statement**, the following information can be given:

The **revenues** are expected to increase 10 % to € 2,200 mill. from year 01 to year 02. The revenues are distributed half-and-half to both business sectors BS1 and BS2. For both business sectors, the price and amount are respectively independent from each other and normally distributed. The following distribution parameters can be estimated on a **yearly basis** for the business sectors:

	BS1:	BS2:
Expected value price:	€ 100.00	€ 200.00
Volatility price:	€ 4.00	€ 6.00
Expected value quantity:	11 mill. pcs.	5.5 mill. pcs.
Volatility quantity:	500,000 pcs.	300,000 pcs.

Both business sectors are strongly positively correlated with each other in the amount of +0.8.

The **production costs** of € 1 bn. include 300 mill. in write-offs for fixed assets. Along with the write-offs, the production costs are primarily made up of material and manufacturing costs (wages and salaries). An increase of 10 % is also expected for the production costs in year 02. Thus the expected value of the production cost for both business sectors together without write-offs is in the amount of € 770 mill. The volatility of the production costs for the year is € 30 mill.

The **sales and administration cost** for the year 02 is calculated with an expected value of € 110 mill. and an associated volatility of € 5 mill. for both business sectors together.

The claimed overdraft in the amount of € 110 mill. for the year 02 is the basis for determining the **interest rate cost** for the operational activities (or the cash flow). The interest rate for utilization amounts to 10 % p. a. The volatility of the daily changes in the 1-month euro money market rate is 0.09 %.

For the **tax expenses**, a **constant tax rate** of 20 % is assumed for the results of normal business activities.

For the **operating risks**, the following observations can be extracted from the loss database for the last five years (multiple losses in one year are separated by a semicolon):

Year:	Internal operating risks:	External operating risks:
1	€ 1 mill.	€ 2 mill.
2	€ 1 mill.	€ 1 mill.
3	–.–	€ 2 mill.; € 1 mill.
4	€ 2 mill.	–.–
5	€ 2 mill.; € 1 mill.	€ 2 mill.

All operating risks are assigned to the entire **business sector** (= BS1 + BS2).

For company-wide **risk aggregation** of the various risk types, the following (estimated) **correlations** are to be taken into account:

Financial risks:	Interest rate risk:	Foreign exchange risk:	Stock price risk:	Default risk:
Interest rate risk:				
Foreign exchange risk:	–0,8			
Stock price risk:	–0,3	0,7		
Default risk:	0,6	0,2	–0,1	
Liquidity risk:	0,3	–0,4	–0,3	0,8

Cash flow risks:	Sales revenues:	Production costs:	Administrative costs:	Interest expense:
Sales revenues:				
Production costs:	0,8			
Administrative costs:	0,2	0,2		
Interest expense:	–0,2	0,7	0,6	
Tax expenses:	0,3	–0,1	–0,2	–0,2

The different types of **liquidity risk** are **not correlated** with each other.

For the aggregation of all performance risks, a correlation of +0.7 is assumed between the **cash flow** and the **operating risks**.

For determining the company-wide overall risk, a correlation of +0.1 is assumed between **performance** and **financial** risks.

The rate for the **risk-free interest** amounts to 3 % p. a.

A **confidence level** of 99 % should always be applied to the calculation of the VaR. For risk reporting to corporate management, **a year** (250 trading days) should be used as the **planning period** (or as the assigned liquidation period).

With that, all the necessary information is given for a risk identification and risk measurement in the next section.

7.2 Risk identification and risk measurement

Risk identification and risk measurement are carried out as described in the case study, using the balance sheet and income statements of Bsp AG.

Risk identification of the **fixed assets** is primarily based on the features of self-use for the production of electrical appliances. Possible depreciation through damage to the fixed assets is captured by the **operating risks**. The depreciation through wear and tear on equipment is captured by the write-off calculations. Investment risk through the purchase of equipment is mirrored in the future cash flow, which is generated by the investment. This risk is modeled by the **cash flow at risk**.

The **financial asset** positions are subject to market price risks. Risk measurement of the **shareholding**, consisting of stocks A1 and A2, by the VaR is unproblematic from the information given above. For the individual stocks respectively, the VaR is

$VaR(A1)$ = € 500,000,000 (risk position=20,000,000 pcs. x € 25.00) x 2.33 (α-quantile) x 0.40 % (volatility) x $\sqrt{250}$ (=liquidation period) = **€ 73,681,069**,
$VaR(A2)$ = € 1,000,000,000,– € x 2.33 x 0.150 % x $\sqrt{250}$ = **€ 55,260,802**.

For the calculation of the stock portfolio VaR, based on the correlation of the stock prices of +0.5 and the associated portfolio weightings, the portfolio volatility is first calculated as

$$s_P = \sqrt{(1/3)^2 \cdot 0.004^2 + (2/3)^2 \cdot 0.0015^2 + 2 \cdot 1/3 \cdot 2/3 \cdot 0.5 \cdot 0.04 \cdot 0.0015} = \mathbf{0.2028\,\%}.$$

The **VaR** for the total **shareholding** based on the portfolio volatility is

VaR(stock portfolio) = € 1,500,000,000 x 2.33 x 0.2028 % x $\sqrt{250}$ = **€ 112,046,112**.

The Component Value at risk is still necessary for the later risk analysis. Calculating the CoVaR requires determining the beta factors for both stocks (see the corresponding formula in the Technical appendix in Section 6.6), as follows:

$$\beta_{A1} = [(1/3)^2 \times 0.004^2 + (1/3) \times (2/3) \times 0.5 \times 0.004 \times 0.0015] / 0.002028^2 = \mathbf{0.5946},$$
$$\beta_{A2} = [(2/3)^2 \times 0.0015^2 + (1/3) \times (2/3) \times 0.5 \times 0.004 \times 0.0015] / 0.002028^2 = \mathbf{0.4054}.$$

Then the following Component VaR values for both stocks come from the beta factors:

$$CoVaR(A1) = 0.5946 \times € 112,046,112 = \mathbf{€\ 66,622,013},$$
$$CoVaR(A2) = 0.4054 \times € 112,046,112 = \mathbf{€\ 45,424,100}.$$

Finally, the premium L, for measuring the liquidity risk when considering market liquidity with regard to disposal of assets, must still be calculated. The following premiums result:

$$L(A1) = 0.5 \times € 500 \text{ mill.} \times 0.001 \times \sqrt{250} = \mathbf{€\ 3,952,847},$$
$$L(A2) = 0.5 \times € 1,000 \text{ mill.} \times 0.001 \times \sqrt{250} = \mathbf{€\ 7,905,694}.$$

Based on the assumption that the various liquidity risks are uncorrelated with each other, the liquidity premium for the entire shareholding is

$$L(stock\ portfolio) = \sqrt{(€\ 3,952,847)^2 + (€\ 7,905,694)^2} = \mathbf{€\ 8,838,835}.$$

With that, the risk measurement for the shareholding is concluded.

For risk measurement of the **fixed-interest federal bonds**, the valuation, i. e. the calculation of the present value, is necessary. The present value (BW) is determined by discounting the cash flow of the bonds, so

Year:	1.	2.	3.	4.	5.
F1:	+€ 30 mill.	+€ 30 mill.	+€ 1,030 mill.		
F2:	+€ 40 mill.	+€ 40 mill.	+€ 40 mill.	+€ 40 mill.	+€ 1,040 mill.
Total:	+€ 70 mill.	+€ 70 mill.	+€ 1,070 mill.	+€ 40 mill.	+€ 1,040 mill.

with the respective term-dependent bond yields (zero bond rates). The present values amount to

$$PV(F1) = \mathbf{€\ 1,000,307,527},$$
$$PV(F2) = \mathbf{€\ 1,003,216,370},$$
$$PV\ (bond\ portfolio) = \mathbf{€\ 2,003,523,897}.$$

In order to calculate the VaR of the bonds, in the first step the respective VaR of the individual terms is calculated according to the simplified formula (see Section 4.1.1). So, for example, the result for bond F1 for the 1. year is:

VaR(F1, 1. year) = [(number of years x present value) / (1 + interest rate of maturity)]
x volatility x α-quantile x liquidation period
= [1 x (€ 30 mill. / 1.025) / 1.025] x 0.020 % x 2.33 x $\sqrt{250}$ = **€ 210,392**.

Analogously, the individual VaR values in € for the other terms and for bond F2 as well as the bond portfolio are as follows:

Year:	1.	2.	3.	4.	5.
F1:	210,392	510,159	30,342,877		
F2:	280,523	680,212	1,178,364	1,737,050	60,560,468
Total:	490,915	1,190,372	31,521,241	1,737,050	60,560,468

In the second step, the VaR of the individual maturities must be considered taking into account the correlations between the maturities. With an assumed correlation of respectively null between all maturities, the roots of the sums of the squared individual VaR values can be summarized from the first to the fifth years. The results are the following summarized VaR amounts:

$$VaR\ (F1) = \text{€ } \mathbf{30{,}347{,}895},$$
$$VaR\ (F2) = \text{€ } \mathbf{60{,}601{,}300},$$
$$VaR\ (bond\ portfolio) = \text{€ } \mathbf{68{,}306{,}913}.$$

Because of the five terms and the consideration of present values, it is not possible to determine the ß-factors using the previous procedures without further work. For this reason, it will be assumed for the sake of simplicity that the volatility of F1 and F2 is given by dividing the VaR by the alpha-quantile and the liquidation period. The following volatilities then result for F1 and F2 in euros:

$$s_{F1} = \text{€ } \mathbf{823{,}764},$$
$$s_{F2} = \text{€ } \mathbf{1{,}644{,}963}.$$

For calculating the portfolio volatility, a correlation of null is likewise assumed as the basis. The resulting portfolio volatility is then

$$s_P = \sqrt{(\text{€ } 823{,}764)^2 + (\text{€ } 1{,}644{,}963)^2} = \text{€ } \mathbf{1{,}839{,}698}.$$

Because of the null correlation, the calculation of the beta factors then simplifies to

$$\text{ß}_{F1} = 823{,}764^2 / 1{,}839{,}689^2 = \mathbf{0.2005},$$
$$\text{ß}_{F2} = 1{,}644{,}963^2 / 1{,}839{,}689^2 = \mathbf{0.7995}.$$

The component value at risk then amounts to

$$CoVaR(F1) = 0.2005 \times €\ 68{,}306{,}913 = €\ \mathbf{13{,}695{,}469},$$
$$CoVaR(F2) = 0.7995 \times €\ 68{,}306{,}913 = €\ \mathbf{54{,}611{,}443}.$$

Analogously to the calculation for the stock portfolio, the premium for the liquidity risk of the bonds is determined as follows:

$$L(F1) = 0.5 \times €\ 1{,}000{,}307{,}527 \times 0.0008 \times \sqrt{250} = €\ \mathbf{6{,}326{,}500},$$
$$L(F2) = 0.5 \times €\ 1{,}003{,}216{,}370 \times 0.0008 \times \sqrt{250} = €\ \mathbf{6{,}344{,}897},$$
$$L(bond\ portfolio) = \sqrt{(€\ 6{,}326{,}500)^2 + (€\ 6{,}344{,}897)^2} = €\ \mathbf{8{,}960{,}041}.$$

With that, the risk measurement of the bonds and also of the overall **financial assets** is **complete**.

The risk measurement of the **current assets** first captures the inventory position. The same applies to the **inventory** as applies to the fixed asset positions. Damage (e. g. by sinking, theft etc.) to inventories is captured by operating risks, and losses from price changes are mapped by procurement risks in the framework of determining the cash flow at risk.

Trade receivables are subject to default risk. In the first step, the calculation of the expected loss (EL) for both borrower groups K1 and K2 is:

$$EL(K1) = 0.5\% \ (=PD) \times 40\% \ (=LGD) \times €\ 200\ \text{mill.}\ (=Credit\ Equivalent) = €\ \mathbf{400{,}000},$$
$$EL(K2) = 1.0\% \ (=PD) \times 50\% \ (=LGD) \times €\ 500\ \text{mill.}\ (=Credit\ Equivalent) = €\ \mathbf{2{,}500{,}000}.$$

In the second step, the calculation of the credit value at risk is carried out. For this, the volatility of the default probability is first calculated:

$$s_{PD}(K1) = \sqrt{PD_{K1} \cdot (1 - PD_{K1})} \ = \ \sqrt{0.5\% \cdot 99.5\%} = \mathbf{7.0534\%},$$

$$s_{PD}(K2) = \sqrt{PD_{K2} \cdot (1 - PD_{K2})} \ = \ \sqrt{1.0\% \cdot 99.0\%} = \mathbf{9.9500\%}.$$

Using the volatility of the default probability, the Credit Value at Risk can then be calculated as

$$CVaR(K1) \ = \ CE \cdot \sqrt{PD \cdot s_{LGD}^2 + LGD^2 \cdot s_{PD}^2}$$

$$= \ CE \cdot \sqrt{0.5\% \cdot 15\%^2 + 40\%^2 \cdot 7.0534\%^2} \ = \ €\ 200\text{mill.} \cdot \sqrt{0.0009085}$$
$$= €\ \mathbf{6{,}028{,}267},$$

$$CVaR(K2) \ = \ CE \cdot \sqrt{1.0\% \cdot 20\%^2 + 50\%^2 \cdot 9.9500\%^2} \ = \ €\ 500\text{mill.} \cdot \sqrt{0.002875}$$
$$= €\ \mathbf{26{,}809{,}513}.$$

From the addition of the expected loss and the credit value at risk, the total VaR of the default risk can be found, thus

$$VaR(K1) = €\,400{,}000 + €\,6{,}028{,}267 = \mathbf{€\,6{,}428{,}267},$$
$$VaR(K2) = €\,2{,}500{,}000 + €\,26{,}809{,}513 = \mathbf{€\,29{,}309{,}513}.$$

A correction of the liquidation period is not necessary here, since the data for a period of one year was collected. For the calculation of the credit portfolio VaR, a correlation of +0.5 between the default probabilities must be taken into account. The calculation of the VaR for the credit portfolio is

$$VaR\,(credit\,portfolio) = \sqrt{VaR\,(K1)^2 + VaR\,(K2)^2 + 2 \cdot VaR(K1) \cdot VaR(K2) \cdot k_{K1,K2}}$$
$$= \mathbf{€\,32{,}996{,}660}.$$

The calculation of the **component value at risk** for the **default risk** of K1 and K2 will not be done, since the deviation between the sums of the individual VaR (=€ 35,737,780) and the credit portfolio VaR under consideration of the correlation (=€ 32,996,660) is not so meaningful as it is e. g. for the bond portfolio. Furthermore, the calculation of the beta factors is not possible without more work because of the special type of calculation required for the credit value at risk. For the later risk aggregation, therefore, a beta factor of 0.15 for borrower group K1 and 0.85 for borrower group K2 will be assumed. This results in the following Component VaR values for K1 and K2:

$$CoVaR(K1) = 0.15 \times €\,32{,}996{,}660 = \mathbf{€\,4{,}949{,}499},$$
$$CoVaR(K2) = 0.85 \times €\,32{,}996{,}660 = \mathbf{€\,28{,}047{,}161}.$$

Due to this assumption, the diversification effect is relatively evenly distributed between both borrower groups.

Finally, for the default risk, it is still necessary to calculate the premium for the associated liquidity risk. The premiums are

L(K1) = € 200 mill. (=repayment) x 1.06 (=loan interest rate) x (60/360) (=period of delay)
x 3% (=refinancing interest rate) x 2% (=probability of delay)
= **€ 21,200**,

L(K2) = € 500 mill. x 1.07 x (120/360) x 3% x 5% = **€ 267,500**,

L(credit portfolio) = $\sqrt{(€\,21{,}200)^2 + (€\,267{,}500)^2}$ = **€ 268,339**.

The total **risk-adjusted lending rate** for K1 and K2 can finally be calculated using the expected loss and the credit value at risk. A detailed description of this calculation (see Section 4.2.3) will be omitted here, since the total risk-adjusted lending

rate represents only additional information for the risk analysis. For the central risk analysis based on the company-wide risk aggregation, only the VaR (see Section 7.3) is required. Based on the information for
- the risk-free interest rate,
- the operating costs,
- the CVaR and the expected loss,
- the required return on equity and
- the profit margin of € 0.00

the risk-adjusted lending rate amounts to **3.511 %** for K1 and **3.975 %** for K2.

The risk measurement of the **foreign currency receivables** is carried out using the base formula for the VaR and comes to:

$$\text{VaR (currency position)} = \text{€ 100 mill.} (= \text{risk position}) \times 0.5\% (=\text{volatility})$$
$$\times \sqrt{250} (= \text{liquidation period}) \times 2.33 (= \alpha\text{-quantile})$$
$$= \underline{\text{€ 18,420,267}}.$$

The premium for the liquidity risk amounts to:

$$L(\text{currency position}) = 0.5 \times \text{€ 100 mill.} \times 0.0005 \times \sqrt{250} = \underline{\text{€ 395,285}}.$$

There are no risks for the **liquid funds**. With that, all asset risks are identified and measured on the basis of the VaR concept.

There are no risks for the **liabilities** except for the overdraft facilities in the amount of € 100 mill. The interest change risk on the overdraft is accounted for by the interest expense in the framework of the cash flow at risk. The capture of the passive liquidity risks is taken into account by the selected confidence level of 99 %. The confidence level of 99 % corresponds to a default probability of 1 %. The default probability of 1 % is required for a rating class of "AAa" from rating agencies. This requirement would be fulfilled if all company risks were completely covered by the equity based on the confidence level of 99 %. This will be carried out in the framework of the risk analysis (see Section 7.3).

Risk measurement of the **profit and loss account** positions is carried out by using the cash flow risk computation. To this end, the VaR of the individual elements of the cash flow are calculated and then merged into the cash flow at risk using the respective correlations.

For calculating VaR of the **revenue** (=RE), the expected value ($=r_{RE}$) and volatility of the revenues ($=s_{RE}$) are first determined using the parameters for price and quantity. The expected value of the revenues divided according to business sector (=BS) amounts to:

r_{RE} (BS1) = r_M(BS1) × r_P(BS1) = 11 mill. pcs. × € 100 = **€ 1,100 mill.**,
r_{RE} (BS2) = r_M(BS2) × r_P(BS2) = 5.5 mill. pcs. × € 200 = **€ 1,100 mill.**

The volatility of the revenues is

$$s_{RE} = \sqrt{r_P^2 \cdot s_M^2 + r_M^2 \cdot s_P^2 + s_P^2 \cdot s_M^2}$$

and the following volatilities result for the business sectors:

$$s_{RE}(BS1) = \sqrt{100^2 \cdot 500,000^2 + 11,000,000^2 \cdot 4^2 + 4^2 \cdot 500,000^2} = \underline{\textbf{€ 66,633,325}},$$

$$s_{RE}(BS2) = \sqrt{200^2 \cdot 300,000^2 + 5,500,000^2 \cdot 6^2 + 6^2 \cdot 300,000^2} = \underline{\textbf{€ 68,499,927}}.$$

The revenues VaR values for the business sectors can be calculated as follows using the volatility:

VaR (RE, BS1) = € 66,633,325 × 2.33 (= α-quantile) = **€ 155,255,647**,
VaR (RE, BS2) = € 68,499,927 × 2.33 (= α-quantile) = **€ 159,604,830**.

The calculation of the VaR of the total revenues of both business sectors together is:

VaR (revenues) = $\sqrt{155,255,647^2 + 159,604,830^2 + 2 \cdot 155,255,647 \cdot 159,604,830 \cdot 0.8}$
= **€ 298,706,042**.

The associated volatility of the revenues can be determined from the VaR of the total revenues and amounts to:

$$s_{RE} = \text{€ } 298{,}706{,}042 / 2.33 = \underline{\textbf{€ 128,200,018}}.$$

The expected value of the total revenues arises from the addition of the expected values of both business sectors and amounts to:

$$r_{RE} = \text{€ } 1{,}100{,}000{,}000 + \text{€ } 1{,}100{,}000{,}000 = \underline{\textbf{€ 2,200 mill.}}$$

In order to calculate the Component VaR for the individual business sectors, the beta factors must first be calculated again:

$ß_{RE}$(BS1) = (66,633,325² + 0.8 × 66,633,325 × 68,499,927) / 128,200,018² = **0.4923**,
$ß_{RE}$(BS2) = (68,499,927² + 0.8 × 66,633,325 × 68,499,927) / 128,200,018² = **0.5077**.

The Component VaR amount to

$$CoVaR(RE, BS1) = 0.4923 \times €\,298{,}706{,}042 = \mathbf{€\,147{,}060{,}825},$$
$$CoVaR(RE, BS1) = 0.5077 \times €\,298{,}706{,}042 = \mathbf{€\,151{,}645{,}217}.$$

For the **production costs** (=PC), the expected value and volatility come to

$$r_{PC} = \mathbf{€\,770\ mill.},$$
$$s_{PC} = \mathbf{€\,30\ mill.}$$

The VaR for the production costs amounts to both business sectors together:

$$VaR(PC) = €\,30\ mill. \times 2.33 = \mathbf{€\,69.9\ mill.}$$

For the **sales and administration costs** (=SAC), the expected value according to the description of the case study is

$$r_{SAC} = \mathbf{€\,110\ mill.}\ \text{and the volatility is}$$
$$s_{SAC} = \mathbf{€\,5\ mill.}$$

This gives the VaR for the sales and administration costs as:

$$VaR(SAC) = €\,5\ mill. \times 2.33 = \mathbf{€\,11.65\ mill.}$$

The expected value of the **interest expense** (=IE) is made up of the constant (claimed) credit sum in the amount of € 110 mill. and an interest rate of 10 % p. a. together.

$$r_{IE} = €\,110\ mill. \times 10\% = \mathbf{€\,11\ mill.}$$

The associated standard deviation of the interest expense projected onto a year amounts to

$$s_{IE} = €\,110\ mill. \times 0.09\% \times \sqrt{250} = \mathbf{€\,1{,}565{,}327}.$$

The associated VaR of the interest expense is:

$$VaR(IE) = €\,1{,}565{,}327 \times 2.33 = \mathbf{€\,3{,}647{,}213}.$$

The basis for calculating the **tax expenses** (=TE) is the **result of normal business activities** (=RB). First, therefore, the expected value and the volatility of the results of business activities must be determined. The expected value comes from adding or subtracting the expected value of the individual components of the results and amounts to:

$$r_{RB} = r_{RE} - r_{PC} - r_{SAC} - r_{IE} = €2{,}200 \text{ mill.} - €770 \text{ mill.} - €110 \text{ mill.} - €11 \text{ mill.} = \underline{\underline{€1{,}309 \text{ mill.}}}$$

Calculating the volatility of the results of normal business activities is carried out by multiplying the variance-covariance matrix with the unity vector (see Section 6.6). The variance-covariance matrix consists of the variances of the individual components of the results and the covariances that are calculated from the given correlations between the components. A detailed representation of the matrix calculation will be omitted for the sake of clarity. The volatility of the normal business activities amounts to

$$s_{RB} = \underline{\underline{€\,105{,}679{,}230}}.$$

The expected value of the tax expenses is

$$r_{TE} = 20\,\% \times €\,1{,}309 \text{ mill.} = \underline{\underline{€\,261.8 \text{ mill.}}}$$

The volatility for the tax expenses is calculated as follows, using the algorithm for random variables (see Section 5.4):

$$s_{TE} = \sqrt{20\,\%^2 \cdot €\,155{,}398{,}332^2} = \underline{\underline{€\,21{,}135{,}846}}.$$

The VaR of the tax expenses thus amounts to:

$$\mathrm{VaR}(TE) = €\,21{,}135{,}846 \times 2.33 = \underline{\underline{€\,49{,}246{,}521}}.$$

With the expected values and the volatilities of the individual components, the **Cash Flow at Risk** can finally be calculated. The calculation is carried out analogously to the procedure for determining the results of the daily business activities. The expected value of the **cash flow** (=CF) amounts to:

$$\begin{aligned} r_{CF} &= r_{RE} - r_{PC} - r_{SAC} - r_{IE} - r_{TE} \\ &= €\,2{,}200 \text{ mill.} - €\,770 \text{ mill.} - €\,110 \text{ mill.} - €\,11 \text{ mill.} - €\,261.8 \text{ mill.} = \underline{\underline{€\,1{,}047.2 \text{ mill.}}} \end{aligned}$$

The cash flow volatility and the associated beta factors of the cash flow components are again calculated by multiplying the variance-covariance matrix by the unity vector (see also the cash flow calculation in Section 5.2.3 and 6.3). For the volatility, the matrix calculation gives the value

$$s_{CF} = \underline{\underline{€\,99{,}028{,}953}}.$$

That gives a Cash Flow at Risk of

$$CFaR = €\ 166{,}653{,}331 \times 2.33 = \mathbf{€\ 230{,}737{,}461}.$$

The matrix calculation (see Section 6.6) delivers the following beta factors and the resulting Component Value at Risk:

$ß_{RE}$	=	1.2703,	CoVaR(RE) =	1.2703 × € 230,737,461	=	**€ 293,105,814**,
$ß_{PC}$	=	−0.2220,	CoVaR(PC) =	−0.2220 × € 230,737,461	=	**−€ 51,229,392**,
$ß_{SAC}$	=	−0.0091,	CoVaR(SAC) =	−0.0091 × € 230,737,461	=	**−€ 2,109,089**,
$ß_{IE}$	=	0.0075,	CoVaR(IE) =	0.0075 × € 230,737,461	=	**€ 1,730,195**,
$ß_{TE}$	=	−0.0466,	CoVaR(TE) =	−0.0466 × € 230,737,461	=	**−€ 10,760,066**.

The sum of the individual component values at risk again gives the cash flow at risk in the amount of € 230,737,461.

The last risk category is represented by the **operational risks**. The distribution of the **loss numbers** is determined by observing the loss database. This is divided up by internal and external risks and aggregated for both risk types.

Loss numbers:	Internal:	External:	Aggregated:
0:	20 %	20 %	0 %
1.	60 %	60 %	20 %
2:	20 %	20 %	60 %
3:	0 %	0 %	20 %
Expected value:	1,0	1,0	2,0

The **loss amount distribution** is constructed similarly.

Loss amount:	Internal:	External:	Aggregated:
€ 1 mill.:	60 %	40 %	50 %
€ 2 mill.:	40 %	60 %	50 %
Expected value:	−€ 1.4 mill.	−€ 1.6 mill.	−€ 1.5 mill.

By combining all possibilities of loss frequency and loss amount and determining the associated probabilities, the **distribution** of the **overall loss** and the associated cumulative probabilities can be calculated.

7.2 Risk identification and risk measurement

Total loss:	Internal:		External:		Aggregated:	
	Distribution:	Cumulative probability:	Distribution:	Cumulative probability:	Distribution:	Cumulative probability:
€ 0:	20.00 %	20.00 %	20.00 %	20.00 %	0.00 %	0.00 %
€ 1 mill.:	36.00 %	56.00 %	24.00 %	44.00 %	10.00 %	10.00 %
€ 2 mill.:	31.20 %	87.20 %	39.20 %	83.20 %	25.00 %	35.00 %
€ 3 mill.:	9.60 %	96.80 %	9.60 %	92.80 %	32.50 %	67.50 %
€ 4 mill.:	3.20 %	100.00 %	7.20 %	100.00 %	22.50 %	90.00 %
€ 5 mill.:	0.00 %	100.00 %	0.00 %	100.00 %	7.50 %	97.50 %
€ 6 mill.:	0.00 %	100.00 %	0.00 %	100.00 %	2.50 %	100.00 %
Expected value:	−€ 1.4 mill.		−€ 1.6 mill.		−€ 2 mill.	

The expected values of the total loss are obtained by multiplying the respective expected values of the loss frequency by the expected value of the loss amount. Through linear interpolation, for a confidence level of 99 %, the VaR values of the internal operating risks (=O-Int), the external operating risks (=O-Ext) and the total operating risks (=O-Tot) are as follows:

$$VaR\ (O\text{-}Int) = €\ 3{,}687{,}500.00,$$
$$VaR\ (O\text{-}Ext) = €\ 3{,}861{,}111.11,$$
$$VaR\ (O\text{-}Tot) = €\ 5{,}600{,}000.00.$$

The associated **operational VaR** values are calculated by subtracting the respective expected values from the VaR. The operational VaR values are not included, however, because they are not explicitly required for the risk analysis. Much more important for the risk analysis are the Component VaR for the operational risk. The calculation of the associated beta factors is not possible on the basis of the full enumeration implemented above without further work. The diversification effect, which results from the summation of the individual risks minus the VaR for the total operational risk, is nonetheless considerable. For this reason, it will be assumed for the sake of simplicity that the beta factors for the internal and external operating risks respectively amount to 0.5. Then the Component VaR values result as follows:

$$CoVaR(O\text{-}Int) = €\ 2{,}800{,}000,$$
$$CoVaR(O\text{-}Ext) = €\ 2{,}800{,}000.$$

With that, all risks are identified and measured. An **overview** of the **results** is shown in Table 7.3. The VaR values are listed in the "individual VaR" column, without consideration of the diversification effects. The summarization (for the stock or bond portfolio) is carried out through simple addition, i. e. based on a correlation of +1. The diversification effects are considered in the "Component VaR" column, according to the above calculation of the respective beta factors.

For the **aggregation** of the different **liquidity types** based on the **component value at risk**, the beta factors were calculated for the given correlation of null. The sum of the different liquidity risks in the amount of € 12,595,062, taking into account the diversification effect, for a correlation of null, results from the root of the sum of the squared individual VaR. The beta factors then result from the ratios of the squared individual VaR and the squared total Component VaR. The Component VaR for the liquidity risk of e. g. stocks is calculated as follows:

$$\beta_{Lstocks} = (€\ 8{,}838{,}835)^2 / (€\ 12{,}595{,}062)^2 = \mathbf{0.49248093}$$
$$Component\ VaR_{Lstocks} = 0.49248093 \times €\ 12{,}595{,}062 = \mathbf{€\ 6{,}202{,}828}.$$

The revenues for the individual business sectors BS1 and BS2 are not listed in the table for the sake of clarity.

Tab. 7.3: Results of the risk measurement for Bsp AG in €

	Business sector (BS1 + BS2):		Financial management:	
	Individual VaR:	Component VaR:	Individual VaR:	Component VaR:
Stock price risk:				
Stock portfolio:			128,941,871	112,046,112
A1:			73,681,069	66,622,013
A2:			55,260,802	45,424,099
Interest rate risk:				
Bond portfolio:			90,949,195	68,306,913
F1:			30,347,895	13,695,469
F2:			60,601,300	54,611,443
Default risk:				
Credit portfolio:			35,737,780	32,996,660
K1:			6,428,267	4,949,499
K2:			29,309,513	28,047,161
Foreign exchange risk:				
US-$-€-position:			18,420,267	18,420,267

Tab. 7.3 (continued)

	Business sector (BS1 + BS2):		Financial management:	
	Individual VaR:	Component VaR:	Individual VaR:	Component VaR:
Liquidity risk:				
Stocks:			8,838,835	6,202,828
Bonds:			8,960,041	6,374,112
Receivables:			268,339	5,717
Currency positions:			395,285	12,406
Liquidity overall:			18,462,499	12,595,062
Cash flow risk:				
Sales revenues:	298,706,042	293,105,814		
Production costs:	69,900,000	−51,229,392		
Administrative costs:	11,650,000	−2,109,089		
Interest expense:	3,647,213	1,730,195		
Tax expenses:	49,246,521	−10,760,066		
Cash Flow at Risk:	433,149,776	230,737,461		
Operational risks:				
Internal:	3,687,500	2,800,000		
External:	3,861,111	2,800,000		
Operational risk total:	7,548,611	5,600,000		

These results of the risk measurement form the basis for the risk analysis in the last section.

7.3 Risk analysis

For the risk analysis, in the first step the various risks of the **associated profits** must be provided. For this, the various risk types for the **financial risks** are based on the expected profits.

For the **shareholdings**, the expected profits consist in the expected dividends of € 0.50 per stock from A1 (or € 0.30 per stock from A2). From that, a profit of € 10 mill. results for stock A1 and for A2 in the amount of € 15 mill. Profits from price increases (such as for bonds and foreign-exchange positions) are not expected.

Expected profits for the **bonds** come from the coupons. The interest payments on bond F1 are targeted in the amount of € 30 mill. and for F2 in the amount of € 40 mill.

For the **trade receivables**, the contractually agreed loan interest represents the expected profits in the amount of € 12 mill. for K1 and € 35 mill. for K2.

The profit from the **foreign-exchange position** comes from investment at the interest rate of 3 % in US-$, so € 3 mill. (or US-$ 3.75 mill.).

Further consideration must be given for the risk category of **liquidity risks**. The liquidity risks cannot be directly assigned to any profit. However, the market liquidity (see Section 4.2.3) is tightly bound with the respective asset positions and in the case of a divestment would itself be central. For this reason, the measurement of the liquidity risk is carried out in the form of a premium on the VaR. It is therefore plausible to divide the **profits** from the asset position **proportionally** between the Component VaR of the asset position and the Component VaR of the associated liquidity risk. If the CoVaR of the asset position amounts to e. g. € 90,000 and the CoVaR for the market liquidity risk amounts to € 10,000, then an expected profit of € 10,000 is proportionally divided. So a profit of € 9,000 would be apportioned to the market risk of the asset position and a profit of € 1,000 would be apportioned to the liquidity risk of this position.

In Table 7.4, a profit of € 25,000,000 is shown for the stock portfolio overall, which comes from the dividend payments on stocks A1 and A2. Based on the Component VaR, the stock price risk amounts to (=stock price risk + liquidity risk of stocks) € 112,046,112 / (€ 112,046,112 + € 6,202,828) = 94.7544 % percent of the overall risk. As a result, the proportional profit for the stock portfolio announced to € 23,688,608 (94.7544 % of € 25,000,000) and for the **liquidity risk of the stocks** it amounts to € 1,311,392 (€ 25,000,000 − € 23,688,608).

The profit allocation for the **performance risks** is carried out for the cash flow using the expected value of the individual components.

For the **revenues**, based on an expected sales increase of 10 %, there is an expected value of € 2,200 mill.

The **production costs** have an expected value of −€ 770 mill. As is clear from the negative sign, what is involved here is not a profit but rather costs or expenses.

The expected **sales and administration cost** amounts to −€ 110 mill. and the expected value of the **interest expense** amounts to −€ 11 mill. Finally, a **tax expenses** of −€ 261.8 mill. is expected.

Adding the expected values of the individual components, gives an **expected cash flow** in the amount of **+€ 1,047.2 mill.**

The **operating risks** are not assigned to any profit. Possible costs for management of operating risks (personnel costs) are contained in the business sector administration cost.

The CoVaR for the overall financial risks and the performance risks must be calculated in order to determine the RoRaC values. Calculating the total financial risk is carried out analogously to the liquidity risk aggregation based on the Component

VaR, as described above. However, in contrast to the liquidity risks (which assumed a respective correlation of null), the given correlations between the different financial risks (interest rate risk, liquidity risk and so on) described in the case study must be taken into account. This is carried out through the **variance-covariance matrix**. On the diagonal of the variance-covariance matrix, instead of the squared volatilities, are the squared Component VaR (e. g. for the interest rate risk € 68,306,913²). Above and below the diagonals are the covariances converted from the given correlations based on the CoVaR, for example, for the interest change risk and the exchange rate risk: −0.8 x € 68,306,913 x € 18,420,267. By multiplying the transposed unity vector with the variance-covariance matrix and then multiplying the result again by the unity vector, one gets the squared total Component VaR (see Section 6.6). The root of this result then delivers the **Component VaR** of the total **financial risk** in the amount of **€ 132,091,908**. The grand total of the individual financial Component VaR amounts to € 231,769,952. The diversification effect between the individual financial risk types is considerable at around € 100 mill.

The total **performance risk** can be determined to be

$CoVaR\ (performance\ risks) =$
$\sqrt{€\ 230{,}737{,}461\ 2 + €\ 5{,}600{,}000\ 2 + 2 \cdot €\ 230{,}737{,}461 \cdot €\ 5{,}600{,}000 \cdot 0.7}$
$= €\ 234{,}691{,}538$

using the correlation of +0.7 between the cash flow risk and the operating risks.

Finally, analogously to the Component VaR, the **overall business risk** is calculated as follows for a correlation of +0.1 between financial and performance risks:

$CoVaR\ (overall\ business\ risk) =$

$$\sqrt{€\ 234{,}691{,}538^2 + €\ 132{,}091{,}908^2 + 2 \cdot €\ 234{,}691{,}538 \cdot €\ 132{,}091{,}908 \cdot 0.1}$$
$$= €\ 280{,}586{,}102.$$

Using these summarized risks and the associated profits, the RoRaC results can now be specified on all aggregation levels through simple division of the profits by the associated CoVaR values.

Finally, for the **assessment** of the **risk bearing capacity**, the Component VaR values are divided by the total equity in the amount of € 7,000 mill.

Overall results of the above calculations in the framework of the risk analysis are summarized in Table 7.4, which forms the basis for a comprehensive risk analysis.

In the first step, the extent of the respective **diversification effects** can be assessed using the comparison of the individual VaR, and possible **limitations** based on the VaR can be established.

With the **financial risks**, because of the positive correlation the diversification effect is smaller for the stocks and the default risk than it is for the bond portfolio and the liquidity risks (for which a correlation of null was assumed). As a possible example for the limitation of, for example, interest change risk, a limitation of € 30 mill. for F1 and € 60 mill. for F2 can be established from the individual bond portfolio VaR. A limitation based on the Component VaR would be carried out for the total bond portfolio and, for example, amount to only € 70 mill. (instead of € 90 mill.). For the overall financial risk overall, there is a large diversification effect which rests on the accumulation of various correlations. On the one hand, diversification effects arise on the portfolio level within the individual risk types (stocks, bonds, loans); on the other hand, the correlations between the various risk types are considered during the aggregation into overall financial risk. In particular, the diversification effects have a considerable impact on the aggregation into overall risk due to the partially negative correlations.

Tab. 7.4: Individual VaR, Component VaR, profits in €, RoRaC and equity utilization of Bsp AG

Risk type:	Individual VaR:	Component VaR:	Profits:	RoRaC:	Equity utilization:
Stock price risk:			25,000,000		
Stock portfolio:	128,941,871	112,046,112	23,688,608	0.2114	1.60 %
A1:	73,681,069	66,622,013	9,220,254	0.1384	0.95 %
A2:	55,260,802	45,424,099	14,468,355	0.3185	0.65 %
Interest rate risk:			70,000,000		
Bond portfolio:	90,949,195	68,306,913	64,025,419	0.9373	0.98 %
F1:	30,347,895	13,695,469	28,802,102	2.1030	0.20 %
F2:	60,601,300	54,611,443	35,223,317	0.6450	0.78 %
Default risk:			47,000,000		
Credit portfolio:	35,737,780	32,996,660	46,991,858	1.4241	0.47 %
K1:	6,428,267	4,949,499	11,998,779	2.4242	0.07 %
K2:	29,309,513	28,047,161	34,993,079	1.2477	0.40 %
Foreign exchange risk:			3,000,000		
US-$-€-position:	18,420,267	18,420,267	2,997,981	0.1628	0.26 %
Liquidity risk:					
Stocks:	8,838,835	6,202,828	1,311,392	0.2114	0.09 %
Bonds:	8,960,041	6,374,112	5,974,581	0.9373	0.09 %
Receivables:	268,339	5,717	8,142	1.4241	0.00 %

Tab. 7.4 (continued)

Risk type:	Individual VaR:	Component VaR:	Profits:	RoRaC:	Equity utilization:
Currency positions:	395,285	12,406	2,019	0.1628	0.00 %
Liquidity overall:	18,462,499	12,595,062	7,296,133	0.5793	0.18 %
Cash flow risk:					
Sales revenues:	298,706,042	293,105,814	2,200,000,000	7.5088	4.19 %
Production costs:	69,900,000	−51,229,392	−770,000,000	15.0304	−0.73 %
Administrative costs:	11,650,000	−2,109,089	−110,000,000	52.1552	−0.03 %
Interest expense:	3,647,213	1,730,195	−11,000,000	−6.3577	0.02 %
Tax expenses:	49,246,521	−10,760,066	−261,800,000	24.3307	−0.15 %
Cash Flow at Risk:	433,149,776	230,737,461	1,047,200,000	4.5385	3.30 %
Operational risks:					
Internal:	3,687,500	2,800,000	0	0.0000	0.04 %
External:	3,861,111	2,800,000	0	0.0000	0.04 %
Aggregated:	7,548,611	5,600,000	0	0.0000	0.08 %
Financial risks total:	292,511,612	132,091,908	145,000,000	1.0977	1.89 %
Performance risks total:	440,698,387	234,691,538	1,047,200,000	4.4620	3.35 %
Business risks total:	733,210,000	280,586,102	1,192,200,000	4.2490	4.01 %

The diversification effects for the **performance risks** (47 % = [€ 440,698,387 − € 234,691,538] / € 440,698,387) are somewhat smaller than for the financial risks (55 %). Within the cash flow risk, the diversification effect is small due to the high beta factor of 1.2703 for the revenues. This is overcompensated in the cost components, which is expressed in negative beta factors and negative Component VaR values for production costs, administration cost and tax expenses (see the explanations to Cash Flow at Risk in Section 5.2.3 and 6.3). The diversification effects are therefore correspondingly high for these cost components. With the operating risks, there is a clear diversification effect. Due to the observed absolute damage amounts of the operating risk, this effect is nonetheless not especially weighted for performance risks overall.

The aggregation of financial and performance risks into the overall **business risk** shows a strong effect of the correlations in the end. So, the sum of the individual VaR values adds up to € 733 mill., while by contrast the company-wide Component VaR only amounts to € 281 mill. The diversification effects thus operate on a considerable scale, which must be taken into account in every case.

In the second step, the **RoRaC** values are analyzed based on the allocated profits.

The **stock portfolio** clearly shows a smaller RoRaC value than the **bond portfolio**. This is based on the smaller dividend return compared to the coupon yield on the bonds in proportion to the respective Component VaR. This would shift in favor of the stock portfolios if a possible price gain were considered for the stocks. An average rate of return of 0 % was assumed. The high RoRaC value of bond F1 is based on two effects. For one thing, the shorter maturity has a risk mitigating effect. For another thing, the largest part of the diversification effect on the bond portfolio is on bond F1. However, in comparison to that, F1 has only a slightly lower coupon yield.

The high RoRaC values for the **default risk** are especially noticeable. These are based on the lending rates obtained, which clearly lie above the respective risk-adjusted lending rates and thus realize a high profit margin. The risk-adjusted lending rate amounts to 3.511 % (3.9753 %) for borrower K1 (K2), compared to a realized lending rate for K1 (K2) of 6 % (7 %).

The **foreign currency position** shows a smaller RoRaC value. The foreign-currency position, however, in contrast to the stock and bond risk, is not targeted and deliberately constructed, but rather results from the export activities of Bsp AG. Against this background, the low RoRaC value has a smaller significance than the RoRaC values of the stocks and bonds.

The various types of **liquidity risk** have the same RoRaC values as the portfolios of the respective asset positions (stocks, bonds, loans). This rests on the distribution of the profits proportionally to the Component VaR. Only the RoRaC value of the overall liquidity risk has relevance to the risk analysis, due to the lack of correlation between the individual types of liquidity risk. Nonetheless, only limited action recommendations can be derived from this, since the liquidity risk is tightly bound with the respective asset position. The liquidity risk (of market liquidity) can thus only be managed through the asset position.

From the aggregation of the individual financial risk types comes a RoRaC value of 1.0977 for the overall **financial risk**. This value must next be compared to the RoRaC value of the **performance risks**.

For the analysis of the RoRaC values of the **cash flow risk**, the special features of the cash flow calculation and its individual components as well as the respective profit allocation must be taken into account.

The RoRaC of 7.5088 for the revenues, which at first glance is very high, arises in the form of the expected revenues through the profit allocation, without considering the costs or expenses. This will be taken into account by the RoRaC calculation of the production cost, the administration costs, the interest expense and the tax expenses. The Component Value at Risk values of the individual **cost and expense components** are negative apart from the interest expense, which results in positive RoRaC values. The RoRaC values of the cash flow, therefore, cannot be meaningfully compared with each other and with the RoRaC values of the asset positions. For a cost-risk analysis, the individual VaR without proportional diversification effects can be used as a replacement. The ratio of individual VaR to cost or expense amounts is most unfavorable for interest expense and tax expenses. Here, measures could be applied using suitable control instruments.

From the RoRaC of the cost components and the RoRaC of the revenues comes a cash flow RoRaC in the amount of 4.5385. This value must still be supplemented by the RoRaC of the **operating risks**. The operating risks are not set against any profits and costs. Thus the RoRaC values are null. By aggregating the operating risks with the cash flow risks, the RoRaC of the overall performance risks is slightly lowered to 4.4620. With that, it is possible to compare the **performance** area with the **financial activities** of Bsp AG. The RoRaC of the performance area amounts to approximately 4.4 times the RoRaC values of the financial risks. A possible measure which can be derived from this result would be the improvement of financial activities through risk mitigation, for example, by deploying derivatives. Another possibility would be to reduce the financial activities or the asset positions in order to invest these funds in the performance sector.

Finally, on the highest aggregation level, the financial and performance risks and profits are tied to the overall **company risk** or company profit. Although the RoRaC of the financial activities is clearly smaller than that of the performance activities, the RoRaC is slightly reduced by the company-wide aggregation to 4.2490. The diversification effect through the company-wide risk aggregation does not compensate for the impact of the smaller RoRaC values of the financial risk.

In analyzing the company-wide RoRaC values it appears that the **company profit** for the year 02 is significantly higher than the profit according to the income statement for the year 01. The difference (between € 741.6 mill. for year 01 and € 1,192.2 mill. for year 02) arises through the following factors:

- **Depreciation** of financial assets (€ 50 mill.) and fixed assets (€ 300 mill.) are not taken into account in the profit planning for the year 02, since the depreciation to the fixed assets was covered under the risk aspects of the cash flow at risk, and the depreciation to financial assets was taken into account by the corresponding VaR of the asset positions.
- In the profit planning for year 02, only the interest expense in the amount of € 11 mill. (instead of € 70 mill. for year 01) from the overdraft facilities for the operating business is considered. For the interest expense of the remaining positions, from long-term liabilities towards credit institutions and from bond issues, no interest change risk is applied due to the long-term fixed interest period.
- For the **cash flow** of year 02, an increase of 10 % is assumed. From that comes a profit increase of € 109.2 mill. compared to year 01 (10 % of € 742 mill. + € 300 mill. depreciation of fixed assets + € 50 mill. depreciation of financial assets)
- The effects of the higher profits due to the three above-mentioned factors are at the same time compensated by the increased **tax expenses** (from € 185.4 mill. to € 261.8 mill.)

For an **assessment** of the **overall company**, the **realized return on equity** is customarily compared to the **return on equity required** on the financial markets. For the year 01, the return on equity targeted by Bsp AG amounts to 10.59 % (€ 741.6 mill. / € 7,000 mill.). With that, the required return on equity of 10 % is reached or even slightly exceeded. The return on equity planned for the year 02 cannot be meaningfully compared with the required return on equity or the return on equity realized in year 01 because of the profit of € 192.2 mill. determined above. The planned profit for the year 02 is calculated with the objective of determining the most consistent and plausible RoRaC value. For the year 02 profit, therefore, only the profits or costs which can also be matched to a corresponding risk are taken into account. However, parts of this profit determination deviate considerably from the profit calculation on the income statement (or according to HGB).

Thus only the RoRaC is appropriate for a conclusive company assessment under consideration of the business risks. For a comparison with other companies, the average RoRaC values of the industry (electrical appliance manufacturer) must be consulted. The **RoRaC** value is considerably more **relevant** for this than the return on equity. So the Bsp AG can get a better financial classification with a realized return on equity of 10.59 % and a RoRaC of 4.2490 than a comparable company with a return on equity of likewise 10.59 % and a RoRaC value of, for example, only 2.12. In this case, the same return on equity is realized under acceptance of a significantly higher risk, which is more economically unfavorable.

In conclusion, the **risk bearing capacity** of Bsp AG will be judged by comparing the Component VaR with the equity (= **equity utilization**). The equity cost also helps to evaluate the coverage of the passive **liquidity risks** (for the borrowing). The business risks only burden the Bsp AG equity by total of 4.01 %. The passive liquidity risks are thus fully covered by the available equity. Due to the low equity utilization, only the coverage of the risk types with the largest equity utilization is still of interest in the framework of the risk analysis. The claim by the cash flow at risk in the amount of 3.30 % represents by far the highest equity cost for Bsp AG. The remaining equity utilization is primarily caused by the stock and bond portfolio (1.6 % or 0.98 %).

With the assessment of the risk-bearing capacity, the **risk analysis** for Bsp AG is **concluded** as far as possible with the information given above for Bsp AG (see Section 7.1) and the methods given in this book.

In the framework of a **perspective** and **possibilities for improvement**, the following problem areas can be mentioned:
- The **VaR calculation** of complex asset positions such as e. g. **derivatives,** for which evaluation models with several different risk factors are applied.
- The statistically more precise consideration of **special distributions** for specific risk types (e. g. the statistically exact consideration of the left skew for operational and credit risks).

- The fundamental treatment of deviations from the theoretical standard normal distribution compared to the empirical distributions in the form of, for example, **asymmetry** and/or **kurtosis** in the framework of the VaR calculation.
- The **risk aggregation** was based on strongly **simplified assumptions** that, for example, the aggregated distribution is always normally distributed. This requires likewise even more precise statistical scrutiny, in particular with reference to the folding (merging) of different distribution types.

List of References

Alexander, Carol: "Market Risk Analysis: Volume I: Quantitative Methods in Finance", Wiley, 2008, (2.7, 4.5).

Alexander, Carol: "Market Risk Analysis: Volume IV: Value-at-Risk Models", Wiley Finance Series, 2008, (2.7).

Allen, Steven: "Financial Risk Management: A Practitioner's Guide to Managing Market and Credit Risk", Wiley Finance, 2nd edition, 2012, (1.4).

Angermüller, Niels O./Eichhorn, Michael/Ramke, Thomas: "Lower Partial Moments: Alternative oder Ergänzung zum Value at Risk?", in: Finanz Betrieb, Heft 3, S. 149–153, 2006, (2.7).

Arnell, Nigel: "A Short Guide to Climate Change Risk", Routledge, New York, 2016, (5.3).

Baesch, Anja: "Analytische Berechnung des OpVaR", in: Zeitschrift für das gesamte Kreditwesen, S. 1284–1286, 2004, (5.3).

Balz, Enno.: "Finanzmarktregulierung nach der Finanzmarktkrise – Vorschläge für eine Neuordnung der internationalen Finanzarchitektur", Hans Böckler Stiftung, Düsseldorf, 2011, (4.5).

Bangia, Anil/Diebold, Frank/Schuermann, Til: "Liquidity on the Outside", in: Risk, Heft 12, S. 68–73, 1999, (4.5).

Bank for International Settlements: "Basel III Leverage Ratio Framework and Disclosure Requirements", January 2014, (4.5).

Bank for International Settlements: "Operational Risk – Supervisory Guidelines for the advanced Measurement Approaches", June 2011, (5.3).

Barfield, Richard: "Practitioner's Guide to Basel III and beyond", London Sweet & Maxwell, 2011, (4.5).

Barthel, Hans-Ulrich: "Ansätze zur integrierten Betrachtung von Zins- und Bonitätsänderungsrisiken", in: Eller, Roland u. a. (Hrsg.): "Handbuch Gesamtbanksteuerung Integration von Markt-, Kredit- und operationalen Risiken", Schäffer-Poeschel, Stuttgart, S. 3–24, 2001, (6.5).

Bartram, Söhnke M.: "Verfahren zur Schätzung finanzwirtschaftlicher Exposures von Nichtbanken", in: Johanning, Lutz/Rudolph, Bernd: "Handbuch Risikomanagement", Band II, Uhlenbruch, S. 1267–1294, 2000, (5.3).

Basel Committee on Banking Supervision: "An Explanatory Note on the Basel II IRB Risk Weight Functions", Bank for International Settlements, Basel, 2005, (4.5).

Beeck, Helmut/Kaiser, Thomas: "Quantifizierung von Operational Risk mit Value– at–Risk", in: Johanning, Lutz/Rudolph, Bernd: "Handbuch Risikomanagement", Band I, Uhlenbruch, S. 633–653, 2000, (5.3).

Beike, Rolf/Schlütz, Johannes: "Finanznachrichten lesen – verstehen – nutzen: Ein Wegweiser durch Kursnotierungen und Marktberichte", Schäffer Poeschel, 5. Auflage, 2010, (4.5).

Bellini, Tiziano: "Stress Testing and Risk Integration in Banks: A Statistical Framework and Practical Software Guide (in Matlab and R)", Elsevier, London, 2016, (6.5).

Bernhardt, Thomas/Erlinger, Daniel/Unterrainer, Lukas: IFRS9: The New Rules for Hedge Accounting from the Risk Management's Perspective", Oxford Journal of Finance and Risk Perspectives, no. 53, p. 1–14, 2016, (4.5).

Blattner, Peter: "Internationale Finanzierung: Internationale Finanzmärkte und Unternehmensfinanzierung", Oldenbourg Wissenschaftsverlag, München, 1997, (4.5).

Bloss, Michael/Ernst, Dietmar/Häcker, Joachim/Sörensen, Daniel: "Financial Engineering", Oldenbourg Verlag, München, p. 501–506, 2012, (1.4)

Bookstaber, Richard: "Global Risk Management: Are We Missing the Point?" in: Journal of Portfolio Management 23 (Spring), S. 102–107, 1997, (2.7).

Brandimarte, Paolo: "Handbook in Monte Carlo Simulation: Applications in Financial Engineering, Risk Management, and Economics". Wiley, 2014, (5.3).
Brealey, Richard A./Myers Stewart C./Allen, Franklin: "Principles of corporate finance", McGraw Hill Education, 12th ed., 2016, (4.5).
Brett, Michael: "How to Read the Financial Pages", Random House Business Books, 5th ed., 2003, (4.5).
Brunel, Vivien: "Operational Risk Modelled Analytically", Risk 27, no. 7 (July 2014), p. 55–59, 2014, (5.3).
Brunetti, Aymo.: "Wirtschaftskrise ohne Ende – US-Immobilienkrise Globale Finanzkrise Europäische Schuldenkrise", hep, Bern, 3. Auflage, 2012, (4.5).
Brunnermeier, Markus K.: "Deciphering the Liquidity and Credit Crunch 2007–2008", Journal of Economic Perspectives, no. 23, p. 77–100, 2009, (4.5).
Bühler, Wolfgang: "Risikocontrolling in Industrieunternehmen", in: Börsig, Clemens./Coenenberg, Adolf G. (Hrsg.): "Controlling und Rechnungswesen im internationalen Wettbewerb", Stuttgart, S. 205–233, 1998, (5.3).
Burger, Anton/Buchhart, Anton: " Risiko-Controlling", Oldenbourg Verlag, 2002, (1.4).
Burghof, Hans-Peter/Henke, Sabine/Rudolph, Bernd u. A. (Hrsg.): "Kreditderivate. Handbuch für die Bank- und Anlagepraxis", Schäffer Poeschel, 2. Auflage, 2005, (4.5).
Burkholder, Nicholas C.: "Outsourcing: The Definitive View, Applications and Implications", Wiley, Hoboken, New Jersey, 2006, (3.5).
Butler, Kirt C.: "Multinational Finance – Evaluating the Opportunities, Costs, and Risks of Multinational Operations, Wiley Finance, 6th ed., 2016, (4.5).
Capinski, Marek/Zastawniak, Tomasz: "Mathematics for Finance: An Introduction to Financial Engineering", Springer, London, 2nd edition, 2011, (2.7).
Carbon Trust: "Brand value at risk from climate change", London, 2005, (5.3).
Cech, Christian/Fortin, Ines: "Messung der Abhängigkeitsstruktur zwischen Markt- und Kreditrisiko", in: Wirtschaft und Management, S. 65–70, November 2005, (6.5).
Cottin, Claudia/Döhler, Sebastian: "Risikoanalyse – Modellierung, Beurteilung und Management von Risiken mit Praxisbeispielen, Springer Spektrum, Wiesbaden, 2. Auflage, 2013, (2.7).
Crouhy, Michel/Galai, Dan/Mark, Robert: "The Essentials of Risk Management", McGraw Hill Education, New York, 2nd edition, 2014, (1.4).
Crouhy, Michel/Galai, Dan/Mark, Robert: "A comparative analysis of current credit risk models", in: Journal of Banking & Finance, Heft 24, S. 59–117, 2000, (4.5).
Damodaran, Aswath: "Strategic Risk Taking – A Framework for Risk Management", Pearson Education, New Jersey, 2008 (5.3, 6.5).
De Grauwe, Paul/Ji, Yuemei: "Self-Fulfilling Crises in the Eurozone: An Empirical Test", CEPS Working Document no. 366, June 2012, (4.5).
Deimel, Klaus/Isemann, Rainer/Müller, Stefan: "Kosten- und Erlösrechnung", Pearson Studium, 2006, (6.5).
Dent, Kieran/Westwood, Ben: "Stress Testing of Banks: An Introduction", Bank of England Quarterly Bulletin, 3rd Quarter, Vol. 56, Issue 3, p. 130–143, 2016, (4.5).
Deutsch, Hans-Peter: "Monte-Carlo-Simulation in der Finanzwelt", in: Johanning, Lutz/Rudolph, Bernd: "Handbuch Risikomanagement", Band II, Uhlenbruch, S. 1267–1294, 2000, (5.3).
Diederichs, Marc: "Risikomanagement und Risikocontrolling", Vahlen, München, 3. Auflage, 2012, (6.5).
Diggelmann, Patrick: "Value at Risk. Kritische Betrachtung des Konzepts, Möglichkeiten der Übertragung auf den Nichtfinanzbereich", Versus Verlag, 1999, (2.7).
Doff, Rene: "Risk Management for Insurers", Risk Books, London, 3rd ed., 2015, (3.5).
Dowd, Kevin: "Beyond Value at Risk", John Wiley and Sons, 1999, (2.7).

Dresel, Tanja: "Die Quantifizierung von Länderrisiken mit Hilfe von Kapitalmarktspreads", in: Johanning, Lutz/Rudolph, Bernd: "Handbuch Risikomanagement", Band I, Uhlenbruch, S. 579–606, 2000, (4.5).

Du, Wenxin/Schreger, Jesse: "Local Currency Sovereign Risk", in: Journal of Finance 71, no. 3 (June 2016), p. 1027–1070, 2016, (4.5).

Dullien, Sebastian/Schwarzer, Daniela: "Umgang mit Staatsbankrotten in der Eurozone", SWP-Studie, Berlin. Juli 2010, (4.5).

Ebert, Christof: "Outsourcing kompakt – Entscheidungskriterien und Praxistipps für Outsourcing und Offshoring von Softwareentwicklung", Spektrum Akademischer Verlag, 3. korrigierter Nachdruck, 2011, (3.5).

Ebke, Werner. F./ Seagon, Christoper/Blatz, Michael (Hrsg.): "Internationale Finanzkrise – Erfahrungen, Lehren, Handlungsbedarf", Nomos, Baden Baden, 2012, (4.5).

Ehrmann, Harald: "Risikomanagement in Unternehmen – Mit Basel III, S. 233 ff., Kiehl, Herne, 2. Auflage, 2012, (4.5).

Eisele, Burkhard: "Value-at-Risk-basiertes Risikomanagement in Banken", Deutscher Universitätsverlag, Wiesbaden 2004, (6.5).

Eitemann, David K./Stonehill, Arthur I./Moffett Michael H.: "Multinational Business Finance", Pearson, 14th ed., 2016, (4.5).

Eller, Roland/Heinrich, Markus u. a.(Hrsg.): "Handbuch Derivativer Instrumente: Produkte, Strategien, Risikomanagement", Schäffer Poeschel, Stuttgart, 3. Auflage, 2005, (3.5).

Elliott, Douglas J./Litan, Robert E.: "Identifying and Regulating Systemically Important Financial Institutions: The Risks of Under and Over Identification and Regulation", Brookings Working Paper, January 2011, (4.5).

Elschen, Rainer/Lieven, Theo (Hrsg.): "Der Werdegang der Krise – Von der Subprime- zur Systemkrise", Gabler, Wiesbaden, 2009, (4.5).

Elton, Edwin J./Gruber, Martin J./Brown, Stephen J./Goetzmann, William N.: "Modern Portfolio Theory and Investment Analysis", Wiley, 2002, (4.5).

Farny, Dieter: "Versicherungsbetriebslehre", Verlag Versicherungswirtschaft, 5. Auflage, 2011, (3.5).

Ferretti, Paola: "New Perspectives on the Bank-Firm Relationship : lending, management and the impact of Basel III", Cham Palgrave Macmillan, 2016, (4.5).

Financial Crisis Inquiry Commission: "The Financial Crisis Inquiry Report", Official Government Edition, 2011, (4.5).

Fink, Dietmar/Köhler, Thomas/Scholtissek, Stephan: "Die dritte Revolution der Wertschöpfung", Econ, 2004, (3.5).

Franke, Günter: "Gefahren kurzsichtigen Risikomanagements durch Value-at-Risk", in: Johanning, Lutz/Rudolph, Bernd (Hrsg.): "Handbuch des Risikomanagements", Band 1, S. 53–85, Uhlenbruch Verlag, 2000, (2.7).

Gorard, Stephen: "Revisiting a 90-year-old debate: the advantages of the mean deviation", in: http://www.leeds.ac.uk/educol/documents/00003759.htm, (2.7).

Gordy, Michael B.: "A comparative anatomy of credit risk models", in: Journal of Banking & Finance, Heft 24, S. 119–149, 2000, (4.5).

Gundlach, Matthias/Lehrbass, Frank: "CreditRisk+ in the Banking Industry", Springer Finance, 2004, (4.5).

Gup, Benton E.: "The financial and Economic Crisis: An International Perspective", Edward Elgar Publishing, 2010 (4.5).

Hager, Peter: "Corporate Risk Management – Cash Flow at Risk und Value at Risk", Band 3, Bankakademie Verlag, 2004, (5.3).

Hakenes, Hendrik/Wilkens, Sascha: "Der Value-at-Risk auf Basis der Extremwerttheorie", in: Finanz Betrieb, Heft 12, S. 821–829, 2003, (2.7).

Haney, Mark H.: "Teaching the concept of Investment Risk through Spreadsheet Monte Carlo Simulations", in: Journal of the Academy of Business Education, Winter 2016, Vol. 17, p. 236–256, 2016, (5.3).
Hansjürgens, Bernd/Antes, Ralf (Editors): "Economics and Management of Climate Change – Risks, Mitigation and Adaptation", Springer, New York, 2008, (5.3).
Hartmann-Wendels, Thomas/Pfingsten, Andreas/Weber, Martin: "Bankbetriebslehre", Springer Gabler, Berlin Heidelberg, 6. Auflage, 2015, (4.5).
Hasenmüller, Philipp: "Unternehmensrisiko Klimawandel – Risiken managen und Chancen strategisch nutzen", Gabler, Wiesbaden, 2009, (5.3).
Hauser, Stefan: "Management von Portfolios festverzinslicher Wertpapiere", Fritz Knapp Verlag, 1992, (4.5).
Heidorn, Thomas: "Finanzmathematik in der Bankpraxis – Vom Zins zur Option", Gabler, Wiesbaden, 5. Auflage, 2006, (4.5).
Hennersdorf, Angela/Fehr, Mark: "Die zehn wichtigsten Fragen zum Stresstest", in: Die Wirtschaftswoche, Heft 43, S. 64–66, 20. 10. 2014, (4.5).
Hermes, Heinz-Josef/Schwarz, Gerd: "Outsourcing-Chancen und Risiken, Erfolgsfaktoren, rechtssichere Umsetzung", Haufe Verlag, 2005, (3.5).
Hoitsch, Hans-Jörg: "Kosten- und Erlösrechnung", Springer, Berlin, Heidelberg, 2004, (6.5).
Hölscher, Reinhold/Kalhöfer, Christian/Bonn, Rainer: "Die Bewertung operationeller Risiken in Kreditinstituten", in: Finanz-Betrieb, Heft 7–8, S. 490–504, 2005, (5.3).
Hölscher, Reinhold: "Von der Versicherung zur integrativen Risikobewältigung: Die Konzeption eines modernen Risikomanagements", in: Hölscher, Reinhold/Elfgen, Ralph (Hrsg.): "Herausforderung Risikomanagement-Identifikation, Bewertung und Steuerung industrieller Risiken", Gabler, Wiesbaden, S. 3–31, 2002, (6.5).
Holton, Glyn A.: "Value-at-Risk. Theory and Practice", Academic Press, 2nd ed., 2009, (2.7).
Horngren, Charles T./Datar, Srikant M./Rajan, Madhav: "Cost Accounting – A Managerial Emphasis", Global Edition, Pearson Education Limited, 15th ed., 2015, (6.5).
Hull, John C.: "Risk Management and Financial Institutions", Wiley, Hoboken, New Jersey, 4th ed., 2015, (2.7, 3.5, 4.5, 5.3).
Hull, John C.: "Optionen, Futures und andere Derivate", Pearson Studium, 8. Auflage, 2012, (3.5, 4.5).
Hull, John C.: "Options, Futures, and Other Derivatives", Prentice Hall, 8th Edition, 2011, (3.5, 4.5).
Hull, John, C.: "Risikomanagement – Banken, Versicherungen und andere Finanzinstitutionen", Pearson Studium, München, 2014, (2.7).
Jorion, Philippe: "Financial Risk Manager Handbook", Wiley, Hoboken, New Jersey, 6th edition, 2011 (1.4, 2.7, 4.5, 5.3).
Jorion, Philippe: "Value at Risk: The New Benchmark for Managing Financial Risk", McGraw-Hill, 3. Auflage, 2006, (1.4, 2.7).
Kadelbach, Stefan.: "Nach der Finanzkrise – Rechtliche Rahmenbedingungen einer neuen Ordnung", Nomos, Baden Baden, 2012, (4.5).
Keitsch, Detlef: "Risikomanagement", Schaeffer-Poeschel, Stuttgart, 2004, (5.3).
Klauck, Kai-Oliver/Stegmann Claus: "Basel III – Vom regulatorischen Rahmen zu einer risikoadäquaten Gesamtbanksteuerung", Schäffer-Poeschel, Stuttgart, 2012, (4.5).
Kremers, Markus: "Risikoübernahme in Industrieunternehmen – Der Value-at Risk als Steuerungsgröße für das industrielle Risikomanagement, dargestellt am Beispiel des Investitionsrisikos", in: Hölscher, Reinhold (Hrsg.): Schriftenreihe Finanzmanagement, Bd. 7, Sternenfels, Berlin, 2002, (5.3).
Kromphardt, Jürgen (Hrsg.): "Die aktuelle Finanz- und Wirtschaftskrise und ihre Überwindung", Metropolis, Marburg, 2013, (4.5).

Kruschwitz, Lutz/Wolke, Thomas: "Duration und Convexity", in WiSt Heft 8, S. 382–387, August 1994, (4.5).

Kruschwitz, Lutz: "Finanzierung und Investition", Oldenbourg Wissenschaftsverlag, München, 6. Auflage, 2010 (4.5).

Kruschwitz, Lutz: "Finanzmathematik – Lehrbuch der Zins-, Renten-, Tilgungs-, Kurs- und Renditerechnung", Oldenbourg, München, 5. Auflage, 2010, (4.5).

Kühlmann, Torsten M./Haas, Hans-Dieter (Hrsg.): "Internationales Risikomanagement – Auslandserfolg durch grenzüberschreitende Netzwerke", Oldenbourg Verlag, München, 2009, (4.5).

Kumarasiri, Jayanthi/Gunasekarage, Abeyratna: "Risk Regulation, Community Pressure and the Use of Management Accounting in Managing Climate Change Risk: Australian Evidence", in: Accounting and Risk, The British Accounting Review, January 2017, 49 (1), p. 25–38, 2017, (5.3).

Löffler, Andreas/Wolke, Thomas: "Variance Minimizing Strategy and Duration", Arbeitspapier HU Berlin, 1996, (4.5).

Longin, Francois M.: "Extreme Events in Finance: A Handbook of extreme value theory and its Applications", Wiley, Hoboken, New Jersey, 2017, (2.7).

Mahammadzadeh, Mahammad: "Risikomanagement: Bewältigung von Klimarisiken in Unternehmen – Bedeutung und Möglichkeiten", in: uwf 19, S. 101–108, 2011, (5.3).

Malz, M. Allan: "Financial Risk Management: Models, History and Institutions", Wiley Finance, 2011, (1.4)

Markowitz, Harry M.: "Portfolio Selection", Journal of Finance 7, no. 1 (March 1952), p. 77–91, 1952, (4.5).

McNeil, Alexander J./Frey, Rüdiger/Embrechts, Paul: "Quantitative Risk Management – Concepts, Techniques and Tools", Princeton University Press, Princeton and Oxford, 2015, (2.7, 4.5, 6.5).

Menk, Michael T./Warkentin, Sergej.: "IFRS 9 im Spannungsfeld von Risikomanagement und Aufsicht, in: Die Bank, Heft 9/14, S. 14–19, 2014, (4.5).

Mennell, Stephen: "What Economists forgot (and what Wall Street and the City never learned): A Sociological Perspective on the Crisis in Economics", in: History of the Human Sciences, Vol. 27(3), p. 20–37, 2014 (4.5).

Miller, Michael B.: "Mathematics and Statistics for Financial Risk Management", Wiley Finance, 2nd ed., 2014, (2.7).

Müller, Stefan/Brackschulze, Kai/Mayer-Friedrich, Matija D.: "Finanzierung mittelständischer Unternehmen nach Basel III – Selbstrating, Risikocontrolling und Finanzierungsalternativen", S. 24 ff., C. H. Beck, Franz Vahlen, München, 2. Auflage, 2011, (4.5).

Neckel, Sighard: "Der Gefühlskapitalismus der Banken: Vom Ende der Gier als ‚ruhiger Leidenschaft'", in: Leviathan, Heft 1 März 2011, S. 39–53, 2011, (4.5).

Nguyen, Tristan/Romeike, Frank: "Versicherungswirtschaftslehre", Springer Gabler, Wiesbaden, 2012, (3.5).

Oehler, Andreas/Unser, Matthias: "Finanzwirtschaftliches Risikomanagement", Springer, Berlin, 2. Auflage, 2013, (4.5).

Onischka, Mathias: "Definition von Klimarisiken und Systematisierung in Risikokaskaden", Diskussionspaper des Projektes Mainstreaming von Klimarisiken und -chancen im Finanzsektor, Wuppertal Institut für Klima, Energie, Umwelt, 2009, (5.3).

Peccia, Tony: "Designing an operational framework from a bottom-up perspective", in: Alexander, Carol: "Mastering Risk Volume 2", Pearson, 2001, (5.3).

Penza, Pietro/Bansal, Vipul K.: "Measuring Market Risk with Value at Risk", Wiley, New York, 2000, (2.7).

Perridon, Louis/Steiner, Manfred/Rathgeber, Andreas W.: "Finanzwirtschaft der Unternehmung", Vahlen, München, 16. Auflage, 2012, (4.5).

Pfingsten, Andreas u. a.: "Armutsmaße als Downside-Risikomaße: Ein Weg zu Risikomaßen, die dem Value-at-Risk überlegen sind", in: Johanning, Lutz/Rudolph, Bernd (Hrsg.): "Handbuch des Risikomanagements", Band 1, S. 85–107, Uhlenbruch Verlag, 2000, (2.7).

Poddig, Thorsten/Dichtl, Hubert/Petersmeier, Kerstin: "Statistik, Ökonometrie, Optimierung", Uhlenbruch Verlag, 2. Auflage, 2001, (2.7).

Poitras, Geoffrey: "Commodity Risk Management", Routledge, New York, 2013, (5.3).

Pojasek, Robert B.: "Organizational Risk Management and Sustainability: A Practical Step-by-Step Guide", Taylor&Francis Inc., 2017, (1.4).

Richardson, Clarence H./Miller, Isaiah Leslie: "Financial Mathematics", Ulan Press, 2012, (4.5).

Rogler, Silvia: "Risikomanagement im Industriebetrieb", DVU, 2002, (5.3).

Rudolph, Bernd: "Lehren aus den Ursachen und dem Verlauf der internationalen Finanzkrise", in: zfbf 60, S. 713–741, November 2008, (4.5).

Saita, Francesco: "Value at Risk and Bank Capital Management : Risk Adjusted Performances, Capital Management and Capital Allocation Decision Making", Academic Press Advanced Finance Series, Amsterdam, 2007, (6.5).

Sartor, Franz J./Bourauel, Corinna: "Risikomanagement kompakt – In 7 Schritten zum aggregierten Nettorisiko des Unternehmens, Oldenbourg Wissenschaftsverlag, München 2013 (1.4).

Saunders, Anthony/Allen, Linda: "Credit Risk Management In and Out of the Financial Crisis: New Approaches to Value at Risk and Other Paradigms", Wiley Finance, 3rd ed., 2010, (4.5).

Saunders, Anthony/Cornett, Marcia Millon: "Financial Markets and Institutions", McGraw Hill Education, 6th edition, 2015, (3.5).

Schäfer, Dorothea: "Banken: Leverage Ratio ist das bessere Risikomaß", in: DIW Wochenbericht, S. 11–17, Heft Nr. 46, 2011, (4.5).

Schierenbeck, Henner/Lister, Michael: "Risikomanagement im Rahmen der wertorientierten Unternehmenssteuerung", in: Hölscher, Reinhold/Elfgen, Ralph (Hrsg.): "Herausforderung Risikomanagement – Identifikation, Bewertung und Steuerung industrieller Risiken", Gabler, Wiesbaden, S. 181–203, 2002, (6.5).

Schierenbeck, Henner: "Ertragsorientiertes Bankmanagement", Band I, 8. Auflage 2003, (4.5).

Schmeisser, Wilhelm/Mauksch, Carola: "Kalkulation des Risikos im Kreditzins nach Basel II", in: Finanz Betrieb, Heft 5, S. 296–310, 2005, (4.5).

Scholtissek, Stephan: "New Outsourcing – Die dritte Revolution der Wertschöpfung in der Praxis", Econ, 2004, (3.5).

Schulte, Michael/Horsch, Andreas: "Wertorientierte Banksteuerung II: Risikomanagement", Frankfurt School Verlag, 4. Auflage, 2010, (4.5).

Schweitzer, Marcell/Küpper, Hans-Ullrich: "Systeme der Kosten- und Erlösrechnung", Vahlen, München, 10. Auflage, 2011, (6.5).

Servigny, Arnaud de/Renault, Olivier: "Measuring and Managing Credit Risk", McGraw-Hill, 2004, (4.5).

Shapiro, Alan: "Multinational Financial Management", Wiley, 10th ed., 2013, (4.5).

Sharpe, William F.: "Capital Asset prices: A Theory of Market Equilibrium under Conditions of Risk", Journal of Finance 19, no. 2 (September 1964), p. 425–442, 1964, (4.5).

Smith, Greg: "Why I Left Goldman Sachs: A Wall Street Story", Grand Central Publishing, New York, Boston, 2012 (4.5).

Spellmann, Frank/Unser, Matthias: "Zinsänderungsrisiko und Bonitätsänderungsrisiko integriert betrachtet – ein Überblick über den Stand der Literatur", in: Oehler, Andreas (Hrsg.): "Credit Risk und Value-at-Risk Alternativen", Schäffer-Poeschel, S. 260–279, 1998, (6.5).

Sperber, Herbert/Sprink, Joachim: "Internationale Wirtschaft und Finanzen", Oldenbourg, München, 2. Auflage, 2012, (4.5).

Stern, Nicholas: "The Economics of Climate Change – The Stern Review", Cambridge University Press, 2007, (5.3).

Stulz, Rene M.: "Risk Management & Derivatives", South-Western, 2002, (3.5).

Toksöz, Mina: "Guide to Country Risk: How to identify, manage and mitigate the risks of doing business across borders", The Economist, 2014 (4.5).

Uhlir, Helmut/Steiner, Peter: "Wertpapieranalyse", Physica-Verlag, Heidelberg, 4. Auflage, 2001, (2.7, 4.5).

Vanini, Ute: "Risikomanagement – Grundlagen, Instrumente, Unternehmenspraxis", Schäffer-Poeschel Verlag, Stuttgart, 2012, (1.4).

Weistroffer, Christian: "Systemisch relevante Finanzinstitute", in: Deutsche Bank Research, 3. 11. 2011, (4.5).

Wolf/Runzheimer: "Risikomanagement und KonTraG. Konzeption und Implementierung", Gabler Verlag, Wiesbaden, 5. Auflage, 2009, (5.3).

Wolke, Thomas: "Finanz- und Investitionsmanagement im Krankenhaus", MWV, Berlin, 2010, (4.5).

Wolke, Thomas: "Bewertung von Staatsanleihen", in: WISU, Heft 5/12, S. 671–674, 2012, (4.5).

Wolke, Thomas: "Die Fallstudie – Risikoanalyse eines Aktienportfolios anhand von Portfoliotheorie, Beta-Faktor, Value at Risk und Return on Risk adjusted Capital", in: WISU, Heft 7/14, S. 886–889, 2014, (2.7).

Wolke, Thomas: "Duration&Convexity", Dissertation, FU Berlin, 1996, (4.5).

Wolke, Thomas: "The Functioning of Government Bonds – The Example of Greece and Vietnam", in Economic Development Review, January 2011, S. 31–36, 2011, (4.5).

Wondrak, Bernhard: "Management von Zinsänderungschancen und –risiken", Physica-Verlag, 1986, (4.5).

Wüst, Kirsten: "Risikomanagement – Eine Einführung mit Anwendungen in Excel", UVK Lucius Verlagsgesellschaft, Konstanz, 2014, (2.7).

Zeranski, Stefan: "Liquidity at Risk zur Steuerung des liquiditätsmäßig-finanziellen Bereichs von Kreditinstituten", Verlag der Gesellschaft für Unternehmensrechnung und Controlling m. b. H., 2005, (4.5).

Zündel, Caroline: "Yield curve shifts and the selection of immunization strategies: Importance of Duration and Convexity in the selection process Portfolio immunization against interest rate risks", Akademikerverlag, 2016, (4.5).

Glossary

Backtesting: testing the statistical precision of the VaR using historical data
Bund-Future: exchange-traded forward transaction with German government bonds as the basis instrument
CAPM: expected return on a stock in relation to the risk-free investment return and a risk premium for the systematic risk
Cash flow at Risk: value at risk of the cash flow
Cash flow: cash-relevant indicator for assessing the solvency of business
Commodities price risk: negative deviation from a planned target amount due to uncertain future developments in the procurement price
Component Value at Risk: value at risk of an individual position, reduced by the proportionate diversification effect
Convexity: an indicator for the curvature of the present value function
Correlation coefficient: a normalized statistical measure between +1 and −1 for considering the relationships between two figures
Country risk: lack of readiness by a foreign state to make currency available for redemption and interest payments
Covariance: statistical measure for considering the relationships between two figures
Credit derivative: transfer of credit risk to a guarantor against payment of premium
Credit Value at Risk: VaR for the default risk
Currency options: the right to buy or sell currency positions at a particular time point in the future
Default risk: default on interest and redemption payments in the credit business
Diversification effect: risk mitigation from combining of specific asset positions
Exchange rate risk: negative deviation from a planned target due to uncertain future developments on the exchange rates
Expected change in assets: sum of the possible changes in assets multiplied by their respective likelihoods of occurrence
Expected loss: sum of the possible losses multiplied by their respective likelihoods of occurrence
Forward exchange transaction: the commitment to buy or sell currency positions at a particular time point in the future
Future: commitment to buy or sell a specified number of financial securities on a particular date in the future
Incremental value at risk: increase of the value at risk through absorption of an additional risk position
Insurance: contractual agreements between insurance beneficiary and an insurance company against payment of an insurance premium to provide an agreed insurance benefit if an insured event occurs
Interest change risk: market rate-related asset risks in the form of interest surplus risks and/or present value risks
Liquidity at risk: VaR for the amount of the disbursement surplus of banks
Liquidity risk: possible losses that arise from a company not meeting its financial obligations
Lower Partial Moments: analysis instrument for the properties of the distribution function under the loss limit
Macaulay duration: average capital commitment of an interest rate position
Marginal VaR: a factor for a possible increase in portfolio risk
Maximal loss: the largest possible damage or loss of an asset position
Modified duration: Measured value for the amount of the interest change risk of interest rate positions

Money market: the market on which banks (interbank market) mutually make short-term loans to each other
Mortgage loan: loans that are secured by property as collateral
Operational risks: the danger of losses through internal or external events
Option: the right to buy or sell a specific basis title in the future
Portfolio return: sum of the weighted returns of all individual portfolio positions
Portfolio: mixture of several asset positions
Present value: sum of the future cash flows that have been discounted to today's date
Real estate price risk: negative deviation from a planned target amount due to uncertain future developments in real estate prices for real estate investment
Risk management: measurement and control of all business risks company-wide with consideration of possible synergies
RoRaC: relationship of profit to component value at risk (Return on Risk adjusted Capital)
Sensitivity: measure for the sensitivity of asset positions to changes in one or more influencing factors
Sharpe Ratio: relationship of stock prices minus the risk-free interest rate to volatility
Stock price risk: negative deviation from a planned target amount based on uncertain future developments in stock prices
Stress tests: procedures for identifying and managing situations which could cause extraordinary losses
Swaps: exchange transactions in the future for exploiting comparative advantages on financial or commodities markets
Value at risk: maximum asset loss for a specific confidence level and a specific liquidation period
Volatility: statistical measure for the average deviation around the mean

Index

A

Accessoriness 183
Adverse selection effect 175
Aggregation level 300
Asset backed securities 204
Asset quality review 207

B

Backtesting 56
– definition 56
– disadvantages 58
– example 57
Bad banks 209
Balance sheet analysis 171
Bank insolvency 208
Bank resolution mechanism 208
Bank stress test
– basic scenario 208
– deficiencies 232
– stress scenario 208
Bank stress tests 207
Basel I 225
Basel II 225
– approaches for risk differentiation 225
– standard approach 226
Basel III 2, 225, 226
– CRD IV, CRR 227
– deficiencies 233
Basket credit default swap 186
Behavioral economics 215
Beta factor
– calculation 47
Bond portfolio 129
– example calculation 133
– features 132
Bonus payments 212
Bootstrap method 138
Bottom-up approach 250
Bund-Future 144
– characteristics 145
– definition 144
– example 144
– features 144
Business ethics 215
Business psychology 215

C

Capital Asset Pricing Model 162
– beta factor 162
– definition 163
– example calculation 163
– premises 165
– risk control 165
– RoRaC 165
Capital buffer
– anti-cyclial 227
– conservation 227
Capital market union 217, 232
Carbon Trust 263
Case study 317
– description 317
– risk analysis
  – individual results 337
  – overall results 342
– risk identification, risk measurement 323
Cash flow 278
– calculation 279
– components 279
– definition 278
Cash flow at risk 278
– calculation
  – properties 285
– calculation methods 280
– control 286
– definition 280
– example calculation 280
Cash flow mapping 129
– example 130
Cash flow risks 114
Causation principle 7, 294
Climate change risks 261
– challenges 261
– measurement 263
– risk compensation 264
– risk control 264
– risk limitation 264
– risk premium 263
– risk provision 264
– risk shifting 264
– risk transfer 264
– risk types 261
Cluster 28
Collateral 180
Commercial code 2
Commercial credits 168

Commodity futures 270
Commodity price risk 268
– definition 268
– properties 268
Company liquidity 195
Component Value at Risk 49
– calculation 49
– definition 49
– negative values 305
– properties 50
Comprehensive assessment 207
Confidence level 31
Control principle 7, 295
Convexity 124
– definition 124
– estimation of present value change 126
– features 127
Core capital 227
Corporate bonds 117
Corporate governance code 2
Corporate management 88
Correlation coefficient 38
– calculation 38
– definition 38
– examples 39
– properties 39
Counterparty risk 229
Country risk 190
– analysis 190
– control 193
– example 191
– interaction country default and borrower default
  – example calculation 192
– interaction country risk and borrower 192
– measurements methods 190
– properties 190
Coupon effect 118
Covariance 37
– definition 37
– interpretation 38
Cover capital 73
Credit default option 134
Credit default swap 185
Credit derivatives
– cluster risks 186
– compensation 184
– credit event 184
– definition 182

– delineation market price risks 183
– maturity 184
– nominal volume 184
– premium 184
– principles 183
– reference instrument 184
Credit equivalent 170
Credit exposure 170
Credit insurance 182
CreditMetrics 187
Credit options 184
Credit portfolio models 187
Credit report 171
CreditRisk+ 187
Credit spread 174
Credit spread option 184
Credit swaps 184
Credit value adjustment 229
Credit value at risk 176
– calculation 177
– distribution
  – left skewed 177
– example calculation 177
– liquidity-adjusted 199
– RoRaC 179
Currency forward transaction 150
– control possibilities 153
– definition 150
– example 151
– features 150
– financial hedge 151
– forward rate 152
– implicit forward exchange rate 151
– swap rate risk 153
Currency option
– definition 154
– example 154
– features 155
– profit and loss profile 154
Currency swap 149
– disadvantages 150
– functioning 149
Customer contract 278

D
Deadline risk 195
Default risk
– aggregate transaction 187
  – analysis 188

– calculation of credit portfolio 187
– example calculation 189
– RoRaC 189
– concept 168
– definition 168
– general measurement 169
– individual transaction 169
  – analysis 171
  – control 180
  – control instruments 180
  – instruments 171
  – limit systems 181
  – risk compensation 182
  – risk transfer 182
Delivery risk 266
Demand risk 266
Density function
– empirical 27
– theoretical 27
Deposit guarantee directive, european 209
Derivatives 96
Differences
– average 15
Diversification effect 45
– application areas 93
– consideration 1
– definition 44
– difficulties 94
– exploitation 93
– properties 45
– proportional 50
Dodd-Frank act 2
DRS 20 311
Duration 122
– derivation 122
– Macaulay
  – definition 136
  – example calculation 136
– modified
  – definition 122
  – example calculation 122
  – features 123
  – present value change 123

E
Economic sociology 215
Elasticity 24
Equity capital 73
– increase 89

Equity costs 226
Equity coverage 226
Equity ratio 227
EURIBOR 118
European banking supervision 208
European bank union 208
Exchange rate insurance 148
Exchange rate risk 145
– currency position 146
– definition 145
– features 146
– risk shifting 148
– risk transfer 148
– strategic 145
  – example 147
– transaction risks 146
– translation risks 145
– types 145
– volatility 146
Expected asset change 14
Expected loss 12, 170
– advantages 12
– disadvantages 13
– example 12, 170
Expected value
– non-zero 32
Exposure at default 170

F
Factoring 96
Fair value 106
Fat tails 63, 218
Financial crisis 202
– causes 204
  – categories 205
– dangers 203
– definition 203
– harmonization 231
– laws and regulations 206
– regulatory arbitrage 231
– solution approaches 206
Financial instruments directive, european 210
Financial market stabilization fund 208
Financial planning 201
– daily liquidity position 201
– long-term 201
– short-term 201
Financial reporting 209
Financial value risks 114

Financing-cost risk 196
Fiscal policy 221
– framework conditions 221
Foreign exchange transfer risk 190
Forward interest rates 138
Forwards 110
Franchising 96
Fulfillment risk 271
Full enumeration 252
Futures 107
– characteristics 109
– definition 107
– example 108
– features 108

G
Generally accepted accounting principles 2
German accounting standard 2, 311
– contents 311
– result 311
Government bonds 117
– example 119
Government debt crisis 204
– causes 204
Granularity principle 171

H
High frequency trading act 211
Historical simulation 52
– approaches of VaR calculation 53
– example 52
– properties 54
Human misconduct 214

I
ICAAP 207
IFRS 7 312
IFRS 9 2, 210, 312
Immunization 134
– disadvantages 138
– end value 136
  – example calculation 137
  – method 136
  – planning horizon 137
– present value 134
  – convexity 135
  – method 134
– significance 134
Incremental value at risk 48

– calculation 48
Institutional remuneration directive 213
Insurance 95, 97
– collective 98
– definition 97
– granularity principle 99
– premium differentiation 99
– principle 98
– RoRaC 99
Integration solution 293
Interest exposure 116
Interest rate 117
– coupon interest 118
– discounting factors 118
– risk-free 178
– sensitivity 122
– variable, floating 118
– zero coupon 118
Interest rate futures 143
Interest rate options
– example 142
– features 143
– functioning 141
– profit and loss profile 142
Interest rate position 116
Interest rate risk
– definition 116
– example calculation 121
– expansive monetary policy 126
– features 124
– types of interest 117
Interest rate swap 138
– comparative advantage 139
– example 139
– functioning 139
Interest rate volatility 116
Intrinsic value 106
Investment risks 195

K
KonTraG 2

L
Leasing 96
Legal risks 260
Lending rate 175
– components 175
– risk adjusted 175
– risk-adjusted

– example calculation 179
Leptokurtosis 63
Leverage ratio 228
Limits 90
– limit system
  – example 92
  – value at risk 91
– nominal 90
– scenario 91
– sensitivity 91
– stop-loss 91
Liquidation period 30
Liquidity at Risk 197
Liquidity coverage ratio 229
Liquidity risk 193
– control 201
  – financial planning 201
  – liability-side liquidity risks 202
– definition 194
– liability-side 196
– measurement
  – bid-ask spread 197
  – calculation 198
  – deadline risks 198, 202
  – example 198
  – example calculation deadline risk 199
  – liability-side liquidity risks 199
  – problems 196
– measurement of liquidity credit value at risk 199
– types 194
Loss 176
– expected 176
– unexpected 176
Loss database 252
Loss given default 170
Lower partial moments 59
– application on crises 62
– basic principle 59
– definition 59
– example calculation 60
– orders 59
– properties 62

M
MaRisk 207
Market failure 215
– examples 216
– solution approaches 216

Marketing tools 278
Market interest rate method 176
Market liquidity 194, 197
Market portfolio 162
Market price risks 115
– subdivisions 115
Market value 118
Maximum loss 10
– advantages 11
– disadvantages 11
– example 10
Minimum capital requirements 225
Mistaken decisions 219
– control functions 222
– politicians 219
Monetary policy 220
– effects 220
Monitoring 188
Monte Carlo simulation 54, 272
– Cholesky decomposition 55
– method 54
– properties 273

N
Natural hedging 95
– exchange rate risk 148
– RoRaC 95
Natural risks 260
Net interest income 117
Net stable funding ratio 229
Normal distribution 26
– assumption 33
– theoretical 27

O
Off-balance sheet transactions 212
Operating costs 176
Operational risks 70, 248
– analysis 257
– definition 248
– external 248
  – control 259
– internal 248
  – control 258
– measurement
  – aggregation 257
  – approaches 250
  – disadvantage 257
  – example calculation 253

– methods 250, 251
– problems 249
Operational Value at Risk 257
Opportunity interest rate 176
Option pricing models 106
Options 100
– call option
  – example 101
– covered 107
– definition 100
– functioning 101
– properties 100
– put option
  – example 103
  – properties 106
– uncovered short sellings 103
Organizational structure 294

P
Personnel risks 258
Planning horizon 286
Portfolio 34
– compensation effect 37
– return 35
– short sales 36
– volatility 36
– weights 35
Portfolio return
– aggregated 37
Portfolio structure
– interpretation 42
Portfolio volatility
– calculation 42
Present value
– example calculation 120
Price-sales function 272
Probability of default 169
Procedural organization 295
Process risks 258
Procurement risks 266
– control 270
– definition 266
– measurement
  – approach 268
  – example 269
– production factors 267
– types 266
Profit aggregation 299, 301
Profit analysis 309

Profit and loss profile 101
Profit expectations 74
Profit margin 178
Prolongation risk 196
Purchasing risk 271

Q
Qualitative risk measurement 69
– example calculation 70
– necessity 69
– scoring models 70
Quantile 28

R
Rating agencies 173
– external 173
– Fitch Ratings 173
– Moody's 173
– regulations 217
– Standard&Poor's 173
Rating classification 173
– possibilities 173
Rating procedures 171
Real estate price risk 166
– application of VaR concept 167
– capital investment 166
– characteristics 166
– definition 166
– features 167
– own use 166
Refinancing 176
– rate 176
– structure-congruent 176
Regulatory arbitrage 225
Repayment rate 170
Return
– logarithmic 23
Return on equity
– required 178
Return on Risk adjusted Capital 75
– definition 75
– example calculation 75
Return-risk diagram 158
Revenues 272
Risk 1
– definition 1
– financial 114
– performance 248
– performance-related 114

– political 190
– procurement 265
– sales 265
– systematic 162
– unsystematic 162
Risk aggregation 299, 301
– example 300
– example calculation 303
– special cases 302
Risk analysis 73, 335
– criteria for the procedure 308
– phase 5
– properties 77
Risk attitude 161
Risk avoidance 90
Risk control 88
– phase 5
Risk controlling 1
– example 296
– functions 291
– phase 5
– term 291
Risk distribution 93
– RoRaC 93
Risk exposure 24
Risk identification
– phase 4
– tools 5
Risk limitation 90
– limit types 90
– types of limits 90
Risk limitation act 2
Risk management 1
– connections financial crisis 223
– economic reasons 3
– legal framework 2
– process 4
– reasons 1
– technological advances 3
– term 1
Risk measurement 9
– phase 4
Risk position 30
Risk premium 175
Risk provision 89
– collaterals 90
– risk bearing capacity 89
– RoRaC 89
Risk report 310

– external 310
Risk shifting 94
– RoRaC 95
Risk structure 17
Risk transfer 95
Risk types 5
– classification 8
– systemization 6
Root function 30
RoRaC 75

S
Salary payments 213
Sales risks 271
– control 277
– definition 271
– measurement
   – analytical calculation 274
   – example 273
   – features 272
– types 271
Scenario analyses 66
Scoring models
– characteristics 72
Security Market Line 164
Sensitivity 24
– analysis 24
– application 25
Separate banking act 213
Separation concept 293
Sharpe ratio
– definition 74
– disadvantages 75
– example calculation 75
Short selling 211
Simulation procedures 272
Skewness 63
Solvency II 2
Sovereign risk option 184
Stability mechanism, european 209
Standard normal distribution 28
Standard risk costs 176
State insolvency 209
Stock futures 165
Stock options 165
Stock price return 18
– calculation 18
– volatility 19
Stock price risk 157

- definition 157
- distinction to credit risk 157
- portfolio theory 158
  - assumptions 161
  - example 158
  - inefficient portfolios 159
  - minimal volatility 159
  - properties 160
  - RoRaC 161
Storage risk 266, 271
Stress test
- definition 66
- example calculation 67
- properties 68
Supplementary capital 227
Supplier contracts 271
Swap rate risk 153
Swaps 110
- advantages 112
- basic principle 110
Syndicated loans 182
Systemic relevance 203
Systemic relevance banks 234
System risk 259

T
Top-down approach 250
Total capital ratio 227
Total loss absorbing capacity 229
Total return swap 185
- applications 186
- functioning 186
Transformation curve 158
Transport risk 266, 271

V
Value at Risk 25
- analytic method 51
- approximation method 52
- Calculation for a sample portfolio 43
- calculation methods 51
- concept 25
- criticism 63
- foreign exchange positions 156
- historical simulation 52
- individual risk position 30
- interest positions
  - correlation 131
  - example calculation 128
- Interest positions 127
- interpretation 32
- linearising 51
- liquidity-adjusted 198
- marginal 46
  - calculation 46
  - example 47
- objectives 26
- parametric calculation method 31
- portfolio 34
- properties of individual risk positions 33
- sample portfolio 43
- simple definition 30
- statistical foundations 26
- variance-covariance method 51
Variance 16
Volatility 16
- definition 17
- disadvantages 23
- estimate 23
- example 16
- implied 23
- Interpretation 17
- problems 22

W
Weather derivatives 264
Worst-case scenarios 66

Y
Yield curve 119
- parallel shift 121

Z
Zero bonds 118